Introducing Sociology for AS level
2nd edition

For Eirene

Ken Browne

Introducing
Sociology
for AS level

polity

First published in 2006 by Polity Press
Reprinted 2006

Polity Press
65 Bridge Street
Cambridge CB2 1UR, UK

Polity Press
350 Main Street
Malden, MA 02148, USA

ISBN-10: 0-7456-3559-8
ISBN-13: 978-07456-3559-0
ISBN-10: 0-7456-3560-1 (pb)
ISBN-13: 978-07456-3560-6 (pb)

A catalogue record for this book is available from the British Library.

Typeset in 9.5pt on 13pt Utopia
by Servis Filmsetting Ltd, Manchester
Printed and bound in Hong Kong by SNP Best-Set Ltd.

For further information on Polity, visit our website: www.polity.co.uk

Contents

Detailed Chapter Contents

Acknowledgements

I'D like to thank the anonymous readers approached by Polity, who provided me with some very constructively critical and supportive comments, many of which I have incorporated into the finished text, and Eirene Mitsos, Ian Bottrill and Austin Covington for some useful help and ideas.

Ken Pyne has drawn some new cartoons to illustrate ideas in the text, and he has once again shown himself to be excellent at interpreting my vague suggestions, and I thank him for being so responsive.

My AS- and A-level students at North Warwickshire and Hinckley College have helped me in judging the level and accessibility of the text, and the effectiveness of some of the activities and questions.

I would like to thank Emma Longstaff, Sarah Dancy, Neil de Cort, Breffni O'Connor and also Ann Bone for her informed and professional copy-editing.

I am grateful to Penguin Books, Tom Shakespeare, the Joseph Rowntree Foundation, the Ford Motor Company, and Richard Reeves, who gave me permission to reproduce copyright material. AQA examination questions are reproduced by permission of the Assessment and Qualifications Alliance. The source of copyright material is acknowledged in the text. Should any copyright holder have been inadvertently overlooked, the author and publishers will be glad to make suitable arrangements at the first possible opportunity.

AS Sociology

THIS book is based on four main assumptions:

1. That many students find sociology A-level courses very difficult and confusing compared to GCSE, particularly in the first year.
2. That many students find the wealth of theories, research and data in A-level sociology confusing, often finding it difficult to see their way through this intellectual maze, and easily getting lost in a range of detail which obscures rather than enhances understanding. These problems are likely to be more pronounced on a one-year AS-level course.
3. That, with AS level, students will need a straightforward textbook which will bring them from GCSE to AS level within one year.
4. That many students don't read nearly as much as teachers think they should.

This book therefore takes a straightforward and instrumental approach. It provides comprehensive coverage for AS Sociology, and is primarily a student book. It aims to give students the knowledge and understanding necessary to successfully achieve an AS qualification in sociology. It aims to help in the development of the skills of identification, analysis, interpretation and evaluation, though these skills are often best developed in the classroom, through discussion and individual or group activities. There is a range of activities to develop these skills in the main chapters covering the various subject areas, many of which could be developed into coursework proposals. This book aims to achieve a simple, concise and readable approach to subject content, while still maintaining the integrity of the subject and recognizing some of its complexities.

The book is based mainly on the AQA specification, but much of the material can also be used for the OCR specification, particularly the chapters on the family, the mass media, and sociological methods.

The AS specification

The AQA AS syllabus involves the following units:

Unit 1

Any *one* from these:

- Families and households
- Health
- Mass media

One data response/structured question. One question on each topic. Each question in six parts – four short questions adding up to 20 marks + two 'mini-essays' each out of 20 marks. Total marks = 60. 35 per cent of AS level and 17.5 per cent of A level. Exam is 1¼ hours.

Unit 2

Any *one* from these:

- Education
- Wealth, poverty and welfare
- Work and leisure

One data response/structured question. One question on each topic. Each question in six parts – four short questions adding up to 20 marks + two 'mini-essays' each out of 20 marks. Total marks = 60. 35 per cent of AS level and 17.5 per cent of A level. Exam is 1¼ hours.

Unit 3W

Sociological methods

One data response/structured question. One question only on the paper, in six parts – four short questions adding up to 20 marks + two 'mini-essays' each out of 20 marks. Total marks = 60. 30 per cent of AS level and 15 per cent of A level. Exam is 1 hour.

or

Unit 3C

Coursework task

> Submitted coursework proposal –
> 1,200 words.

This book covers all the subject requirements for the AS exam, but students only have to study a minimum of one subject area for each unit, giving students a choice of areas on each paper.

Assessment

At AS Sociology, students are assessed on two main objectives:

1 *Knowledge and understanding*

This involves sociological theories, concepts and research, and an understanding of how sociologists use a range of methods and sources of information.

Knowledge and understanding is likely to be tested in *questions* by the use of words like:

Outline	Explain
Examine	Describe
Discuss	Give reasons for

2 *The application of the skills of identification, analysis, interpretation and evaluation*

This involves things like being able to recognize and criticize sociologically significant information, to 'make sense of' data, to recognize the strengths and weaknesses of sociological theories and evidence, and to reach conclusions based on the evidence and arguments presented.

The skills of *identification and interpretation* are likely to be tested in *questions* by the use of words like:

Identify	Illustrate
Give an example	Suggest
How might . . .?	In what ways . . .?
With reference to item A	

The skills of *analysis and evaluation* are likely to be tested in *questions* by the use of words like:

Assess	Evaluate
To what extent . . .?	How useful . . .?
Critically discuss	Compare and contrast
. . . for and against the view . . .	

To show the examiner that you are using the skill of *analysis* you might consider using the following words and phrases:

the relevance of this is	this indicates
this is similar to/different from	so
therefore	this means/does not mean
hence	a consequence of
the implication of	the contrast between
put simply	

For *evaluation skills*, you might use the following words and phrases:

a strength/weakness of this	an argument for/against
an advantage/disadvantage of	the importance of
this is important because	this does not take account of
however	alternatively
a criticism of this is	others argue that
a different interpretation is provided by . . .	on the other hand
the problem with this is	this does not explain why . . .
to conclude	this argument/evidence suggests

Two themes

There are two themes or threads that run through the whole AS (and A-level) course:

- socialization, culture and identity
- social differentiation, power and stratification

These are not expected to be taught as specific subjects, but rather themes that should be referred to throughout the course. For example, in the family unit, you might consider the socialization of children, or inequalities of power and status between men and women. In the poverty unit, you might consider issues like the way children are socialized into the 'culture of poverty' or a dependency culture, or the way that the poor lack the power and resources to challenge and change their position. In education, you might consider the role of the hidden curriculum or the labelling process in forming student identities, or how the education system contributes to reproducing an unequal society.

Key skills

All AS- and A-level students now have to include key skills as part of their courses. The core key skills are:

- communication
- application of number
- information technology

The way key skills are developed and assessed is likely to vary between different schools and colleges. However, the AS Sociology course provides a range of opportunities for developing key skills and providing assessment evidence. For example, contributing to discussions, making presentations, reading and pulling information together, and writing different types of document (such as essays, research outlines, or questionnaires) would contribute to the communication element. The application of number is likely to be developed in any kind of survey work done in your course which involves selecting samples or evaluating results obtained. Information technology skills are likely to be developed through using IT, such as the internet, to search for, explore and select information, and through using computers to present information, including text, numbers and pictures or charts. Some useful websites, with a brief description, are listed later, and others are referred to in activities throughout the book.

How to use this book

Each chapter of this book is designed to be more or less self-contained, and to cover the knowledge and skills required to achieve success at AS-level Sociology. *All students should read chapter 1*, as it lays out some important introductory ideas which are developed and referred to in later chapters.

Important terms are printed in **blue type** when they first appear in the text, or in **bold type** in the page margins. These are normally explained in the text, and listed at the end of the chapter. They are also included in a comprehensive glossary at the end of the book. Unfamiliar terms should be checked in the glossary or index for further explanation or clarification. The contents pages or the index should be used to find particular themes or references. The bibliography consists of all research referred to in the book, in case you should wish to explore any of the studies further. Suggestions for coursework proposals are included at the end of the chapters below, except for chapters 1 and 8. Many of the activities included in the book also provide opportunities for further development into coursework proposals.

Chapter summaries outline the key points that should have been learnt after reading each chapter. These should be used as checklists for revision – if you cannot do what is asked, then refer back to the chapter to refresh your memory. The glossary at the end of the book also provides both a valuable reference source and a revision aid, as you can check the meaning of terms. Two typical examination questions are included at the end of every chapter, except for chapter 1. Students should attempt these under timed conditions, both as practice and to gauge how ready they are for the examination in that unit.

Useful websites

The internet is a valuable source of information for sociologists, and for exploring the topics in this book. However, there is a lot of rubbish on some internet sites, and information should be treated with some caution. Internet site addresses often change or disappear, but below are a few sites that are very well run, kept very up to date, and which carry an excellent range of contemporary information, articles and statistics of relevance to the topics covered in this book. The information found on them can generally be regarded as accurate and trustworthy, and used by sociologists as evidence or to develop arguments. Other useful websites are referred to throughout this book.

Current affairs and useful general information

www.google.com is one of the best search engines to search for topics generally. Try this for any research topic – putting 'UK' at the end of your search phrase usually helps, e.g. 'poverty uk'.

www.guardian.co.uk – this is the site of the *Guardian* newspaper, which is packed with useful stuff.

www.bbc.co.uk – the BBC. This is widely regarded as one of the best websites in the world, so you're bound to find something useful.

Sociology for schools and colleges

www.sociology.org.uk – an excellent sociology site created for GCSE, AS and A-level students, and run by Chris Livesey.

www.atss.org.uk – the site of the ATSS (Association for the Teaching of the Social Sciences). You will find a range of material, including worksheets, notes, and a list of websites of use to sociologists.

www.chrisgardner.clara.net – part of the National Grid for Learning, this is a Sociology Learning Support site, with some good online quizzes.

Government and other 'official' sites

www.statistics.gov.uk – the site of the Office for National Statistics, which contains a huge range of contemporary data on all the topics covered in this book.

www.statistics.gov.uk/census2001 – the Office for National Statistics 2001 census site.

www.direct.gov.uk – the British government site is an excellent starting point for locating all government ministries and departments.

Families and Households

www.nfpi.org – the National Family and Parenting Institute.

Health

www.dh.gov.uk – the Department of Health.

www.who.int/en/ – the site of the World Health Organization.

Mass Media

www.ofcom.org.uk – the Office of Communications – the media regulator.

www.pcc.org.uk – the Press Complaints Commission.

www.cultsock.ndirect.co.uk/MUHome/cshtml/index.html – a site containing just about everything you need on the mass media, for both teachers and students.

www.aber.ac.uk/media/index.html – a site at the University of Wales, Aberystwyth with lots of useful analysis and information.

Education

www.dfes.gov.uk – the Department for Education and Skills (DfES), for all information on education.

www.standards.dfes.gov.uk – the Standards site of the DfES.

Wealth, poverty and welfare

www.dwp.gov.uk – the Department for Work and Pensions, where the latest benefit and poverty statistics are available, as well as the 'Targeting benefit fraud' site.

www.jrf.org.uk – the site of the Joseph Rowntree Foundation, the best site for finding out all the latest research about poverty and inequality.

www.cpag.org.uk – the site of the Child Poverty Action Group, the major campaigning group against poverty.

www.newint.org – the site of the *New Internationalist* magazine, where global poverty and international inequalities between nations are discussed.

www.socialexclusionunit.gov.uk – the Social Exclusion Unit at the Office of the Deputy Prime Minister.

Work and leisure

www.tuc.org.uk – the site of the Trades Union Congress, a useful site for exploring trade union and labour force issues.

CHAPTER 1

Introducing Sociology

KEY ISSUES

- What is sociology?
- Sociology and common-sense and naturalistic explanations
- Key introductory ideas
- Sociological perspectives
- Sociological problems, social problems and social policy

IN this chapter the focus is on introducing sociology and some of the key terms, ideas and sociological approaches which will be referred to throughout this book. It is an important chapter which will help to lay the groundwork for later chapters. It is therefore worth spending some time on learning the main points covered.

Newcomers to sociology often have only quite a vague idea of what the subject is about, though they often have an interest in people. This interest is a good start, because the focus of sociology is on the influences from society which shape the behaviour of people, their experiences and their interpretations of the world around them. To learn sociology is to learn about how human societies are constructed and where our beliefs and daily routines come from; it is to re-examine in a new light many of the taken-for-granted assumptions which we all hold, and which influence the way we think about ourselves and others. Sociology is above all about developing a critical understanding of society. In developing this understanding, sociology can itself contribute to changes in society, for example by highlighting and explaining social problems like divorce, ill-health and poverty. The study of sociology can provide the essential tools for a better understanding of the world we live in, and therefore the means for improving it.

What is sociology?

Sociology is the systematic (or planned and organized) study of human groups and social life in modern societies. It is concerned with the study of social institutions. These are the various organized social arrangements which are found in all societies. For example, the family is an institution which is concerned with arrangements for marriage, such as at what age people can marry, whom they can marry and how many partners they can have, and the upbringing of children. The education system establishes ways of passing on attitudes, knowledge and skills from one generation to the next. Work and the economic system organize the way the production of goods will be carried out, religious institutions are concerned with people's relations with the supernatural, and the law is concerned with controlling and regulating the behaviour of people in society. These social institutions make up a society's social structure – the building blocks of society.

> **Social institutions** are the various organized social arrangements which are found in all societies.

Sociology tries to understand how these various social institutions operate, and how they relate to one another, for example the way in which the family might influence how well children perform in the education system. Sociology is also concerned with describing and explaining the patterns of inequality, deprivation and conflict which are a feature of nearly all societies.

> **Social structure** refers to the social institutions and social relationships that form the 'building blocks' of society.

Sociology and common sense

Sociology is concerned with studying many things which most people already know something about. Everyone will have some knowledge and understanding of family life, the education system, work, the mass media and religion simply by living as a member of society. This leads many people to assume that the topics studied by sociologists and the explanations sociologists produce are really just common sense: what 'everyone knows'.

This is a very mistaken assumption. Sociological research has shown many widely held 'common-sense' ideas and explanations to be false. Ideas such as that there is no real poverty left in modern Britain, that the poor and unemployed are inadequate and lazy, that everyone has equal chances in life, that the rich are rich because they work harder, that men are 'naturally' superior to women, that sickness and disease strike people at random have all been questioned by sociological research. The re-examination of such common-sense views is very much the concern of sociology.

A further problem with common-sense explanations is that they are very much bound up with the beliefs of a particular society at particular periods of time. Different societies have differing common-sense ideas. The Hopi Indians' common-sense view of why it rains is very different from our own – they do a rain dance to encourage the rain gods. Common-sense ideas also change over time in any society. In Britain, we no longer burn 'witches' when the crops fail, nor see mental illness as evidence of 'satanic possession', but seek scientific, medical or psychiatric explanations for such events.

Not all the findings of sociologists undermine common sense, and the work of sociologists has made important contributions to the common-sense understandings of members of society. For example, the knowledge most people have about the changing family in Britain, with rising rates of divorce and growing numbers of lone parents, is largely due to the work of sociologists. However, sociology differs from common sense in three important ways:

Objectivity means sociologists should approach their research with an open mind – a willingness to consider *all* the evidence, and to have their work available for scrutiny and criticism by other researchers.

Value freedom means sociologists should try not to let their prejudices and beliefs influence the way they carry out their research and interpret evidence.

- Sociologists use a sociological imagination. This means that, while they study the familiar routines of daily life, sociologists look at them in unfamiliar ways or from a different angle. They ask if things really are as common sense says they are. Sociologists re-examine existing assumptions, by studying how things were in the past, how they've changed, how they differ between societies and how they might change in the future.
- Sociologists look at evidence on issues before making up their minds. The explanations and conclusions of sociologists are based on precise evidence which has been collected through painstaking research using established research procedures.
- Sociologists strive to maintain objectivity and value freedom in their work.

Sociology and naturalistic explanations

Naturalistic explanations are those which assume that various kinds of human behaviour are natural or based on innate (inborn) biological characteristics. If this were the case, then one would expect human behaviour to be the same in all societies. In fact, by comparing different societies, sociologists have discovered that there are very wide differences between societies in customs, values, beliefs and social behaviour. For example, there are wide differences between societies in the roles of men and women and what is considered appropriate 'masculine' and 'feminine' behaviour. This can only be because people learn to behave in different ways in different societies. Sociological explanations recognize that most human behaviour is learnt by individuals as members of society, rather than something with which they are born. Individuals learn how to behave from a wide range of social institutions right through their lives. Sociologists call this process of learning socialization.

Some key introductory ideas

Socialization, culture and identity

Socialization is the lifelong process by which people learn the culture of the society in which they live. Socialization is carried out by agencies of socialization, like the family, the education system, religious institutions or the mass media.

Culture is socially transmitted (passed on through socialization) from one generation to the next.

Socialization plays a crucial part in forming our identities. Identity is about how we see and define ourselves – our personalities – and how other people see and define us. For example, we might define ourselves as gay, black, a Muslim, Welsh, English, a woman, a student or a mother. Many aspects of our individual identities will be formed through the socialization process, with the family, friends, school, the mass media, the workplace and other agencies of socialization helping to form our individual personalities. Figure 1.1 illustrates the various factors which influence our identities and how others see us, and many chapters in this book refer to aspects of this socialization process, and the formation of our identities.

However, while lifelong socialization plays a very important part in forming our identities, individuals also have the free will to enable them to 'carve out' their own personal identities and influence how others see

Socialization is the lifelong process of learning the culture of any society.

The term **culture** refers to the language, beliefs, values and norms, customs, dress, diet, roles, knowledge and skills which make up the 'way of life' of any society.

Identity is concerned with how individuals see and define themselves and how other people see and define them.

them, rather than simply being influenced by them. Individuals are not simply the passive victims of the socialization process. Figure 1.1 shows a range of factors which influence our identities. Note the arrows go both ways, suggesting that while individual identities are formed by various forces of socialization, the choices individuals and groups make and how they react to these forces can also have an influence. For example, while the mass media might influence our lifestyles, attitudes and values, and how we see ourselves and how others see us, individuals may also react to what they read, see or hear in the media in different ways. A woman from a minority ethnic background may define herself as black or Asian, but she may also see herself mainly as a woman, a mother, a teacher or a Muslim. Similarly, we have some choices in the consumption goods we buy, the clothes we wear, and the leisure activities we choose to follow. Through these choices, we can influence how others see us, and the image of ourselves we project to them. Individuals may also have multiple identities, presenting different aspects of themselves in different ways to different groups of people. People may therefore not adopt the same identity all the time, and different people will see them in different ways.

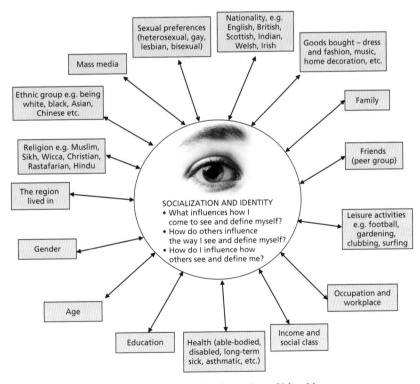

Figure 1.1 Some social influences on the formation of identities

Activity

Refer to figure 1.1 and:

1 Suggest one example in each case of how the various factors may influence the individual's sense of identity.
2 Suggest five ways in which individuals can influence how others see them.
3 Describe the five most important factors you think have influenced how you define yourself and how others see you. Explain your answer with examples.
4 Suggest three ways you can influence how others see and define you, such as a particular 'type' of person, e.g. 'trendy', 'odd', 'sporty', 'Goth', etc.
5 Give examples of ways you try to present different identities to different groups of people. How and why do you do this?

Roles, role models and role conflict

Roles are very like the roles actors play in a theatre or television series. People in society play many different roles in their lifetimes, such as those of a man or a woman, a child and an adult, a student, a parent, a friend, and work roles like factory worker, police officer, or teacher. People in these roles are expected to behave in particular ways. The police officer who steals, the teacher who is drunk in the classroom or the parent who neglects his or her children are clearly not following the behaviour expected in these roles, and these examples show how important these expectations of others are.

Roles are often learnt by copying or imitating the behaviour and attitudes of others. Children, for example, will often learn how to behave by copying the behaviour of their parents, teachers or friends. Those whose behaviour we consciously or unconsciously copy are known as **role models**.

One person plays many roles at the same time. For example, a woman may play the roles of woman, mother, student, worker, sister and wife at the same time. This may lead to **role conflict**, where the successful performances of two or more roles at the same time may come into conflict with one another.

A woman who tries to balance, and is often torn apart by, the competing demands of being a night-class student, having a full-time job, looking after children and taking care of a dependent elderly mother illustrates this idea of role conflict.

Values and norms

Values provide general guidelines for behaviour. In Britain, values include beliefs about respect for human life, privacy and private property, about

> **Roles** are the patterns of behaviour which are expected from people in different positions in society.

> **Role models** are the patterns of behaviour which others copy and model their own behaviour on.

> **Role conflict** is the conflict between the successful performance of two or more roles at the same time, such as worker, mother and student.

> **Values** are general beliefs about what is right or wrong, and about the important standards which are worth maintaining and achieving in any society or social group.

Role conflict for working women

the importance of marriage and the importance of money and success.
While not everyone will always share the same values, there are often
strong pressures on people to conform to some of the most important
values in any society, which are often written down as **laws**. These are
official legal rules which are often based on matters that many people
think are very important. Laws against murder and theft, for example,
enforce the values attached to human life and private property in our society. Laws are formally enforced by the police, courts and prisons, and
involve legal punishment if they are broken.

    Norms are social rules which define the correct and acceptable behav-
iour in a society or social group to which people are expected to conform.
Norms are much more precise than values: they put values (general guidelines) into practice in particular situations. The norm that someone
should not generally enter rooms without knocking reflects the value of
privacy, and rules about not drinking and driving reflect the values of
respect for human life and consideration for the safety of others. Norms
exist in all areas of social life. In Britain, those who are late for work, jump
queues in supermarkets, laugh during funerals, walk through the streets
naked or never say hello to friends when they are greeted by them are likely
to be seen as unreliable, annoying, rude or odd because they are not
following the norms of expected behaviour. Norms are mainly informally
enforced – by the disapproval of other people, embarrassment or a 'telling
off' from parents or others. **Customs** are norms which have lasted for a
long time and have become a part of society's traditions – kissing under

the mistletoe at Christmas, buying and giving Easter eggs or lighting candles at Divali are typical customs found in Britain.

Values and norms are part of the culture of a society, and are learned and passed on through socialization. They differ between societies – the values and norms of an African tribe are very different from those of people in modern Britain. They may also change over time and vary between social groups even in the same society. In Britain, living together without being married – a cohabiting relationship – is much more accepted today than it was in the past, and wearing turbans – which is seen as normal dress among Sikh men – would be seen as a bit odd among white teenagers.

Social control

Social control is the term given to the various methods used to persuade or force individuals to conform to the dominant social norms and values of a society, and to prevent **deviance** – a failure to conform to social norms.

Processes of social control may be formal, through institutions like the law or school rules, or they may be informal, through peer group pressure, personal embarrassment at doing something wrong, or the pressure of public opinion.

Sanctions are the rewards and punishments by which social control is achieved and conformity to norms and values enforced. These may be either **positive sanctions**, rewards of various kinds, or **negative sanctions**, various types of punishment. The type of sanction will depend on the seriousness of the norm: positive sanctions may range from gifts of sweets or money from parents to children, to merits and prizes at school, to knighthoods and medals; negative sanctions may range from a feeling of embarrassment, to being ridiculed or gossiped about or regarded as a bit eccentric or 'a bit odd', to being fined or imprisoned.

> **Social control** is the term given to the various methods used to persuade or force individuals to conform to the dominant social norms and values of a society.
> **Deviance** is the failure to conform to social norms.
> **Sanctions** are the rewards and punishments by which social control is achieved and conformity to norms and values enforced. **Positive sanctions** are rewards of various kinds. **Negative sanctions** are various types of punishment.

Activity

1 Identify three important values in Britain today and three norms relating to these values. Suggest ways in which these norms and values are enforced.
2 Identify at least four roles that you play, and describe the norms of behaviour to which you are expected to conform in each case.
3 Describe the sanctions you might face if you failed to conform to the norms you have identified.
4 Identify how the successful performance of one role might conflict with the successful performance of another.

Social class, social mobility and status

A **social class** is a group of people who share a similar economic situation, such as a similar occupational level, income and ownership of wealth.

Social class is a term you will read a lot about in sociology, including in this book. It is often used in a very general and imprecise way. Social class is generally associated with inequality in industrial societies.

Often occupation, income and ownership of wealth are closely related to each other and to other aspects of individuals' lives, such as how much power and influence they have in society, their level of education, their social status, their type of housing, car ownership, leisure activities and other aspects of their lifestyle.

Life chances are the chances of obtaining those things defined as desirable and of avoiding those things defined as undesirable in any society. **Social mobility** refers to the movement of groups or individuals up or down the social hierarchy, from one social class to another.

An individual's social class has a major influence on his or her **life chances**. Life chances include the chances of obtaining things like good quality housing, a long and healthy life, holidays, job security and educational success, and avoiding things like unemployment, ill-health and premature death. **Social mobility** refers to the movement of groups or individuals up or down the social hierarchy, from one social class to another.

To help you to understand the different social classes in modern Britain, the following simplified classification will suffice for the purposes of this book:

The **working class** consists of those working in manual jobs, involving physical work and, literally, work with their hands, such as factory or labouring work.
The **middle class** consists of those in non-manual work – jobs that don't require heavy physical work and are usually performed in offices and involve paperwork or computer work.
The **upper class** consists of those who are the main owner's of society's wealth. It includes wealthy industrialists, landowners and the traditional aristocracy.
The **underclass** is the social group right at the bottom of the social class hierarchy, consisting of those who are in some ways cut off from or excluded from the rest of society.

- The **working class** is one of the largest social classes, referring to those working in manual jobs – jobs involving physical work and, literally, work with their hands, like factory or labouring work.
- The **middle class** is also a large class, and refers to those in non-manual work – jobs which don't involve heavy physical effort, and which are usually performed in offices and involve paperwork or ICT (information and communication technology) of various kinds. Some argue that those in the lowest levels of non-manual work, such as supermarket check-out operators and those in routine office work, should really be included in the working class, as their pay and working conditions are more like those of manual workers than like those of many sections of the middle class.
- The **upper class** is a small class, and refers to those who are the main owners of society's wealth, including wealthy industrialists, landowners and the traditional aristocracy. Often these people do not work for others, as their assets are so large that work is not necessary to survive.
- The **underclass** is a small class, and refers to a group of people who are right at the bottom of the class structure, and whose poverty often excludes them from full participation in society. The term 'underclass' is used in different ways, and is a controversial concept. It is discussed more fully in chapter 6 on wealth, poverty and welfare.

Figure 1.2 overleaf illustrates the class structure of modern Britain, and is a useful guide to the use of social class in this book.

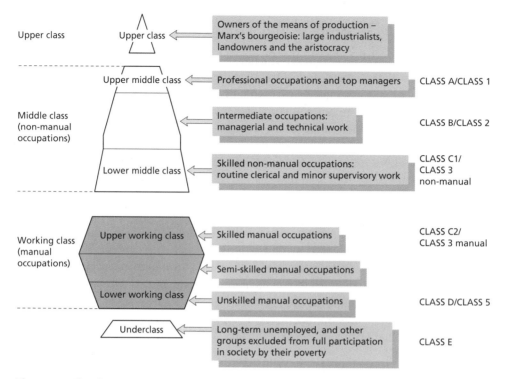

Figure 1.2 The class structure

The term **status** is used in sociology in two main ways. It is often used to refer to the role position someone occupies in society, like a father, worker or consumer. It is also sometimes used to refer to the ranking of individuals in society according to the differing amounts of prestige or respect given to different positions by other members of that group or society – people's social standing in the eyes of others.

Three other concepts you will come across in sociology, and which are also referred to widely in this book, are those of **ethnicity**, **minority ethnic group**, and **gender**.

> **Status** sometimes refers to the role position someone occupies in society, but more commonly refers to the amount of prestige or social importance a person has in the eyes of other members of a group or society.
>
> **Ascribed status** is status given by birth or family background and which, in general, cannot be changed by individuals. Examples of such status include a person's age, ethnic group, sex, or place or family of birth.

Activity

Using the word list below, fill in the blanks in the following passage. Each dash represents one word. (The words are given in the correct order on p. 490.)

identity	social structure	values
social control	norms	social mobility
status	working class	role conflict
value freedom	ascribed status	status
social class	positive	upper class
achieved status	socialization	objectivity

Achieved status refers to any social position or position of prestige that has been achieved by an individual's own efforts, such as through education, skill and talent, promotion at work and career success.

ethnicity	roles	underclass
minority ethnic group	social institutions	negative sanctions
social classes	deviance	life chances
gender	social classes	

Sociology involves studying the social world, but as sociologists are themselves part of this social world, they need to take care that they look at things in a detached and impartial way. They should approach research in an open-minded way, considering all the evidence before making up their minds. This is known as _____. They should also try not to let their own beliefs and prejudices influence their research. This_____ _____ is important if sociology is to be seen as something more than newspaper journalism.

Society is constructed of a range of _____ _____, like the family, religion, the education system and the law. These make up the _____ _____ – the 'building blocks' of society. Sociologists generally believe that people learn the culture of their society, and this learning process is known as _____. For example, males and females often learn to behave in different ways. This difference is known as _____. The learning process influences the formation of the individual's _____ – how they see and define themselves and how others see and define them. _____ refers to the shared culture of a social group which gives its members a common identity in some ways different from other social groups. If a group has a cultural identity different from the majority population of a society, such as black and Asian groups in Britain, it is known as a _____ _____ _____.

Everyone in society is expected to behave in particular ways in particular situations, and these patterns of expected behaviour are known as _____, but sometimes these come into conflict with each other, causing _____ _____. Every society has sets of guidelines for behaviour. _____ establish the important standards about what is important in a society and what is right or wrong. _____ provide rules about how to behave in particular situations. People are encouraged to conform to these rules by _____ _____, which is carried out by a range of rewards and punishments known as _____ and _____ _____. Non-conformity to social rules is known as _____.

A _____ _____ is a group of people who share a similar economic situation, and this can have an important influence on their chances of obtaining the desirable, and avoiding the undesirable, things in life – their _____ _____. The two largest _____ _____ are the _____ _____ and the middle class. The main owners of society's wealth are known as the _____ _____, while the very poorest group which is excluded from full participation in society by poverty is known as the _____. Sometimes people can move up or down between _____ _____, and this is known as _____ _____. Some people and some positions in society are ranked by others in terms of different amounts of prestige or respect, and this is known as _____. If this is given by birth or family background, it is known as _____ _____. However, some people can achieve their _____ through their own individual efforts and talents. This is known as _____ _____.

Ethnicity refers to the shared culture of a social group which gives its members a common identity in some ways different from other social groups.

A **minority ethnic group** is a social group which shares a cultural identity which is different from that of the majority population of a society, such as African-Caribbean, Indian Asian and Chinese ethnic groups in Britain.

Gender refers to the culturally created differences between men and women which are learnt through socialization, rather than simply **sex** differences, which refer only to the biological differences between the sexes.

Sociological perspectives

A **sociological perspective** is simply a way of looking at society. New-comers to sociology often find the different perspectives in sociology difficult, as there appears to be no 'right answer'.

A useful insight might be gained from the following situation. Imagine there are five people looking at the same busy shopping street – a pick-pocket, a police officer, a roadsweeper, a shopper and a shopkeeper (see cartoon). The pickpocket sees wallets sticking out of pockets or bags, and an opportunity to steal. The police officer sees potential crime and disorder. The road sweeper sees litter and garbage left by everyone else. The shopper might see windows full of desirable consumer goods to buy, and the shop-keeper sees only potential customers, and possibly shoplifters. All are view-ing the same street, but are looking at different aspects of that street. What they see will depend on their 'perspective' – what they're looking for. They might all be seeing different things, but you can't really say any of their views is more correct than another – though you might think some views provide a more truthful, rounded and fuller description of the street than others do.

Sociological perspectives are basically similar, in that they are the differ-ent viewpoints from which sociologists examine society. We might say that different sociological perspectives, and the different research methods

> A **perspective** is a way of looking at something. A **sociological perspective** involves a set of theories which influences what is looked at when studying society.

People may view the same scene from different perspectives

they lead to, simply emphasize and explain different aspects of society. Often, debates between and criticisms of these different perspectives help us to understand social issues much more clearly.

Sociological perspectives are often best understood by looking at particular areas, and this book will illustrate them in various chapters, particularly those on the family and education. However, what follows is an introduction to some of these perspectives.

Sociological perspectives centre on the themes of how much freedom or control the individual has to influence society. To what extent is the individual's identity moulded by social forces outside her or his control? How much control does the individual have over these social forces, and how free are individuals to form their own identities?

There are two main approaches here:

- the sociology of system, often referred to as structuralism.
- the sociology of action – social action or interpretivist theories.

Structuralism

Structuralism is a perspective which is concerned with the overall structure of society, and sees individual behaviour moulded by social institutions like the family, the education system, the mass media and work.

Structuralism is concerned with the overall structure of society, and the way social institutions, like the family, the education system, the mass media and work, act as a constraint on, or limit and control, individual behaviour. Structuralist approaches have the following features:

- The behaviour of individual human beings and the formation of their identities are seen as being a result of social forces which are external to the individual – the individual is moulded, shaped and constrained by society through socialization, positive and negative sanctions, and material resources like income and jobs. For example, institutions like the family, the education system, the mass media, the law and the workplace mould us into our identities. According to the structuralist approach, the individual is like a puppet, whose strings are pulled by society. We might see people almost like jelly, poured into a 'social mould' to set.
- The main purpose of sociology is to study the overall structure of society, the social institutions which make up this structure, and the relationships between these social institutions (or the various parts of society) such as the links between the workplace and the economy, the political system, the family, the education system and so on. The focus of sociology is on the study of social institutions and the social structure as a whole, not on the individual. This is sometimes referred to as a **macro approach**.

A **macro approach** focuses on the large-scale structure of society as a whole, rather than on individuals.

There are two main varieties of structuralism: functionalism (consensus structuralism) and Marxism (conflict structuralism)

Activity

1 To what extent is our behaviour moulded by social forces beyond our control? Try to think of all the factors which have contributed to the way you are now, and which prevent you from behaving in any way you like. You might consider factors like the influences of your parents and family background, the mass media, experiences at school, your friendship groups, income and so on.

2 Imagine you were creating an ideal society from scratch. Plan how you would organize it, with particular reference to the following issues:
   - the care and socialization of children
   - the passing on of society's knowledge and skills from one generation to the next
   - the production of food and other goods necessary for survival
   - how you would allocate food and other goods to members of society
   - the establishment and enforcement of rules of behaviour
   - how you would deal with people who didn't conform to social rules
   - how you would coordinate things and resolve disputes between members of society

3 Consider how your ideal society is similar to, or different from, the organization of contemporary Britain. How would you explain these differences?

Functionalism (consensus structuralism)

Functionalism sees society built up and working like the human body, made up of interrelated parts which function for, or contribute to, the maintenance of society as a whole. For example, in order to understand the importance of the heart, lungs and brain in the human body, we need to understand what function or purpose each carries out and how they work together in providing and maintaining the basic needs of human life. Similarly, functionalists argue that any society has certain **functional prerequisites** (certain basic needs or requirements) that must be met if society is to survive. These include the production of food, the care of the young and the socialization of new generations into the culture of society. Social institutions like the family or education exist to meet these basic needs, in the same way as we have to have a heart and lungs to refresh and pump blood around our bodies.

Just as the various parts of the human body function in relation to one another and contribute to the maintenance of the body as a whole, so, according to functionalist sociology, social institutions meet functional prerequisites, maintaining the social system and order and stability in society. In this view, social institutions like the family, education and work are connected and function in relation to one another for the benefit of

Functionalism is a sociological perspective which sees society as made up of parts which work together to maintain society as an integrated whole. Society is seen as fundamentally harmonious and stable, because of the agreement on basic values (value consensus) established through socialization.
Functional prerequisites are the basic needs that must be met if society is to survive.

Value consensus is a general agreement around the main values and norms of any society.

society as a whole. Stability in society is based on socialization into norms and values on which most people agree. These shared norms and values are known as a **value consensus**. It is this value consensus which functionalists believe maintains what they see as a peaceful, harmonious society without much conflict between people and groups.

> ### Activity
>
> Try to think of all the connections or links you can between the following institutions – for example, how what happens in the family may influence what happens at school and educational achievement:
> - the family and the education system
> - the family and the workplace
> - education and the workplace

Marxism (conflict structuralism)

Marxism is a structural theory of society which sees society divided by conflict between two main opposing social classes, due to private ownership of the means of production.
The **means of production** are the key resources necessary for producing society's goods, such as land, factories and machinery. The private ownership of the means of production enables the owners (employers) to extract surplus value from the workers. **Surplus value** is the extra value added by workers to the products they produce, after allowing for the payment of their wages, and which goes to the employer in the form of profit.

Marxism comes from the work of Karl Marx, who lived from 1818 to 1883. Marxism sees the overall structure of society as primarily determined (or influenced) by the economic system – the **means of production** like the land, factories and offices necessary to produce society's goods. These means of production are privately owned, and most people depend on the owners for employment. Marx argued that workers produce more than is needed for employers to pay them their wages – this 'extra' produced by workers is what Marx called **surplus value**, and provides profit for the employer. For example, in a burger chain, it is the workers who make,

Karl Marx, 1818–1883

cook, package and serve the burgers, but only half the burgers they sell are necessary to cover production costs and pay their wages. The rest of the burgers provide profit for the burger chain owners. This means the workers who produce the burgers do not get the full value of their work, and they are therefore being exploited.

> ### Activity
>
> Do you think those who produce the wealth should get the full share of what they produce? Do you think most goods today are produced because people need them, or because they are persuaded to buy them by advertising? See what other people think about this.

Capitalists and workers   Marx argued that there were two basic social classes in capitalist industrial society: a small wealthy and powerful class of owners of the means of production (which he called the **bourgeoisie** or **capitalists** – the owning class) and a much larger, poorer class of non-owners (which he called the **proletariat** or working class). The proletariat, because they owned no means of production of their own, had no means of living other than to sell their labour, or **labour power** as Marx called it, to the bourgeoisie in exchange for a wage or salary. The capitalists exploited the working class by making profits out of them by keeping wages as low as possible instead of giving the workers the full payment for the goods they'd produced.

The **bourgeoisie** is the class of owners of the means of production.

Capitalists are the owners of the means of production in industrial societies, whose primary purpose is to make profits.

The **proletariat** is the social class of workers who have to work for wages as they do not own the means of production.

Labour power refers to people's capacity to work. People sell their labour power to the employer in return for a wage, and the employer buys only their labour power, but not the whole person.

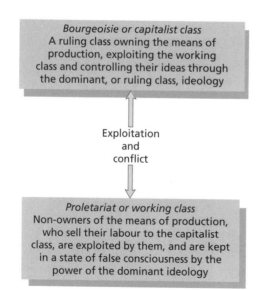

Bourgeoisie or capitalist class
A ruling class owning the means of production, exploiting the working class and controlling their ideas through the dominant, or ruling class, ideology

Exploitation
and
conflict

Proletariat or working class
Non-owners of the means of production, who sell their labour to the capitalist class, are exploited by them, and are kept in a state of false consciousness by the power of the dominant ideology

Figure 1.3 A summary of the Marxist view of society

Class conflict is the conflict that arises between different social classes. It is generally used to describe the conflict between the bourgeoisie and proletariat in Marxist views of society.

Class conflict   Marx asserted that this exploitation created major differences in interest between the two classes, and this created conflict. For example, the workers' interests lay in higher wages to achieve a better lifestyle, but these would be at the expense of the bosses' profits. The bosses wanted higher profits to expand their businesses and wealth, but this could only be achieved by keeping wages as low as possible and/or by making the workers produce more by working harder. The interests of these two classes are therefore totally opposed, and this generates conflict between the two social classes (**class conflict**). Marx believed this class conflict would affect all areas of life.

The **ruling class** is the social class of owners of the means of production, whose control over the economy gives them power over all aspects of society, enabling them to rule over society.

The ruling class   Marx argued that the owning class was also a **ruling class**. For example, because they owned the means of production, the bourgeoisie could decide where factories should be located, and whether they should be opened or closed down, and they could control the workforce through hiring or firing. Democratically elected governments could not afford to ignore this power of the bourgeoisie, otherwise they might face rising unemployment or other social problems if the bourgeoisie decided not to invest its money.

Ideology is a set of ideas, values and beliefs that represents the outlook, and justify the interests, of a social group. The **dominant ideology** is the set of ideas and beliefs of the most powerful groups in society, which influences the ideas of the rest of society. **Ruling class ideology** is the set of ideas of the ruling class.

Dominant ideology   Marx believed the ruling or dominant ideas in any society, what he called the **dominant ideology**, were those of the owning class (hence it is sometimes also called **ruling class ideology**) and the major institutions in society reflected those ideas.

For example, the law protected the interests of the owning class more than it did those of the workers; religion acted as the 'opium of the people', persuading the working class to accept their position as just and natural (rather than rebelling against it), by 'drugging' them and giving hallucinations with promises of future rewards in heaven for putting up with their present suffering; the bourgeoisie's ownership of the mass media meant only their ideas were put forward. In this way, the working class were almost brainwashed into accepting their position. They failed to recognize they were being exploited and therefore did not rebel against the bourgeoisie. Marx called this lack of awareness by the working class of their own interests **false consciousness**.

False consciousness is a failure by members of a social class to recognize their real interests.
Class consciousness is an awareness in members of a social class of their real interests.

Revolution and communism   However, Marx thought that one day the circumstances would arise in which the workers did become aware of their exploitation. They would develop **class consciousness** (an awareness of their real interests and their exploitation) and would join together to act against the bourgeoisie through strikes, demonstrations and other forms of protest. This would eventually lead to a revolution against and overthrow of the bourgeoisie. The means of production would then be put in the hands of the state and run in the interests of everyone, not just of the bourgeoisie. A new type of society – communism – would be created, which would be without exploitation, without classes and without class conflict.

Marx therefore saw society based on the exploitation of one large class by a small group of owners, creating social classes with opposing interests, and inequalities of wealth and power in society. Rather than seeing society functioning harmoniously as the functionalists do, Marxists see society based on conflict between rival social classes (class conflict) with social institutions serving to maintain the interests of a ruling class. However, like functionalists, Marxists see the behaviour of individuals as still largely determined or moulded by social institutions.

> **Communism** refers to an equal society, without social classes or class conflict, in which the means of production are the common property of all.

Activity

Comparing the views of functionalists and Marxists, which view of society do you think provides the most accurate and useful insights into the way British society is currently organized? Is it mainly based on consensus or conflict? Give reasons for your answer, with examples to illustrate the points you make.

Social action or interpretivist theories

Individual behaviour in everyday social situations is the main focus of social action or interpretivist approaches. These theories are concerned with discovering and thereby understanding the processes by which interactions between people (actions between individuals) take place, how people come to interpret and see things as they do, how they define their identities, and how the reactions of others can affect their view of things and the sense of their own identity.

Social action or interpretivist theories include the following features:

- Society and social structures/institutions are seen as the creation of individuals. An emphasis is placed on the free will of people to do things and form their identities, rather than the determinism of structuralism. Determinism means that the activities and identities of individuals are moulded by forces beyond their control, and they have little control or choice in how they behave. It almost suggests people are programmed to behave the way they do by society.

- An emphasis is placed on the individual and everyday behaviour rather than the overall structure of society. The focus of sociology is on the individual or small groups of individuals, not on the social structure as a whole. Rather than studying general trends and the wider

> **Social action theories** or **interpretivist** approaches are perspectives which emphasize the creative action which people can take, making people not simply the passive victims of social forces outside them. Social action theory suggests it is important to understand the motives and meanings people give to their behaviour, and how this is influenced by the behaviour and interpretations of others. The focus of research is therefore on individuals or small groups rather than on society as a whole.

> **Determinism** is the idea that people's behaviour is moulded by their social surroundings, and that they have little free will, control or choice over how they behave.

causes of crime, for example, interpretivists are more likely to study a juvenile gang, to see how they came to be seen and labelled as deviant, and how they themselves see the world. This is sometimes referred to as a micro approach.

- People's behaviour is viewed as being driven by the meanings they give to situations: their definitions of a situation, or the way they see things and therefore behave, become very important. For example, a parent might interpret a baby crying as a sign of tiredness, hunger, fear or illness. The action the parent takes – putting the baby to bed, feeding her, comforting her or taking her to the doctor – will depend on how the parent defines the situation, and to understand the parent's behaviour we have to understand the meaning he or she gives to the baby's crying. In turn, how the parent acts in response to the meaning given to the baby's behaviour is likely to affect the baby's behaviour – whether it stops crying because it is no longer tired, hungry, afraid or ill.
- The main purpose of sociology is to study, uncover and interpret the meanings and definitions individuals give to their behaviour.

> **A micro approach** focuses on small groups or individuals, rather than on the structure of society as a whole.

Activity

1 How do the attitudes and interpretations of other people affect your view of yourself? Give examples to illustrate the points you make.
2 Imagine you wanted to study the family and the education system. Identify three things for each institution you might be interested in if you adopted a structuralist approach, and three things for each institution if you adopted an interpretivist approach.

Symbolic interactionism

Symbolic interactionism is a social action perspective particularly concerned with understanding human behaviour in face-to-face situations, and how individuals and situations come to be defined or classified in particular ways. This is known as **labelling**. It is also concerned with the consequences for individual behaviour of such definitions, since people will behave according to the way they see situations. For example, the sociologist's task is to understand the point of view and experience of, say, the disillusioned and hostile student who hates school, as well as the teachers and others who label him or her as 'deviant'. Sociologists should try to understand how and why teachers classify some students as deviant, and what happens to the behaviour of those students once they have been classified in that way.

> **Symbolic interactionism** is a sociological perspective which is concerned with understanding human behaviour in face-to-face situations, and how individuals and situations come to be defined in particular ways through their encounters with other people.

> **Labelling** refers to defining a person or group in a certain way – as a particular 'type' of person or group.

Structuration: a middle way between structure and action

In real life, society is probably best understood using a mixture of both structural *and* action approaches. In other words, constraints from social structures, like the family, work (and the income it does or doesn't produce), the law and education, limit and control the behaviour of individuals or groups, and have important influences on the formation of individual and group identities. However, individuals can, within limits, make choices within those structures and act accordingly. For example, the school is part of the education system – a social structure. Young people are constrained (forced) by law to go to school, and that school continues to exist even after generations of young people have come and gone. It therefore has an existence separate from the individuals who attend that school at any one time. That structure continues only so long as people support the law and agree to attend school (and some don't) – if everyone stopped sending their children to school, the system would either have to be changed or it would collapse. This shows human beings create and reinforce, or can change or destroy, these structures.

If we take a particular school or group of schools, while they are constrained by the demands of the National Curriculum, the laws on education and the income they have, what happens within each individual school is controlled to some degree by the people within it – governors, students, teachers and parents. If attendance is poor, behaviour dreadful, teaching quality inadequate, exam results a catastrophe, and the school has a weak or incompetent headteacher, we may see this as a 'failing' school. It might be inspected by Ofsted (the Office for Standards in Education), and officially classified as a school requiring 'special measures' to put it right. If parents opt to send their children to another school, it may face declining income, making things worse. As a result, it might face closure.

However, the school might be dramatically improved by teachers and others in the school community working harder to try and turn the school around. We might then eventually see it as a 'good' school. The school might be held up as a showpiece of improvement by the government, and used as a model or 'beacon school' for all other schools to follow. This change shows that within social structures like education, human action – human activity – can make differences by changing those structures.

This means that while people operate within the constraints of the social structure, they can also act, make choices, and sometimes change that social structure. It has to be supported by people, and constantly recreated: parents have to send their children to school because it is against the law not to do so, and most parents don't question this. But they do have to agree to this, and there are lots of cases where parents refuse to

Structuration is an approach between structuralism and social action theory. It suggests that, while people are constrained by social institutions, they also have choice and can at the same time take action to support or change those institutions.

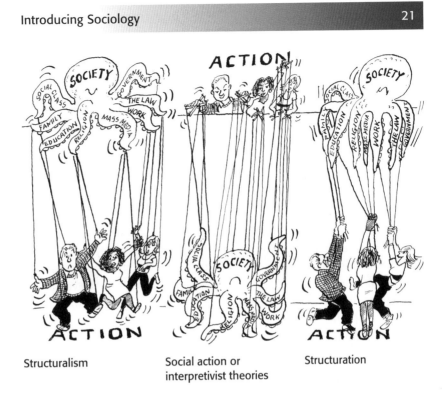

Structuralism

Social action or interpretivist theories

Structuration

send their children to school because they believe there is something wrong with the school. If they refuse, especially a lot of them, then there would undoubtedly be a change in the schooling system.

This third or middle way, between structuralism and action theories, recognizes the importance both of the constraints of social structure and of choice: the actions people can take to accept or change those structures. This is Anthony Giddens's highly influential theory of **structuration**.

The three approaches of structuralism, social action theory and structuration are illustrated in the cartoon.

Activity

Some argue that living in society is like living in a goldfish bowl – you are constrained by the bowl, even though you can't see the glass walls. In the light of what you have read in this chapter, discuss in a group to what extent you think this is an accurate view of society. Give reasons for your answers.

Feminism is a view that examines the world from the point of view of women, coupled with the belief that women are disadvantaged and their interests ignored or devalued in society.

Feminist perspectives

Feminism examines society particularly from the point of view of women. Feminists argue that a lot of mainstream sociology has been focused on the concerns of men – 'malestream sociology' – and has failed to deal with the concerns of women and the unequal position they have traditionally occupied in society. There are a number of strands within feminist approaches, but three of the main ones are Marxist feminism, radical feminism and liberal feminism. Marxist feminism and radical feminism fundamentally challenge the way society is presently organized and seek major social change, while liberal feminism basically accepts the system as it is but seeks to ensure women have equal opportunities with men within that system.

New Right perspectives

The New Right is more a political philosophy than a sociological perspective, and is associated mainly with the years of the Conservative government in Britain between 1979 and 1997. This approach is, however, found in the work of some sociologists, and is referred to in various parts of this book. This approach has four main features:

- *An emphasis on individual freedom*, and the need to reduce the power of the state to the minimum, and reduce control of the individual by unnecessary state interference.
- *Reduced spending by the state*, by making individuals more self-reliant. An example is cutting welfare benefits and encouraging people into work to make them 'stand on their own two feet', and not expect them to be dependent on the state for support if they are physically and mentally capable of supporting themselves.
- *A defence of the free market.* This means that free competition between individuals, companies, schools and other institutions is encouraged, to give individuals maximum choice between competing products, such as in health care and education. An example might be giving parents a free choice of schools as 'consumers' of education, and the right to reject some schools in favour of others, just as people choose between competing products in a supermarket. The selling off of state-owned industries like gas, electricity, water, British Airways, and British Telecom to private companies was seen as a way of introducing competition in these areas, on the assumption more competition would lead to lower prices and better quality services or products.
- *A stress on the importance of traditional institutions and values*, such as traditional family life, and a condemnation of anything that challenges these values. For example, lone parent families have been viciously attacked by the New Right, and blamed for a whole range of social problems, such as poor discipline and underachievement at school, immorality, crime, a culture of laziness, welfare dependency and the lack of a work ethic, and the existence of poverty.

Marxist feminism takes a Marxist approach to the study of women and women's interests, and emphasizes the way in which women are doubly exploited – both as workers and as women.
Radical feminism tends to focus more on the problem of **patriarchy** – the system whereby males dominate in every area of society, such as the family, the workplace and politics. For radical feminists, the main focus is on the problem of men and male-dominated society.
Liberal feminism wants to ensure that women have equal opportunities with men within the present system, through steps such as changes to the law to stop sex discrimination, removing obstacles to women's full participation in society, and better childcare measures so that women can play their full part in paid employment.

The **New Right** approach stresses individual freedom and self-help and self-reliance, reduction of the power and spending of the state, the free market and free competition between private companies, schools and other institutions, and the importance of traditional institutions and values.

Postmodernism

Postmodernism is an approach in sociology, as well as in other subjects, which stresses that society is changing so rapidly and constantly that it is marked by chaos and uncertainty, and social structures are being replaced by a whole range of different and constantly changing social relationships. Societies can no longer be understood through the application of general theories like Marxism or functionalism, which seek to explain society as a whole, as it has become fragmented into many different groups, interests and lifestyles. Society and social structures cease to exist, to be replaced by a mass of individuals making individual choices about their lifestyles.

Postmodernism is most likely to be considered and examined in the second year of an A-level course, rather than at AS level. However, it is included here since you may come across the term in any wider reading you might do, and it is useful to have a bit of background, especially as some postmodernist ideas influence parts of this book.

Postmodernism stresses the chaos and uncertainty in society, and argues that social structures like 'the family' or 'social class' are breaking down. These are replaced by a whole range of different and constantly changing social relationships. Postmodernists argue it is nonsense to talk of an institution called the 'family', for example, as people now live in such a wide range of ever changing personal relationships. Gay and lesbian couples, cohabiting heterosexual couples who do not marry, multiple partners, divorce and remarriage, lone parents, step-parents and stepchildren, dual income families with both partners working, people living alone, people living in shared households with friends, couples who have differing arrangements for organizing household tasks, all mean that any notion of the 'typical family' or 'the family as an institution' is absurd.

Because society is now changing so constantly and so rapidly, societies can no longer be understood through the application of general theories. There can therefore be no 'big' theories (called *meta-narratives*) like Marxism or functionalism, which seek to explain society as a whole, because society has become fragmented into so many different groups, interests and lifestyles that are constantly changing that society is essentially chaotic.

Postmodernists believe there are few of the social constraints on people that structuralist approaches identify, and society and social structures cease to exist – there is only a mass of individuals making individual choices about their lifestyles. People can now form their own identities – how they see and define themselves and how others see and define them – and they can be whatever they want to be. People are free to make choices about their lifestyles, and the image they want to project to other people. Postmodern society involves a media-saturated consumer culture where individuals are free to 'pick 'n' mix' identities and lifestyles, chosen from a limitless range of constantly changing consumer goods and leisure activities, which are available from across the globe.

Activity

Go through the following statements, and classify them as one of the following:

- functionalist
- Marxist feminist
- liberal feminist
- New Right
- Marxist
- radical feminist
- interpretivist

(a) We will challenge all aspects of society not relevant to women, bring about a complete female takeover, eliminate the male sex and begin to create a female world.

(b) The family is one of the main building blocks in creating the shared values which are such an important part of a stable society.

(c) There are conflicts between the rich and the poor in our society. This is hardly surprising, given the richest 10 per cent of the population own over half the country's wealth.

(d) To make sure women have equal opportunities with men, there must be more free childcare provided.

(e) Women are exploited both as women and as workers – they get exploited in paid employment, and they get exploited at home, where they do most of the housework and childcare and get nothing for it.

(f) The ruling ideas in society are those of the ruling class.

(g) Some people may see an amber traffic light as a warning to speed up before it turns red. Others may see it as a sign to slow down before stopping. In order to understand such behaviour, you need to understand the meaning people give to events.

(h) The education system is of major importance in preparing a well-trained and qualified labour force so the economy can develop and grow.

(i) The education system prepares an obedient workforce who won't rock the boat and complain about their exploitation at work.

(j) If you think people are out to get you, even if they're not, then this is likely to affect the way you behave. To understand behaviour, we have to understand people's point of view.

(k) Women will never achieve equality in society so long as men hold all the positions of power in society.

(l) It is in everyone's interests to pull together at work for the benefit of society as a whole.

(m) Despite girls doing better than boys in education now, girls could do better still. We must make sure that any obstacles to girls' progress in school are removed.

(n) We must make sure women get equal pay for equal work.

(o) Some students are almost bound to fail, because teachers give the impression they're thick, and this undermines the self-confidence of the students, who then think it isn't worth bothering.

(p) The welfare state has produced an underclass of people who are idle and don't want to work, and are content to scrounge off overgenerous welfare state benefits rather than get a job to support themselves.

Sociological problems, social problems and social policy

A **sociological problem** is, quite simply, any social issue that needs explaining.
A **social problem** is something that is seen as being harmful to society in some way, and needs something doing to sort it out.

Social problems are nearly all **sociological problems**, but not all sociological problems are social problems. However, very often sociologists have been able to show by research that many social problems are not simply a result of the behaviour of individuals, but are created by wider social factors. A useful example is that of accidents.

Accidents as a social and a sociological problem

Accidents are a social problem, and the accident statistics show a clear social pattern in terms of age, class and gender. For example, young people and old people, the poor and males are more likely to die or be seriously injured because of an accident. Accidents may happen to us individually, and sometimes randomly, but the causes are often socially influenced, by factors such as poor quality housing, inadequate home care for the elderly, low income, dangerous working conditions and a dangerous environment, with busy roads and no safe play areas for children. Accidents provide an often dramatic and tragic but nevertheless excellent example of how seemingly random or individual experiences and events are in fact socially patterned and socially influenced.

The study of accidents shows how clear-sighted C. Wright Mills (1970) was when he wrote about the distinction between 'the personal troubles of milieu' (immediate social surroundings) and 'the public issues of social structure'. Every single accident is a personal experience but the social pattern of these experiences in Britain every year is for all of us a social problem – not least because of the harm they cause and the millions of pounds spent treating them by the National Health Service. This social problem is also a sociological problem – something, which needs explaining by sociologists. The pattern of accident statistics illustrates well Mills's distinction between 'personal troubles' and 'public issues' to which we referred above. To paraphrase Mills, when in a nation of 60 million only one person has an accident, then that is his or her personal trouble, and for its solution we look at the circumstances of that person. But when in a nation of 60 million 8 million have accidents, with a clear social pattern, that is a public issue and a social problem, and we cannot hope to find a solution within the personal situations and characteristics of individuals.

Sociological research has often made major contributions to the **social policy** solutions needed to tackle social problems like accidents, ill-health, crime, poverty or educational failure. However, sociologists also try to explain social issues that aren't social problems, like the improved performance of females in the educational system, or why the birth rate is declining and why people are having smaller families.

> **Social policy** concerns the package of measures taken to solve social problems.

It is this ability of sociology to explain social events and to contribute to the understanding and solution of social problems, and the social policy solutions adopted, which makes it such a worthwhile, useful and exciting subject.

Chapter summary

After studying this chapter, you should be able to:

- explain what is meant by a 'social institution' and 'social structure'
- explain how sociology is different from common-sense and naturalistic explanations
- define the meaning of socialization, culture, identity, roles, role models, role conflict, values, laws, norms, social control, deviance, and positive and negative sanctions, and explain their importance in understanding human behaviour in human society
- explain what is meant by 'social class' and identify the main social classes in contemporary Britain
- explain what is meant by a sociological perspective, and identify the main features of the structuralist approaches of functionalism and Marxism, and the social action or interpretivist approaches, including symbolic interactionism
- explain what is meant by structuration, and how it provides a middle way between structural and action perspectives
- explain the variety of feminist perspectives, and the features of the New Right approach in sociology
- explain what is meant by, and the differences between, a sociological problem and a social problem, and the contribution of sociology to social policy

Key terms

- achieved status
- ascribed status
- bourgeoisie
- capitalists
- class conflict
- class consciousness
- communism
- culture
- customs
- determinism

- deviance
- dominant ideology
- ethnicity
- false consciousness
- feminism
- functional prerequisites
- functionalism
- gender
- identity
- ideology
- interpretivism
- labelling
- labour power
- laws
- liberal feminism
- life chances
- macro approach
- Marxism
- Marxist feminism
- means of production
- micro approach
- middle class
- minority ethnic group
- negative sanctions
- New Right
- norms
- objectivity
- patriarchy
- perspective
- positive sanctions
- postmodernism
- proletariat
- radical feminism
- role conflict
- role models
- roles
- ruling class
- ruling class ideology
- sanctions
- sex
- social action theory
- social class
- social control
- social institution
- social mobility
- social policy
- social problem
- social structure
- socialization
- sociological perspective
- sociological problem
- status
- structuralism
- structuration
- surplus value
- symbolic interactionism
- underclass
- upper class
- value consensus
- value freedom
- values
- working class

Families and Households

What is the family?

A **family** is a social institution consisting of a group of people who are related by **kinship** ties: relations of blood, marriage or adoption.

The family unit is one of the most important social institutions, found in some form in nearly all known societies. It is a basic unit of social organization, and plays a key role in socializing children into the culture of their society.

What is a household?

A **household** simply means one person living alone or a group of people who live at the same address and share living arrangements.

Most families will live in a household, but not all households are families. For example, students sharing a house together make up a household, though they are not a family. Similarly, in pre-industrial Britain, average household sizes were often larger than they are today, but this was generally because they contained domestic servants or other non-family members. Increasingly today, more households are containing people living alone rather than families. In 2005, around one in three households consisted of people living alone.

Different forms of the family and marriage

Even though the family is found in nearly every society, it can take many different forms. Marriage and family life in earlier times in Britain, and today in many other societies, can be organized in quite different ways from family life in modern Britain. Sociologists use a number of different terms to describe the wide varieties of marriage and household type. Table 2.1 overleaf summarizes these varieties.

Is the nuclear family a universal institution?

Functionalist writers like Murdock (1949) suggest that the nuclear family is such an important social institution, playing such vital functions in maintaining society, that it is found in some form in every society. In other words, it is a universal institution. However, although most societies in the world have some established arrangements for the production, rearing and socialization of children, this does not mean that these arrangements always or necessarily involve prime responsibility resting on the family or biological parents. The examples starting on page 32 help to illustrate some alternative arrangements which suggest the family is not always the main way of bringing up children.

Table 2.1. Forms of marriage and household

Forms of:	Description
Marriage:	
Monogamy	One husband and one wife Found in Europe, the US and most Christian cultures
Serial monogamy	A series of monogamous marriages Found in Europe and the US, where there are high rates of divorce and remarriage
Arranged marriage	Marriages arranged by parents to match their children with partners of a similar background and status Found in the Indian subcontinent and Muslim, Sikh and Hindu minority ethnic groups in Britain
Polygamy	Marriage to more than one partner at the same time Includes polygyny and polyandry
Polygyny	One husband and two or more wives Found in Islamic countries like Egypt and Saudi Arabia
Polyandry	One wife and two or more husbands Found in Tibet, among the Todas of southern India, and among the Marquesan Islanders
Family and household structure	
Nuclear family	Two generations: parents and children living in the same household
Extended family	All kin including and beyond the nuclear family
Classic extended family	An extended family sharing the same household or living close by
Modified extended family	An extended family living far apart, but keeping in touch by phone, letters, e-mail, and frequent visits
'Beanpole' family	A multi-generation extended family in a pattern which is long and thin, with few aunts and uncles, reflecting fewer children being born in each generation, but people living longer
Patriarchal family	Authority held by males
Matriarchal family	Authority held by females
Symmetrical family	Authority and household tasks shared between male and female partners
Reconstituted family or stepfamily	One or both partners previously married, with children of previous marriages
Lone parent family	Lone parent with dependent children, most commonly after divorce or separation (though may also arise from death of a partner or unwillingness to marry or cohabit)
Gay male and lesbian family	Same sex couple living together with children
Single person household	An individual living alone

Activity

Refer to table 2.1 and:

1 Interview a few people and try to find out what types of family they live in today. Is there any 'typical' family or is there a variety of family types? Write a report or do a presentation on your findings.

2 Fill in the blanks in the following passage. Each dash represents one word.

The ___ ___ means just the parents and children, living together in one household. This is sometimes called the two-generation family, because it contains only the two generations of parents and children. The ___ ___ is a grouping consisting of all kin. The ___ ___ ___ consists of several related nuclear families or family members who live in the same household, street or area and who see one another regularly. The ___ ___ ___ is one where related nuclear families, although they may be living far apart, maintain close relations made possible by modern communications, such as car travel, phone, letters or e-mail. This is probably the most common type of family arrangement in Britain today.

The ___ ___ is a form of the extended family in a pattern which is long and thin, reflecting the fact that people are living longer but are having fewer children.

The ___ ___ ___ is today largely a result of the rise in the divorce rate, although it may also arise from the death of a partner, the breakdown of cohabiting relationships, or a simple lack of desire to get married. Nine out of ten of these families are headed by women. The ___ ___ is one where one or both partners have been married previously, and they bring with them children of a previous marriage.

It remains a popular impression that the most usual kind of family in contemporary Britain is the ___ ___ where both husbands and wives or cohabiting partners are likely to be wage earners, and to share the housework and childcare. However, some argue that men still dominate in the family and make most of the decisions, and it therefore remains ___ .

___ is the only legal form of marriage allowed in Britain. In modern Britain, most of Western Europe and the United States there are high rates of divorce and remarriage, and some people keep marrying and divorcing a series of different partners. The term ___ ___ is sometimes used to describe these marriage patterns. This type of marriage pattern has been described as 'one at a time, one after the other and they don't last long'!

___ ___ are those where parents organize the marriages of their children to try and ensure a good match with partners of a similar background and status. They are typically found among Muslim, Sikh and Hindu minority ethnic groups. However, this custom is coming under pressure in Britain as younger people demand greater freedom to choose their own marriage partner in the same way as in wider society.

While marrying a second partner without divorcing the first is a crime in Britain, in many societies it is perfectly acceptable to have more than one marriage partner at the same time. ___ is a general term used to describe this form of marriage.

The Nayar

Among the Nayar of south-west India before the nineteenth century there was no nuclear family. A woman could have sexual relations with any man she wished (up to a maximum of twelve) and the biological father of children was therefore uncertain. The mother's brother, rather than the biological father, was responsible for looking after the mother and her children. Unlike our society, where in most cases the biological parents marry, live together and are responsible for rearing their children, among the Nayar there was no direct link between having sexual relations, childbearing, childrearing and cohabitation.

Communes

Communes developed in Western Europe, Britain and the United States in the 1960s, among groups of people wanting to develop alternative lifestyles to those of conventional society because of the political or religious beliefs they held.

> **Communes** are self-contained and self-supporting communities.

Communes often try to develop an alternative style of living and a kind of alternative household, with an emphasis on collective living rather than individual family units. A number of adults and children all aim to live and work together, with children being seen as the responsibility of the group as a whole rather than of natural parents. Many communes tended to be very short-lived, and only a few remain in Britain today.

The kibbutz

In the early kibbutzim, childrearing was separated as much as possible from the marriage relationship, with children kept apart from their natural parents for much of the time and brought up in the children's house by *metapelets*. These were a kind of 'professional parent' combining the roles of nurse, housemother and educator. The role of the natural parents was extremely limited, and they were only allowed to see their children for short periods each day. The children were seen as the 'children of the kibbutz' – they were the responsibility of the community as a whole, which met all of their needs. Children would move through a series of children's houses with others of the same age group until they reached adulthood.

> The Israeli **kibbutz** is a form of commune, and is one of the most famous and successful attempts to establish an alternative to the family. Here, the emphasis is on collective childrearing, with the community as a whole taking over the tasks of the family.

In recent years, the more traditional family unit has re-emerged in the kibbutzim, with natural parents and children sharing the same accommodation, but the kibbutz remains one of the most important attempts to find an alternative to conventional family structures.

Lone parent families

The lone parent family is becoming increasingly common in Western societies, and is usually headed by a woman. Lone parents represent a clear alternative to the conventional nuclear family. This is discussed later in this chapter.

Gay and lesbian families

Same sex (or homosexual) couples with children are becoming more common, though they are still relatively rare. Most same sex couples with children tend to be lesbian couples, that is, two women. However, there are more cases emerging of gay male couples adopting children or having children through surrogate mothers. In May 1999 the Canadian Supreme Court declared that gay couples are no different from heterosexual couples in their ability to share loving relationships, and suffer tragic breakdowns in those relationships like many heterosexual couples. In April 2001 in Amsterdam, Europe's first officially blessed gay weddings took place, as Dutch law granted full equality to same sex couples on issues such as adoption, inheritance, pension rights and tax. The Dutch experience paved the way for greater change and acceptance of gay marriage and family life in the European Union, and in 2004 the Civil Partnership Act gave gay male and lesbian couples in Britain the same legal rights as married couples.

You might argue that gay and lesbian couples are families like any other, but they do offer an alternative to more conventional views of the nuclear family.

Foster care and children's homes

It is worth remembering that a considerable number of children are 'looked after' by local authorities, and brought up by foster parents or in children's homes. This does demonstrate that the link between natural parents and the rearing of children can be, and sometimes is, separated.

Even though the nuclear family is probably one of the main means of bringing up children in the world today, the examples above mean it would be incorrect to assume that the conventional nuclear family is a universal institution. This is particularly the case today, where new forms of relationship are developing, and where the idea of a lifetime relationship is increasingly diminishing as more people have a series of partners during their lifetimes, and abandon traditional styles of family living.

Sociological perspectives on the family

The functionalist perspective

As we saw in the previous chapter, functionalism emphasizes integration and harmony between the different parts of society, and the way these parts work together to maintain society. With regard to the family, functionalists see the family as a vital 'organ' in maintaining the 'body' of society, just as the heart is an important organ in maintaining the human body. Functionalists are interested in the contribution the family makes to satisfying the functional prerequisites, or basic needs, which enable society to survive, and how the family 'fits' with other social institutions (like education or work) so that society functions efficiently and harmoniously.

Murdock argues there are four main functions of the family:

- *Sexual* – expressing sexuality in a socially approved context (note the social disapproval attached to, for example, incest, adultery and homosexuality in many societies).
- *Reproduction* – the family providing some stability for the reproduction and rearing of children.
- *Socialization* – the family is an important unit of primary socialization of children, where children learn socially acceptable behaviour and the culture of their society. This helps to build the shared ideas and beliefs (value consensus) which functionalists regard as important to maintaining a stable society.
- *Economic* – the family provides food and shelter for family members.

Murdock regards these functions as necessary in any society, and he suggests that the nuclear family was found in every society to carry them out. However, as has already been seen, the nuclear family is not the only form of arrangement possible for carrying out these functions, and other institutions and arrangements can and do take them over.

Parsons is an American functionalist writer who examined family life in the 1950s. He argued that there are two basic functions of the family that are found in every society. These are the primary socialization of children and the stabilization of human personalities.

The primary socialization of children

Parsons (1951) sees primary socialization as involving the learning and internalization of society's culture, such as the language, history and values of a society. He argues that society would cease to exist if the

Primary socialization refers to socialization during the early years of childhood (contrasted with **secondary socialization**, when other social institutions exert an ever increasing influence on individuals, such as the school, the peer group and the mass media).

new generation were not socialized into accepting the basic norms and values of society. In his view, this socialization in the family is so powerful that society's culture actually becomes part of the individual's personality – people are moulded in terms of the central values of the culture and act in certain ways almost without thinking about it. Parsons therefore argues that families are factories producing human personalities, and only the family can provide the emotional warmth and security to achieve this.

The stabilization of human personalities

The **sexual division of labour** refers to the way jobs are divided into 'men's jobs' and 'women's jobs'.

In industrial societies, the need for work and money, the lack of power and independence combined with boredom at work, the pressure to achieve 'success' and support the family all threaten to destabilize personalities. Parsons suggests the family helps to stabilize personalities by the sexual division of labour in the family.

The **expressive role** is the nurturing, caring and emotional role.
The **instrumental role** is the provider/breadwinner role in the family.

In Parsons's view, women have an expressive role in the family, providing warmth, security and emotional support to their children and male partner. The male partner carries out an instrumental role as family breadwinner, which leads to stress and anxiety and threatens to destabilize his personality. However, the wife's expressive role relieves this tension by providing love and understanding: the sexual division of labour into 'expressive' and 'instrumental' roles therefore contributes to the stabilization of human personalities.

Criticisms and evaluation of the functionalist perspective

The criticisms made of the functionalist perspective see it as:

Scapegoats are individuals or groups who get blamed for things that aren't their fault.

- *Downplaying conflict* Both Murdock and Parsons paint very 'rosy' pictures of family life, presenting it as a harmonious and integrated institution. However, they downplay conflict in the family, particularly the 'darker side' of family life, such as child abuse and violence against women. Children may become emotionally disturbed by conflict between parents, and children may often be used as scapegoats by parents.
- *Being out of date* Parsons's view of the 'instrumental' and 'expressive' roles of men and women is very old-fashioned. It may have held some truth in the 1950s when many married women were full-time housewives, and men the breadwinners in most households. However, this is clearly not the case today, when most married women are wage-earning breadwinners. Nowadays, both partners are likely to be playing expressive and instrumental roles at various times,

especially if men are taking on greater responsibilities for childcare, as we are sometimes led to believe.

- *Ignoring the exploitation of women*   Functionalists tend to ignore the way women suffer from the sexual division of labour in the family, with their responsibility for housework and childcare undermining their position in paid employment, through restricted working hours because of the need to prepare children's meals, take them to and from school, and look after them when they are ill. Housework also causes stress, leading to mental illness. These concerns are typically raised by feminist writers, discussed below.

- *Ignoring the harmful effects of the family*   Leach (1967) asserts that, in modern industrial society, the nuclear family has become so isolated from kin and the wider community (this is called **privatization**) that it has become an inward-looking institution that leads to emotional stress. Family members expect and demand too much from one another, and this stress generates conflict within the family. He argues that 'Far from being the basis of the good society, the family, with its narrow privacy and tawdry secrets, is the source of all our discontents.' Writers like Laing and Cooper also argue the family can be a destructive and exploitative institution, and Laing sees family life as one of the factors causing the mental illness of schizophrenia among young people. Both writers regard family life as stunting individual development, with the smothering of individuality leading to unquestioning obedience to authority in later life.

> **Privatization** is the process whereby households and families become isolated and separated from the community and from the wider kin, with people spending more time together in home-centred activities.

These criticisms of the functionalist approach suggest we need to think more carefully about the way family life is actually experienced by family members, and particularly to take into account the 'darker side' of family life.

Don't forget you can also criticize the functionalist approach by referring to arguments drawn from other perspectives – like the Marxist and feminist approaches discussed below.

The traditional Marxist perspective

Like functionalists, Marxists adopt a *structural perspective* on the family, looking at how the family contributes to the maintenance of society's structure. However, unlike functionalists, Marxists do not regard the nuclear family as a functionally necessary (and therefore universal) institution. Marxists see the family within the framework of a capitalist society, which is based on private property, driven by profit, and is riddled with conflict between social classes with opposing interests. Marxists argue that the nuclear family is concerned with teaching its members to submit to the capitalist class. Marxists emphasize the ways the family reproduces unequal relationships and works to damp down inevitable social conflict.

Early Marxists like Engels (1820–1895) believed that the monogamous nuclear family developed as a means of passing on private property to heirs. The family, coupled with monogamy, was an ideal mechanism as it provided proof of paternity (who the father was) and so property could be passed on to the right people. Women's position in this family was not much different from that of a prostitute in that a financial deal was struck – she provided sex and heirs in return for the economic security her husband offered.

Althusser, a French Marxist writing in 1971, argued that in order for capitalism to survive, the working class must submit to the ruling class or bourgeoisie. He suggested that the family is one of the main means, along with others such as the education system and the mass media, of passing on the ideology (the ideas and beliefs) of the ruling class. Through socialization into this ideology in the family, the ruling class tries to maintain false class consciousness by winning the hearts and minds of the working class.

Criticisms of the traditional Marxist perspective

The traditional Marxist perspective tends to be a bit old-fashioned. The idea that men marry and have children to pass on property ignores other reasons for getting married. Many women now work and have independent incomes, and in many cases they are more successful than men in some areas of the labour market. Women are therefore far less likely to marry for economic security. Marriage is now less of a social necessity. A 2003 report by the Institute of Education, 'Changing Britain, changing lives', found that people are now more likely to marry for love and affection rather than as a social obligation, with a growing emphasis on the emotional aspects of relationships and personal fulfilment both for men and, especially, for women.

Marxist feminist and radical feminist perspectives on the family

In recent years, feminist writers have probably had more influence on the study of the family than any other perspective. Feminist perspectives are often a more critical development of Marxist views of the family, focusing particularly on the role of the family in the continuing oppression of women. They emphasize the harmful effects of family life upon women.

Not all feminist writings use a Marxist perspective. Many radical feminist writers see patriarchy as the main obstacle to women's freedom – a system of male power and dominance.

Feminist approaches have been extremely valuable in introducing new areas into the study of the family, such as housework and its contribution to the economy; domestic violence; the negative effects of family life on women's careers in paid employment; and the continuing inequality between men and women in the family.

Some of the feminist criticisms of the family are covered in more detail in later sections of this chapter on changes in the family. The following represents a brief outline of the key features of feminist approaches to the family.

Themes in feminist analysis of the family

The family, and particularly women's work in the family, contributes to the maintenance of capitalism in the following ways:

The social reproduction of labour power   The social reproduction of labour power simply means the family provides a place where children can be born and raised with a sense of security, and the ruling class is supplied with a readily available and passive labour force for its factories and offices. The family achieves this in three ways:

- By providing a place for eating, drinking and relaxing, helping to ensure that members of the workforce are able to go to work each day with their ability to work (their labour power) renewed.
- By producing and maintaining labour which is free of cost to the capitalists through the unpaid housework of women (what is called domestic labour), as women are not paid for their labour in rearing children and looking after male partners.
- By socializing children into the dominant ideas in society (the dominant ideology), and preparing them for the necessity and routines of work, such as the need to work for a living, and to be punctual and obedient at work. Through day-to-day relationships in the family, with parents having power and control over their children, and men over women, family members come to accept, often without questioning them, the power inequalities they will face in 'adult' capitalist society. The family therefore lays the groundwork for submission to 'the boss' in later life, and is one of the mechanisms by which capitalism produces and recruits a moulded and obedient workforce.

Social control of the working class   Social control refers to the means of keeping people conforming to the dominant norms and values of society. The expectation that 'good parents' must work to provide material comforts and good life chances for their children helps to keep people in unsatisfying, boring and unrewarding jobs. It is harder for workers to go on strike for higher pay if there is a family to support, because it might mean cuts in the living standards of themselves and their children. This weakens workers' bargaining power at work, and discourages them from taking action that might disrupt the system.

The family can also act as a 'safety valve', providing a release from the tedium, frustration and lack of power and control at work that many workers experience. The family can be a place to escape from the world and relax – a 'sanctuary' into which adults withdraw to recover – and this helps to prevent frustration at work from spilling over into action against the system. This contributes to the stabilization of the capitalist system, to the benefit of the dominant class.

The family as a place of work   Feminist writers were among the first to state that housework is work – as 'real' as waged work outside the home. Housework and childcare in the family, which are mainly performed by women, are unpaid, and not really recognized as work at all. Men are often the ones who gain from this, as it is they who have their meals cooked, their children looked after and their homes kept clean by women's work. Oakley has emphasized that housework is hard, routine and unrewarding (both personally and in a financial sense), and housework remains the primary responsibility of women, though men might sometimes 'help'. This will be examined later in this chapter.

The myth of the 'symmetrical family'   Feminists attack the notion (put forward originally by Young and Willmott in *The Symmetrical Family* (1973)) that there is growing equality between partners in the family. These issues are discussed later in this chapter, but feminists emphasize it is still mainly women who:

- perform most housework and childcare tasks
- make sacrifices to buy the children clothes, and to make sure other family members are properly fed
- are less likely to make the most important decisions in the family
- are more likely to be dependent on men's earnings, as the average pay of women is only about 82 per cent of that of men
- are more likely to give up paid work, or suffer from lost or restricted job opportunities, to look after children, the old, the sick, and male partners. Many women now work both outside the home in paid employment *and* inside the home doing domestic labour. In effect, they have two jobs to their male partner's one
- are more likely to be the victims of domestic violence by men

Criticisms of the Marxist feminist and radical feminist perspectives

Criticisms of the Marxist feminist and radical feminist perspectives point out that:

- Women's roles are not the same in all families. Many families now consist of dual worker couples, with both partners in paid employment.
- These perspectives assume that women are passive victims in the family, and do not have any choices. Some women may choose to become full-time housewives and mothers because they enjoy it and find it fulfilling and rewarding, and they are not forced to do this. Many choose to take paid employment, even though they still have to combine this with the major responsibilities for housework and childcare (see later in this chapter).
- More women are working and have independent incomes, and this means they may have more power in the family than feminist writers imply. That around 70 per cent of divorces are initiated by women shows that women can, and do, escape from relationships which are oppressive.
- Day-to-day relationships in the family are less likely today to create an unquestioning and obedient workforce. Children have much more status and power in the family than they used to, with families becoming more child-centred (see later), and they are exposed to a much wider range of socializing experiences outside the family, such as the mass media. Women too are much more likely to assert themselves in family life.

Feminist approaches to the family provide a healthy antidote to functionalist accounts, which tend to emphasize the 'functional' aspects of the family and downplay the negative side of family life. For feminists, the family and marriage are major sources of female oppression and gender inequalities in society – whether we examine housework, childcare, power and authority or women's employment outside the home.

Table 2.2 summarizes functionalist, Marxist feminist and radical feminist perspectives on the family.

Changes in the family in Britain

The family in Britain has gone through a number of changes since the beginnings of industrialization, and it continues to change today. The extent of some of these changes thought to have occurred in the family has often been exaggerated and misleading conclusions have been drawn.

Table 2.2. Sociological perspectives on the family

Functionalism	Marxist feminism	Radical feminism
The family meets the needs of society by socializing children into shared norms and values, leading to social harmony and stability	The family meets the needs of capitalism by socializing children into ruling class norms and values (the ruling class ideology), leading to a submissive and obedient workforce, with false consciousness, and stability for capitalism	The family meets the needs of patriarchy by socializing children into traditional gender roles, with men as 'breadwinners' and women having responsibility for housework and childcare
The family is a social institution providing security for the conception, birth and nurture of new members of society	The family is a social institution responsible for the reproduction of labour power for capitalism	The family is a social institution responsible for the reproduction of unequal roles for women and men
The sexual division of labour in the family, with men performing instrumental roles and women performing expressive roles, stabilizes adult personalities and thereby helps to maintain a stable society	The male's instrumental role as wage earner maintains the family, pays for the reproduction of labour power and acts as a strong control on workers' behaviour in the workplace, thereby helping to maintain the stability of an unequal, exploitative capitalist society	The sexual division of labour in the family exploits women, since their responsibilities for domestic labour and childcare are unpaid, undermine their position in paid employment and increase dependency on men. It thereby maintains an unequal patriarchal society
The family is a supportive and generally harmonious and happy social institution	The family is an oppressive institution that stunts the development of human personalities and individuality. There is a 'dark side' to family life that functionalist accounts play down	The family is an oppressive institution that benefits men and oppresses and exploits women. There is a 'dark side' to family life that includes violence and abuse against women and children

The key changes commonly thought to have occurred are discussed below, and summarized in figure 2.1 overleaf.

Family change 1: has the family lost its functions?

The family in pre-industrial and early industrial Britain and most other societies traditionally had a number of responsibilities placed upon it – these are the functions it performs in society. They are primarily concerned with its role in the preparation of children to fit into adult society.

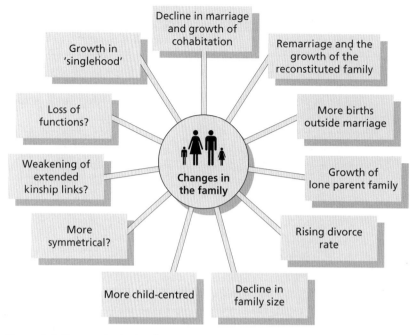

Figure 2.1 Changes in the family

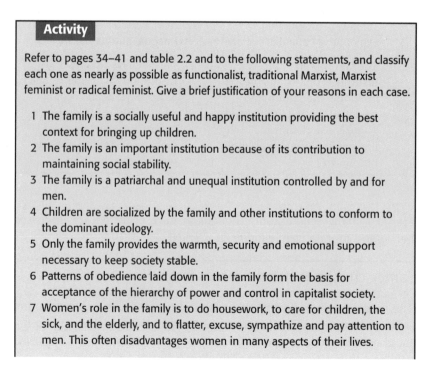

Activity

Refer to pages 34–41 and table 2.2 and to the following statements, and classify each one as nearly as possible as functionalist, traditional Marxist, Marxist feminist or radical feminist. Give a brief justification of your reasons in each case.

1 The family is a socially useful and happy institution providing the best context for bringing up children.
2 The family is an important institution because of its contribution to maintaining social stability.
3 The family is a patriarchal and unequal institution controlled by and for men.
4 Children are socialized by the family and other institutions to conform to the dominant ideology.
5 Only the family provides the warmth, security and emotional support necessary to keep society stable.
6 Patterns of obedience laid down in the family form the basis for acceptance of the hierarchy of power and control in capitalist society.
7 Women's role in the family is to do housework, to care for children, the sick, and the elderly, and to flatter, excuse, sympathize and pay attention to men. This often disadvantages women in many aspects of their lives.

8 The family always benefits either men or capitalism.

9 The image of the caring and loving family ignores the violence against women and the sexual crimes, like rape within marriage, which go on there.

10 The family exists primarily to pass on private property from one generation to the next, and to prepare a submissive and obedient workforce.

11 The family is an important institution in maintaining male power.

12 When wives play their traditional role as 'takers of shit', they often absorb their husbands' anger and frustration at their own powerlessness and oppression in the world of work, and stop rebellion in the workplace.

13 Families are factories producing stable human personalities.

14 It is highly unlikely that any society will find an adequate substitute to take over the functions of the nuclear family.

15 Women's unpaid domestic labour reproduces the workforce at no cost to the capitalist.

Activity

With reference to figure 2.1, discuss with different generations, such as friends, parents and grandparents or great-grandparents, how the family has changed during the course of the last fifty years. If you are in a group, pool all your findings and discuss the changes you have discovered.

The case for the view the family has lost its functions

Functionalist writers, like Parsons and Dennis, argue that with the process of industrialization, many of the functions once performed by the family in pre-industrial society have been removed from the family. These have been transferred to other more specialized institutions, such as the National Health Service and the education and welfare systems. Parsons calls this process **structural differentiation**.

Parsons claims this process of structural differentiation has meant the modern, more specialized family has only two basic functions left: the primary socialization of children and the stabilization of adult personalities.

The case against the view the family has lost its functions

Sociologists like Fletcher (1966) and Shorter deny that the family has lost many of its functions in modern industrial society. They suggest that in pre-industrial and early industrial society poverty meant functions such as welfare, education or recreation were often not carried out. Children were frequently neglected, and male peasants often cared more about their animals than their wives. Fletcher argues that the family now has more, not fewer, responsibilities (functions) placed on it. For example, the

Structural differentiation refers to the way new, more specialized social institutions emerge to take over a range of functions that were once performed by a single institution.

health and welfare functions of the family have been strengthened by the welfare state, and parents today are more preoccupied with their children's health, and retain responsibility for diagnosis of minor illness and referral to doctors and other welfare state agencies. Social services departments, with their powers to intervene in families if children are neglected or abused, have increased the responsibilities on parents, not reduced them.

Fletcher says that although the family may no longer be a unit of production (where family members work together in the home to produce goods), it plays an important economic role as a unit of consumption. The modern family is particularly concerned with raising the living standards of the family and 'keeping up' with the neighbours through buying a whole host of goods targeted at family consumers, such as washing machines, stereo systems, DVD players, computers and package holidays. Marxists see this pressure to purchase consumer goods as a means of motivating workers in boring, unfulfilling jobs.

Feminist writers dispute whether the modern family really has ceased to be a unit of production, since women's unpaid domestic labour (housework and childcare) produces a wide range of goods and services in the family which would prove very expensive if they were provided and paid for outside the family.

The discussion of whether or not the family has lost its functions is outlined in table 2.3.

Table 2.3. The changing functions of the family

Traditional functions of the family	How they have changed
The reproduction and nurturing of children was often seen as the main reason for marriage, as a means of passing on family property and providing a future workforce	There has been a steady increase in the reproduction of children and sexual relations before, alongside and outside marriage
Before industrialization and the growth of factory production in Britain, the family was a unit of production. This means that the family home was also the workplace, and the family produced most of the goods necessary for its own survival. Children would learn the skills needed for working life from their parents, and the family ascribed the occupational roles and status of adults. In other words, children generally followed in their parents' footsteps	Since the early nineteenth century in Britain, work has moved outside the home to factories and offices. Families do not generally produce the goods they need any more – they go out to work for wages so they can buy them. The skills required for adult working life are no longer learnt in the family but at the place of work, at colleges or on government-supported job training schemes. Occupational roles and status in society are less likely to be ascribed by the kinship network, but achieved by individual merit

Table 2.3. (*continued*)

Traditional functions of the family	How they have changed
The family traditionally played the major role in caring for dependent children – that is, those children who were still unable to look after themselves. Before the twentieth century in Britain, most children were often poorly looked after because of poverty	The modern nuclear family gets more help and assistance in maintaining and caring for children through a wide range of state welfare services, such as child tax credits, the social services and growing numbers of pre- and after-school clubs, playgroups and nurseries
The family used to have the main responsibility for health and welfare provision for the young, the old, the sick, the disabled, the unemployed and the poor	The welfare state (established in the 1940s) has taken on some of these responsibilities. The National Health Service, social services departments and other agencies of the welfare state, plus a range of welfare benefits, reduce the dependence on kin for money and support when misfortune strikes
The primary and secondary socialization and social control of children, and their education, used to be performed mainly by the family and close community. Before compulsory schooling was provided by the state in Britain from 1880, many children from working-class families had extremely high illiteracy rates	The family still retains important responsibilities for the socialization, social control and education of young children. However, nurseries, playgroups and the state educational system now help the family with these functions, and the mass media also play an important socializing role. Education is now primarily the responsibility of professional teachers rather than parents, although the family still continues to play an important role in supporting children at school. The family still has important influences on how well a child does at school

---

Activity

1 To what extent do you consider the family has lost its functions? Examine the arguments in table 2.3 and on pp. 43–4, weigh up the strengths and weaknesses of each argument and reach a conclusion. (This is *evaluation*).
2 Do you think the welfare state has placed more or fewer demands on the family? Give reasons for your answer.
3 Look at TV, newspaper or magazine advertising. Can you find any evidence that the image of family life presented in advertising is used as a way of persuading people to buy consumer goods – for example, by making it appear that buying goods will lead to happier lives, or will make children feel more cared for? If you're in a group, collect or record some adverts and discuss them in your group.
4 Do you have any evidence from your own experience of families buying goods to keep up with the neighbours? If so, why do you think they do this?

Family change 2: the decline of the classic extended family and the emergence of the privatized nuclear family?

A second major change in the family to consider is a traditional view that the most common form of the family in Britain changed from the classic extended family before industrialization to the **privatized nuclear family** today. The privatized nuclear family means the modern nuclear family is a very private institution, separated and isolated from its extended kin, and often from neighbours and local community life as well. It has become a self-contained, self-reliant and home-centred unit, with free time spent doing jobs around the house, and leisure time mainly spent with the family. In the privatized nuclear family, family members will often know more, and care more, about the lives of media soap stars and computer game heroes than they do about the real people who live in their street. The privatized nuclear family has been called by Parsons the 'structurally isolated' family, since it has also lost many of its functions and links to other social institutions.

> The **privatized nuclear family** is a self-contained, self-reliant and home-centred family unit that is separated and isolated from its extended kin, neighbours and local community life.

The three stages of family life: the work of Young and Willmott in The Symmetrical Family

Young and Willmott, in *The Symmetrical Family* (1973) argue that the British family has passed through three main historical stages as industrial society developed:

- *Stage 1* was the pre-industrial family. Then, the family was a stable unit, the home and the workplace were combined – the family was a unit of production – and the family was patriarchal, with power and authority held by men.
- *Stage 2* was the early industrial extended family, in the period around 1750–1900. As home and workplace were separated, the family ceased to be a unit of production. Traditional family life was torn apart as family members were forced to move to work to earn their living in the new industrial towns. Conditions of life for the working class were generally grim in the new industrial towns, with unemployment and poverty widespread. The family responded to working-class poverty by extending itself as a support network when faced with hardship and unemployment.
- *Stage 3* involves the transition to the privatized symmetrical nuclear family of today. This transition began around 1900 and represents a family that is once again stable after the disruptive effects of industrialization. This stage 3 symmetrical family has strong bonds between married or cohabiting partners, with the relationship becoming more symmetrical, or equal on both sides. Both partners share household chores, childcare and decision-making, and both partners are more likely to be involved in paid employment. Whether the modern family really is 'symmetrical' is discussed later in this chapter.

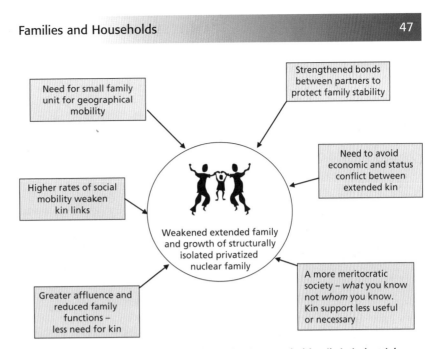

Figure 2.2 Reasons for the decline of the classic extended family in industrial society

Writers like Parsons, Young and Willmott and Fletcher have suggested that it was the industrialization process which brought about these changes, and that the structurally isolated, privatized nuclear family or some form of modified extended family emerged as the main family form in industrial society. According to Parsons, this is because it is well adapted to meet both the needs of industrial society and the needs of individuals.

There are six main reasons why there is thought to have been a decline in extended family life, with the isolated nuclear family 'fitting' industrial society. These are summarized in figure 2.2.

The need in industrial societies for geographical mobility   Modern industrial society has a specialized division of labour, with a wide range of different occupations with different incomes and lifestyles. This means the labour force needs to be geographically mobile – to be able to move around the country to areas where their skills are required, to improve their education or gain promotion. This often involves leaving relatives behind, thus weakening and breaking up traditional extended family life.

The isolated nuclear family is ideally suited to this requirement because it is small in size and it is not tied down by responsibilities for extended kin who, in earlier times, might have been living with them.

The higher rate of social mobility in industrial societies   Social mobility means that people can move up or down the social scale compared to the family they were born into. In pre-industrial society, when social

The **division of labour** is the division of work or occupations into a large number of specialized jobs or tasks, each of which is carried out by one worker or group of workers.

mobility was very limited, most members of an extended family would have had similar education, jobs, incomes and lifestyles, giving them a lot of things in common. In industrial societies, rates of social mobility are higher. This means that different members of the extended family may find themselves in different jobs, with differences in education, income, lifestyle, opportunities, and attitudes and values between kin. These differences weaken relations between kin, as they have less in common.

The growth in people's wealth and income as society has got richer and the welfare state has developed   People have become much better off in industrial society, and the welfare state has taken over a number of functions previously performed by the family, such as in education, health care and welfare. This has reduced dependence on kin for support in times of distress. This further weakens the extended family.

The growth in meritocracy in industrial societies   Industrial societies, which require more skills and education for jobs, are more meritocratic – it is *what* you know, rather than *whom* you know, that is the most important factor in getting jobs.

   Extended kin therefore have less to offer family members, such as job opportunities, reducing reliance on kin. However, while this is true for most people, kin links remain very important in the upper class, for the inheritance of wealth and for access to the top 'elite' jobs.

> A **meritocracy** (or a meritocratic society) is a society where occupational status is mainly achieved on the basis of talent, skill and educational qualifications, rather than whom you know or the family you were born into.

The need to avoid the possibility of economic and status differences in an extended family unit causing conflict and family instability   The different occupations, incomes, lifestyles and statuses of extended family members who live together might be a source of family conflict and instability in an industrial society. In an extended family unit, conflicts might arise over where to live when different job opportunities arise, and over different incomes and lifestyles in the same family unit. The fact that adult children generally move away from the family home in industrial societies to establish their own separate nuclear family units avoids such potential problems.

The need to protect family stability by strengthening the bonds between marriage partners   There is a lack of support from kin in the isolated nuclear family, and Parsons argues this helps to cement family relationships through increasing the mutual dependency of marriage partners. This increases the stabilization of adult personalities, which are under particular stress in the face of the impersonal competitive relations of the wider industrial society as people fight for higher status, more money and promotion at work to support the consumer-led lifestyles of industrial society. Young and Willmott suggest rising living standards have made the home a more attractive place to spend time, and family life has become more home-centred. Free time is spent by both partners doing jobs around the home, watching TV and so on, and the family becomes a self-contained and more intimate unit.

Criticisms

The view that the typical family unit in pre-industrial Britain was the extended family, and that the industrialization process led to the emergence of the isolated nuclear family as the main family form in industrial society, has been criticized on three main grounds.

The typical family before industrialization was never the extended family: the work of Laslett   Laslett, a historian, found there was no evidence to support the view that the classic extended family was widespread in pre-industrial England. He found that between 1564 and 1821, only 10 per cent of households contained kin beyond the nuclear family, and family size was not that different from Britain in the 1960s. Although households were larger in pre-industrial Britain, this was often because they contained non-family members, like domestic servants. Laslett (1965, 1972) suggests that it was not industrialization that produced the nuclear family, but, on the contrary, that the industrialization process was able to proceed more easily because the nuclear family was so common, and fitted neatly with the requirements of the emerging industrial society.

In the early stages of industrialization, the extended family became more common: the work of Anderson   Based on historical research he carried out in Preston, Anderson (1971) suggested that far from encouraging the formation of nuclear families, the early stages of industrialization in England may well have strengthened kinship ties beyond the nuclear family, and encouraged the formation of extended families, especially in the working class. In the absence of the welfare state, and with high unemployment, large families, a high death rate and overcrowded housing, the maintenance of a large kinship network was necessary, because individuals were largely dependent on kin for help in times of hardship and need. The extended family was strengthened as a self-help institution, providing support for the aged, childcare while mothers worked, and help with house rents and with finding work. This was also found in Young and Willmott's stage 2 early industrial family.

There is no 'typical' family type in industrial society   While there may be some evidence that nuclear families have become more common in industrial societies, it would be wrong to suggest that extended family life has completely disappeared in industrial societies, and it is still of great importance in parts of modern Britain. There is also a wide diversity (or range) of family structures besides the isolated nuclear family. The issue of family diversity is discussed later in this chapter.

The continued existence of the classic extended family

While the most common type of family found in modern Britain is the nuclear family or the modified extended family (see below), there is evidence that the classic extended family still survives today in modern Britain in two types of community:

Traditional working-class communities   These are long-established communities dominated by one industry, like fishing and mining, in the traditional working-class industrial centres of the north of England, and also occurring in inner city working-class areas. In such communities, there is little geographical or social mobility, and children usually remain in the same area when they get married. People stay in the same community for several generations, and this creates close-knit community life – it is the type of community shown in TV 'soaps' such as *Coronation Street* or *EastEnders*. Members of the extended family live close together and meet frequently, and there is a constant exchange of services between extended family members, such as washing, shopping and childcare between female kin, and shared work and leisure activities between male relatives. Such extended family life declined in the second half of the twentieth century, particularly in the 1990s, as traditional industries closed down and people were forced to move away in search of new employment.

The Asian community   There is evidence that the extended family is still very common among those who came to Britain in the 1960s and 1970s from India, Pakistan and Bangladesh. The extended family usually centres on the male side of the family, with grandfathers, sons, grandsons and their wives, and unmarried daughters. Such family life continues to be an important source of strength and support in such communities.

The modified extended family

While it is true that most families with dependent children in Britain today are nuclear families, we must not assume that just because family members may live apart geographically, all links with kin are severed and destroyed. Kin beyond the nuclear family still play an important part in the lives of many families, particularly in the early years of relationships when homes are purchased or rented and children arrive. Often, in the age of modern communications and easy transportation, the closeness and mutual support between kin typical of classic extended family life are retained through e-mail, letter writing, telephone and visiting, despite geographical separation. We might therefore conclude that the typical family unit in industrial society is not simply extended or nuclear, but a modified form of the extended family. This modified extended family, as Eugene Litwak called it, is one where related nuclear families, although they may be living far apart geographically, nevertheless maintain regular contact and mutual support made possible by modern communications and easy transportation. This, rather than the isolated nuclear family, is probably the most common type of family arrangement in Britain today.

The 'Beanpole' family: the return of the extended family?

Britain's ageing population means that a growing number of people are reaching old age, and often living well into their eighties and many into their nineties. At the same time, couples are having fewer children and nuclear families are getting smaller. This means that there is an increase in the number of extended three- and four-generation families. There are fewer children in families, but more of them are growing up in extended families alongside several of their grandparents and even great-grandparents. This new shape of the extended family is sometimes called the 'beanpole' family (Brannen, 2003). This is because the family tree is

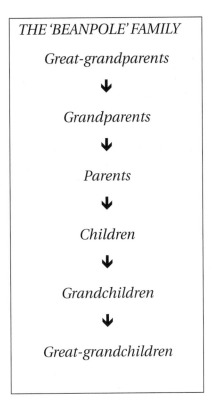

THE 'BEANPOLE' FAMILY

Great-grandparents

↓

Grandparents

↓

Parents

↓

Children

↓

Grandchildren

↓

Great-grandchildren

'thinner' and less 'bushy': fewer brothers and sisters in one generation leads to fewer aunts and uncles in the next. It is also longer, with several generations of older relatives, as people live longer. This trend towards a new emerging 'beanpole' form of the extended family can only be expected to increase with the growing numbers of the elderly, and fewer children being born.

Figure 2.3 summarizes the debates above, and also a range of other changes in the family which are often linked with the move from a pre-industrial to a modern industrial society.

Activity

1 Describe two characteristics of the privatized nuclear family.
2 Give three reasons for the decline of the classic extended family.
3 Explain what is meant by the 'modified extended family'.
4 Write a short essay of about one and half sides answering the following question:
   Critically assess the view that the nuclear family is ideally suited to the needs of an industrial society.

(Note: give arguments and evidence for and against, and reach a conclusion.)

Family change 3: the emergence of the symmetrical family?

Is there more equality between partners in relationships today, or does the family remain a patriarchal, male-dominated unit? There is a common belief that, since the middle of the twentieth century, the relations between male and female partners in the family in Britain have become less patriarchal, or male-dominated, and become much more a 'partnership of equals'. The assumption has been that there has been a change from **segregated conjugal roles** to more **integrated** (or joint) **conjugal roles**. Young and Willmott called this more equally balanced relationship the symmetrical family.

Some of the differences between segregated and integrated conjugal roles are identified in table 2.4 on page 54.

This greater equality in marriage or cohabiting relationships is often thought to be shown by women taking on more 'men's work' (especially working outside the home) and men doing 'women's work' (housework, shopping and childcare), with shared leisure and decision-making. This was often combined with discussion, mainly in the mass media, about the emergence of a so-called 'new man', who was more caring, sharing, gentle, emotional and sensitive in his attitudes to women, children and his own

Conjugal roles simply means the roles played by a male and female partner in marriage or in a cohabiting relationship.
Segregated conjugal roles show a clear division and separation between the male and female roles.
Integrated (or joint) **conjugal roles** show few divisions between male and female partners' roles.

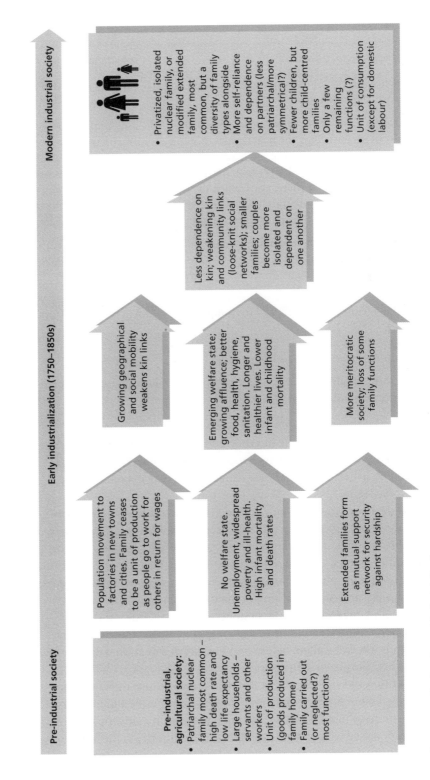

Figure 2.3 The family and industrialization

Table 2.4. Differences between segregated and integrated conjugal roles

Segregated conjugal roles	Integrated conjugal roles
Partners in a married or cohabiting relationship have clearly separated roles.	Partners in a married or cohabiting relationship have interchangeable and flexible roles.
Men take responsibility for bringing in money, major decisions and doing the heavier and more technical jobs around the home, such as repairing household equipment and doing repairs. Women are mainly housewives, with responsibility for housework, shopping, cooking, childcare, etc.; they are unlikely to have full-time paid employment.	Both partners are likely to be either in paid employment or looking for a job. Household chores and childcare are shared, with males taking on traditional female jobs like housework, cooking, shopping, etc., and female partners taking on traditional male jobs, such as household repairs, looking after the car, etc.
Partners are likely to have separate friends and different leisure activities.	Partners share common friends, leisure activities, and decision-making.

emotional needs, and committed to doing his fair share of housework and childcare.

What causes these apparent changes?

The growing equality in family relationships which is thought to be occurring is often explained by several factors:

- Improved living standards in the home, such as central heating, TV, DVDs, computers and the internet, and all the other modern consumer goods, have encouraged husbands and wives, or cohabiting couples, to become more home-centred, building the relationship and the home.
- The decline of the close-knit extended family and greater geographical and social mobility in industrial society have meant there is less pressure from kin on newly married or cohabiting couples to retain traditional roles – it is therefore easier to adopt new roles in a relationship. There are often no longer the separate male and female networks (of friends and especially kin) for male and female partners to mix with. This increases their dependence upon each other, and may mean men and women who adopt new roles avoid being teased by friends who knew them before they got married or started cohabiting (see Bott's research in the box).
- The improved status and rights of women encourage men to accept women more as equals and not simply as housewives and mothers.
- The increase in the number of women working in paid employment has increased women's independence and authority in the family. Where the female partner has her own income, she is less dependent

on her male partner, and she therefore has more power and authority. Decision-making is thus more likely to be shared.

- The importance of the female partner's earnings in maintaining the family's standard of living may have encouraged men to help more with housework – a recognition that the women cannot be expected to do two jobs at once.
- Weaker gender identities. Postmodernists would argue that men and women now have much more choice in how they see themselves and their roles. Couples are free to 'pick 'n' mix' roles and identities based on personal choice, and are therefore less constrained by traditional gender identities. This weakens traditional gender divisions in housework and childcare.

Elizabeth Bott, 'Conjugal roles and social networks' (1957)

Bott tried to explain the apparent changes in conjugal roles. Although her research is old, the theoretical aspects of her work still have some use today.

Bott found that the most important factor influencing whether couples had segregated or integrated conjugal roles was the social network of friends, kin and acquaintances built up by each partner before marriage. Where couples had a tight-knit network, where the members of the network knew each other well and were in regular contact, this helped to reinforce the separation between men's and women's roles. Both husband and wife, or cohabiting partners, had people of their own sex for companionship or help with household tasks, the closeness of the network acted as a form of social control on the couple, and things such as teasing prevented the couple drifting from 'traditional' segregated roles. By contrast, a loose-knit network would make movement towards more role integration easier, because those constraints would be removed.

Using Bott's framework, one would expect that the geographical and social mobility of industrial societies would lead to looser social networks, more reliance on the partners in the relationship, and therefore more role integration.

Criticisms of the view that modern marriages and cohabiting relationships are really more equal

The view that there is more equality in modern family relationships has been subject to very strong criticism, particularly by feminist writers, and there is not really much evidence that the family is now typically 'symmetrical'. The following summarizes several of these criticisms.

Inequalities in the division of labour in the household   Evidence from a number of surveys, including the British Social Attitudes surveys (see

Have conjugal roles really become more equal?

figure 2.4 on page 58), suggests that women still perform the majority of domestic tasks around the home, even when they have paid jobs themselves. This is true even among full-time working women, where one would expect to find the greatest degree of equality. Cooking the evening meal, household cleaning, washing and ironing, and caring for sick children are still mainly performed by women. Data published in 1997 by the Office for National Statistics showed that women spent on average nearly twice as long as men each day (five hours) cooking, cleaning, shopping, washing and looking after the children. Housework is the second largest cause of domestic rows, after money.

Crude indicators are often used to measure integrated roles. For example, shared friends are often seen as evidence of 'jointness', but shared friends may mean the male partner's friends, and involve the woman being cut off from *her* friends, resulting in more dependence on her male partner and greater inequality.

Ann Oakley is a feminist sociologist who did much of the pioneering work on housework and roles in the family in *The Sociology of Housework* (1974). Oakley argues that Young and Willmott's evidence for 'jointness' in *The Symmetrical Family* is totally unconvincing. Seventy-two per cent of married men claimed to 'help their partners in the home in some way other than washing up at least once a week'. As Oakley points out, this could mean anything – a quick pass of the vacuum cleaner, tucking children into bed, making breakfast occasionally, going out with the children on Saturday mornings, or even a man ironing his own trousers. This is hardly convincing evidence for symmetry or equality in marriage, and fewer than three-quarters of husbands in Young and Willmott's research did even this much.

Research on families where both partners are working in full-time career jobs, such as Elston's (1980) research on doctors and Rapoport and Rapoport's (1976) study of professional and business couples, suggests that these professional wives are still expected to take major responsibility for dealing with childcare arrangements, sick children and housework. So women who are in full-time demanding career jobs are still treated primarily as housewives/mothers at home, and this is the group Young and Willmott argued would be most likely to display symmetry in marriage.

How representative is the research on conjugal roles?

The extent to which research on conjugal roles can be applied to the whole population is seriously questionable. For example, Bott's research was based on a small sample of 20 families, research by Oakley on 40 couples, by Boulton on 50 couples, and by Edgell on 38 couples. Much of this research was based in London. These samples are too small and too specific to London to be applied to the whole country. The only survey which can really claim to be representative of everyone is the British Social Attitudes Survey, which uses much larger samples (around 3,000 people) and very careful sampling techniques. These issues are discussed in the final chapter on sociological methods.

Three-quarters of households now have dual incomes, but 2005 research by Susan Harkness at the University of Bristol found that women still take responsibility for most of the housework. This research found it is still mainly women who take time off to look after sick children, including more than half of women who earn the same or more than their partners. Working mothers with children put twice as many hours into housework as their partners, and mothers working full-time in dual earner couples faced long working hours, with the burden of unpaid housework and childcare responsibilities increasing the time pressures for many women. These pressures of housework and childcare on top of full-time careers have led to the suggestion by the *Guardian* newspaper that many full-time married career women effectively have the status of 'married lone parents'.

While there is some evidence of more sharing of childcare than household tasks, Mary Boulton argues that many surveys exaggerate how much childcare men really do. As she sees it, while men may 'help' with childcare, it is their female partners who take the main responsibility for children, often at the expense of other aspects of their lives, like paid employment.

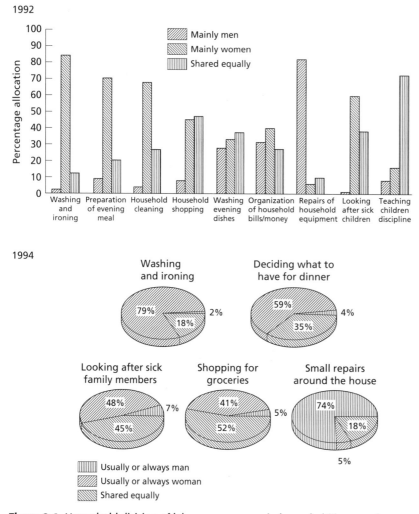

1992

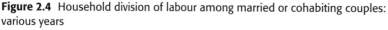

Figure 2.4 Household division of labour among married or cohabiting couples: various years
Source: Based on data from British Social Attitudes surveys (1992, 1994), *Social Trends* (1997) and *British and European Social Attitudes Report* (1998)

A 2005 report by the Institute for Public Policy Research found that while public attitudes increasingly assume a high degree of gender equality in paid work, this does not apply to home and family life. This research found there was still a widely held belief among the public that women should be responsible for the care of the home and young children. Asked about whether mothers should work, 48 per cent thought they should stay at home while children are under school age, with 34 per cent supporting part-time working. This perception disadvantages mothers with full-time careers, harming their promotion prospects.

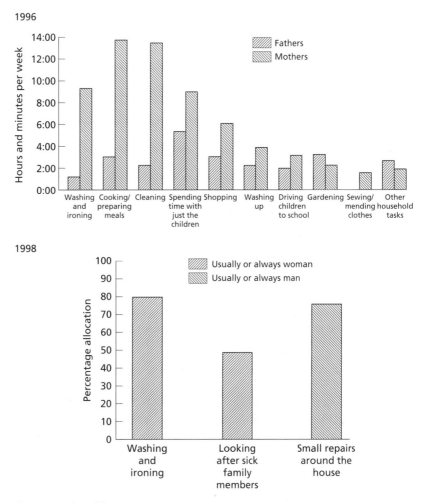

1996

1998

Figure 2.4 *(cont'd)*

It seems that patriarchal ideology still sees housework and childcare as 'women's work', and nothing much has changed since Oakley wrote in *The Sociology of Housework*:

> As long as the blame is laid on the woman's head for an empty larder or a dirty house it is not meaningful to talk about marriage as a 'joint' or 'equal' partnership. The same holds of parenthood. So long as mothers and not fathers are judged by their children's appearance and behaviour . . . symmetry remains a myth.

The unequal distribution of power and authority in marriage and cohabiting relationships   An important issue to consider when assessing whether there is more equality or not in the family is to examine how

Table 2.5. Percentage who never do selected household tasks: United Kingdom, 2001

	Does not do activity	
Activity	Men	Women
Cooking a meal	15	3
DIY repair work	16	46
Gardening	20	22
Non-food shopping	7	3
Food shopping	33	10
Cooking a meal (special occasion)	18	27
Decorating	12	5
Tidying the house	13	4
Helping children with homework	66	60
Washing clothes	39	5
Ironing clothes	42	8

Source: Adapted from UK Time Use Survey, Office for National Statistics

much control over decision-making each partner has. Research in this area suggests:

● Most decisions which couples think of as 'very important', such as moving house or taking out loans, are finally taken by men alone. While some decisions are taken jointly, very few are taken by women alone. Edgell, in *Middle-Class Couples* (1980), found women had sole responsibility for decisions only in relatively unimportant areas like home decoration and furnishing, children's clothes, food and other domestic spending. This was confirmed by a MORI survey conducted for Direct Line Financial Services in June 2000. This found that decisions on major spending (over £1,000) were only made jointly between men and women in 53 per cent of cases. Women made only one in ten of the decisions. In many households, men still hold the purse strings.

● Men are still often the major or sole earners. This puts them in a stronger bargaining position than women, and often puts their female partners in a position of economic dependence.

● There is evidence of widespread male violence in relationships (wife-battering), often resorted to when men are drunk and use their power to try to get women to submit to their wishes. Such violence is all too often not taken seriously by the police or courts, being dismissed as a 'domestic dispute'. This might be interpreted as a view that such violence is almost seen as a 'normal' part of a relationship. Violence in the family is discussed later in this chapter.

Activity

Refer to figure 2.4 and table 2.5. These show the results of surveys which were conducted throughout the 1990s and in 2001. Then answer the following questions:

1 Overall, which household task was the most likely to be performed mainly by women?
2 Overall, which household task was the most likely to be performed mainly by men?
3 Who is most likely to look after sick children or other sick family members?
4 Which household tasks do fathers spend more time on than mothers?
5 Overall, which three households tasks are most likely to be shared equally?
6 When considering whether the time spent on household tasks is fair or not, what other information do you think is required?
7 What percentage of men never iron clothes?
8 What percentage of women never do do-it-yourself repair work?
9 Outline all the evidence in figure 2.4 and table 2.4 which suggests that it is largely a myth that the family is a 'partnership of equals' today?
10 Do a small survey in your own home or in any household where there are children, and find out who performs the various jobs around the home – mainly the man, mainly the woman, or shared equally. You might like to investigate if children do any work.

  (a) Make a note about whether or not one or both partners are working in paid employment, and whether they do this full-time or part-time. Why might this be important information?

  (b) Use the various tasks included in figure 2.4 and table 2.4 to draw up a checklist of jobs. You might also consider some of the following tasks: cleaning floors; cleaning the loo; drawing up the shopping list or working out what's needed when going to the supermarket; changing nappies; bathing the baby; buying children's clothes. You might also consider decision-making in the family, by asking about who finally decides whether to spend a large amount of money (say, over £1,000), buy new furniture, whether and where to go on holiday, whether to buy a new car, deciding on colour schemes when redecorating, deciding what plants to put in the garden, and so on. A further aspect to explore might be who takes responsibility for children, such as making sure they have the right gear for school every day, buying them new shoes, arranging parties and so on.

  (c) Examine your results to see if there is any evidence to suggest family roles are becoming more equal. If you are in a group, bring all the results together and discuss what the evidence shows.

The effects of housework and childcare on women's careers   Women's continuing responsibility for housework and childcare often means women's careers suffer. The constraints these pressures put on the energies of working women, particularly mothers, are seen to be holding back their earning power. Surveys suggest many working women are limited in the jobs they can do and the hours they can work because they are still expected to take the main responsibility for housework and childcare, and to be at home when the children leave for and return from school. These family commitments allow little opportunity for working mothers to concentrate on the actions necessary for progressing their careers, and women consequently have less pay, less security of employment and poorer promotion prospects than men, and this reinforces men's economic superiority and greater authority in the family.

More than four out of five part-time workers are women, and about 40 per cent of women in paid employment work only part-time, compared with about 9 per cent of men. The presence of dependent children (under the age of 18) and the age of the youngest child are the most important factors bearing on whether or not women are in paid employment, and whether they work full-time or part-time. Figure 2.5 illustrates the importance of this link between dependent children and part-time status, and

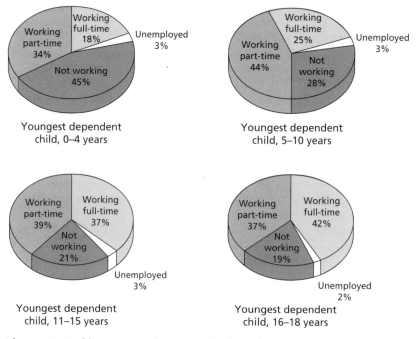

Figure 2.5 Working patterns of women with dependent children: United Kingdom, 2004
Source: Data from Labour Force Survey

provides clear evidence that it is women who retain primary responsibility for childcare.

Activity

Refer to figure 2.5:

1 What percentage of mothers whose youngest child was aged 0–4 years was not working in 2004?
2 Identify two trends which occur as the youngest dependent child gets older.
3 What does figure 2.5 suggest might be the main restriction on mothers with dependent children going out to work? Suggest ways this restriction might be overcome.
4 How do you think having young dependent children might affect the working lives of fathers? Give reasons for your answer.

There is still a lot of male prejudice about women in career jobs and senior positions, and women face a number of disadvantages:

- Women who have children are seen as 'unreliable' by some employers, because of the assumption they will get pregnant again, or be absent to look after sick children.
- Employers are sometimes reluctant to invest in expensive training programmes for women, as they may assume women will leave work eventually to produce and raise children.
- Women with promising careers may have temporarily to leave jobs to have children, and therefore miss out greatly on pay and promotion opportunities. Top jobs require a continuous career pattern in the 20–30 age period, yet these are the usual childbearing years for women, so while men continue to work and get promoted, women miss their opportunities. Women may also find difficulties in attending meetings, and this may affect their chances of promotion.
- Highly qualified women who leave jobs to have children, or who take career breaks to spend time with young children, often face 'hidden discrimination' when they return to their jobs. Gatrell (2004) found many of these returning women, labelled 'jelly heads' by hostile employers, had no other option but to accept a downgraded position if they wished even to stay in their chosen professions, particularly if they asked for more flexible working arrangements to cope with their children. Although downgrading like this is illegal, many women don't fight their cases for fear of being labelled as 'awkward' and consequently facing even further career disadvantages.
- It is mainly women who give up paid work (or suffer from lost/restricted job opportunities) to look after children, the elderly or the sick.

- Married or cohabiting women are still more likely to move house and area for their male partner's job promotion rather than the other way round. This means women interrupt their careers and have to start again in a new job, often at a lower level, while the men are getting promoted at the expense of lost opportunities for their partners.

Domestic labour   Domestic labour refers to unpaid housework and childcare, and, as seen above, most of this still falls to women. This is a clear inequality between men and women, and this problem is made worse by some of the features of domestic labour that make it different from a paid job. These include no pay, no pensions, no holidays, and unlimited working hours. Much of this has been covered in Oakley's work.

These features of domestic labour are illustrated in figure 2.6 on page 66. The Office for National Statistics in 1997 calculated that if the time spent on unpaid work in the home (childcare, washing, ironing, cleaning, shopping and cooking) was valued at the same average pay rates as equivalent jobs in paid employment (for example, if cooking were paid as it is for chefs, or childcare as for nannies and childminders), it would be worth £739 billion a year. The Legal and General insurance company's 'Value of a Mum' survey in 2004 valued domestic labour and childcare at £407 per week, based on an average 64-hour week around the home, including childcare, cooking, cleaning and housekeeping. This is a very modest £6.36 an hour, and probably too low an hourly rate to purchase all these services outside the home. The same survey found that men thought they could pay people half this. Norwich Union's research in 2004 set the value of a mother's contribution to the home at £29,000 a year.

There are differing views about who benefits from domestic labour:

- For *radical feminists*, men are seen as the main people who benefit from domestic labour, since it is overwhelmingly women who do it. From this point of view, the inequalities in domestic labour are part of the problem of patriarchy, with the family seen as a patriarchal unit, institutionalizing, reinforcing and reproducing male power.
- *Marxist feminists* see domestic labour as benefiting capitalism by contributing to the reproduction of labour power. Unpaid domestic labour reproduces the labour force at no cost to the capitalist, through the free production and rearing of children, and support for male workers. From this point of view, the family is a 'social factory', producing human labour power. Domestic labour also contributes to the daily reproduction of the labour force by providing for the physical and mental well-being of family members so they are capable of performing labour each day for the capitalist. However, Marxist

feminists recognize it is also a problem of patriarchy, as it is women who do most of this unpaid work and it is predominantly men who benefit from it.

The emotional side of family life   There is evidence that women take the major responsibility for 'managing' the emotional side of family life. Duncombe and Marsden (1995) found that many long-term relationships were held together by women, rather than men, putting in the emotional work necessary to keep their relationships alive. As well as with their partners, women also seem to be more involved in the emotional aspects of childcare, such as talking to, listening to, understanding and supporting children, including older children. This emotional work also involves liaising between family members when there are rows, and acting as the family mediator. This additional work of women is very much in keeping with the functionalist view that Parsons was talking about in the 1950s when he wrote about the 'expressive' role of women. However, this 'expressive' role of women in the emotional side of family life now often comes on top of their 'instrumental' responsibilities in paid employment and domestic labour. This means many female partners often have three jobs (paid work, domestic labour and childcare, and emotional work) to their male partner's one. That women mainly undertake this aspect of family life is perhaps illustrated by the fact that, after separation or divorce, 40 per cent of fathers lose contact with their children within two years.

Women's triple shift

The points discussed in this section mean many female partners now often have three jobs – paid work, domestic labour and childcare, and emotional work – to their male partner's one. This has sometimes been referred to as women's 'triple shift'.

Social construction
means that the important characteristics of something, such as statistics, health, childhood, old age or what is regarded as deviance, are created and influenced by the attitudes, actions and interpretations of members of society. It only exists because people define it as such.

Family change 4: the changing position of children in the family

The changing status of children

We tend to think of childhood as a clear and separate period of life, with the child's world being different and separate from the world of adults. However, sociologists would argue that childhood is a **social construction**.

This means that the identity and status of children, and childhood as a separate phase of life, have been created by society and social attitudes, and are not simply moulded by biological immaturity.

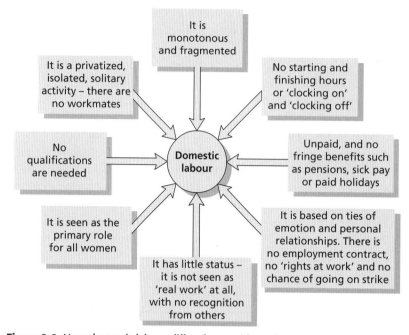

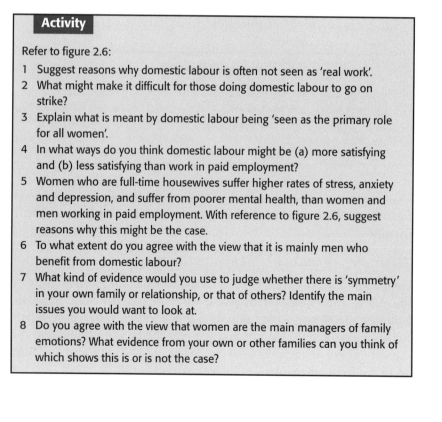

Figure 2.6 How domestic labour differs from paid employment

Activity

Refer to figure 2.6:

1 Suggest reasons why domestic labour is often not seen as 'real work'.
2 What might make it difficult for those doing domestic labour to go on strike?
3 Explain what is meant by domestic labour being 'seen as the primary role for all women'.
4 In what ways do you think domestic labour might be (a) more satisfying and (b) less satisfying than work in paid employment?
5 Women who are full-time housewives suffer higher rates of stress, anxiety and depression, and suffer from poorer mental health, than women and men working in paid employment. With reference to figure 2.6, suggest reasons why this might be the case.
6 To what extent do you agree with the view that it is mainly men who benefit from domestic labour?
7 What kind of evidence would you use to judge whether there is 'symmetry' in your own family or relationship, or that of others? Identify the main issues you would want to look at.
8 Do you agree with the view that women are the main managers of family emotions? What evidence from your own or other families can you think of which shows this is or is not the case?

The notion of childhood as a distinctive phase of life between infancy and adulthood is a relatively modern development. Philippe Ariès (1973) showed that in medieval times childhood did not exist as a separate status. Children often moved straight from infancy, when they required constant care, to working roles in the community. Children were seen as 'little adults'. They did not lead separate lives, and mixed with adults. None of the things we associate with childhood today, like toys, games, books, music, special clothes, schooling and so on existed.

Ariès showed that the social construction of childhood was linked to industrialization. With industrialization, work moved outside the family home. Restrictions on child labour in mines and factories during the nineteenth century isolated most children from the 'real world' of adult work and responsibilities. The growing speed of technological change meant parents were frequently unable to pass on the knowledge and skills required for working life, and the requirements for a literate and numerate labour force in part led to the development of compulsory education from 1880. These changes made children dependent on parents or other adults. There then emerged a new conception of a phase of 'childhood', with children lacking in power and dependent on and supported by adults. This period of dependency is ever lengthening today, as more young people spend time in education and training.

Children and the family in the nineteenth century

In the nineteenth century, the father and husband was the head of the family – it was a patriarchal unit – and fathers often had a great deal of authority over other family members. He would often have little involvement in the care of his children. Children might see relatively little of their parents and, generally, children had low status in the family and were expected 'to be seen and not heard'.

Children and the family in the twentieth and early twenty-first centuries

During the course of the twentieth century and in the early twenty-first, families have become more child-centred, with family activities and outings often focused on the interests of the children. The amount of time parents spend with their children has more than doubled since the 1960s, and parents are more likely to take an interest in their children's activities, discussing decisions with them and treating them more as equals. Often, the children's welfare is seen as the major family priority, frequently involving the parents in considerable financial cost and sacrifice.

The causes of child-centredness

There are a number of reasons why families are more centred on children:

- Families have got smaller since the end of the nineteenth century, and this means more individual care and attention can be devoted to each child.

- In the nineteenth century, the typical working week was between 70 and 80 hours for many working-class people. Today it is more like 44 hours (including overtime), and is tending to get shorter. This means parents have more time to spend with their children.

- Increasing affluence, with higher wages and a higher standard of living, has benefited children, allowing more money to be spent on them and their activities.

- The welfare state provides a wide range of benefits designed to help parents care for their children, and has increased demands on parents to look after their children properly. Social workers, for example, have an extensive range of powers to intervene in families on behalf of children, and have the ultimate power to remove children from families if parents fail to look after them properly. The Children Acts of 1989 and 2004 established children's legal rights, and there is now a Minister for Children and a Children's Commissioner to champion the views of children and protect and promote their interests.

- Paediatrics, or the science of childhood, developed in the twentieth century, with a wide range of research and popular books suggesting how parents should bring up their children to encourage their full development. The nurturing, protection and education of children are now seen as a vital and central part of family life, with 'parenting skills' and early years education now recognized as an important aspect of children's educational and social development.

- Compulsory education and more time spent in further education and training have meant young people are dependent on their parents for longer periods of time. Tuition fees for higher education and the abolition of student grants have recently extended this period of dependency of young people on their parents. In this respect, 'childhood', and the dependency on adults it involves, has itself been extended.

- Children's lives have become more complex, with more educational, medical and leisure services for them. This frequently involves parents in ferrying children to schools, cinemas, friends and so on.

- Growing traffic dangers and parental fears (largely unjustified) of assaults against their children have meant that children now travel more with parents rather than being left to roam about on their own as much as they used to.

- Large businesses have encouraged a specific childhood consumer market. Businesses like Mothercare, Toys "Я" Us and Nike, and publishers and the music industry aim at the childhood consumer market, encouraging children to consume, and parents to spend to satisfy their children's demands. 'Pester power', where advertisers target children to pester their parents into buying them CDs, clothes, toys and so on, is now an important feature of the advertising business.

Despite this growth of child-centredness, we need to be aware of the way children are rapidly becoming exposed to a range of experiences that they share with adults, such as the mass media, especially television, videos and DVDs. This may be eroding the cultural divisions between childhood and adult status.

On the other hand, the rapid pace of technological and social change often means that children are more up to date than their parents. Computer technology and use of the internet are good examples of this, as children are often far more adept at using these than their parents. The internet particularly gives young people access to a range of knowledge and imagery of which their parents in many cases have little awareness. This creates the possibility that young people will increasingly develop a culture that parents find goes beyond their comprehension or experience, and is far more in tune with the future than the culture of their parents. This may make parental involvement with their children's activities more difficult, and create a barrier between parents and children.

We must also remember that, although the status of children in the family has improved this century in Britain, child-centredness doesn't

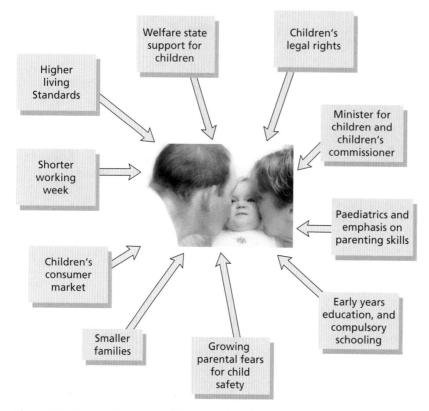

Figure 2.7 Reasons for a more child-centred society

Activity

1. Explain in your own words what is meant by 'childhood is a social construction'.
2. Suggest two reasons why childhood is a relatively modern invention.
3. Identify and explain three ways in which the position of children has changed in the last hundred years.
4. Suggest and explain two ways in which the difference between 'childhood' and 'adulthood' may be changing.

---

mean all children are well looked after. Abuse and neglect are all too common experiences for some children. This is discussed later in this chapter, in the section on the 'darker side' of family life.

Family change 5: the decline in average family size

Over the last century, the **birth rate** has been declining in Britain, from 28 per 1,000 in 1902 to about 11 per 1,000 in 2005.

> The **birth rate** is the number of live births per thousand of the population each year.

This has meant that average family and household size has been dropping, from around 6 children per family in the 1870s to an average of around 1.8 children per family in 2004. The average household size in Britain has also almost halved in the last hundred years, from around 4.6 people to around 2.3 people per household in 2004. The trend towards smaller families, and more people living alone, explains this reduction in average household size.

The reasons for smaller families

Contraception   More effective, safer and cheaper methods of birth control have been developed in the last century, and society's attitudes to the use of contraception have changed from disapproval to acceptance. This is partly because of growing secularization, and the declining influence of the church and religion on people's behaviour and morality. The availability of safe and legal abortion since 1967 has also helped in terminating unwanted pregnancies. Family planning is therefore easier.

> **Secularization** is the process whereby religious thinking, practice and institutions lose social significance.

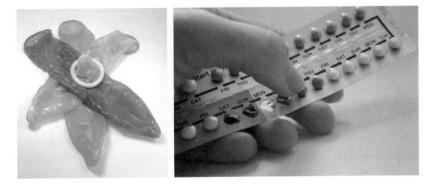

The compulsory education of children   Since children were barred from employment in the nineteenth century, and education became compulsory in 1880, they have ceased to be an economic asset that can contribute to family income through working at an early age. Children have therefore become an economic liability and a drain on the resources of parents, because they have to be supported for a long period in compulsory education, and often in post-16 education and training. Parents have therefore begun to limit the size of their families to secure for themselves and their children a higher standard of living. The move to a more child-centred society has assisted in this restriction of family size, as smaller families mean parents can spend more money and time on and with each child.

The changing position of women   The changing position of women, particularly in the last century, has involved more equal status with men and greater employment opportunities. Women today have less desire to spend long years of their lives bearing and rearing children, and many wish to pursue a career of their own. While most women do eventually have children, there is a growing proportion who are choosing not to do so. For example, 20 per cent of 35-year-old women in 1989 were childless, compared to 12 per cent in 1979. Around one in five women currently reaching the end of their childbearing years is childless, compared to one in ten born in the 1940s, and nearly 25 per cent of women born in 1973 are expected to be still childless at age 45. This trend towards childlessness can be expected to continue with women's growing position in paid employment.

The declining infant mortality rate   In the nineteenth century, the absence of a welfare state meant many parents relied on their children to care for them in old age. However, many babies failed to survive infancy, and it was often uncertain whether children would outlive their parents. Parents therefore often had many children as a safeguard against some of them dying. The decline in the **infant mortality rate** and the overall **death rate** has meant that fewer people die before adulthood and old age, so parents no longer have more children as security against only a few surviving. In addition, the range of agencies which exist to help the elderly today mean people are less reliant on care from their children when they reach old age.

> The **infant mortality rate** is the number of deaths of babies in the first year of life per 1,000 live births per year.
> The **death rate** is the number of deaths per 1,000 of the population per year.

A geographically mobile labour force   Industrial societies generally require a geographically mobile workforce, that is, a workforce that can easily move to other areas for work or promotion. This may have been a factor in encouraging smaller families, because they can more easily pack up and move elsewhere.

Changing values   Parenthood involves greater pressure on couples, a lifelong commitment, a loss of freedom and independence, and sacrifices like cuts in money to spend on consumer goods and the loss of time for leisure and pleasure. In the postmodern age, where consumer values dominate and people seek to develop their identities through their consumer spending and leisure choices, couples are becoming more reluctant to have children.

Family change 6: the rising divorce rate

One of the most startling changes in the family in Britain in the last century has been the general and dramatic increase in the number of marriages ending in divorce, with a similar trend found in many Western industrialized countries. The number of divorces rose from 27,000 in 1961 to around 167,000 by 2005; during the 1960s the number doubled, and

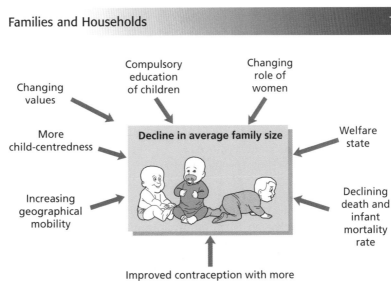

Figure 2.8 Reasons for the decline in the birth rate and smaller family size

---

Divorce and 'broken homes'

Divorce is the legal termination of a marriage, but this is not the only way that marriages and homes can be 'broken'. Homes and marriages may be broken in 'empty shell' marriages, where the marital relationship has broken down but no divorce has taken place. Separation – through either choice or necessity (like working abroad or imprisonment) – may also cause a broken home, as may the death of a partner. So homes may be broken for reasons other than divorce, and divorce itself is often only the end result of a marriage which broke down long before.

The **divorce rate** is the number of divorces per 1,000 married people per year.

then doubled again in the 1970s. Britain has one of the highest **divorce rates** in the European Union. About 40 per cent of new marriages today are likely to end in divorce, and, if present rates continue, more than one in four children will experience a parental divorce by the time they are 16.

Divorce statistics

Divorce statistics are presented in three main ways:

- *the total number of divorce petitions per year* (the number of people applying for a divorce but not necessarily actually getting divorced)
- *the total number of decrees absolute granted per year* (the number of divorces actually granted)
- *the divorce rate* (the number of divorces each year per thousand married people in the population)

Divorce statistics must be treated with considerable caution, and assessed against changing legal, financial and social circumstances, if misleading conclusions about the declining importance of marriage and the family are to be avoided. The increase may simply reflect easier and cheaper divorce procedures enabling the legal termination of already unhappy 'empty shell' marriages rather than a real increase in marriage breakdowns. It could be that people who in previous years could only separate are now divorcing as legal and financial obstacles are removed.

Divorce statistics only show the legal termination of marriages. They do not show:

- the number of people who are separated but not divorced
- the number of people who live in 'empty shell marriages' – many couples may want to split up but are deterred from doing so by their roles as parents
- how many 'unstable' or 'unhappy' marriages existed before divorce was made easier by changes in the law and changing social attitudes to divorce

These points could mean *either* that divorce figures underestimate the extent of family and marriage breakdowns *or* that rising divorce rates only reflect legal changes and do not represent a real increase in marital instability.

There are two broad groups of reasons for the increase in the divorce rate: changes in the law which have gradually made divorce easier and cheaper to get; and changes in society which have made divorce a more practical and socially acceptable way of terminating a broken marriage. These are discussed in the next sections, and figure 2.9 on page 77 summarizes these changes.

Changes in the law as a reason for the rising divorce rate

Changes in the law over the last century have made divorce easier and cheaper to get, and have given men and women equal rights in divorce. This partly accounts for the steep rise in the divorce rate over the last fifty years, particularly in the 1970s and 1980s. These changes in the law are listed in the box. However, changes in the law reflect changing social attitudes and norms, and there are a number of wider social explanations that must also be considered.

Changes in society as a reason for the rising divorce rate

The changing role of women   This is a very important explanation for the rising divorce rate. Around three-quarters of divorce petitions (requests to a court for a divorce) are initiated by women, and around three out of four of all divorces are granted to women. This suggests more women than men are unhappy with the state of their marriages, and are more likely to take the first steps in ending them. This may well be because

A brief history of the divorce laws

Before 1857, divorce could only be obtained by the rich, since each divorce needed a private Act of Parliament. As a result, there were very few divorces. Since that time, changes in the law have made it easier to get a divorce over about the last sixty years.

- *The Matrimonial Causes Act of 1857* made divorce procedure easier and cheaper, but it was still beyond the financial means of the lower middle class and working class. Men had more rights in divorce than women, and divorce was only possible if it could be proved in court that a 'matrimonial offence' such as adultery, cruelty or desertion had been committed. Even by 1911, there were only about 600 divorces a year.

- *The Matrimonial Causes Act of 1923* gave women equal rights with men in divorce for the first time, and therefore gave more women the opportunity to terminate unhappy marriages.

- *The Legal Aid and Advice Act of 1949* gave financial assistance with the costs of solicitors' and court fees, which made it far more possible for working-class people to cope with the costs of a divorce action.

- *The Divorce Law Reform Act of 1969*, which came into effect in 1971, was a major change. Before the 1969 Act, a person wanting a divorce had to prove before a court that his or her spouse had committed a 'matrimonial offence', as mentioned above. This frequently led to major public scandals, as all the details of unhappy marriages were aired in a public lawcourt. This may have deterred many people whose marriage had broken down from seeking a divorce. Also, marriages may have broken down – become 'empty shell' marriages – without any matrimonial offence being committed. The 1969 Act changed all this, and made 'irretrievable breakdown' of a marriage the only grounds for divorce. It is now no longer necessary to prove one partner 'guilty' of a matrimonial offence: it simply has to be demonstrated that a marriage has broken down beyond repair. After 1971, one way of demonstrating 'irretrievable breakdown' of a marriage was by two years of separation. This change in the law led to a massive increase in the number of divorces after 1971.

- *The Matrimonial and Family Proceedings Act of 1984* allowed couples to petition for divorce after only one year of marriage, whereas previously couples could normally divorce only after three years of marriage. This led to a record increase in the number of divorces in 1984 and 1985.

- *The Family Law Act of 1996* came into effect in 1999. This increased the amount of time before a divorce could be granted to eighteen months, introduced compulsory marriage counselling for a 'period of reflection', and required children's wishes and financial arrangements for children to be agreed before a divorce was granted. This was an attempt to stem the rising number of divorces by increasing the time for 'cooling off'. These compulsory counselling sessions were later abandoned because it was found they were more likely to encourage people to go through with a divorce, even when they were initially uncertain.

women's expectations of life and marriage have risen during the course of the last century, and they are less willing to accept a traditional house-wife/mother role, with the sacrifices of their own leisure activities, careers and independence this involves.

The employment of married women has increased over the last century. For example, in 1931 only 10 per cent of married women were employed, but this had gradually risen to about 75 per cent by the end of the twentieth century. This has increased their financial independence, and reduced the extent of dependence on their husbands. There is also a range of welfare state benefits to help divorced women, particularly those with children. Marriage has therefore become less of a financial necessity for women, and this makes it easier for women to escape from unhappy marriages.

Rising expectations of marriage   Functionalist writers like Parsons and Fletcher argue that the divorce rate has risen because couples (especially women) expect and demand more in their relationships today than their parents or grandparents might have settled for. Love, companionship, understanding, sexual compatibility and personal fulfilment are more likely to be the main ingredients of a successful marriage today. The grow-ing privatization and isolation of the nuclear family from extended kin and the community have also meant that couples are more likely to spend more time together. The higher expectations mean couples are more likely to end a relationship which earlier generations might have tolerated.

This functionalist approach suggests that higher divorce rates therefore reflect better quality marriages. This view of the higher expectations of marriage is reflected in the fairly high rate of remarriage among divorced people. In other words, families split up to re-form happier families – a bit like 'old banger' cars failing their M.O.T. test, being taken to the scrapyard and being replaced with a better quality car, thereby improving the general quality of cars on the road.

Growing secularization   Secularization refers to the declining influence of religious beliefs and institutions. Writers such as Goode (1971) and C. Gibson (1994) argue that this has resulted in marriage becoming less of a sacred, spiritual union and more a personal and practical commitment which can be abandoned if it fails. Evidence for this lies in the fact that more than 60 per cent of marriages today no longer involve a religious ceremony. The church now takes a much less rigid view of divorce, and many people today probably do not attach much religious significance to their marriages.

Changing social attitudes   Divorce has become more socially accept-able, and there is less social disapproval and condemnation (stigmatizing)

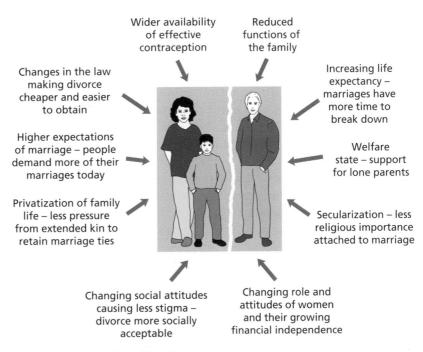

Figure 2.9 Causes of the rising divorce rate

of divorcees. Divorce no longer hinders careers through a public sense of scandal and outrage. As a result, people are less afraid of the consequences of divorce, and are more likely to seek a legal end to an unhappy marriage rather than simply separating or carrying on in an 'empty shell' marriage.

The greater availability of, and more effective, contraception The greater availability of and more effective contraception has made it safer to have sex outside the marital relationship, and with more than one person during marriage. This weakens traditional constraints on 'fidelity' to a marriage partner, and potentially exposes relationships to greater instability.

The growth of the privatized nuclear family Functionalists contend that the growing privatization and isolation of the nuclear family from extended kin and the community in industrial society has meant it is no longer so easy for marriage partners to seek advice from or temporary refuge with relatives. This isolation can also increase the demands and expectations of each partner in a marriage. There is also less social control from extended kin pressuring couples to retain marriage ties. In this sense, there is both more pressure on marriage relationships arising from the points above, and fewer constraints preventing people abandoning marriage, and increasingly the decision whether to divorce or not lies with the married couple alone.

The reduced functions of the family   As we saw earlier in this chapter, some functionalist writers argue that, with industrialization, a number of family functions transferred to other social institutions. This has perhaps meant that marriage has become less of a necessity, and there are fewer bonds linking marriage partners. Love, companionship, understanding, sexual compatibility and personal fulfillment are more likely to be the main ingredients of a successful marriage today, and if some or all of these disappear, there may be nothing much left to hold the marriage together.

Increasing life expectancy   People live to a greater age today than they did in the early years of the twentieth century, and this means the potential number of years a couple may be together, before one of them dies, has increased. This gives more time for marriages to 'go wrong' and for divorces to occur. It has been suggested that the divorce courts have taken on the role in finishing unhappy marriages once performed by the undertaker!

Variations in divorce rates between social groups

While divorce affects all groups in the population, there are some groups where divorce rates are higher than the average. Teenage marriages are twice as likely to end in divorce than those of couples overall, and there is a high incidence of divorce in the first five to seven years of marriage and after about ten to fourteen years (when the children are older or have left home). The working class, particularly semi-skilled and unskilled, has a

---

Activity

1   Suggest reasons why the following groups might be more 'at risk' of divorce than other groups in the population:
   - teenage marriages
   - childless couples
   - couples where each partner is from a different social class or ethnic background
2   Suggest reasons why women are more likely to apply for divorce than men.
3   Refer to figure 2.10, which shows the different numbers and reasons for divorce by husbands and wives:
   (a) Which reason for divorce shows the largest difference between husbands and wives?
   (b) Approximately how many more divorces were granted to wives than husbands?
   (c) Outline the main differences in the reasons for divorce by husbands and wives, and suggest explanations for them. What conclusions might you draw about the different behaviour of men and women in marriage?

Divorces granted:

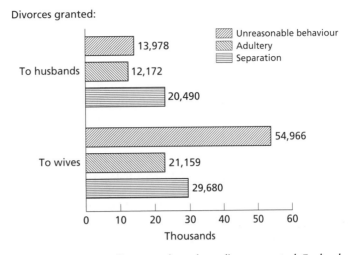

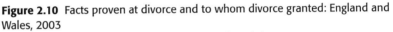

Figure 2.10 Facts proven at divorce and to whom divorce granted: England and Wales, 2003
Source: Data adapted from Office for National Statistics

higher rate of divorce than the middle class. Childless couples and partners from different social class or religious backgrounds also face a higher risk of divorce, as do couples whose work separates them for long periods. The rising divorce rate therefore does not affect all groups of married people equally, and some face higher risks of divorce than others.

Family change 7: remarriage and the growth of the reconstituted family

While marriage is still the usual form of partnership between men and women, marriages where it is the first time for both partners are declining substantially. The number of these has more than halved since 1970. Just over two-fifths of marriages now involve a remarriage for one or both partners, mainly reflecting the increase in the divorce rate. A lot more divorced men remarry than divorced women, reflecting women's greater dissatisfaction or disillusionment with marriage. This is perhaps not surprising, given the way women often have to balance the triple and competing demands of paid employment, domestic labour and childcare, and emotional 'management' of the family.

These trends have meant that there are more reconstituted families (sometimes called 'stepfamilies') with step-parents, stepchildren, and stepbrothers and stepsisters arising from a previous relationship of one or both partners. Stepfamilies are the fastest growing family type. Stepfathers are more common than stepmothers, since most children remain with the mother after a break-up, and around nine out of ten stepfamilies consist of a couple with at least one child from a previous relationship of the woman. This reflects the fact that it is nearly always women who gain custody of children in the event of a relationship breakdown. One in six men in their thirties are now stepfathers, raising other men's children – nearly double the proportion in the mid-1990s. Official estimates suggest there are around half a million stepfamilies with dependent stepchildren in Britain, and around three-quarters of a million children live in such families.

Family change 8: the growth of the lone parent family

One of the biggest changes in the family has been the growth of the lone parent family (also known as the single parent or one parent family). The percentage of lone parent families has tripled since 1971, and Britain has one of the highest proportions of lone parent families in Europe. More than one in four of all families with dependent children were lone parent families in 2004 – nine out of ten of them headed by women. Nearly one in four (23 per cent) of dependent children now live in such families, compared to just 7 per cent in 1972.

Why are there more lone parent families?

The rapid growth in the number of lone parent families can be explained by a number of factors, some of which have already been discussed earlier in explaining the rising divorce rate. These include:

- *The greater economic independence of women.* Women have greater economic independence today, both through more job opportunities and through support from the welfare state. This means marriage, and support by a husband, is less of an economic necessity today compared to the past.
- *Improved contraception, changing male attitudes, and fewer 'shotgun weddings'.* With the wider availability and approval of safe and effective contraception, and easier access to safe and legal abortion, men may feel less responsibility to marry women should they become pregnant, and women may feel under less pressure to marry the future father. There are therefore fewer 'shotgun weddings'.
- *Reproductive technology is available to women,* enabling them to bear children without a male partner, through surrogate motherhood and fertility treatments like IVF (in vitro fertilization).
- *Changing social attitudes.* There is less social stigma (or social disapproval and condemnation) attached to lone parenthood today. Women are therefore less afraid of the social consequences of becoming lone parents.

Those with 'New Right' views particularly blame the generosity of the welfare state for the growth in lone parenthood. Writers such as Charles Murray (1990) argue that generous welfare benefits encourage women to have children they could not otherwise afford to support. This is often linked to the idea of the underclass, which is discussed in chapter 6.

The growth in lone parenthood has been seen by some as one of the major signs of the 'decline' of conventional family life and marriage. Lone parent families – and particularly lone never-married mothers – have been portrayed by some of the media and conservative politicians of the 'New Right' as promiscuous parasites, blamed for everything from rising juvenile crime through to housing shortages, rising drug abuse, educational failure of children and the general breakdown of society. The problems created by lone parenthood, particularly for boys, are usually explained by the lack of a male role model in the home, and consequently inadequate socialization.

Lone parenthood has therefore been presented as a major social problem, and there have been **moral panics** about lone parenthood in the mass media.

> A **moral panic** is a wave of public concern about some exaggerated or imaginary threat to society, stirred up by exaggerated and sensationalized reporting in the mass media.

In an effort to cut the welfare costs to the state of lone parents, the Child Support Agency was established in 1993. This was designed to encourage absent fathers to take financial responsibility for their children, thereby reducing benefit costs to the state. There have been a number of attempts to encourage lone parents to support themselves through paid employment. For example, since 1997 a new Childcare Tax Credit to help with the costs of childcare has been introduced, along with a national childcare strategy to ensure good quality affordable childcare, the expansion of nursery places for children aged 3 and 4, and more pre- and after-school clubs. These policies arise from the fact that it is the lack of affordable childcare that is the major deterrent to lone parents working. The national minimum wage helps to avoid the exploitation of lone parents, who are mainly women, by unscrupulous employers, and the New Deal for Lone Parents enabled many lone parents to find paid employment.

Nailing the myths

Never-married lone mothers only account for less than half of all lone parents, with lone parenthood mostly arising from divorce, separation or widowhood, as figure 2.11 overleaf shows. Even among never-married lone mothers, the vast majority cohabited with the father and have registered his name on the child's birth certificate.

The problems allegedly created by absent fathers have been questioned on the grounds that it is not the presence or absence of a father that is important, but whether fathers actually involve themselves in the children's upbringing. There are probably many fathers in two-parent families as well who fail to involve themselves in the care and discipline of their children,

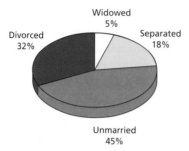

Figure 2.11 Lone mother families with dependent children, by marital status: Great Britain, 2003
Source: Data from Labour Force Survey

Activity

1 Suggest reasons why, in the event of divorce, women are more likely than men to be given custody of the children.
2 Suggest explanations why most lone parent families are headed by women.
3 To what extent do you agree with the following statements, and why?
   - 'A lone mother can bring up her child as well as a married or cohabiting couple'
   - 'People who want children ought to get married'
   - 'To grow up happily, children need a home with both their mother and father'
4 What are the advantages and disadvantages of lone parenthood compared to two-parent families?
5 Suggest reasons why the stereotypes held by professionals (like teachers, police officers and social workers) might mean children from lone parent families are more likely (a) to underachieve in education, and (b) to be overrepresented in the official crime statistics.
6 Try the following websites, and identify five issues that seem to be of particular concern to lone parents. Describe each issue briefly, and outline any solutions that are suggested.

   www.gingerbread.org.uk
   www.lone-parents.org.uk
   www.oneparentfamilies.org.uk

---

and problems like juvenile delinquency are likely to arise in any household where children are inadequately supervised and disciplined. This problem, often blamed on lone parenthood, is therefore just as likely to occur among two-parent families. A Home Office report has found no difference in the crime rates between youngsters from lone-parent and two-parent families. Even if there were such a link, it is likely to be caused by poverty rather than lone parenthood – because lack of childcare facilities means many lone parents have to depend on inadequate state benefits to live, and lone parents are more likely to live in overcrowded or poor quality housing. This probably explains other factors linked in the popular imagination to lone parenthood, such as lower educational achievement.

A misleading myth is that of lone teenage mothers getting pregnant to jump the queue for social (council and housing association) housing. There is very little evidence for this. A 1999 report from the National Council for One Parent Families pointed out that the average age of a lone parent is 34, and that at any one time, less than 3 per cent of all lone parents are teenagers. Research in 1996 commissioned by the Economic and Social Research Council found that only 10 per cent of the small minority of women who were not in a regular relationship with the father when they became mothers were living alone with their child in social (council) housing six months after the birth. Many live with their parents, and many single, never-married parents have been in cohabiting relationships which break down. In effect, this is no different from marriages that break down.

Family change 9: the decline in marriage and the growing incidence and acceptance of cohabitation

The decline of marriage and the growth of living together before or outside marriage were two of the major social changes at the turn of the twenty-first century. Marriage rates are declining in Britain, and there are more and more couples cohabiting rather than seeking official recognition of their relationships through marriage. In 2002, there were 250,000 marriages in England and Wales – 19 per cent fewer than in 1991, and the lowest number ever. Over a quarter of non-married males and females were cohabiting in 2003–4. A number of these included people who were separated but not divorced. By the early 2000s, the majority of people in first marriages had lived with their partner beforehand, and cohabitation is now the norm rather than the exception. Seven in every ten couples married in 2000 gave identical addresses, and this 'living in sin' included 56 per cent of those getting married in a religious ceremony. There are well over a million and a half cohabiting couples who have refused to tie the marriage knot – more than one in ten of all couples. Around 11 per cent of dependent children are now being brought up by unmarried, cohabiting couples. Many cohabiting relationships eventually end up in marriage – about 60 per cent of first-time cohabitations turn into marriages.

The reasons for the decline of marriage and growing cohabitation have been considered earlier, including:

- The changing role of women, whose growing economic independence has given them more freedom to choose their relationships.

- The growing divorce rate, and the message it is sending out to potential marriage partners.
- Growing secularization.
- Changing social attitudes and reduced social stigma. Young people are more likely to cohabit than older people, and this may in part reflect the evidence that older people compared to younger people are more likely to think that 'living together outside marriage is always wrong'. This reveals more easygoing attitudes to cohabitation among the young, showing the reduced social stigma attached to cohabitation.
- The greater availability of, and more effective, contraception.
- Higher expectations of marriage.

Activity

Drawing on the points in this section, but explaining them more fully, write a short essay of about one side of A4 paper explaining why marriage is in decline, and why cohabitation is becoming more common and accepted.

Family change 10: the growth in 'singlehood' – living alone

About one in three households today contains only one person, compared to one in twenty in 1901. Around half of these households are over pensionable age (age 60 for women, 65 for men), compared to two-thirds in 1971. This means there is a growth in the number of younger people living alone. This trend can be explained by the decline in marriage, the rise in divorce and separation, and the fact that people are delaying marriage or cohabitation until they are older. There are twice as many men as women living alone in the 25–44 age group, but there are twice as many women as men aged 65 and over, because women live longer than men. Longer lives, particularly for women, explain the increase in the number of pensioner one-person households.

Family change 11: more births outside marriage

Around four in every ten births are now outside marriage – about five times more than the proportion in 1971. Despite the record numbers of children being born outside marriage, nearly 80 per cent of those births in 2004 were registered jointly by the parents. Both parents in three out of four of these cases gave the same address. This suggests the parents were cohabiting, and that children are still being born into a stable couple relationship, even if the partners are not legally married.

The explanations for the increase of births outside marriage are very similar to those for the increase in the divorce rate, the decline in the marriage rate and the increase in cohabitation, which were discussed above.

Family diversity and the myth of the 'cereal packet' family

The popular impression that many people have of the family in Britain at the turn of the twenty-first century has been described as the 'cereal packet family'. This is the **stereotype** often promoted in advertising and other parts of the mass media, with 'family size' breakfast cereals, toothpaste and a wide range of other consumer goods.

This popular 'happy family' image often gives the impression that most people live in a 'typical family' with the following features:

- It is a privatized, nuclear family unit consisting of two parents living with one or two of their own natural dependent children.
- These parents are married to one another, and neither of them has been married before.
- The husband is the 'breadwinner' and responsible for family discipline, with the wife staying at home and primarily concerned with

A **stereotype** is a generalized, oversimplified view of an institution or social group.

The 'cereal packet' family, with a working father in a first marriage to a home-based mother, caring for their own two natural children, makes up only about 5 per cent of all households

housework and childcare (expressing herself through 'maternal love'), or perhaps doing some part-time paid employment to supplement the family income.

This image also often includes ideas that this family is based on romantic love, as well as love of children (particularly maternal love), and that it is a nurturing, caring and loving institution – a safe and harmonious refuge from an uncaring outside world.

It is this 'cereal packet' stereotype of the 'typical family' that is found in family ideology. This is discussed later in this chapter.

This stereotype of the 'typical family' is very mistaken, because there are a wide range of households and family types in contemporary Britain. This is known as family diversity.

> **Family ideology** is that dominant set of beliefs, values and images about how families are and how they *ought* to be.

Why is the 'cereal packet' stereotype misleading?

The 'cereal packet' stereotyped 'conventional' or 'typical' family is very misleading because, as discussed earlier in this chapter, there have been and continue to be important changes in family patterns, and there is a wide range of family types and household arrangements in modern Britain. This growing diversity of relationships that people live in shows that traditional family life is being eroded as people constantly develop new forms of relationship and choose to live in different ways. The meaning of 'family' and 'family life' is therefore changing for a substantial number of parents and children.

Households and families

Figure 2.12 shows the different types of household in Britain in 2004, and what percentages of people were living in them. In 2004, only 22 per cent of households contained a married or cohabiting couple with dependent children, and only 37 per cent of people lived in such a household. Meanwhile, 29 per cent of households consisted of one person living alone, and at least 68 per cent of households had no dependent children in them. Twelve per cent of people lived in lone parent families, and 10 per cent of households were lone parent families. This alone shows that the 'cereal packet' image of the nuclear family does not represent the arrangement in which most people in Britain live.

Families with dependent children

Figure 2.13 examines families with dependent children. This shows that in 2003, about 25 per cent of such families were lone parent families, with nearly nine out of ten of them headed by women. Although a married or cohabiting couple headed 75 per cent of families with dependent

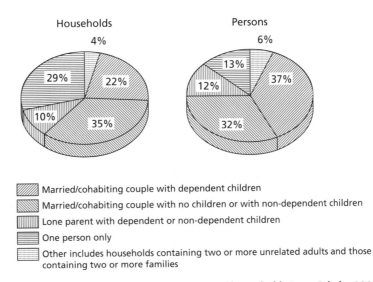

Households
4%

Persons
6%

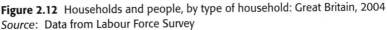

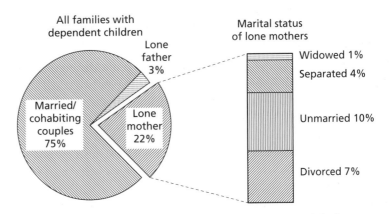

Married/cohabiting couple with dependent children

Married/cohabiting couple with no children or with non-dependent children

Lone parent with dependent or non-dependent children

One person only

Other includes households containing two or more unrelated adults and those containing two or more families

Figure 2.12 Households and people, by type of household: Great Britain, 2004
Source: Data from Labour Force Survey

Figure 2.13 Families with dependent children, by family type and, for lone mothers, by marital status: Great Britain, 2003
Source: Data from Labour Force Survey

Activity

Refer to figures 2.12 and 2.13

1 What percentage of households in 2004 consisted of one person only?
2 What percentage of people in 2004 were living in households consisting of a married or cohabiting couple with no children or with non-dependent children?
3 In 2003, what percentage of all families with dependent children were headed by a lone mother who was widowed?
4 What was the main cause of lone motherhood?
5 Suggest reasons why so many people seem to believe that the 'cereal packet' family is the most common type of family.

children, this doesn't mean that most of these families conformed to the 'cereal packet' image.

- A number of these families involved a cohabiting rather than a married relationship. Twelve per cent of women with dependent children were cohabiting in 2001. Such arrangements do not conform to the 'cereal packet' stereotype.
- A number were reconstituted families, in which one or both partners were previously married. More than two in five marriages currently taking place will end in divorce, and more than 40 per cent of all marriages now involve remarriage for one or both partners. About 10 per cent of all families with dependent children were stepfamilies in the early 2000s.
- Most of these families were dual worker families, where both parents were working. In 2003, about 65 per cent of couples with dependent children were both working. As figure 2.5 (on page 62) showed, large numbers of mothers with dependent children work in paid employment, with the numbers increasing as children get older. In 2003, about 65 per cent of all women with dependent children were working. This often involves complex and costly alternative arrangements for childcare while both parents are working.

The 'cereal packet' 'happy family' stereotype of family ideology, of a working father married to a home-based mother caring for two small children made up in 2003 only about 5 per cent of all households.

Cultural diversity

Cultural diversity refers to differences in family lifestyles between ethnic and religious groups.

South Asian families   Ballard (1982) found extended family relationships are more common in minority ethnic groups originating in South Asia, from Pakistan, Bangladesh and India. Such families are commonly patriarchal in structure, with seniority going to the eldest male, and males in general. A report in 2000 from the Institute for Social and Economic Research, *Family Formation in Multicultural Britain,* found the highest rates of marriage were among Pakistani and Bangladeshi women (three-quarters were married by age 25, compared to half of white women), and virtually all South Asians with a partner were in a formal marriage. A majority of Bangladeshi and Pakistani women reported their primary activity to be looking after the house and family. In many ways, the traditional British 'cereal packet' family of a working male married to a home-based female is more likely to be found among Pakistanis and Bangladeshis than any other ethnic group. Divorce rates are low in such families because of strong social disapproval and a wide support network of kin for families under stress. Arranged marriages are still common in such communities.

African-Caribbean families African-Caribbean families are often centred on the mother, who is in many cases the main breadwinner. Lone parenthood is higher among African-Caribbean mothers than any other ethnic group – over half of African-Caribbean families with children are lone parents, and there are low marriage rates. This partly reflects a cultural tradition, but also high rates of black male unemployment and men's inability and reluctance to support families. African-Caribbean families often belong to a female network of friends and kin to support women with children.

Class diversity

Class diversity refers to differences between middle-class and working-class families. For example, extended families are still found in traditional working-class communities, and the nuclear family may be more common in middle-class families. Differences in income will also lead to differences in lifestyle between such families.

Life cycle diversity

Life cycle diversity refers to the way families may change through life, for example as partners have children, as the children grow older, and eventually leave the home, as partners separate and form new relationships, as people grow old and have grandchildren, etc. All these factors mean the family will be constantly changing. For instance, levels of family income will change as children move from dependence to independence, levels of domestic labour and childcare will differ, and levels of participation in paid employment will alter, particularly for women, depending on the absence or presence of children and the children's age. Figure 2.14 overleaf shows an example of a family life cycle.

Regional diversity

Regional diversity refers to the way family life differs in different geographical locations around the country. Eversley and Bonnerjea (1982) suggest there are distinctive patterns of family life in different areas of Britain. For example, on the south coast there is a high proportion of elderly couples; older industrial areas and very traditional rural communities tend to have more extended families; and the inner cities have a higher proportion of families in poverty and lone parent families.

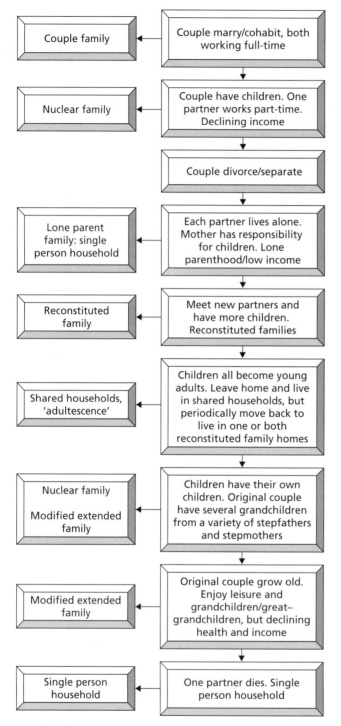

Figure 2.14 A family life cycle

Shared households and 'families of choice'

Shared households are becoming much more common, particularly among young people. Sue Heath (2004) has described how young people are now less likely to follow the traditional route of living at home, leaving school, going into a job or higher education, and then 'settling down' into a married or cohabiting couple relationship. Increasingly, they are adopting a wider range of living arrangements before forming couple relationships later in life. This transitional period between youth and adult roles has been described as 'kidulthood' or 'adultescence'. These transitional living arrangements might include living alone, going back to live with their parents, or living in shared households with their peers. There may often be a greater loyalty among young people to their friends than to their family. Such shared households, where people choose to live with and form relationships with a group of people with whom they have closer relations than with their families of birth, have therefore sometimes been called 'families of choice' (although they are not strictly speaking 'families' as they are not based on kinship relations). Such households may involve shared domestic life (cooking, eating and socializing together), and shared leisure, sporting activities and holidays.

Such households are on the increase because of the high costs of buying or renting houses, the growing numbers of young people entering higher education, and the desire of young people to explore alternative living arrangements rather than simply 'settle down' into a conventional couple household.

Figure 2.15 overleaf summarizes the range of family diversity in contemporary Britain.

Activity

1. Identify all the ways that family life might change during its life cycle.
2. Suggest three ways the rising divorce rate contributes to family diversity in contemporary Britain.
3. Suggest differences you might expect to find between working-class and middle-class families.
4. Identify and explain three reasons why the conventional nuclear family no longer remains the norm in contemporary Britain.
5. Write an essay of about one and a half sides of A4 paper answering the following question:
   Discuss the view that there is no 'typical' family or household in Britain today.

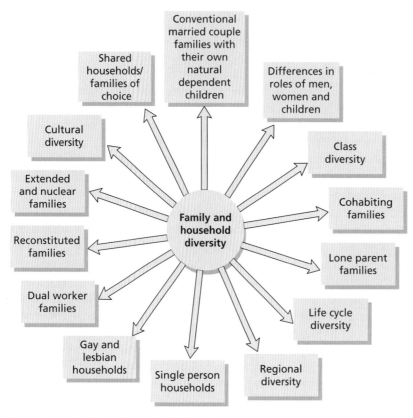

Figure 2.15 Family and household diversity

The 'darker side' of family life

The 'cereal packet' image of the 'typical family' has already been questioned on a number of levels, but the view often put forward by functionalists of the warm and supportive 'happy family' has been questioned on a more fundamental level by many writers, particularly feminists.

While the family may often be a warm and supportive unit for its members, it can also be a hostile and dangerous place. The growing privatization of family life can lead to emotional stress in the family. Family members are thrown together, isolated from and lacking the support of extended kin, neighbours and the wider community. Tempers become easily frayed, emotional temperatures and stress levels rise, and – as in a pressure cooker without a safety valve – explosions occur, resulting in family conflict. This may lead to violence, divorce, and psychological damage to children, perhaps even mental illness and crime.

The breakdown of marriages which leads to divorce is often the end result of long-running and bitter disputes between partners. The intense emotions involved in family life often mean that incidents that would appear trivial in other situations take on the proportion of major confrontations inside the family. The extent of violence in the family is coming increasingly to public attention, with rising reports of sexual and physical abuse of children, emotional neglect of children, the rape of wives by their husbands, and wife and baby battering. One in four murders takes place in the family. This is the darker side of family life.

Because of the private nature of the family, accurate evidence on the extent of violence and abuse inside the family is difficult to obtain, and fear or shame means that it is almost certain that many such incidents are covered up.

The abuse of children

There are several different types of abuse of children, as figure 2.16 shows. *Sexual abuse* refers to adults using their power to perform sex acts with children below the age of consent (age 16 for heterosexual and lesbian acts and age 18 for male homosexual acts). *Physical abuse* refers to non-sexual violence. *Emotional abuse* refers to persistent or severe emotional ill-treatment or rejection of children, which has severe effects on their emotional development and behaviour. *Neglect* refers to the failure to protect children from exposure to danger, including cold and starvation, and failing to care for them properly so that their health or development is affected.

A report in 2000 from the NSPCC (the National Society for the Prevention of Cruelty to Children), *Child Maltreatment in the United Kingdom,*

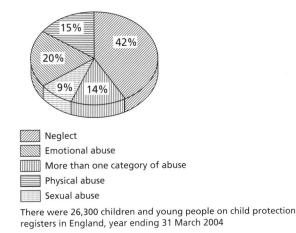

Neglect
Emotional abuse
More than one category of abuse
Physical abuse
Sexual abuse

There were 26,300 children and young people on child protection registers in England, year ending 31 March 2004

Figure 2.16 Children and young people on child protection registers, by category of abuse: England, year ending 31 March 2004
Source: Department for Education and Skills (DfES)

found that around 10 per cent of children suffered serious abuse or neglect at home, with most of it committed by natural parents. In 2005, the most comprehensive survey ever of teenagers and domestic abuse, conducted by the teen magazine *Sugar* in association with the NSPCC, found one-fifth of teenage girls were hit by parents – a quarter of them regularly. In 2004, statistics from the Department for Education and Skills (DfES) showed there were 26,300 children and young people under the age of 18 on child protection registers in England because of various forms of abuse. There were 6,600 children registered for physical injury or sexual abuse, 11,000 for neglect, and a further 5,100 for emotional abuse.

This was just for England, and only for abuse which was brought to the attention of social services departments. It is very likely that much abuse goes on that is undiscovered. Some indication of this is shown by statistics from ChildLine, the free confidential counselling service for children, established in 1986. ChildLine has counselled well over a million children and young people, and almost one in five of the calls received has been about sexual and physical abuse.

Domestic violence

There is widespread evidence of violence by men and women against their partners. It is estimated that one in four women, and one in six men, will suffer some form of domestic violence at some point in their relationships. Most of the assaults and physically most violent incidents – 89 per cent – are committed by men against their female partners. Each year about 150 people are killed by a current or former partner, and 80 per cent of them are women. Domestic violence accounts for an estimated 30 per cent of all violent crime, and about 650,000 incidents are recorded by the police each year, with around four out of five of the victims being women. Around 45 per cent of all violent crime experienced by women is domestic, and esti-mates suggest there may be as many as 6.5 million violent incidents each year. It is women who are most likely to experience domestic violence, to experience repeated violence, and to sustain injuries requiring medical treatment. Female victims of domestic violence will suffer an average of 35–37 assaults for an average period of seven years before informing any agency. Every year in England and Wales, approximately 63,000 women and children spend at least one night in a refuge. For many women, home is neither a secure nor a safe place to be.

Such violence is often not taken very seriously by the police or courts, being dismissed as a 'domestic dispute' – which seems to suggest violence in the family, and particularly against women, is seen in some quarters as an acceptable and normal part of a relationship. Certainly the type of physical violence carried out in the family, mainly by male partners, would quite probably result in prosecution and imprisonment if it was carried out against a stranger outside the family. Nonetheless, an estimated two-thirds of victims of domestic violence do not seek help because they are afraid the violence will get worse, are ashamed, or see it as a private matter, and only about a quarter of all domestic violence incidents are reported to the police.

Statistics such as these, and the widespread growth of refuges for battered women since the 1970s (in 2003, there were around 500 refuges in England and Wales), reflect the extent and seriousness of the problem of violence in the home, particularly against women, much of which goes unreported and undiscovered.

Despite the high level of violence against women in married and cohabiting relationships, many women do not leave their violent partners. This is often because of fear, shame and embarrassment, financial insecurity, lack of alternative housing and concerns about disruption to their children's lives.

Disturbingly, many young women today still seem to believe that violence and aggression are acceptable parts of relationships. The 2005 survey conducted by *Sugar* magazine, referred to above, found that 16 per cent of teenage girls had been hit by a boyfriend – a quarter of them regularly. Yet over two-thirds of the girls who had been hit then stayed with their boyfriends. Of all the teenage girls who replied to the survey, 43 per cent thought it acceptable for a boyfriend to get aggressive, and 6 per cent thought it was OK for a boy to hit his girlfriend, for reasons such as cheating on him, flirting with someone else or if she was 'dressing outrageously'. Over 40 per cent of all the girls said they would 'consider giving a boy a second chance if he hit them'.

Rape in marriage

Rape is when someone is forced to have sex against her or his will, often accompanied by the actual or threatened use of violence. Estimates suggest more than one in four women has been raped, with most rapes being committed by men on their female partners. Nearly half of these rapes within marriage are accompanied by the actual or threatened use of violence, and one in five wives suffer physical injury.

Such sexual violence in the family, then, would appear to be disturbingly common, but it was only as recently as 1991 that rape within marriage was confirmed as a criminal offence by the Court of Appeal.

Activity

Go to www.womensaid.org.uk (the Women's Aid site), or www.crimereduction.gov.uk (search 'domestic violence') and find out the extent of domestic violence and the policy measures being taken to combat it.

Feminist explanations for domestic violence

Radical feminists explain domestic violence as a result of patriarchy. In a society where men dominate women, violence is often used by men, often when they are drunk, to control and intimidate women, and to keep them in a state of submission. Marxist feminists are likely to emphasize structural factors as well. These include social deprivation (which may, for example, generate stress and disputes about money), a culture of violence – particularly in some parts of the working class – and the generally lower status of women in society. Both radical feminists and Marxist feminists would agree that domestic violence stems from structural inequalities in society, and that only by improving the position of women in society generally, and making housing and employment policies and the legal system more responsive to domestic violence and the needs of women, will domestic violence be tackled at its roots.

Activity

1 Why do you think child abuse and domestic violence statistics are likely to understate the extent of these social problems?
2 Do you think domestic violence by women against men is more or less likely to be reported than domestic violence by men against women? Give reasons for your answer.
3 How would you define child abuse? Do you think ideas about what child abuse is have changed over time? Give reasons for your answer.
4 What difficulties do you think sociologists might face in trying to research the areas of child abuse and domestic violence?
5 What explanations might there be for child abuse?

Family ideology

Family ideology refers to a dominant set of ideas, beliefs and images about family life, family structure and family relationships which suggest what the ideal family is and how family life ought to be lived. At the heart of this ideology is the patriarchal 'cereal packet' family model discussed earlier. This family is seen as the 'normal' family, and a symbol of natural, wholesome goodness, and supporting such a traditional family and parental responsibilities is often seen as crucial to maintaining moral values in society. Family ideology represents a powerful view of how people should lead their lives, even if this ideology does not reflect the reality of how most people do actually live their lives.

As seen earlier, this 'cereal packet' image no longer corresponds to the typical household unit, and does not reflect the reality of everyday experience for the majority of families or people. Writers such as Barrett and McIntosh (1982) have argued that this stereotype found in family ideology is patriarchal, harmful and anti-social:

- *It is patriarchal* because it involves the exploitation of women through the triple burden of domestic and emotional labour in the family, on top of paid employment. This benefits men to the disadvantage of women. Women remain disadvantaged in paid work compared to men because of their assumed or actual responsibilities for house- work, childcare and looking after other dependants, like disabled or elderly relatives. This increases women's dependency on men in relationships.
- *It is harmful* because it suggests that those living in other relation- ships, or living alone, are somehow deviant, are a threat to 'normal' family life and lack any meaningful relationships in their lives. Every time politicians or policy-makers make appeals to 'strengthen the family', they are at the same time condemning those who live outside such a family, such as lone parents, lesbian and gay male couples, and those living alone. Lone parents, particularly, have been subject to attack by conservative politicians and the mass media because they are seen as 'inadequate' units for bringing up children, and the source of a range of social problems. Attacks on gays are often justified by the threat they are perceived to present to 'normal' heterosexual relation- ships found in family ideology. Yet those living outside conventional families now make up a substantial proportion of the population. The stereotype is also harmful because it pretends there is no 'darker side' of family life, as discussed above, and prevents such issues being treated as seriously as they should be, at great cost to the women and children who are mainly the ones victimized in the family. The stereo- typed image of family ideology overlooks the way women become isolated at home with children, or struggle to combine paid work with childcare, situations which may be very stressful and lead many women towards tranquillizer use and mental illness. Lone parent and other non-conformist household units may face discrimination by social workers, teachers, the police and magistrates, and therefore face higher risks of labelling or stereotyping, with children being branded failures at school, or being taken into care, or arrested and prosecuted because they are seen as 'deviant'.
- *It is anti-social*, because it devalues life outside the family. Much of social life today centres around family activities, and it is often difficult for those outside such conventional arrangements to partici- pate. For example, schools are organized in such a way that it is difficult for lone parent families and dual worker families to combine

paid work with childcare. Package holidays are overwhelmingly geared to families, and those who are lone parents or who live alone may often find it difficult to get the same financial deals as family groups. Family ideology separates people from one another – from 'us' in the family and 'them' outside the family, and therefore sets up barriers between people. It devalues life outside the family, and discourages alternative forms of household organization and relationships between people from developing, such as same sex relationships, lone parenthood, communal living or serial monogamy.

Politics, social policy and the family

Debates over family life have become a major feature of politics in Britain. The family ideology and 'family values' discussed above have had important consequences for government social policies on the family. Both Labour and Conservative politicians have expressed similar views on the importance of the family, and both have sought to strengthen the traditional family. Both main parties, and particularly the Conservative Party, have tended to support family ideology's 'cereal packet' view of the traditional family, to see it as one of society's central and most important institutions, and to encourage support for living in traditional family units. They see the family as being 'under threat' from increasing divorce rates, rising numbers of lone parents and births outside marriage, with the growing diversity of alternative lifestyles undermining the stability of society and generating serious moral decline. Wider social problems like teenage pregnancies, sexual promiscuity, educational failure, welfare dependency, poverty, drug abuse and crime and delinquency have all at one time or another been blamed on the failure of the family. The blame generally falls on the inadequate socialization and supervision of children by parents, and in some cases the lack of a male role model for boys.

The similarity of Labour and Conservative approaches was made very clear in the 1997 general election manifestos. The Conservative Party manifesto stated: 'The family is the most important institution in our lives. It offers security in a fast-changing world . . . Conservatives believe that a healthy society encourages people to accept responsibility for their own lives . . . we want families to help themselves.' The Labour Party manifesto made very similar points: 'We will uphold family life as the most secure means of bringing up our children. Families are the core of our society. They should teach right from wrong. They should be the first defence against anti-social behaviour. The breakdown of family life damages the fabric of our society . . .' Things continued in a similar vein in 2001, with the Labour manifesto saying: 'Strong and stable family life offers the best possible start to children. And marriage provides a strong foundation for stable relationships. The government supports marriage. But it has to do more than that. It must support families, above all families with children.' The 2001 Conservative manifesto similarly headlined that 'Common sense means strengthening the family' and 'support for marriage'.

In the 2005 election, the Conservative Party manifesto – at around nineteen pages of text the shortest in forty years – had little to say about family values, but nonetheless managed to include sixteen references to the family. This included 'rewarding families . . .', 'trust families . . .', 'working families', 'help families', 'enabling families' and 'giving more power to . . . families'. The 112-page Labour manifesto of 2005 seemed to signal for the first time a recognition of the growing diversity of family forms, with more emphasis placed on the care, protection and development of children rather than the social institution in which they are raised. Nonetheless, the manifesto contained around thirty-six references to the family, including references to 'a typical family', 'family doctors', 'family incomes', 'family-friendly government' and family prosperity', and made clear statements that 'strong families are the bedrock of a strong society', and 'the financial support we are giving families, along with new rights to flexible working and access to childcare, are all designed to support family life'.

Activity

1 There is a vast array of laws and government policies that affect families, and relationships within them. Explore some of the following websites and identify three policies or laws that affect family life, explaining in each case how they affect families and family roles and relationships. Be prepared to search and follow links. For instance:

   www.nfpi.org (the National Family and Parenting Institute)
   www.surestart.gov.uk
   www.homeoffice.gov.uk/crime/domesticviolence
   www.everychildmatters.gov.uk
   www.ondivorce.co.uk

2 What are the political parties currently saying about family roles and relationships? Go to the websites of the political parties below, and briefly outline two policies on the family and family roles and relationships. Identify any differences you can between them. Look for a 'policy' heading or button, but be prepared to search (try 'policy', 'manifesto', or 'family' first)

   www.labour.org.uk (the Labour Part)
   www.libdems.org.uk (the Liberal Democrats)
   www.conservatives.com (the Conservative Party)

Only the Liberal Democrats explicitly recognized that 'in the twenty-first century, the modern British family comes in many different shapes and sizes. We are no longer a nation that has one universal family structure.' But they nonetheless still felt it necessary to produce a special 'Manifesto for families' for the 2005 general election, and still emphasized that their policies were 'all designed to increase support for families and maintain the family's central place in our society'.

So, despite a changing world where a majority of the population no longer live in families, or families with dependent children, family life still seems to be central to the thinking of the major political parties.

Is the family a declining social institution?

We have seen how complex the question of 'family' has become today. The activity below will help you to decide whether or not the conventional family is a declining institution.

Activity

Below are fourteen statements. Some provide evidence for, and some against, the view that the conventional family is in decline, and some might be used in a conclusion.

1   First mark each statement 'for decline', 'against decline' or 'conclusion'.
2   Match up the competing arguments for and against which seem most linked to each other.
3   Using the material below, and the 'organizing work' you have just done, and drawing on ideas of your own and what you've read in this chapter, write a short essay (about one and a half to two sides) answering the question:
    To what extent is the family in Britain a declining social institution?
    Include arguments for and against, and reach a conclusion.

(a) Marriages today are more likely to be based on love and companionship rather than the custom and necessity of the past. Of all divorced people, 75 per cent remarry, a third of them within a year of getting divorced. This shows that what they are rejecting is not the institution of marriage itself but a particular marriage partner – they divorce hoping to turn an unhappy marriage into a new, happier one. The marriages that exist today are therefore probably much stronger and happier than ever, since unhappy relationships are easily ended by divorce.

(b) Postmodernists suggest that the traditional family unit is dead, with people choosing to live in a wide variety of household and family arrangements, which are constantly changing. It therefore no longer makes sense to talk of the family unit as a key institution in contemporary societies.

(c) It doesn't really matter whether or not couples are married or have been married before, or whether there is one parent or two. Though the form of the family will keep on changing, the importance of the family lies in its role as a stable and supportive unit for one or two adults, whether of the opposite or same sex, and their dependent children. In that sense, the ideal of the family perhaps still remains intact.

(d) There are well over a million and a half cohabiting couples who have refused to tie the marriage knot – about one in ten of all couples. This is expected to rise to 1.7 million by 2020, making up around one in seven of all couples. Over a quarter of all non-married people were cohabiting in 2002. Living together before or outside marriage was one of the major social changes of the late twentieth century.

(e) What really seems to be happening is not so much that the family and marriage are in decline but that they are changing. People are choosing to live in a diversity of relationships and household types. There are more lone parent families, more reconstituted families, more gay male and lesbian families, more experiments in living together before marriage, and fewer people prepared to marry simply to bring up children. Nevertheless, marriage remains an important social norm, and strong pressures from parents, peer groups and the responsibilities brought about by the birth of children continue to propel most people into marriage.

(f) It is estimated that more than 40 per cent of marriages will end in divorce, with almost one in four children experiencing a parental divorce by their sixteenth birthday.

(g) Many of those who cohabit eventually marry – about 60 per cent of first-time cohabitations turn into marriages – and about 75 per cent of the population have been married by the age of 50. It would appear that marriage remains an important social institution, even in the light of the high divorce rate and previous experience of living together outside marriage.

(h) Despite the record numbers of children being born outside marriage, about 80 per cent of those births in 2004 were registered jointly by the parents, and both parents in three out of four of these cases gave the same address. This suggests that most children are still being born into a stable relationship, and live in family situations with concerned parents who are simply reluctant to tie the legal marriage knot. Most dependent children still live in families headed by a married or cohabiting couple.

(i) About 40 per cent of births are outside marriage today.

(j) The failure of the family has been blamed for a wide range of social ills, such as declining moral standards, social disorder, drug abuse, rising crime rates, vandalism, football hooliganism, educational failure and increasing levels of violence in society.

(k)	The Policy Studies Institute has calculated that if these trends continue, by the year 2010 the majority of couples will cohabit before marriage, the majority of marriages will end in divorce followed by remarriage, and nearly all births will be outside marriage.

(l)	The causes of those social problems all too often blamed on the family are many and complex, and those who blame the family are often searching for simple solutions to complex problems.

(m)	Statistics like these have made the state of the family a major battleground for politicians, with the suggestion that the very existence of the family is threatened by rising rates of divorce, cohabitation, lone parenthood and reconstituted families.

(n)	In Britain today, a quarter of families with dependent children have just one parent.

(o)	Although the divorce rate has gone up, the evidence suggests that it is easier divorce laws, the growing economic independence of women, reduced social stigma and more sympathetic public attitudes which have caused this, rather than more marriage breakdowns. In the past, many couples may have been condemned by legal and financial obstacles and social intolerance to suffer unhappy 'empty shell' marriages or to separate without divorcing. If the law were changed to make divorce harder to get, couples would continue to separate without divorcing

Chapter summary

After studying this chapter. You should be able to:

- describe the different forms of marriage, the family and household
- identify arguments about the universality of the nuclear family
- explain and criticize the functionalist, Marxist, Marxist feminist and radical feminist perspectives on the family
- examine the arguments about whether or not the family has lost its functions
- critically discuss how industrialization changed the family, particularly the debate over the change from a classic extended family to an isolated nuclear family
- critically examine the links between the isolated nuclear family and industrial society
- examine the view that roles in marriage and cohabiting relationships have become more equal
- examine the ways in which women's responsibilities for housework and childcare undermine their positions in paid employment
- identify the features of domestic labour, and how these differ from paid work

- identify and explain the main changes in the position of children in the family
- explain why average family size has decreased, and why women are having fewer, or no, children
- explain the reasons for the rising divorce rate, the emergence of the reconstituted family and the groups most 'at risk' of divorce
- explain why there has been a large increase in the number of lone parent families
- explain why there has been a decline in marriage, the growth of cohabitation and more people living alone
- explain why there are more births outside marriage
- describe and explain why the 'cereal packet' family is a myth, and identify the diversity of family and household forms in Britain
- identify and discuss the 'darker side' of family life
- explain what is meant by 'family ideology' and critically discuss its main features
- discuss political views of the family and social policies and laws affecting families
- examine the arguments and evidence for and against the view that the family and marriage are of declining social importance

Key terms

- arranged marriage
- 'beanpole' family
- birth rate
- classic extended family
- commune
- conjugal role
- death rate
- division of labour
- divorce rate
- domestic labour
- expressive role
- extended family
- family
- family ideology
- household
- infant mortality rate
- instrumental role
- integrated conjugal role
- kibbutz
- kinship
- matriarchy
- meritocracy
- modified extended family
- monogamy
- moral panic
- nuclear family
- patriarchy
- polyandry
- polygamy
- polygyny
- primary socialization
- privatization
- privatized nuclear family
- reconstituted family
- scapegoat
- secondary socialization
- secularization
- segregated conjugal role

- serial monogamy
- sexual division of labour
- social construction
- stereotype
- structural differentiation
- symmetrical family

Coursework suggestions

1   Investigate how far conjugal roles have really become more integrated, by carrying out a series of interviews with a sample of families to discover how housework and childcare is divided up between women and men in the home – try to interview each partner separately. You might use unstructured interviews to find out how partners feel about the division of household and childcare tasks, and how fair or unfair they think it is.
2   Interview a sample of people from different generations, and give a first-hand account of how they feel family life has changed over a period of time.
3   Carry out a survey among different age groups within the Asian community to see how they feel about arranged marriages.
4   Interview some lone parents, and ask them about the advantages and disadvantages of lone parenthood.
5   Investigate attitudes to marriage or cohabitation among a sample of men and women who live alone.
6   Interview some cohabiting couples about why they have chosen not to marry.

Exam Questions

FAMILIES AND HOUSEHOLDS

Time allowed: 1 hour 15 minutes   **Total for this Question:** *60 marks*

Item A

From the late nineteenth century, there was a major change in family size. In the 1890s the infant mortality rate began to fall rapidly. We might expect this to result in an increase in family size, yet in fact there was a fall in the birth rate from about 1870, a trend which had major implications for family life.

Women who married in the 1860s averaged 5.7 live births. By the 1920s the number of live births per woman was down to 2.2. After fluctuating somewhat during the mid-twentieth century, it dropped below   5
2.0 in the early 1970s, has stayed there ever since and is now around 1.7 live births per woman. Sociologists are interested in the reasons for these changes and several social and economic factors have been suggested.

Item B

With industrialization and the rise of individual wage-labour, the dependencies that held the extended family together no longer applied. In particular, as family members no longer depended on common property for their well-being, as they had in family farming, each individual was freer to further his or her own economic interests independently of other family members. There was little to tie adult generations together, and little need for siblings to cooperate. As a result, it was argued, the nuclear family came   5
to replace the extended family as the main form of household structure as industrialization gathered pace. Increasingly, as Parsons puts it, the nuclear family became 'structurally isolated'. However, the historical basis for these claims has been questioned.

Source: Adapted frm G. Allan, *Kinship and Friendship in Modern Britain* (Oxford University Press) 1996

(a) Explain what is meant by the term ' "structurally isolated" ' nuclear family (**Item B**, line 7).   *(2 marks)*
(b) Explain the difference between the infant mortality rate and the birth rate (**Item A**, lines 1–3). *(4 marks)*
(c) Suggest **three** reasons why birth rates have fallen since the nineteenth century (**Item A**, lines 4–8). *(6 marks)*
(d) Identify **two** laws or government policies that may affect roles and relationships within the
     family and briefly describe how each of these does this.   *(8 marks)*
(e) Examine the contribution of feminist sociologists to the study of family life.   *(20 marks)*
(f) Using material from **Item B** and elsewhere, assess the view that industrialization led to the
     nuclear family replacing the extended family as the main form of household structure
     (**Item B**, lines 5–6).   *(20 marks)*

(AQA AS Unit 1 January 2001)

FAMILIES AND HOUSEHOLDS

Time allowed: 1 hour 15 minutes   **Total for this Question:** *60 marks*

Item A

The last 30 or 40 years have seen major changes in family life in industrial and post-industrial countries. The formation and break-up of relationships is one area of change. In the UK, the number of first marriages has halved since the 1970s and the number of divorces has risen about six-fold since 1961. Meanwhile, cohabitation has been rising rapidly since the 1980s and is set to account for about half of all unmarried adults by 2021.   5

Childbearing and childrearing is another area of change. Forty per cent of all births now occur to unmarried women, while about three in ten children grow up in either a reconstituted family or a lone parent family (usually female-headed). Women are also now having fewer children than in the past.

However, changes such as the increased numbers of divorces, lone parent families or births outside marriage do not necessarily mean that the family is in decline.   10

Item B

About three-quarters of married or cohabiting women in the UK are now working, as against less than half in 1971. Some sociologists argue that this trend towards both partners working is leading to more equal relationships. For example, Jonathan Gershuny found that men whose wives worked full-time did significantly more domestic work than men whose wives did not. He explains this trend in terms of a gradual change in values and role models and argues that couples are adapting to more women working   5 full-time by sharing domestic tasks more equally. However, he found that men and women still take responsibility for different tasks.

Gershuny's view is an optimistic one, similar to Willmott and Young's 'march of progress' view that conjugal roles are becoming more symmetrical. Rosemary Crompton accepts Gershuny's findings. However, she explains them differently, in terms of women's earning power rather than changing values.   10

(a) Explain what is meant by a 'reconstituted' family (**Item A**, line 7).   *(2 marks)*

(b) Suggest **two** reasons why the number of first marriages has fallen (**Item A,** line 3).   *(4 marks)*

(c) Suggest **three** reasons why women are 'now having fewer children than in the past' (**Item A**, line 8).   *(6 marks)*

(d) Identify and briefly explain **two** reasons why 'changes such as the increased numbers of divorces, lone parent families or births outside marriage do not necessarily mean that the family is in decline' (**Item A**, lines 9–10).   *(8 marks)*

(e) Examine the different functions performed by the family for individuals and for society.   *(20 marks)*

(f) Using material from **Item B** and elsewhere, assess the effect upon couples' relationships of women's involvement in paid work.   *(20 marks)*

(AQA AS Unit 1 January 2005)

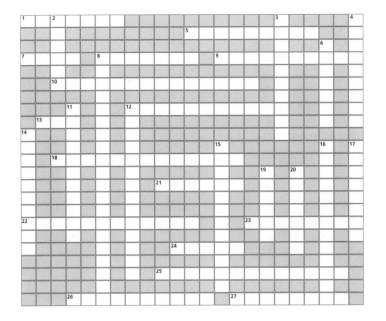

Across

1) Israeli alternative to the nuclear family (7)
5) The term used to describe an individual or group of people living under the same roof (9)
7) She first identified the importance of social networks in understanding roles in the family (4)
8) An American functionalist writer who thought families were 'factories producing human personalities' (7)
9) The opposite to an instrumental role (10)
10) In marriage, one at a time, one after the other and they don't last long! (6, 8)
12) The number of divorces per 1000 married people (7, 4)
13) These families with same sex parents have a happy name (3)
18) A family type involving the remarriage of one or both partners and the children of a previous marriage (13)
21) She was one of the first to study the sociology of housework (6)
22) One of the fastest growing forms of family relationship and unlikely to be regarded as 'sinful' (12)
23) This legal bonding is in decline (8)
24) A writer who argued 'the family . . . is the source of all our discontents' – sounds like a bloodsucker (5)
25) A two-generational family (7, 6)
26) A family form usually arising from death of a partner, divorce or choice (4-6)
27) This approach challenged the male view of the family (8)

Down

2) Around 40 per cent of these take place outside marriage (6)
3) The people we learn from by imitating their behaviour (4, 6)
4) These children are below working age and rely on their families to support them financially (9)
6) Relations of blood, marriage or adoption (7)
8) The process of learning the culture of society within the family (7, 13)
11) A type of family where there are similar roles performed by each partner (11)
12) Technical term for housework (8, 6)
14) Where males are dominant (10)
15) The traditional family stereotype (6, 6)
16) The term used to describe relationships between husband and wife (8, 5)
17) A nuclear family with vertical or horizontal extensions (8)
19) A male partner who takes an active role in housework (3, 3)
20) The legal termination of a marriage (7)

The solution is on p. 490.

Health

What is meant by 'health', 'illness' and 'disease'?

Health is probably easiest to define as 'being able to function normally within a usual everyday routine'.
Disease generally refers to a biological or mental condition, such as high blood pressure, a faulty heart or chemical imbalances in the body, which usually involves medically diagnosed symptoms.
Illness refers to the subjective feeling of being unwell or in ill-health – a person's own recognition of lack of well-being. It is possible both to have a disease and to not feel ill, and to feel ill and not have any disease.

The definitions of health, illness and disease are not simple matters. What counts as health and illness varies between individuals, between different social groups within a single society, such as between men and women, and between societies. Views of acceptable standards of health are likely to differ widely between the people of a poor African country and Britain. Even in the same society, views of health change over time. At one time in Britain, mental illness was seen as a sign of satanic possession or witchcraft – a matter best dealt with by the church rather than by doctors. Similarly, what were once seen as personal problems have quite recently become medical problems, such as obesity, alcoholism and smoking.

There is no simple definition of illness, because for pain or discomfort to count as a disease it is necessary for someone to diagnose or label it as such. There are also subjective influences on health: some of us can put up with or ignore pain more than others; some feel no pain; and many of us will have different notions of what counts as 'feeling unwell'. Individuals will define and respond to health in different ways. For example, older people may define 'good health' as not having too many aches and pains, and having energy levels that enable them to go about their daily tasks, or being well enough to run their own homes. Younger people may define good health as being well enough to go clubbing or take part in sport.

We can also change our views of the state of our health depending on our choices and situations. For example, we might be too ill to go to school or college, but well enough to go clubbing.

This means health is a relative concept, which will vary according to the age, lifestyle, personal circumstances, culture and environment in which people live. There are strong subjective (personal) influences on health, and whether a person sees himself or herself as healthy or not will depend on how well they are able to function within their own everyday routines.

So what counts as 'health' and 'illness' can be considered as a **social construction** – a result of individual, social and cultural interpretations and perceptions.

> **Social construction** means that the important characteristics of something, such as statistics, health, illness or disability, are created and influenced by the attitudes, actions and interpretations of members of society.

Activity

The United Nations World Health Organization defines health as 'a state of complete physical, mental, and social well-being, and not merely the absence of disease or infirmity'. Some have argued that this definition goes far beyond a realistic definition of health, as it implies not simply the absence of disease, but also a personally fulfilling life.

1 Discuss how the World Health Organization's definition of health might apply to the health of the long-term unemployed in Britain.
2 Using the World Health Organization's definition, how might the definition of 'good health' differ between:
   (a) people who live in a poor African country and those who live in modern Britain?
   (b) people in Britain who live in an isolated village in the country and those who live in a town?
3 How do you think the society we live in influences people's ideas of what counts as health and illness?
4 Discuss the view that 'good health is simply a state of mind'.

Disability

Disability is often linked with illness, helplessness and weakness. Most of us learn about disability as part of the socialization process, rather than as a result of personal experience. Media images of disability are often linked with socially unacceptable behaviours, or suggest we have good reasons to fear people with disabilities, especially those with mental or behavioural difficulties, or who display violent or inexplicable behaviour. For example, the Glasgow Media Group found in *Message Received* (Philo, 1999) that media reporting portrayed a high level of violence as associated with mental illness, especially schizophrenia.

> **Disability** is defined by the Disability Discrimination Act 1995 as 'a physical or mental impairment which has a substantial and long-term adverse effect on [your] ability to carry out normal day-to-day activities'.

There are clearly some physical or mental impairments, such as loss of use of limbs or sight, or brain damage, that will mean some people will find more difficulty in carrying out everyday tasks than others.

However, **impairment** is not the same as disability. Tom Shakespeare (1998) suggests that disability should be seen as a social construction – a problem created by the attitudes of society and not by the state of our bodies. Shakespeare argues that disability is created by societies that don't take into account the needs of those who do not meet with that society's ideas of what is 'normal'. Whether someone is disabled or not is then a social product – it is social attitudes which turn an impairment into a disability, because society discriminates against them. For example, people parking on pavements makes it difficult for those in wheelchairs or the blind to get by; buildings may make access difficult or impossible for those who have lost the use of their lower limbs and need wheelchairs to aid their mobility. People who are short-sighted only become disabled if they have no access to glasses to correct their sight, or if documents are printed in small type or colours which people with visual impairments find hard to read. Workplaces can be disabling if adjustments to the working environment are not made to enable people with impairments to perform their jobs successfully. With the ageing population (a growing proportion of elderly people in the population), all of us will, if we live long enough, eventually become disabled unless social attitudes

> An **impairment** is some abnormal functioning of the body or mind, arising from birth or from injury or disease.

Activity

'People become disabled, not because they have physical or mental impairments, but because they have physical or mental differences from the majority, which challenges traditional ideas of what counts as "normal". Disability is about the relationship between people with impairment and a society which discriminates against them. People are disabled by society, not by their bodies. Disability is about discrimination and prejudice . . . Understanding disability is about flexing the sociological imagination – turning personal troubles into public issues.'

(Adapted from an unpublished paper by Tom Shakespeare, 26 Jan. 2001)

1   Do you agree with the view that people are disabled by society and the attitudes of others rather than by the state of their minds or bodies? What evidence can you think of for and against this view?

2   Explain in your own words what you think Shakespeare means when he says: 'Understanding disability is about . . . turning personal troubles into public issues.'

3   What kinds of impairments in our society create disadvantages for those who have them? What steps might be taken to remove these disadvantages facing people with some impairments?

change and society adapts to the needs of those with physical or mental impairments.

The medical and social models of health

As seen above, there are different meanings attached to 'health'. There are two main approaches to health arising from different views of what the causes of ill-health are, and the policies needed to solve it. These two competing models of health are often referred to as the medical (or biomedical) and social models of health.

The medical (biomedical) model of health

This is the model of health which has underlined the development of Western medicine, and is the main approach found in the National Health Service. This model sees health in terms of the absence of disease, with ill-health arising from identifiable biological or physical causes. The main aim of medicine, and modern health care systems like the NHS, is there-fore to diagnose and tackle these physical symptoms.

Main features of the medical model

- Disease is seen as mainly caused by biological factors, together with the recent emphasis on personal factors such as smoking and diet. Health is defined as the absence of disease or disability.
- The human body is seen as working like a machine which occasional-ly 'breaks down'. In the same way as a car that has broken down, 'body mechanics' (doctors) apply their expert medical knowledge to diag-nose the biological or chemical processes that have caused the sick-ness. Doctors are then able to treat and cure the disease they have identified, through medical or surgical treatments in 'body shops' – clinical situations like doctors' surgeries and hospitals.
- The causes of ill-health are seen as arising either from the moral fail-ings of the individual (such as smoking too much, not eating the right food, or not getting enough exercise) or from random attacks of dis-ease. This is a bit like blaming car breakdowns on poor maintenance and lack of proper servicing, or because of faulty parts and bad luck.
- Scientific medicine is seen as the way to solve health problems. This means good health depends on the availability of trained medical personnel, medical technology, operating theatres, drugs and so on. Medicine is seen as in itself a 'good thing', and the more of it there is, the better people's health will be.

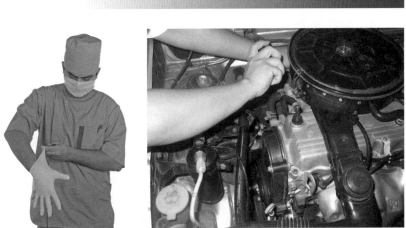

The medical model of health views the human body as working like a machine that occasionally breaks down, with doctors like mechanics, fixing it in 'body shops' like surgeries and hospitals

---

Activity

1 Suggest five ways those adopting the medical model might tackle the issue of improving a society's health.
2 Do you think there are any problems with an approach to improving health which concentrates only on the medical treatment of individuals? What other factors might also be important in influencing the state of our health?

Criticisms of the medical model

- It suggests that health can be defined objectively, as the absence of disease. However, what counts as 'good health' is, as shown above, socially constructed – a product of social influences and not simply biological ones.
- The focus on treating the symptoms of disease in the body by the application of medical knowledge, drugs and surgery ignores the wider social conditions that may have created these symptoms in the first place. These might include factors such as hazardous work environments, poor quality food, poverty or environmental pollution.
- It serves the interests of doctors, and gives them a great deal of power. Doctors have a legal monopoly over treatment, and other alternative approaches, like acupuncture or homeopathy, have traditionally been downgraded and dismissed as ineffective. However, the British Medical Association in 2001 finally conceded that complementary medicines can be integrated into conventional patient care, and called for greater cooperation between practitioners of orthodox and complementary medicine.

The medical model of health tends to concentrate on rescuing sick individuals, rather than looking at health education, preventive measures and the social causes which make people sick in the first place

- It suggests resources are best channelled into medical science, new drugs and medical technology, and 'state of the art' high-tech hospitals. Health education and preventative medicine are therefore not given the resources needed. This is like standing by a river bank and constantly hauling people out of the water, without asking who is throwing them into the river in the first place.

- It suggests the medical and nursing professions are generally doing a good job. However, writers like Illich (1976) have argued that medicine sometimes does more harm than good. Illich calls this **iatrogenesis**, which suggests that medical intervention, surgery and drugs can actually have more harmful effects than the condition they are meant to be curing. Some tranquillizers, for example, are addictive, and feminists have been particularly critical of mastectomy (the surgical removal of breasts) as a treatment for breast cancer. In 2001, there were major public concerns (largely unjustified) about the safety of the MMR (mumps, measles and rubella) vaccination.

- The identification of health care with medical care has led to a 'pill for every ill' syndrome. There is a growing trend towards the medicalization of health care. The drug industry, for example, produces medication for all sorts of ailments. Every condition is given a medical label,

Iatrogenesis is any harmful mental or physical condition induced in a patient through the effects of treatment by a doctor or surgeon.

and new 'diseases' are constantly being 'invented' which may be primarily social rather than biological in character. Examples might include stress, anxiety and depression arising from difficulties at work or unemployment, eating disorders like bulimia or anorexia, and the way some 'naughty children' are now labelled as suffering from 'emotional and behavioural difficulties' (EBD) or attention deficit disorder (ADD) or hyperactivity disorder.

- Illness and disease do not strike at random, out of the blue. They follow consistent social patterns. Ill-health is not simply a matter of fate or bad luck, but very much a product of the society and social circumstances in which a person lives.

- The model suggests disease is abnormal, has a clearly identifiable biological cause, and that measures can be taken to treat and cure it. However, Steve Taylor has shown that this model of health is inadequate and increasingly under attack because:

  - Infectious diseases like smallpox, typhoid and cholera have been replaced by degenerative diseases such as cancer and heart disease as the main killers of people in the twentieth and twenty-first centuries. Modern medicine has often proved unable to provide cures for these new diseases. Medicine is almost completely ineffective in curing some new diseases like AIDS (Acquired Immune Deficiency Syndrome) or vCJD (variant Creutzfeldt–Jakob disease), though there is a constant pursuit of cures, such as the use of combination drugs for AIDS. There is still no cure for the common cold or flu.

  - Researchers like McKeown (1976) have shown that doctors are not (solely) responsible for improving life expectancy and health. Improvements in social conditions, such as public sewers and clean water are far more important.

Life expectancy is an estimate of how long people can be expected to live from a certain age.

Iatrogenesis in Britain

The harmful effects of medical treatment are reported widely in the media, with horror stories of people having the wrong legs amputated or healthy kidneys removed, patients dying because of HIV/AIDS or septicaemia occurring as a result of transfusions of contaminated blood, GPs failing to identify tumours, children dying after incompetent heart surgery, brain damage arising from overdoses of prescribed medicines, wrongly administered injections causing death and disability, and people dying from general anaesthetics in dental surgeries. A Department of Health report in 2000, *An Organisation with a Memory*, admitted that every year:

- Over 400 people die or are seriously injured in 'adverse' events involving medical devices.

- Nearly 10,000 people experience serious adverse reactions to drugs. At least thirteen patients have died or been paralysed since 1985 because a drug was wrongly administered by spinal injection.
- Hospital-acquired infections (HAI) cost the NHS around £1 billion a year. The House of Commons Public Accounts Committee in 2000 reported that MRSA – the 'superbug' immune to antibiotics – and other HAIs affect up to 100,000 hospital patients every year, and that 5,000 of them die in England alone.
- Around 1,150 people who have been in recent contact with mental health services commit suicide.
- Medical negligence claims cost the National Health Service around £400 million.
- Adverse events, in which patients are harmed, occur in more than 10 per cent of admissions to NHS hospitals – 850,000 each year. The estimated cost of this was put at £2 billion, at least, in additional days spent in hospital. Half of these adverse events were preventable.
- 8 per cent of adverse events may result in death, and 6 per cent in permanent disability – amounting to over 34,000 preventable deaths and 25,000 preventable permanent disabilities every year.

The report recognized that these figures underestimated the true scale of the problems. To tackle the high level of negligence claims against the NHS, the National Patient Safety Agency was set up in 2001, modelled on the Air Accidents Investigation Branch.

Activity

Do you believe you are safe in the hands of doctors and other medical professionals? Do you have any personal experience of medicine being of little help to you? Are there currently any stories of medical negligence around that you are aware of? Collect together information, and discuss it in your group.

The social model of health

The social model of health highlights the way that social factors are involved in both defining health and the causes of ill-health. This model is the main alternative to the medical model, and recognizes there are important social influences on health which the medical model ignores. The Acheson Report (1998) made a powerful case that many of the factors causing ill-health are rooted in social inequality, and therefore recognized the importance of the social dimensions of health.

Features of the social model of health

- 'Health' and 'illness' are not seen simply as medical or scientific facts. Health is a relative condition. What is defined as health depends on what is regarded as 'normal' in a particular society, and this will vary over time and between cultures, and between individuals in the same culture.
- A choice exists whether someone sees himself or herself as ill or not. Those with power can choose whether or not to classify someone as ill. In most cases, 'those with power' means doctors and other medical experts. What counts as health and sickness is as much about the power of medical professionals as it is about biology.
- Medical science is not the detached objective science the medical model implies. It is influenced by wider social and economic considerations, rather than simply the treatment of biological disease. Drug companies and medical technology manufacturers are likely to have important influences on the way doctors go about their work.
- A strong emphasis is placed on the social causes of health and ill-health, and on how society influences health. Patterns of health and illness cannot simply be explained and treated individually, but should be understood within the social and economic environment in which they occur. It is not just chance individuals who become sick through bad luck, but whole groups of people who are more at risk of ill-health. There is a pattern of social class, gender and ethnic inequalities in health. This suggests that it is social and environmental factors that make some groups of people more vulnerable to disease than others, and not simply lightning bolts from the blue hurled out by nature at unfortunate and randomly chosen individuals.

Limitations of the social model

It is important to recognize the social dimensions of health, and the ways conceptions of health and illness are socially constructed. However, there

---

Activity

1 List six social and environmental factors you think influence health, and identify in each case how they affect health.
2 How would you set out to improve society's health if you were particularly concerned with tackling the social and environmental causes of ill-health?
3 Go to www.dh.gov.uk (the website for the Department of Health) and search for three policies being followed by the government to improve the health of Britain. Explain how each of the policies you identify might improve health.

is a danger of overemphasizing these social aspects at the expense of the medical approach. Medicine has contributed to improvements in health, even if not as much as some doctors might claim. Childhood immunization against diseases such as tuberculosis, polio, smallpox, measles, mumps and rubella (German measles) have reduced these diseases, and in some cases wiped them out in modern Britain. Antibiotics have proved very effective in treating many infections, and medicine has effective treatments for broken bones. Most of us therefore derive some benefit from cures, and knowledge through health education about preventing disease, which come from scientific medicine.

Becoming a health statistic

The main ways used to measure the extent of health and illness are morbidity (the extent of disease) and mortality (death) statistics. Major concerns have been raised over the *validity* (or truthfulness) of these statistics. Morbidity statistics will depend on the diagnostic skills of doctors, since their decisions will affect how the symptoms are classified (e.g. as pneumonia or AIDS). Statistics on causes of death will also depend on the doctor's interpretation of what the cause of death is.

Many sociologists argue health statistics are simply social constructions, rather than being valid in providing a true picture of the pattern of health. Health statistics must therefore be treated with considerable care.

The social construction of health statistics

- Health statistics depend on people persuading doctors they are ill, and are therefore simply a record of doctors' judgements and decision-making.
- Doctors may diagnose illnesses incorrectly, reflecting the state of the doctor's knowledge. Records of illnesses may not be accurate. For example, there may have been many AIDS deaths recorded as pneumonia or other diseases before AIDS was 'discovered' in the 1980s.
- Not all sick people go to the doctor, and not all people who persuade doctors they are ill are really sick.
- Private medicine operates to make a profit, and therefore is perhaps more likely to diagnose symptoms as a disease.

Official health statistics have been described as a 'clinical iceberg', as it is estimated that only about 10 per cent of illness is reported to doctors, with most concealed beneath the surface.

The process of becoming ill is not as simple and straightforward as it might seem. People often have choices over whether to report themselves sick or not. People may respond to the same symptoms in different ways. While some may seek medical help, others may choose to ignore their symptoms. They may look for alternative non-medical or less serious explanations for them: bronchitis may become simply a 'smoker's cough', and possible brain tumours may be dismissed as 'headaches'.

Often, whether an individual goes to the doctor or not will depend on the responses of other people, such as whether they can put up with a person's moaning any longer, or whether the individual's friends can continue to play sport with them or not. It may be difficulties experienced with looking after children while feeling unwell, pressures from friends and family, or health scare stories in the media, the costs of taking time off work and so on which finally persuade people to go to the doctor. These examples suggest it may be difficulties in coping with an illness, rather than the illness itself, which bring people to seek medical attention.

For people to be labelled as 'sick' – and to be recorded as a health statistic – there are at least four stages involved:

Stage 1: Individuals must first recognize they have a problem.
Stage 2: They must then define their problem as serious enough to take to a doctor.
Stage 3: They must then actually go to the doctor.
Stage 4: The doctor must then be persuaded that they have a medical or mental condition capable of being labelled as an illness requiring treatment.

Activity

1 List all the factors you can which might influence each of the four stages involved in labelling someone 'sick', and which lead some people to visit the doctor and others not to. For example, in stage 1, you might consider a person's ability to continue his or her responsibilities to friends and family, pressure from relatives, friends and employers, etc. Draw on your own experiences of what makes you decide whether you are ill, and whether or not to go to see the doctor.

2. Discuss in a group what you think the most common influences on going (or not going) to the doctor might be.

Medicine and social control: the sick role

Social control is concerned with maintaining order and stability in society. Parsons, writing from a functionalist perspective, argues that sickness is really a form of deviance, which threatens the stability of society. This is because those who are classified as sick are able to avoid their normal social responsibilities, like going to work, school or college, or looking after the family. If too many people did this, then society would collapse – imagine a school or factory where the teachers, students, managers or workers were always off ill. Ill-health is therefore something that needs to be kept within careful limits to avoid undermining social order and the smooth functioning of society. Parsons sees the **sick role** as fulfilling this purpose.

The sick role provides an escape route for individuals from everyday responsibilities. This is because, when people are sick, they can reasonably abandon normal everyday activities, and often others will take over their responsibilities so that they are able to recover.

> The **sick role** refers to the pattern of behaviour which is expected from someone who is ill.

Features of the sick role

Parsons suggests the sick role involves both rights and obligations for those who are sick.

Rights

● Depending on the illness, individuals are excused normal social activities, such as going to school or work. This requires approval by others such as teachers, employers and family members. The doctor often plays a key role in this process, by diagnosing the person as 'really ill', and issuing sick notes.

● Individuals are not seen as personally to blame for their illness, nor are they expected to be solely responsible for their recovery by a sheer act of will. There is a recognition they will need help to recover. Relatives, friends and doctors are often very critical of those they see as responsible for their own illness, and excessive drinking and drug overdoses often don't get much sympathy from the medical profession.

Obligations

● The sick person must see his or her sickness as an undesirable state, and individuals have an obligation to want to 'get well', and ensure their sickness state is only a temporary one.

● When necessary, sick people are expected to seek and accept medical help and cooperate in their treatment to get well. In other words, sick

---

Activity

Do you think everyone who is ill can or should adopt the sick role? Try to think of individuals or groups whose circumstances might make it difficult for them to do so. Give reasons for your answers.

people are expected to do what the doctor orders, and they cannot expect sympathy and support if they don't try to get well. Those refusing medical treatment are unlikely to have their illnesses recognized as genuine sickness. Even if people don't want to call in the doctor because they don't see their illness as serious enough to do so, they are still expected to stay in bed, take non-prescription medicines, or take it easy in an effort to recover.

Parsons argues these obligations are necessary to stop people getting into a subculture of sickness, where sickness, dependence on others and apathy are seen as a normal and desirable state. Such a subculture would disrupt the smooth running of society. People must therefore be obliged to get well and resume their everyday responsibilities as quickly as possible.

Doctors as gate-keepers

Gate-keeping is the power of some people, groups or organizations to limit access to something valuable or useful. For example, doctors act as gate-keepers as they have the power to allow or refuse entry to the sick role.

Doctors and other medical professionals play a key role in the social control of the sick by acting as **gate-keepers** of entry to the sick role – doctors are the ones who legitimize (justify) sickness by officially classifying it as such. For example, doctors can stop people taking more than a few days off work on the grounds of illness by refusing to issue sick notes. The doctor's role is to cure the sick and get them back to normal, and sort out those who are really sick from hypochondriacs, malingerers and skivers who try to evade their responsibilities by faking illness.

Doctors play an important part in social control of the sick and access to the sick role

Criticisms of Parsons and the sick role

- Not everyone who feels ill adopts the sick role, perhaps because they don't like or are afraid of doctors or cannot afford to have time off work. Lone parents may not be able to afford the luxury of adopting the sick role as they have to continue looking after their children.
- Not everyone who is ill gets the sympathy of others and avoids the personal blame implied in the rights of the sick role. For example, AIDS, heart disease brought on by smoking, drug abuse and alcohol poisoning often bring little sympathy from others as they are seen as self-inflicted.
- Some diseases, like mental illness and AIDS, involve high degrees of stigma (social disapproval, rejection and inferior status), and sufferers may wish to conceal public knowledge of their illness. They may therefore wish to avoid adopting the sick role because of the consequences of doing so.
- Some illnesses or disorders are not curable, and it may be better for both the individual and society to avoid the sick role and try to carry on with normal life as much as possible. This might well apply to those with terminal illnesses, various forms of impairment, such as blindness or loss of limb functions, or conditions like heart disease or diabetes.
- The sick don't always act as the well-behaved, passive and obedient patients implied by the sick role. They may well refuse to cooperate with doctors, challenge diagnoses and the doctor's authority, and ask for 'second opinions'. The relationship between doctors and patients is changing, and patients now have access to much more information about medical treatments through the internet, and services such as NHS Direct. This means doctors no longer have the monopoly of medical knowledge they once enjoyed.

The power of the medical profession

Doctors play a key role in controlling the sick and legitimizing (justifying) sickness by their gate-keeping function in relation to the sick role. It is doctors who have the power to confirm or deny that people have a genuine illness, and who put them on an approved programme of treatment.

This gives doctors a great deal of power and authority over patients. Patients themselves are very vulnerable when they are sick, and they are often liable to face intimate medical examinations. Functionalist writers like Parsons therefore argue that there is a high level of trust involved in the doctor–patient relationship, and the patient's interests must be protected.

Protecting the patient?

Parsons and other functionalist writers suggest that the following features of the medical profession protect the interests of patients, such as by protecting the confidentiality of their consultations and maintaining high standards of treatment:

- Doctors have a long period of training, giving them the specialized and expert knowledge and the wide range of diagnostic skills necessary to treat their patients effectively.
- Doctors need legal permission to practise medicine. This monopoly protects the patient from unqualified 'cowboy' doctors.
- Doctors are mainly concerned with patient care, rather than personal gain.
- Doctors are bound by a code of professional ethics, which puts the interests of the patient first and leaves doctors open to disciplinary action if they fail in their duty to patients. The General Medical Council does occasionally 'strike doctors off' the medical register in cases of medical incompetence or breaches of appropriate professional behaviour.

Because of these features of the medical profession, doctors are given high status in society, with high salaries to match. They are also trusted with high levels of independence to get on with their work of curing people.

These functionalist views have not gone unchallenged.

Criticisms of the medical profession

- Because of their long training, and specialized knowledge and skills, doctors have high levels of independence in their work. This means there is little control by others over what they do and often incompetent doctors remain undiscovered and unchallenged. Dr Harold Shipman achieved notoriety as Britain's worst serial killer, killing 215 patients between 1975 and 1998. While Shipman was something of an exception in the medical profession, the Shipman public inquiry was told the independence given to doctors undermined safeguards for patients against an incompetent doctor or, as in this case, a determined killer.
- The professional code of ethics means doctors are forbidden to criticize the work of other doctors publicly. This makes it very difficult for patients to complain about and expose medical incompetence.
- Because they have a monopoly over medical treatment, practitioners of alternative medicine of which the British Medical Association does

not approve are seen as giving inferior treatments, even though these might benefit patients. This same monopoly of treatment ensures doctors can maintain their high salaries.

- As seen earlier when discussing iatrogenesis, doctors and nurses don't always do a good job, and may actually do more harm than good to patients' health. Feminist writers have been particularly critical of the medical profession, and the way childbirth and pregnancy have come to be defined as medical problems, to be dealt with as an illness and treated clinically at the doctors' convenience. This takes control over childbirth away from women, and turns what should be a natural process into a medical procedure.

- Most doctors work within the framework of publicly funded health care, like the National Health Service or GP's surgeries. Concern over the costs of treatment may mean doctors do not always provide the best care, but may go for cheaper, less effective treatments.

The erosion of medical power?

The power of the medical profession is being eroded to some degree. This is because many of the new diseases in contemporary society are degenerative diseases for which there are no medical cures. In such circumstances, doctors are of less use to patients, and people often turn to alternative medicines. The rise of these alternatives was given extra force when the House of Lords recognized in 2000 that there was scientific evidence that some, such as acupuncture and herbal medicine, could be effective, and the British Medical Association has now accepted the usefulness of certain alternative treatments.

Patients are demanding much more from their doctors and nurses, and have growing knowledge of what medical treatments are effective and what they should be entitled to. More patients are questioning the competence of doctors, and losing confidence in them. This is reflected in rising numbers of complaints against medical professionals, with complaints about doctors to the General Medical Council reaching an all-time high in 2000. Patients now have the right to see their medical records, and doctors are facing growing threats of legal action when care is inadequate or when mistakes are made.

In the National Health Service, managers and administrators, rather than doctors, often make the major decisions about the types and costs of medical care provided. These factors are changing the balance of power between patients and doctors in the patient's favour, giving patients more rights through complaints procedures, and undermining the status of doctors.

Reforms in the National Health Service in the early 2000s aimed to provide more personalized health services for individuals, with the health care system fitting the needs of individuals rather than the other way round, giving patients more control over their medical treatment.

Public confidence in the medical profession is being eroded by medical 'scandals' of various kinds. An example of this was the wave of public revulsion and distrust arising from the scandal at Alder Hey hospital in Liverpool in 2001, when the organs of dead children were routinely removed during post-mortem examinations and stored for research purposes, without the prior consent of the parents.

Further lack of confidence in medicine arises from the return of diseases which were once thought nearly extinct in Britain. For example, tuberculosis has returned as a significant disease. In 2001 there was the worst outbreak of tuberculosis in Britain for twenty years in a secondary school in Leicester, with a further outbreak among children at a school in Newport, South Wales. TB in England has increased by 25 per cent over the last ten years, and around 350 people in England die each year from the disease.

Activity

Consider the following extract from a speech by the former Health Secretary, Alan Milburn, in January 2001:

'In this country we can no longer accept the traditional paternalistic attitude of the NHS, that the benefits of medicine, science and research are somehow self-evident regardless of the wishes of patients or their families . . . the health of the patient belongs to the patient, not to the health service. I want the balance of power in the NHS to shift decisively in favour of the patient, not to pitch patients against doctors but to put the relationship between patients and the health service on a more modern footing.'

1   What changes would you recommend to be introduced to shift the balance of power in favour of the patient, rather than doctors?

2   Go to www.dh.gov.uk, do a search on 'choice' or 'patient choice' and identify three steps the government has taken to implement such changes.

Marxist approaches to health and medicine

Marxists like Navarro (1976) adopt a social model of health, and are very critical of the biomedical model. Marxists argue:

● The medical model of health suggests ill-health is caused by either random attacks of disease or the failure of individuals to follow a healthy lifestyle. This puts the blame on individuals when ill-health is really caused by social influences in an unequal society, such as low pay, unemployment and poverty, unhealthy food, environmental pollution and hazardous workplaces. The state doesn't tackle the real social causes of ill-health, and allows companies to continue making profits out of health-damaging products, like tobacco, alcohol and 'junk' food.

- The National Health Service helps to keep the workforce fit, and this caring face of capitalism conceals the exploitation of the working class by the owning class.
- Doctors are agents of social control – gate-keepers who control access to the sick role and therefore keep the workforce at work in the interests of capitalists.
- The definition of health and the provision of health care are concerned with protecting the interests of the dominant class in an unequal capitalist society. Medicine is mainly concerned with providing capitalists with a healthy workforce.
- The focus on medical treatment, rather than the prevention of ill-health, supports big business in the form of drug and medical technology companies. These companies are mainly concerned with making profits out of ill-health, not reducing it.

How society influences health

The list you made in the Activity may have reminded you of a number of ways that social factors influence health. That health is the product of society rather than simply of biology or medicine is shown by historical evidence that patterns of disease change over time. While the message has been that medicine can cure us, all the major advances in health have occurred before medical intervention. In Britain, the elimination or substantial reduction of the killer infectious diseases of the past, such as tuberculosis (TB), pneumonia, cholera, typhoid and diphtheria, all took place before the development of modern medicine. It was social changes such as better diet, clean water supplies, sewage disposal, improved housing and general knowledge about health and hygiene that improved health,

---

Activity

Make a list of as many environmental, political, social and economic factors affecting health as you can think of, such as unemployment, pollution or poor housing. Explain in each case how the factors you identify might influence health. Refer to figure 3.1 to help you in this.

Figure 3.1 Some key influences on health

rather than medical improvements like antibiotics and vaccines. This is shown especially in the less developed countries today, where the major advances in health have come about as a result of simple preventive measures such as clean water and sewage control, where vaccines have been less effective because of malnutrition, and where medicines are often not affordable because of the high prices charged by international drug companies. Doctors and medical treatment have therefore not had the impact on health they often claim, and it is incorrect to assume that medicine has been largely responsible for the most significant improvements and promotion of health. Improvements in health are due to wider social, economic and environmental factors, and not simply medical ones.

Changes which occurred during the nineteenth century and the first half of the twentieth century illustrate this well.

Improvements in health in the nineteenth and early twentieth centuries

In the nineteenth century, adult and child mortality (death rates) started to fall, and this was accompanied by a large and rapid population increase. For a long time this was thought to be due to the development of medicine. However, McKeown (1976) showed that the role of medicine in reducing morbidity and mortality rates in the nineteenth and twentieth centuries had been massively exaggerated. It is now agreed that these changes were due to a number of social and economic changes and the general improvement in living standards. These included:

- *Public hygiene* The movement for sanitary reform and public hygiene in the nineteenth century helped to develop a clean and safe environment and higher standards of public hygiene. Pure drinking water, efficient sanitation and sewage disposal, paved streets and highways all helped to reduce deaths from infectious diseases.

- *Better diet*   Being well fed is the most effective form of disease prevention, as shown in less developed countries today where vaccination programmes are not as successful as they should be because children are poorly nourished. The high death rates of the past were mainly due to hunger or malnutrition, which led to poorer resistance to infection. The nineteenth and early twentieth centuries saw improved communications, technology and hygiene enabling the production, transportation and import of more and cheaper food. Wages improved, and higher standards of living meant better food and better health.
- *Safer and more effective contraception*   This led to smaller families, enabling a better diet and health care for children. It also improved the health of women, who spent less time childbearing.
- *Housing legislation*   This increased public control over standards of rented housing, which helped to reduce overcrowding and the spread of infectious diseases between family members and in the close community.
- *The war effort*   During the First World War (1914–18) unemployment was virtually eliminated. As part of the war effort, rents were controlled, food rationing was introduced and minimum wages were established in agriculture. The resulting decline in poverty cut childhood deaths, especially among the families of unskilled workers in urban areas.
- *General improvements in living standards*   Higher wages, better food, clothing and housing, laws improving health and safety at work, reduced working hours, and better hygiene regulations in the production and sale of food and drink all improved health.

All the above suggest that good health is more the result of government policy decisions and of economic development than simply of individual initiative or medical intervention.

The new 'disease burden'

The infective diseases of the nineteenth century were often called the 'diseases of poverty' since most victims were malnourished and poor. These have been replaced by 'diseases of affluence' – a result of eating too much poor quality food, a lack of exercise, and smoking and drinking too much.

Around one in five people in the United Kindom were officially classified as obese in 2005, and the World Health Organisation predicts that almost 50 per cent of children could be obese by 2025 through a combination of junk food and lack of exercise. Obesity is much more common among the most deprived sections of society

A well-balanced diet is necessary for good health, and the lack of one makes people more vulnerable to disease. Despite the wealth of modern industrial societies, there is a problem of malnutrition, in the form not of too little food, as you find in less developed countries, but too much of the wrong sort. As a result, advanced industrial societies experience health problems rarely found in simpler rural societies. The new 'disease burden' includes obesity and degenerative (worsening) diseases like cirrhosis of the liver, certain cancers, heart disease, respiratory diseases and diabetes. These kill or disable more people than they did in the past, and many more people are becoming chronically ill for longer periods in their lives than they did in the past.

What are the causes of these new diseases?

It is generally accepted that the causes of these new diseases of affluence are mainly social and environmental, and therefore preventable. Public concerns over the food supply have been rising. There were major scares over BSE ('Mad cow disease') in beef in the 1990s, and the linked human equivalent vCJD (variant Creutzfeldt–Jakob disease) had killed 152 people in Britain up to November 2005. *E. coli* food poisoning outbreaks in 1996–7 killed twenty people, and many worry about GM (genetically modified) crops and foods, while the effects on health of the use of growth-promoting drugs in chickens was of continuing concern in the early 2000s. Between 1989 and 1999, cases of food poisoning serious enough to be reported to a doctor nearly doubled, and the Food Standards Agency estimates there are 5.5 million cases of food poisoning in Britain each year. Some doctors have linked the rise of asthma to poor diet, with insufficient fruit and vegetables. The rise in heart disease has been blamed on factors such as smoking, stress, an inactive life style (too many couch potatoes!) and a diet high in sugar, salt and fats but low in fibre. A 1997 British government report, *Nutritional Aspects of the Development of Cancer*, estimated that up to 70 per cent of cancer cases were linked to the type of food people ate. Diet was seen as ten times more important than the effects of job-related causes and of smoking on all cancers. The *Lancet* medical journal reported in 2003 that women eating too much food high in fat, such as butter, milk, meat, burgers, crisps, biscuits and cakes, were more likely to get breast cancer than others whose fat intake was low. A *Lancet* report in 2005 said that one-third of cancer deaths worldwide were caused by diet, lifestyle factors like smoking and alcohol, and physical inactivity and environmental pollution.

The British are now eating a more highly processed diet than at any time in history. We consume a whole range of factory-produced food, which is often low in nutritional value and may well be harmful to health because of additives like flavourings, colourings, preservatives and various drugs. Revelations that large food-processing companies were 'bulking up' chicken destined for schools, hospitals and restaurants with poultry skin, beef bits and pig waste were of major concern in 2003. Highly processed junk food reinforces the trend towards a high-sugar, high-salt and high-fat diet which is low in vitamins, minerals, protein and fibre. Research in 2003 suggested that high doses of fat and sugar in fast and processed foods could be as addictive as nicotine and even hard drugs, causing hormonal changes creating a need for even more high-fat foods and generating obesity as a growing health problem.

Inequalities in health

Social class inequalities in health

Official statistics reveal massive class inequalities in health. These inequalities are often referred to as the 'health divide'. Nearly every kind of illness and disease has a class aspect. Poverty is the major driver of ill-health, and poorer people tend to get sick more often, to suffer more years in poor health and to die younger than richer people. Those who die youngest are people who live on benefits or low wages in poor quality housing and who eat cheap, unhealthy food. Lifestyle choices related to poor health, like smoking, alcohol misuse, obesity, poor diets and lack of exercise, are all more common among the most deprived sections of society.

A 1995 Department of Health report noted that if everyone was as healthy as the middle class, there would have been 1,500 fewer deaths a year among children under the age of one, and 17,000 fewer deaths among men aged 20–64. In 2005, the Office for National Statistics reported that people in the most prosperous neighbourhoods of England enjoyed seventeen more years of fit and active life than those in the poorest.

The Black Report (1980) and The Health Divide (1987)

Social class inequalities in health were first most clearly revealed in the Black Report of 1980. This report was so contentious and carried such a strong condemnation of health inequalities that the government never published it. Only 260 duplicated copies were made available, and it was released just before August Bank Holiday weekend – when it was guaranteed to get the absolute minimum of publicity. The Black Report was followed up in 1987 by *The Health Divide*, which confirmed yet again the pattern of social inequalities in health. As with the Black Report, there was strong evidence of official connivance in suppressing the findings of *The Health Divide*; as Townsend and his colleagues noted (1990), there was 'an attempted cover-up of unpalatable information about the nation's health'.

The Health of the Nation (1992)

The Health of the Nation, published by the Department of Health in 1992, set out the main strategy for improving the health of people in England until 1997. The strategy identified five key areas of ill-health: coronary heart disease and stroke; cancer; mental illness; HIV/AIDS and sexual health; and accidents – all major causes of premature death or avoidable ill-health and offering significant scope for improvement in health. It set targets in these areas, and monitored progress towards them.

The Acheson Report (1998)

Both the Black Report and *The Health Divide* were based on the social model of health, and the Acheson Report followed in their footsteps in recommending more help for the poor as a means of improving health. The Acheson Report confirmed earlier findings of wide social class inequalities in health, and helped to establish the framework for future health policies. These policies were unveiled in the 1998 Department of Health paper *Our Healthier Nation*, and *Saving Lives* a year later.

Our Healthier Nation (1998) and Saving Lives (1999)

Although overall trends show an improvement in health since the 1970s, with life expectancy increasing and infant mortality falling, these overall trends mask the fact that the health of the poor has failed to keep up with the improvements of the most prosperous sections of society. In fact, the health gap between those at the top and those at the bottom of the social scale has actually been widening since the last quarter of the twentieth century. The Labour government, in its 1998 paper *Our Healthier Nation*, and *Saving Lives* a year later, finally officially recognized these social class inequalities in health, and the social, environmental and economic causes of ill-health. These documents laid the basis for government health policy for the years ahead.

Our Healthier Nation pointed out that:

> the poorest in our society are hit harder than the well off by most of the major causes of death. Poor people are ill more often and die sooner. The life expectancy of those higher up the social scale (in professional and managerial jobs) has improved more than those lower down (in manual and unskilled jobs). This inequality has widened since the early 1980s.

Figure 3.2 shows some of these social class inequalities, which provide strong evidence that it is society and the way it is organized that influences health, rather than simply our biological make-up.

Explanations for social class inequalities in health

The causes of ill-health are complex, and there are clearly some influences on health which go beyond social factors. The ageing process and our genetic inheritance do have important influences on our health, though health education awareness, access to health, leisure and social services and a range of other social factors have an impact on how effectively we cope with them.

There are four main types of explanation for social class inequalities in heath: artefact, natural or social selection, cultural or behavioural, and material or structural explanations.

The artefact explanation This suggests that health inequalities between social classes are artificial rather than real – a manufactured explanation

---

Activity

Study figure 3.2:

1　Which disease shows the greatest difference in deaths between social class 5 and social class 1?
2　Which disease shows the smallest difference in deaths between social class 1 and social class 5?
3　Which social class shows the lowest deaths from lung cancer?
4　Identify two patterns shown in figure 3.2.
5　Which social class for deaths from what disease is exactly in line with the number expected from the population as a whole?

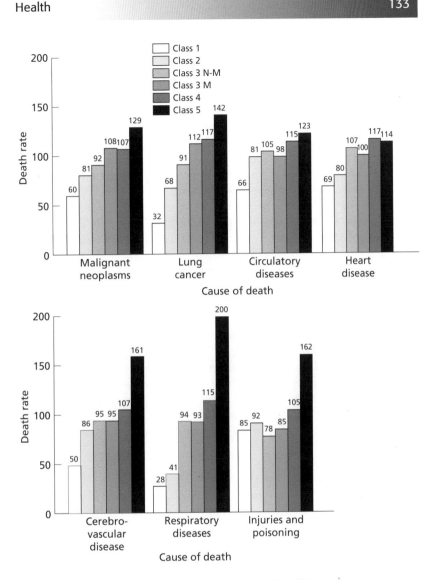

The average expected from the population as a whole is 100.
Death rates are higher than expected above 100, and lower than expected below 100.
Classes 1, 2 and 3 N-M are non-manual middle-class occupations, and 3 M, 4 and 5 are
manual working-class occupations.

Figure 3.2 Mortality (1976–1989) of men aged 15–64 at death, by cause of death
and by their social class in 1971
Source: Data from *Population Trends 80*

arising only because of distortion and bias in the way statistics are used,
and the way the link between social class and health is measured. The
apparent link between poor health and social class is simply because the
number of lower working-class occupations is getting smaller, and those
left in these occupations tend to be older than those in other social classes,

---

The extent of social class inequalities in health in contemporary Britain

- The death rate in class 5 (unskilled manual workers) is about twice that of class 1. A person born into social class 1 (professional) lives, on average, about seven years longer than someone in social class 5.
- In the first year of life, for every five children who die in class 1, eight die among unskilled workers. The risk of dying before the age of 5 is twice as great for a child born into social class 5 than for social class 1, and children from poorer backgrounds are five times more likely to die as a result of an accident than children from better-off families.
- Men and women in class 5 have twice the chance of dying before reaching retirement age than people in class 1. About 90 per cent of the major causes of death are more common in social classes 4 and 5 than in other social classes.
- Lung cancer and stomach cancer occur twice as often among men in manual jobs as among men in professional jobs. Four times as many women die of cervical cancer in social class 5 as in social class 1.
- Working-class people, especially the unskilled, go to see doctors far more often and for a wider range of health problems than do people in professional jobs.
- Semi-skilled and unskilled workers are more likely to be absent from work through sickness than those in professional and managerial jobs. Long-standing illness is around 50 per cent higher among unskilled manual workers than for class 1 professionals.
- All of the above are worse for the long-term unemployed and other groups in poverty.

---

with younger people going into new skilled or non-manual occupations. It is therefore only to be expected that those in such occupations will suffer poorer health, because the people left are older. This explanation is rejected by sociologists, since social class inequalities in health remain even after using a number of different methods of measurement.

The natural or social selection explanation   This explanation suggests that people in lower social classes are there because of their poor health, with their lack of physical strength, vigour and fitness stopping them getting into, and hanging on to, higher social class jobs. Poor health acts as a 'filter', with poor health causing their low social class, rather than their social class causing their ill-health. Society is seen as based on 'survival of the fittest', with the most unhealthy people inevitably ending up in the lowest social classes, while those in good health succeed in society and achieve the highest rewards. This explanation is rejected by sociologists, because most adult health problems seem to arise among those coming from already deprived backgrounds, and there is significant evidence to show that poor health is a result of deprived circumstances rather than a cause of them. There are also some people in higher social classes who suffer poor health, and people in lower social classes who enjoy good health, so good or poor health cannot by itself explain a person's social class position.

The following two types of explanation for social class inequalities in health are those firmly rooted in society itself.

Cultural or behavioural explanations – blaming the victims   Cultural explanations suggest that those suffering from poorer health have different attitudes, values and lifestyles which mean they don't look after themselves properly. Health inequalities are rooted in the unhealthy behaviour and lifestyles of individuals, and individuals can and should tackle them themselves by making voluntary efforts to change. Examples might include smoking too much, consuming too much alcohol, using too much salt or sugar, eating 'junk food' and not enough fresh fruit and vegetables, or not bothering to take any exercise.

These types of factors are linked to a variety of conditions, including heart disease, cancer, strokes, bronchitis and asthma. *Our Healthier Nation* estimates that alcohol abuse, for example, leads to around 40,000 deaths a year, and that a third of all cancers are the result of a poor diet.

Cultural explanations essentially place the blame on individuals themselves, in what are called 'victim blaming' theories. However, as Townsend and his colleagues (1990) pointed out:

> While some of the links between deprivation and ill-health are still very poorly understood, life style is clearly far from being the whole answer . . . some people have more freedom than others by virtue of their individual situation and circumstances to choose a healthy lifestyle, the unlucky ones being restrained from adopting a healthier life, even when they would wish to do so, by income, housing, work and other social constraints.

The way material factors can influence lifestyles and health choices was well illustrated in *Our Healthier Nation*:

> low income, deprivation and social exclusion all influence smoking levels. It's harder to stop smoking when you're worrying about making ends meet . . . If the nearest supermarket is miles away or the bus doesn't go there when you can, it can be difficult to buy food which is cheap and healthy; if the street outside your home is busy with traffic or there are drug dealers in the park then it's safer to keep the kids in front of the TV than let them out to play.

The Black Report and *The Health Divide* both pointed out that class differences in health remained even when lifestyle factors were taken into account, and many class differences were not related to factors such as smoking, drinking and other lifestyle choices. It is for all these reasons that sociologists have generally given more emphasis to material, social and economic explanations rather than cultural explanations for social class inequalities in health.

> ### Activity
>
> 1 To what extent do you think health and illness are the responsibility of individuals and the lifestyle choices they make?
> 2 What problems might there be for an approach to improving a society's health which focused only on the behaviour and choices of individuals?

Material or structural explanations – blaming social conditions   Material or structural explanations – about the means available to the individual and the structure of the society – suggest that those suffering poorer health do so because of the inequalities of wealth and income in Britain. Those suffering poorer health lack enough money to eat a healthy diet, have poor housing, dangerous or unhealthy working conditions, live in an unhealthy local environment and so on.

The Black Report concluded that 'while genetic and cultural or behavioural explanations played their part, the predominant or governing explanation for inequalities in health lay in material deprivation'. *Our Healthier Nation* recognized this link between poverty and ill-health:

> it is clear that people's chances of a long and healthy life are basically influenced by how well off they are . . . This means tackling inequality which stems from poverty, poor housing, pollution, low educational standards, joblessness and low pay. Tackling inequalities generally is the best means of tackling health inequalities in particular.

Figure 3.3 on page 138 identifies a range of possible factors which might explain health inequalities.

The Black Report, *The Health Divide*, the Acheson Report, *Our Healthier Nation* and *Saving Lives* provided so much evidence of the link between social class and the 'health divide' in Britain that it is doubtful whether any rational person could seriously deny it. As Dr John Collee said in the *Observer* newspaper in 1992:

> Forget everything else I have written on the subject. There is one piece of health advice which is more effective than all the others. One guaranteed way to live longer, grow taller, avoid chronic illness, have healthier children, increase your quality of life and minimize your risk of premature death. The secret is: *be rich.*

The inverse care law

Tudor-Hart first identified the inverse care law in 1971. This suggests that health care resources tend to be distributed in inverse proportion to need. This means that those whose need is least get the most resources, while those in greatest need get the least. Social class differences in health are therefore made worse through inequalities in the National Health Service. Why is this?

- Poorer areas have fewer GP practices – so there are fewer doctors for those who are most likely to get ill.
- Poorer people are more likely to be dependent on public transport, and so spend greater time travelling to hospitals and GPs, but they are also more likely to lose pay if they have to take time off work.

In contrast, those in the middle class:

- have more knowledge of illness and how to prevent it
- know more about the health services available and therefore get better service
- are more likely to fight against inadequate medical services
- are more self-confident, effective and assertive in dealing with doctors, and therefore get longer consultations, ask more questions, receive more explanations from their doctors and are more likely to be referred for further treatment
- have more money, so they are better able to jump NHS waiting lists by using private medicine

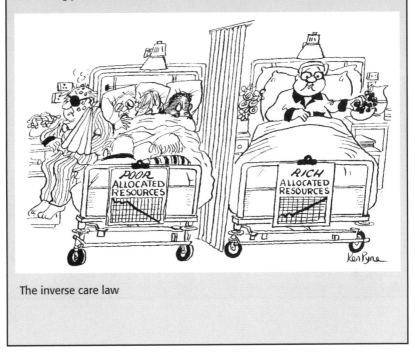

The inverse care law

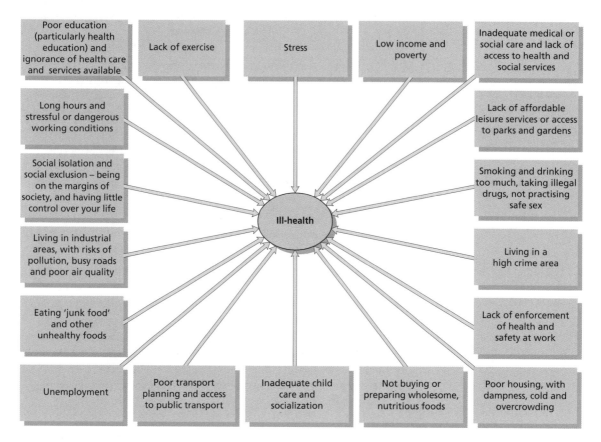

Figure 3.3 Cultural and material influences on health

Activity

Study figure 3.3 and answer the following questions:

1   Suggest ways each factor might explain social class inequalities in health.
2   Try to divide the explanations into 'cultural' and 'structural/material' explanations.
3   Suggest ways the cultural explanations might be influenced by structural/material factors.
4   Do you think cultural or structural/material explanations (or a bit of both) are better in explaining health inequalities? Give reasons for your answer.
5   Which of these factors do you think society can help to tackle, and which do you think are individual problems which only individuals themselves can solve?

Inequality kills

The importance of the social causes of ill-health is illustrated well by Richard Wilkinson (1996). Wilkinson has argued that health differences cannot be explained simply by material deprivation, such as poverty, but that social cohesion is itself a significant factor. Social cohesion means the extent to which people stick together and identify with each other in a sense of community. Wilkinson suggests that large income differences between social groups divide people from one another, and lead to a lack of social cohesion. Social inequalities, and the social divisions they create, can in themselves have poor effects on health, even among those who are not especially poor in income terms. He concludes that 'societies with narrower income differences are likely to be more socially cohesive and consequently more healthy'. In other words, the more equal a society is, the healthier it is, and a sense of community and social cohesion can in themselves improve health.

Tackling social class inequalities in health

The Acheson Report, *Our Healthier Nation* and *Saving Lives* laid the basis for government health policy for the years ahead. Their proposals marked a significant change in the focus of health policy away from curative to preventative medicine – from the medical to a social model of health.

There is now recognition by government of the important influence of social deprivation on health, and that social class inequalities in health are very much products of society rather than of simply biological factors, with social and economic life having major influences on the patterns of illness and death. As *Our Healthier Nation* concluded, 'the link between poverty and ill-health is clear. In nearly every case the highest incidence of illness is experienced by the worst off social classes.'

The social, economic and environmental causes of ill-health are complex, and often involve a range of factors, such as poor housing and education, poverty, unemployment or low pay, fear of crime, and social exclusion. The government has recognized that tackling health inequalities involves a range of linked policies, including measures to improve employment opportunities, together with action on crime, poverty, housing and education, as well as on health itself. These policies include, for example, the New Deal for Communities, Neighbourhood Renewal, and the SureStart programme for children's early years.

At the beginning of the twenty-first century, the government set itself a range of targets to tackle inequalities in health, and there have been many new policies developed. An NHS Plan was developed to tackle inequalities through more effective prevention and improved care for disadvantaged

populations. Two key Department of Health 'action' documents were produced: *Tackling Health Inequalities: A Programme for Action* (2003) and *Choosing Health* (2004).

These policies and targets had three main aims:

- to improve the health of the population as a whole by increasing the length of people's lives and the number of years people spend free from illness
- to prevent inequalities in health worsening by improving the health of the poorest fastest
- to narrow the health gap between the richest and the poorest

Two particular targets were set to help achieve these:

- by 2010, to reduce by at least 10 per cent the gap in infant mortality between routine non-manual and manual groups and the population as a whole

- by 2010,to reduce by at least 10 per cent the gap between the fifth of areas where people have the lowest life expectancy at birth and the population as a whole

Four national priority areas for health improvement were established:

- heart disease and stroke
- accidents
- mental health
- cancer

The government recognized that to achieve these targets and aims, a wide range of public and private agencies would need to work together, such as GPs, clinics and NHS hospitals, government departments, community and leisure centres, schools and workplaces, and the food industry. To address the underlying causes of ill-health, and to improve the health of the poorest 30–40 per cent of the population where the greatest burden of disease exists, a wide range of policies has been adopted. The table in the activity shows some of these policies.

Activity

Go through the list of policies below. Explain in each case how the policy might help to reduce social class inequalities in health. Three are already done for you, as examples.

Go to www.dh.gov.uk and find out how much progress has been made on three of these policies and how successful they have been. Try searching on 'inequalities' or 'health improvement' to start. Words in *italics* refer to specific programmes or policies that can be searched for.

Policy	How it might help to reduce social class inequalities in health
1 Halve the number of children in poverty by 2010, and eradicate child poverty by 2020.	Poverty is a major cause of ill-health. Tackling child poverty is likely to improve the health of the most disadvantaged children, making them healthier as adults and giving them more opportunities to be successful in society.
2 Improve sexual health, by promoting safe sex and contraception.	These are likely to reduce sexually transmitted infections, such as HIV/AIDS, and unplanned pregnancies. The least educated are more likely to lack awareness of these issues.

Policy	How it might help to reduce social class inequalities in health
3 Develop *Healthy Living Centres* (over 350 in 2005) across the UK in areas of greatest deprivation.	This would improve health and fitness by making gyms and fitness centres accessible to those people who may find existing facilities too expensive, off-putting or difficult to get to. These are often the most disadvantaged. This would rectify the current situation, where – in keeping with the inverse care law – middle-class customers dominate health and leisure centres.
4 Develop a national *Healthy Schools* programme, to encourage schools to raise awareness of health issues, and promote better health through healthy eating and lifestyles.	
5 Reduce smoking.	
6 Reduce teenage pregnancy, through the *Teenage Pregnancy Strategy*, in particular through action in neighbourhoods with high teenage conception rates.	
7 Improve access to, and the quality of, antenatal care, and early years support for children and families in disadvantaged areas, through programmes such as *SureStart*.	
8 Improve the physical activity of the population.	
9 Improve environmental health and reduce the risk of accidents in the home and on the road.	
10 Improve the quality and energy efficiency of housing, particularly in social (council and housing association) housing in the most disadvantaged areas, through programmes such as *Neighbourhood Renewal* (see figure 3.4) and the *UK Fuel Poverty Strategy*.	

Policy	How it might help to reduce social class inequalities in health
11 Tackle alcohol misuse.	
12 Improve mental health and mental well-being.	
13 Provide more information about the health risks of obesity, poor diet and lack of exercise, and action that people can take themselves to improve their health.	
14 Develop better labelling on the nutrition content of packaged food, showing which foods can make a positive contribution to a healthy diet (and which don't).	
15 Reduce crime, the fear of crime, and drug misuse.	
16 Improve educational attainment and skills among disadvantaged groups.	
17 Reduce unemployment, and improve the income of the most disadvantaged groups.	

All of the measures identified in the activity to create a healthier nation and reduce inequalities in health depend on resources, on commitment and on cooperation between the official providers of health care and the public. Tackling health inequalities only through the health service is unlikely to work. It may be the job of the National Health Service to resuscitate people once they have been rescued from drowning, but it is the job of everyone else to prevent them from drowning in the first place. If people don't want to 'get healthy' – as actress Anna Friel once said, 'I smoke because I'm still young enough to feel immortal'– it is hard to see what any government can do. However, health policy at the beginning of the twenty-first century has finally recognized that so long as inequalities of wealth, income, education, occupation, opportunity and social privilege continue, so will inequalities in health. As the government itself recognized in *Our Healthier Nation*, 'tackling inequalities generally is the best means of tackling health inequalities in particular.'

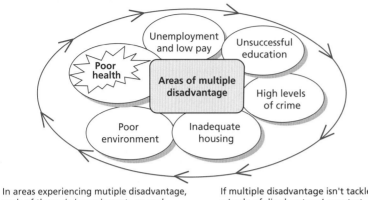

In areas experiencing mutiple disadvantage, each of these six issues impacts on and feeds the others – tackling one by itself will be most unlikely to succeed

If multiple disadvantage isn't tackled then a 'cycle of disadvantage' can start, making 'breaking out' of it very difficult indeed

Figure 3.4 What's involved in neighbourhood renewal? Areas of multiple disadvantage and the 'cycle of disadvantage'

Activity

Refer to figure 3.4 and:

1 Explain how each of the six issues identified 'impacts on and feeds the others'.
2 Explain why 'tackling one by itself will be most unlikely to succeed'.
3 Explain why a 'cycle of disadvantage' can start if all the issues are not tackled, and why 'breaking out' of it can then become very difficult.
4 Identify and explain three cultural factors that may affect a person's health.
5 Identify and explain three material explanations for social class inequalities in health.
6 Explain what is meant by the 'inverse care law'.
7 In about one and a half to two sides of A4 paper, answer the following essay question:

Assess sociological explanations for social class differences in health and illness.

Gender differences in health

As well as a pattern of social class differences in health, there is also a big difference between the health of men and women. At all ages, women's death rates are much lower than men's. Men's death rates are almost double those of women in every class and on average women lived five years longer than men in 2003. Almost two-thirds of deaths before the age of 65 are male, and two-thirds of people aged over 65 are women.

Activity

Refer to the box below

1 Which of the reasons given for women living longer than men do you think is most important? Put them in order of importance, giving your reasons.
2 Do you think men's 'macho' behaviour is an important factor in shortening their lives? Suggest evidence for or against this from your own experiences.
3 'The growing equality of women with men is a threat to women's health.' Explain this statement. Do you agree? How might this situation be avoided (apart from stopping women becoming more equal!)?

Why do women live longer than men?

- Evidence suggests that boys are the weaker sex at birth, with a higher infant mortality rate – male babies are more likely to die in the first year of life. Women seem to have a better genetic resistance to heart disease than men.
- The process of gender role socialization means men are more likely to be brought up to shrug off illnesses, they are more likely to drink and smoke (with all the consequences for health), are more aggressive and take more risks, are less careful in what they eat, and are not socialized to show their emotions as much as women and so have fewer outlets for stress.
- Women are more involved in family health, as they are more likely to be involved in nurturing and caring roles in the family, and sensitive to illness. Women are the biggest users of the health service, both for themselves and because it is generally women who organize the rest of the family going to the doctor's.
- Women are socialized to 'take care of themselves' more than men, and they are more likely to visit doctors, which may mean they receive better health care. Sometimes working fewer hours means women have more opportunity to visit doctors.
- Men generally live more hazardous lives than women. The more dangerous occupations are more likely to be done by men, such as construction work, and therefore men are more at risk of industrial accidents and diseases. In the home, men are more likely to do the dangerous and risky jobs, such as jobs using ladders and climbing on the roof. Men also make up the majority of lorry and car drivers and motor-cyclists, and are therefore more at risk of death through road accidents.
- Men are more likely to work full-time and to work longer and more unsociable hours, such as overtime working and shift work, which can be harmful to health.
- Men retire later than women (age 65 compared to 60). Evidence suggests that the later retirement age of men could be an important factor in reducing their life expectancy (note: women's retirement age is planned to increase to 65 in the period between 2010 and 2020).

Are women healthier than men?

The answer to whether women are healthier than men is 'yes' if we use only the indicators of death rates and life expectancy. However, statistics show that men, who in general die younger, don't seem to experience as much ill-health during their lives as women who live longer. Women are the major users of health care services and apparently get sick more often than men.

Compared to men, women:

- go to the doctor about 50 per cent more often between the ages of 15 and 64
- report more head and stomach aches, high blood pressure and weight problems
- consume more prescription and non-prescription drugs
- are admitted to hospital more often and have more operations
- go to see doctors about conditions like insomnia, tension headache and depression (which are often labelled as 'mental illness') about twice as often
- receive far more prescriptions for tranquillizers, sleeping pills and antidepressants
- are off work with reported sickness more often and spend more days in bed

Why do women apparently suffer more sickness?

There are particular features in women's lives compared to men's that may make them more vulnerable to sickness.

Stress   Many women suffer a triple burden of being low-paid workers, carrying responsibilities for housework and childcare, and managing family emotions. In many cases this involves having to manage limited household budgets with pressure to make ends meet, and working long days with little time to relax.

Poverty   Women are more likely to experience poverty than men, because they are more likely to be lone parents, and because they live longer than men while being less likely to have employers' pensions or savings for old age. In low income households, it is usually women who go without to ensure other family members get enough to eat. Women are therefore likely to suffer the effects of poverty more directly than men.

Domestic labour   Domestic labour (housework) is rarely fulfilling (for further discussion on this, see chapter 2 on the family and households). Depression may be linked to the unpaid, repetitive, unrewarding and low status nature of housework in a society where only paid employment is really respected. The high accident rates at home might be influenced by the isolated nature of housework.

Socialization   Women are socialized to express their feelings and talk about their problems more than men. Since women are generally the ones who 'manage' family health matters, they are often more aware of health and health care matters. Women may therefore be more willing than men to report physical and mental health problems. The higher rates of recorded illnesses among women could then be due, not necessarily to greater health problems than men, but to women's greater willingness to admit to them and to take them to doctors. While women go to doctors for prescribed drugs like tranquillizers, men opt for non-prescribed drugs like alcohol. Men's higher death rates may simply be because they bottle everything up until it is too late.

Different diagnoses   Due to gender roles, it may be that women are more willing to report symptoms of mental illness. Doctors are more likely to see symptoms reported by women as mainly mental, while men's are seen as physical. Women are therefore more likely to be diagnosed as depressed or suffering from anxiety than men. Until recently, women had a much higher chance than men of being institutionalized in mental hospitals.

Activity

1   Refer to the list of four stages and the activity on page 119 and suggest
    reasons why women might be more likely to end up as a health statistic
    than men.
2   Discuss the explanations suggested above for women apparently suffering
    more sickness than men. Do you think women really do suffer more ill-
    health, or do you think they are simply more open and honest about it than
    men?

Feminist approaches to health

Feminist writers, like Ann Oakley (1984), Nicky Hart (1985) and Hilary
Graham (1993) have been very critical of the biomedical approach to
health and the patriarchal nature of the medical profession. They are
particularly critical of the way pregnancy and childbirth have come to be
seen as medical problems (this is sometimes called the 'medicalization of
childbirth') and the way they have been dealt with as an illness, rather than
a natural process, and treated clinically at times suited to doctors. For
example, births may be induced and babies delivered by caesarean operations at times to suit the working hours of hospitals and doctors rather than
the needs of the mother and baby. A survey for *Mother and Baby* magazine
in 2005 found that just 43 per cent of the 96 per cent of expectant mothers
giving birth in hospital had the same midwife throughout their labour, and
half described their postnatal care as 'not kind or compassionate'.

Feminist writers point to patriarchy in the medical profession and the
drug and medical technology industry, with women marginalized in
many aspects of health care. For example, midwives (nearly all women)
are supervised by mainly male obstetricians and gynaecologists, around
74 per cent of whom were men in 2004. Nurses, around 90 per cent of
whom are women, have lower status than doctors – around 65 per cent of
whom are men – and there is a large body of research evidence which
suggests that men have greater career success in the nursing profession
than women. Women dominate in the lower levels of every aspect of the
National Health Service. Feminists also point out, for example, that
contraception is mainly aimed at women rather than men. What male
contraception there is has few side-effects. In contrast to this, contraception for women does have harmful effects, with worries, for example, that
certain contraceptive pills might be linked to higher risks of cancer, and
IUDs (intrauterine devices) and caps leaving women vulnerable to infections. Is this because men dominate the development of contraceptive
technologies?

Feminist writers are also, of course, concerned with the general issues of
women's health discussed above. Marxist feminists focus more closely on

the particular impact of social inequality in general on the health of the lives of women in the working class and minority ethnic groups.

Ethnic inequalities in health

Social class and gender are not the only important social inequalities in health; there are also some differences between ethnic groups. As with social class, social and economic factors, rather than culture and biology, are the main factors explaining the poorer health of minority ethnic groups in Britain.

Explanations

Three main kinds of explanations have been given for the health disadvantages of minority ethnic groups.

Language and culture   Asian women are less likely to visit ante- and postnatal clinics, which helps explain their higher levels of infant mortality. Many Asian women speak poor English, possibly creating difficulties in obtaining treatment, advice and guidance from health workers. This is made worse by the lack of translation services in the NHS. Despite big improvements, there is still a lack of information available in minority ethnic group languages.

Some findings on minority ethnic group inequalities

Compared to the white majority ethnic group:

- People from African-Caribbean, Indian, Pakistani and Bangladeshi backgrounds are all more likely to suffer and die from TB, liver cancer or diabetes.
- Africans and African-Caribbeans are more likely to suffer from strokes and hypertension.
- Asians (Indians and Pakistanis) suffer more heart disease and are more likely to die from it.
- Indians and African-Caribbeans are more likely to be compulsorily admitted to hospital for mental illnesses, and once there receive less sympathetic and harsher forms of treatment. African-Caribbeans are more likely to be diagnosed as schizophrenics and compulsorily committed to mental hospitals for this.
- Most ethnic minorities show higher rates of stillbirths, perinatal deaths (dying at birth or within the first week of life), neo-natal deaths (within a month) and infant mortality (within a year of birth).
- Most minority ethnic groups have higher rates of mortality.
- African-Caribbeans, Pakistanis and Bangladeshis are between 30 and 50 per cent more likely to suffer ill-health.

Asian women often prefer to see female doctors, and many find it difficult talking to male and white doctors. However, the number of female GPs is lowest in those areas with the largest concentrations of Asian households.

Health professionals are often not familiar enough with the religious, cultural and dietary practices of different ethnic groups, hence their concerns may not be understood, nor their needs met.

Racism, poverty and deprivation   Many of the health problems of some minority ethnic groups arise for the same reasons as social class inequalities, because they are likely to be among the poorest groups in society. Racism in society means some minority ethnic groups are more likely than white people to find themselves living in the worst housing, and to be unemployed or working for long hours in low paid jobs, in hazardous and unhealthy environments. Such conditions create stressful, unhealthy lives. Racism and poverty are the twin planks of ill-health in minority ethnic groups.

Diet   Rickets (which can lead to difficulties in walking) is found more commonly in the Asian community. This is probably due to vitamin D deficiency and there has been much discussion about how to intervene in the diet of Asian children to remedy this. Higher levels of heart disease may arise from aspects of the high-fat Asian diet, which also generates higher levels of obesity – itself a cause of heart disease.

Inequalities of access to health care

The National Health Service is the main source of formal, clinical health care for most people. However, this does not mean everyone has equal access to health services, and services do vary in the quality of care provided.

There are four major areas of inequality.

Funding

Despite the shift in health policy away from the curative medicine of the medical model towards a greater emphasis on preventative medicine based on the social model of health, the 'acute' sector (hospitals) still gets the most attention and funding. This is often at the expense of other services, such as chiropody and mental illness, and services geared towards the particular needs of groups like adults with learning difficulties and minority ethnic groups. Standards of care are therefore not as good, nor as responsive as they should be.

Geography

Modern 'high-tec' hospitals and numbers of GPs are concentrated in urban areas, disadvantaging people living in the countryside. Specialist hospitals and units, such as heart and cancer units, are not spread equally across the country. Health care provision is better in the more affluent south of England than the disadvantaged areas of the north, producing a north–south divide in access to health care. For example, the House of Commons Public Accounts Committee reported in 2005 that people in the cities of northern England were almost twice as likely to die of cancer as those in affluent areas of the south, in what has been called a 'postcode lottery'. Those in the south get faster access to diagnostic tests, scans, anti-cancer drugs and chemotherapy.

These differences could be because of social class factors rather than simply geography, as these areas contain a higher proportion of people from lower social classes. Nonetheless, the industrial areas of northern England and Wales have fewer and older hospitals, fewer and less adequate specialized facilities, such as for cancer or kidney treatments, fewer hospital beds per head of population, and higher patient/doctor ratios.

Social class

There are differences in health care provision for different social classes, and the evidence suggests that this inequality has not been significantly reduced since the introduction of the National Health Service. For the majority of cancers, there is a five-year gap in the survival rates between the better and worst off. Working-class children, even though they suffer more illnesses and accidents, are less likely to be taken to the doctor than those from the middle class, or for dental checks and treatment. Health services in working-class areas are often less accessible and of poorer quality. There are fewer GPs per head of population in working-class areas, despite higher levels of sickness, and middle-class patients are likely to demand, and get, more time with their doctors. This means working-class people may not get the same quality of consultation and treatment as the middle class. The discussion earlier in this chapter on social class inequalities in health, and the inverse care law, explains many of the reasons why those from the poorest social groups have less opportunity to access the health services.

Disability

'A disability can make you invisible to the health service and normal medical care.' This is what Peter Cardy, chief executive of the MS (Multiple Sclerosis) Society, said to the *Guardian* newspaper in November 2000 to describe the way many disabled people do not have adequate access to medical treatment or equipment. The same article reported a survey by the disability organization SCOPE in 2000 that found 47 per cent of people who cannot use speech were being denied access to electronic communication aids. People with MS have been denied drugs, such as beta-interferon, that might reduce their suffering. Women with MS are often not given routine gynaecological checks. People with disabilities are also regularly excluded from routine treatment because of difficulties in travelling to a health centre or dentist.

The Royal College of Physicians has recommended that people with learning disabilities have annual health checks, but in many cases this is not happening, even though such people are more vulnerable to hearing problems, heart disease and epilepsy. *Treat Me Right!*, a 2004 report by Mencap, a charity supporting those with learning disabilities, found that people with a learning disability often die younger than other people, and suggested part of the reason for this was because many of them get poorer health services than other people. In a survey by Mencap, 90 per cent of GPs said they found it harder to diagnose people with a learning disability, and 75 per cent said they had received no training in treating such patients. Seventy per cent of GP surgeries had no information that those with learning disabilities could easily understand. Some GPs do not understand their needs, and think that all the health problems people with a learning disability have are a result of their disability, and so they do not take their health problems as seriously as they would if they were presented by someone without such a disability. The report called for better training in learning disability for all health care staff in order to cut the number of premature deaths.

Mental illness

An estimated one in six people of working age suffers some form of mental illness, from depression, through disabling anxiety disorders, to schizophrenia and, for a tiny minority, dangerous and severe personality disorder (DSPD – these are popularly known as 'psychopaths'). Yet, despite being relatively common, mental illnesses are often seen and treated quite differently from physical ones. The mentally ill often face discrimination at every level of society, because mental illness is among the most stigmatized and misunderstood of illnesses. This is because it involves behaviour we find very hard to understand, and because it does not have any obvious physical symptoms. Research by the Mental Health Foundation charity in April 2001, *Is Anybody There? A Survey of Friendship and Mental Health*, found that four in ten people with mental health problems were worried about telling friends about their problems, and one in three felt friendships had become strained, or lost, because of their mental illness. They felt their friends would not understand, or were likely to react negatively, because of the continuing stigma attached to mental illness.

People are likely to see mental illness as less 'real' than physical illness. There is, as a consequence, frequently a greater reluctance by other people to accept the legitimacy of the sick role, even though some mental illness, like some kinds of depression, does have a biological basis.

What is mental illness?

Mental illness has been defined as 'a state of mind which affects the person's thinking, perceiving, emotion or judgement to the extent that she or he requires care or medical treatment in her or his interests or in the interests of other persons'.

Mental illness might therefore be seen as any mental disorder affecting the behaviour and personality of an individual so as to prevent him or her functioning adequately within their society. Mental illnesses can range from anxiety and mild depression, through behavioural and emotional problems like eating disorders, to personality disorders and severe neurotic and psychotic disorders.

Care in the community

In the past, the seriously mentally ill were treated in large long-stay psychiatric hospitals, but now, except for the most serious cases, they are more likely to be cared for in the community. Community care involves those who are mentally ill living as much as possible within a 'normal' community, alongside members of the public who are not mentally ill. They are generally cared for and supported in smaller community-based units, or cared for by the family or through GPs. The move to 'care in the community' was prompted by the desire to reduce spending on large-scale hospital care, and the desire to avoid the negative effects that long-stay psychiatric hospitals had on the patients, and the often quite frightening situations that patients faced in them from other mentally ill patients. The underfunding of community care led to a series of scandals arising from inadequate care and supervision by welfare agencies, and a lack of liaison between local authorities and health authorities. However, care in the community provides an important means for people with mental health problems to receive support and treatment in conditions as near 'normal' as possible, and to help them cope with the difficulties they face in a safe context – for both themselves and the public at large.

The biomedical approach to mental illness

In the past, mental illness was often explained as being the result of possession by evil spirits, the Devil, or the work of witches. However, it is now seen as a medical problem, to be treated using the biomedical approach. This involves the use of drugs or other medical or surgical treatments, in clinical environments (psychiatric hospitals), to attempt to cure the illness.

The challenge to the biomedical approach: the social pattern of mental illness

There is, as in other aspects of health, a social pattern to mental illness. This challenges the biomedical model, since it would appear that mental illness affects social groups differently, and is linked to social conditions. It therefore cannot stem simply from biological factors, where a more random pattern would be expected. For example:

● The working class is diagnosed as suffering more mental illness than the middle class, and working-class mothers report more depression than middle-class mothers. This may reflect higher levels of poverty and family stress. Class differences in the treatment given, such as admittance to NHS psychiatric hospitals (where they will become a health statistic) rather than unrecorded private psychotherapy or psychiatric treatments at home or in private clinics, may also explain this difference.

● More women than men suffer, or at least report, mental illness.

● People of African-Caribbean origin are more likely to be diagnosed as schizophrenic and compulsorily committed to psychiatric hospitals.

● Suicide and depression is more common among young unemployed males.

● African-Caribbeans and some Asian groups suffer higher levels of mental illness, possibly explained by racism, combined with social deprivation.

These social patterns of mental illness have led some researchers to suggest that not only is mental illness caused by social factors, like racism, stress, unemployment and poverty, but that the definition of mental illness itself is created by society – a social construction.

The social construction of mental illness

The decision about whether someone is mentally ill or not involves other people, such as partners, family, friends, workmates and doctors, making judgements about whether someone's behaviour is so outside the boundaries of normal behaviour, so strange, unusual, bizarre or frightening, that it presents a problem for either the individual concerned or other people.

The definition of mental illness therefore rests on what people see as normal and socially acceptable behaviour, and on those people then defining some forms of behaviour as unacceptable deviance. This obviously prompts the question of how the notions of 'normal' and 'abnormal' behaviour are established, and therefore what is and isn't classed as 'mental illness'. This is no easy matter, since what is regarded as abnormal or 'mad' in one society or group may be seen as perfectly normal in another, and notions of normality and deviance change over time. For example, agoraphobia (fear of open spaces) is only seen as a mental illness because other people don't regard staying indoors all the time as normal behaviour.

Certainly the label of 'mental illness' has been used to condemn deviant (non-conformist) behaviour. For example, some young women were once put in mental hospitals simply because they were unmarried mothers, and opponents of the former Communist regime in the Soviet Union (now Russia and its neighbouring countries) were once seen as 'mad' to oppose the government and put in mental hospitals for 'treatment'. Even today in Britain we find an increasing medicalization of odd behaviour so that, for example, 'naughty' children are often labelled as suffering from Emotional and Behavioural Difficulties or Attention Deficit Disorder. How often do many of us dismiss people whom we think of as strange, with odd views or bizarre behaviour, as 'crazy'?

The work of Scheff

These issues have led researchers, such as Scheff and Szasz, to claim that what we call mental illness is a social construction – simply a label applied by others, and particularly those with power such as doctors, politicians and the mass media, to those whose behaviour they cannot make sense of, or dislike, or of which they disapprove. It is a label applied to those who display unacceptable forms of deviance which go against the dominant norms in any society.

Thomas Scheff (1966) sees what is called 'mental illness' as a label to explain away, and justify treatment of, bizarre behaviour that cannot be explained or made sense of in any other way. The label 'mental illness' is applied to rule-breaking and odd behaviour which takes place in unapproved contexts, and which might pose a threat to the smooth running of society.

Scheff argues that most people at some time go through stages of stress, anxiety or depression, or show signs of odd or bizarre behaviour. In the majority of cases other people do not label this as evidence of mental illness, and it is dealt with through the normal sick role. A few days off work, a change in social circumstances or a holiday is often enough to deal with these problems. It is only when others label this behaviour as evidence of mental illness that it begins to have important consequences for individuals.

Scheff argues that once others begin to see behaviour as so bizarre, frightening or intolerable that it is seen as a sign of mental illness, then stereotypes of mental illness we have all learnt since childhood – like the 'nutter' or the 'loony' – come into play. The patient then acts according to the stereotype she or he has learnt to expect of the mentally ill. Others react in terms of the same stereotyped expectations. Psychiatrists confirm the 'insane' label, psychiatric treatment begins, and the deviant label of 'mentally ill' is firmly established. People labelled in such a way are thus thrown into the 'insanity role'. Those labelled as mentally ill often have little choice but to accept the label, as refusal of it and of the treatment ('there's nothing wrong with me') is interpreted by others as yet further confirmation of their illness.

The work of Szasz

Szasz (1972), like Scheff, argues that mental illness is not really an illness at all, but a label used by powerful or influential people to control those who are seen as socially disruptive or who challenge existing society or the dominant ideas in some way. Szasz says that it is the views and reactions of others that lead to the mental illness label being applied, and not the abnormal behaviour itself that makes us 'mad'. What we define as 'mental illness' or 'madness' cannot therefore be treated or cured, as the problem lies with the attitudes of other people, not with the behaviour itself.

The work of Goffman

Goffman, in *Asylums* (1961), is concerned with the consequences that follow for those individuals whose behaviour has been labelled as a mental illness. Goffman suggests that once a person is labelled as 'mentally ill' and chooses or is forced to enter a psychiatric hospital as a patient, then the insanity role is confirmed and the career of the psychiatric patient begins.

Goffman argues that psychiatric hospitals develop their own subculture, where people don't get cured but learn to 'act mad' according to the label that has been attached to them. This reduces their chances of release and makes it difficult for them to re-enter 'normal' society successfully. He therefore suggests that hospitals for the treatment of mental illness are more likely to create the behaviour they are supposed to be curing, making release and a return to normality even more difficult.

Mortification is a process whereby a person's own identity is replaced by one defined by an institution, such as a psychiatric hospital or prison.

Entering a mental hospital – mortification   Entering a mental hospital involves what Goffman calls a process of **mortification**, where the patient's own identity is replaced by one defined by the institution. This is to encourage the patient to conform to the hospital regime. It involves things like removing personal clothing and possessions, lack of privacy, making the patient follow hospital routines, obeying staff and so on.

In these circumstances, Goffman suggests patients may respond to the institution and the label applied to them in various ways:

- *Withdrawal*   Patients keep themselves to themselves – behaviour which is interpreted as part of the illness, confirming the label.
- *Rebellion*   Patients challenge the institution – which is interpreted as part of the illness, but suggests more treatment is needed.
- *Institutionalization*   Patients accept they are mentally ill, feel more secure in hospital and scared of the outside world, and want to remain in hospital.
- *Conversion*   Patients accept their new roles and rules, and creep to staff as a 'model patient'.
- *Playing it cool*   Patients keep their heads down and don't break rules so they can hang on to what's left of their own identity.

Goffman argues that the label of 'mentally ill' carries with it a stigma – a sign of social disapproval, rejection and inferiority – that has severe consequences for people so labelled, even when they have been 'cured'. For example, some employers are reluctant to employ people who have a history of mental illness. This means that, even if patients are released, they are likely to face the social stigma attached to being a 'former mental patient'.

The work of Rosenhan

Rosenhan's research 'On being sane in insane places' (1973) showed how unreliable diagnoses of mental illness were. This research confirmed the views of Scheff, Szasz and Goffman that mental illness is basically a label placed on behaviour by others.

Rosenhan in 1972 was interested in discovering how the staff of mental hospitals in the United States made sense of perfectly sane 'patients' who, unknown to staff, faked the symptoms of schizophrenia by claiming to hear a voice saying 'thud'. Nine people (including Rosenhan himself) prepared themselves by not washing, shaving on cleaning their teeth for five days before going to the hospitals. All were diagnosed as schizophrenics and admitted to hospital. Once admitted, they behaved normally, and said the voice wasn't bothering them any more. All the pseudopatients were perfectly healthy, but were nonetheless kept in hospital for many days, and aspects of their perfectly normal lives before being admitted to

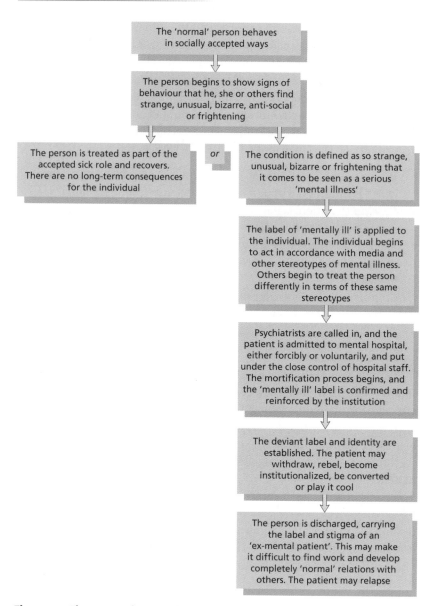

Figure 3.5 The career of a mental patient

hospital were reinterpreted as signs of their apparent illness. Rosenhan took many notes while in hospital, and this was also interpreted by staff as part of his illness, labelled as 'writing behaviour'.

Rosenhan then reversed the experiment, telling hospital staff they could expect an undisclosed number of patients who would be faking illness. The staff eventually thought they had identified forty-one fake patients, but all those they identified were actually genuine patients who wanted help, and Rosenhan had in fact not sent any fake patients at all. Rosenhan's work illustrated very clearly that the attachment of the label 'mentally ill' is a fairly arbitrary and inaccurate process. This is a matter of concern given the stigma that is attached to mental illness, and the consequences that may flow once the label is applied.

Rosenhan revisited

Rosenhan's experiment hit the world of psychiatry like a bombshell, and resulted in changes in the way diagnoses of mental illness were made. Contemporary psychiatrists are convinced that what happened with Rosenhan and his fellow pseudopatients could not happen in the twenty-first century. However, in 2002, the experiment was repeated by the psychologist Lauren Slater. She followed the same procedures as Rosenhan, not washing and so on for five days before going to the hospital, and claimed, like Rosenhan, that 'I'm here because I'm hearing a voice and it's saying "thud"'. Like Rosenhan's pseudopatients, Slater had no other symptoms of mental illness or physical ill-health. She was initially diagnosed as having post-traumatic stress disorder, and then as suffering psychosis and depression. She visited eight hospitals, and while she was not admitted, she was prescribed a total of twenty-five antipsychotic and sixty antidepressant drugs. Like Rosenhan thirty years earlier, her non-existent condition was misdiagnosed and mislabelled.

For further information, see 'Into the cuckoo's nest', *Guardian* 31 Jan. 2004, an edited extract from *Opening Skinner's Box: Great Psychological Experiments of the Twentieth Century* by Lauren Slater (London: Bloomsbury 2004).

Primary deviance is deviant behaviour which is not publicly labelled as deviant.

Activity

1 To what extent do you agree with the view that mental illness is simply a social construction?
2 Do you think the media present negative stereotypes of those with mental illness? Try to find evidence from recent media reporting.
3 Primary deviance is the type of deviant behaviour we might all display from time to time with few, if any, social consequences, because other people either don't know about it or don't see it as very important. Secondary deviance is when that behaviour is seen by others, and labelled as deviant or unacceptable behaviour with a need for action to be taken. Suggest how the concepts of primary and secondary deviance might be applied to the cases of those displaying symptoms of mental illness.

Secondary deviance is deviant behaviour which is labelled as such by others.

Criticisms of the social construction approach to mental illness

The work of writers like Scheff, Szasz, Goffman and Rosenhan has been criticized for the small scale of their studies, which may therefore not be representative of all institutions involved with mental health.

The view that mental illness is simply a social construction – a response to the interpretations of other people – ignores the fact that for many people it is a real illness, often causing a great deal of distress both for individuals and their families and friends. In such circumstances, psychiatric help and medical treatment can sometimes be effective. Nonetheless, the views of writers like Scheff, Szasz, Goffman and Rosenhan do raise serious questions about the way we think about, define and label 'mental illness'. The study of mental illness shows yet again that there are significant social aspects to health which are as important as biological or physical causes.

Activity

1   Conduct a small survey in your school or college, exploring attitudes to mental illness. Ask about things that interest you, but you might consider some of the following issues:
    - whether the welfare state should provide the best possible care for people with mental illness
    - whether the people in your survey think the mass media give unfair treatment to those with mental illnesses
    - whether they believe anyone can become mentally ill
    - what they think the causes of mental illness are
    - whether anyone with a history of mental health problems should be excluded from taking up some jobs
    - whether care units for people with psychiatric problems should be located in residential neighbourhoods
    - whether people with mental illness should live as part of a normal community
2   Analyse and discuss your findings. What do these show about public attitudes to mental illness?
3   In about two sides of A4 paper, answer the following essay question:
    Examine the view that mental illness is primarily a social construction.

Conclusion

This chapter has shown that health, illness, disease and disability, and inequalities in health, are very much products of society rather than of simply biological factors. Social and economic life has major influences on the patterns of illness and death. So long as inequalities of wealth, income, education, occupation and social privilege continue, so will inequalities in health.

Chapter summary

After studying this chapter, you should be able to:

- explain what is meant by 'health', 'illness', 'disease' and 'disability'
- identify and explain the difference between the medical and social models of health, and criticize both
- suggest the reasons why some people may seek medical or psychiatric help while others may not
- identify some problems with health statistics
- explain what is meant by the 'sick role', and identify its rights and obligations
- identify and criticize the role of doctors in social control
- outline Marxist and feminist contributions to the study of health and health care
- identify and explain a range of social factors which influence health and disease
- explain social class, gender and ethnic inequalities in health, including inequalities of access to health care
- identify some policies to tackle health inequalities
- explain different sociological approaches to the study of mental illness, including the view that it might be seen as a social construction

Key terms

- disability
- disease
- gate-keeping
- health
- iatrogenesis
- illness
- impairment
- inverse care law
- life expectancy
- mortification
- primary deviance
- secondary deviance
- sick role
- social construction

Coursework suggestions

1. Carry out a survey among men and women to find out when they were last ill enough to take time off work, school or college, when they last visited the doctor, and how many times a year they visit the doctor. See if there are any differences between men and women. You could also do the same type of survey to identify any differences between social classes or ethnic groups.

2. Using secondary sources, try to find out if there are differences in the health of people in various areas of your city or county, or in the

country as a whole, for example between richer and poorer areas. Draw on the material in this chapter to try to explain your findings.

3 Investigate how social class, gender, lifestyle, people's occupations, poverty, ethnicity, or other material and cultural factors affect health.

4 Investigate a sample of people's attitudes to mental illness, and discuss any stereotypes you might identify.

A number of the activities in this chapter could also be developed for coursework.

Exam Questions

HEALTH

Time allowed: 1 hour 15 minutes   **Total for this Question:** *60 marks*

Item A

Not all members of society are equally well served by the health care system. There are ethnic, social class, regional, gender and age differences in access to and usage of health care. Such differences and inequalities are found across a wide range of different types of health care. For example, one study found that among males, 22 per cent of both the 0–4 and the 75+ age groups had consulted a GP within the last 14 days, as against only 9 per cent of males aged 16–44. Similarly, rates of treatment for mental illness,   5 and the types of treatment received, show significant differences between different social groups. For example, women are more likely than men to be prescribed psychotropic (mind-altering) drugs, and black and older women are more likely to be offered only physical treatments rather than psychotherapy.

Unfortunately, many of those groups with the worst health chances are precisely the groups who gain least from the health care system. For example, members of ethnic minority groups may have health care   10 needs that are different from, or greater than, the rest of the population, yet they are often less well served by the NHS.

Item B

Cultural and behavioural explanations of class inequalities in health and illness argue that different social classes behave differently and that these behavioural differences lead to differences in health. For example, only 4 per cent of women of the professional class smoke during pregnancy, as against 26 per cent of women of the unskilled manual class. This behavioural difference between the classes may help to account for differences in the health of babies born to women of different classes. For example, in   5 general, the lower the social class of the mother, the greater the risk of premature birth and low birth weight and the higher the infant mortality rate, including the rate of 'cot deaths' (sudden infant death syndrome). Cultural explanations of health inequalities go further, arguing that these behavioural differences result from cultural differences between the classes.   9

(a) Explain what is meant by 'the infant mortality rate' (**Item B,** line 7).   *(2 marks)*
(b) Suggest **two** reasons for differences in consultation rates between different age groups
  (**Item A,** lines 4–5).   *(4 marks)*
(c) Suggest **three** reasons why members of ethnic minority groups may have different health
  care needs from those of the rest of the population (**Item A,** lines 10–12).   *(6 marks)*
(d) Identify and briefly explain **two** reasons why rates of treatment for mental illness, and/or the
  types of treatment received, 'show significant differences between different social groups'
  (**Item A,** lines 5–6).   *(8 marks)*
(e) Examine the role of the medical profession in society.   *(20 marks)*
(f) Using material from **Item B** and elsewhere, assess cultural and behavioural explanations
  of social class differences in health and illness.   *(20 marks)*

(AQA AS Unit 1 May 2003)

HEALTH

Time allowed: 1 hour 15 minutes   **Total for this Question:** *60 marks*

Item A

Working-class patients make more use of GP services than middle-class patients, in that they see their GPs more frequently. However, when we take account of their higher levels of ill-health, they make less use of GP services (and health services generally) in relation to their needs than middle-class patients. And once they are at the surgery, they spend less time in consultations with their GP on average than middle-class patients do.   5

A further striking class difference in health care is the uptake of different kinds of services. Middle-class people make greater use of preventative services (such as routine medical check-ups) than working-class people. Findings such as these have led some sociologists to argue that an inverse care law exists in relation to social class.

Item B

Labelling theory sees people's behaviour and identity as shaped by the labels that others attach to them. In many cases, labelling creates a self-fulfilling prophecy in which the individual comes to live out the label that they have been given. As applied to mental illness, labelling theory argues that those who are defined as mentally ill and treated as such by others may come to accept the label.

This is particularly likely when those attaching the label, such as psychiatrists and hospital staff, have   5 the power to make it stick. For example, Goffman argues that admission to mental hospital is accompanied by a series of 'degradation rituals' that strip patients of their original identity and seek to impose a new one, that of 'mental patient'. However, although many patients do accept this identity and become 'institutionalised', with no desire ever to leave hospital, others 'play it cool' or even rebel against the label.   10

(a) Explain what is meant by the 'inverse care law' (**Item A,** line 8).   *(2 marks)*
(b) Suggest **two** examples of 'preventative services' **apart from** routine medical check-ups
(**Item A,** line 7).   *(4 marks)*
(c) Suggest **three** reasons why working-class people may have 'higher levels of ill-health' than
middle-class people (**Item A,** line 2).   *(6 marks)*
(d) Identify and briefly explain **two** reasons for class differences in the amount of time that
patients spend in consultations with GPs.   *(8 marks)*
(e) Examine reasons for gender differences in health chances and health care.   *(20 marks)*
(f) Using material from **Item B** and elsewhere, assess the view that mental illness is the result
of labelling by the medical profession.   *(20 marks)*

(AQA AS Unit 1 May 2004)

The Mass Media

The power of the media: key questions

The term 'mass media' refers to forms of communication which are directed at large mass audiences without any personal contact. The main media of mass communication include terrestrial (earth-based), cable and satellite television, radio, newspapers and magazines, books, cinema, videos/DVDs, advertising, CDs, video games and the internet.

In Britain, over 85 per cent of the population watch television seven days a week, with those over 16 spending nearly half of all free time watching it, and around 12.5 million newspapers are sold every day. Digital broadcasting is leading to the creation of literally hundreds of cable and satellite television channels. The media have become a gigantic international business, with instant news from every part of the globe. International marketing of TV programmes and films to international audiences is backed by huge investments. The internet has millions more people going online every year, providing instant access to colossal amounts of information and entertainment from the entire globe. The speed of technological change is now so great that the world is rapidly becoming a 'global village', with many people exposed to the same information and messages through mass media which cut across all national frontiers. This is part of what is known as globalization, which refers to the way societies across the globe have become increasingly interdependent, and are exposed to the same cultural products across the world. This is considered later in the discussion of mass culture.

Globalization refers to the growing interdependence of societies across the world, with the spread of the same culture, consumer goods and economic interests across the globe.

The media have therefore become important sources of information, entertainment and leisure activity for large numbers of people, and they have also become key agencies of secondary socialization and informal education, often with an important formative influence on the individual's sense of identity and consumer spending choices. Most of our taken-for-granted knowledge and our opinions and attitudes are based, not on personal experience, but on evidence and knowledge provided by newspapers and television. Indeed, if the media didn't report an event, the only people likely to know about it would be those who were actually involved. For most of us, the mass media are our only source of evidence, and they colour, shape and even construct our view of the world.

If most of our opinions are based on knowledge obtained second-hand through the mass media, then this raises important issues about the power of the media to mould and shape our lives and identities. Most people think and act in particular ways because of the opinions they hold and the knowledge they have. However, do the mass media inform us about everything, or do they 'filter' information, obscuring the truth and giving false, distorted or exaggerated impressions of what is happening in the world? Do they favour some points of view over others, favouring the more affluent over the poor, for example? Do they misrepresent or stereotype some social groups, like women, minority ethnic groups or the disabled? The main mass media are privately owned and controlled, and run to make a profit. What effect does this pattern of ownership have on the content of the media? Does it create bias in them? Do the mass media actually have any influence on people? These are the sorts of questions which have interested sociologists and which will be explored in this chapter.

Bias means that a subject is presented in a one-sided way, favouring one point of view over others, or ignoring, distorting or misrepresenting some issues, points of view or groups compared to others.

Activity

1 List all the ways you think the mass media influence you in your life, such as your knowledge about current affairs, opinions, tastes in music and fashion, and your views of different social groups, such as women and men, minority ethnic groups, the disabled, the elderly, etc.
2 Do you think the media have a large effect on your beliefs and values, your sense of identity and your consumer choices? What other influences on your beliefs and values might also be important?

Formal controls on the media

Although the mass media in Britain are formally free to report whatever they like, and the government has no power in normal times to stop the spreading of any opinions by using censorship, there are some formal limits to this freedom.

The law

The law restricts the media's freedom to report anything they choose in any way they like. The principal legal limits to the media's freedom are shown in the box overleaf.

Ofcom

In 2003, Ofcom (the Office of Communications) was established as a powerful new regulator of the mass media, with responsibilities across television, radio, telecommunications and wireless communication services. This has responsibility for:

● furthering the interests of consumers
● securing the best use of the radio spectrum

- ensuring that a wide range of television, radio, electronic media and communications networks are available in the UK, with high quality services having a broad appeal
- protecting the public from any offensive or potentially harmful effects of broadcast media, and to safeguard people from being unfairly treated in television and radio programmes

---

Legal limits to the media's freedom

- The *laws of libel* forbid the publication of an untrue statement about a person which might bring him or her into contempt, ridicule, dislike or hostility in society.
- The *Official Secrets Acts* make it a criminal offence to report without authorization any official government activity which the government defines as an 'official secret'.
- *Defence Advisory or 'DA' notices* are issued by the government as requests to journalists not to report certain news items if the government believes it to be 'against the national interest'. These usually concern military secrets and other information which might be useful to an 'enemy'.
- The *Race Relations Acts* forbid the expression of opinions which will encourage hatred or discrimination against people because of their ethnic group.
- The *Obscene Publications Act* forbids the printing of anything that the High Court considers to be obscene and indecent, and likely to 'deprave and corrupt' the public.
- *Contempt of Court* provision forbids the reporting and expression of opinions about cases which are in the process of being dealt with in a court of law.

Activity

Go to www.ofcom.org.uk and identify and briefly describe four issues that Ofcom is currently dealing with.

The BBC

The BBC is a largely state-funded body, which operates under a charter and is controlled by a board of governors whose members are appointed by the Queen on the advice of government ministers. It is partly regulated by Ofcom, and partly by the board of governors, which is meant to represent the public interest, particularly the interests of viewers and radio listeners. The BBC is financed by the state through the television licence fee, plus income from a series of private spin-off companies, which top up the licence fee income with substantial profits. The state can therefore have some control over the BBC by refusing to raise the licence fee. Although the BBC is not a private business run solely to make a profit like the independent commercial broadcasting services (independent TV and radio), and is not dependent on advertising for its income, it still has to compete with commercial broadcasting by attracting audiences large enough to justify the licence fee.

Independent broadcasting

Independent broadcasting includes all the non-BBC television and radio stations. These are regulated by Ofcom, which licenses the companies which can operate in the private sector, and is responsible for the amount, content, quality and standard of advertising and programmes on independent television and radio, and for dealing with any complaints.

The Press Complaints Commission

The Press Complaints Commission is a voluntary body appointed by the newspaper industry itself to maintain certain standards of newspaper journalism. It deals with public complaints against newspapers, but it has no real power to enforce effective sanctions as a result of these complaints.

Ownership of the mass media

The mass media are very big business. The ownership of the main mass media in modern Britain is concentrated in the hands of a few large companies, which are interested in making profits. This concentration of ownership is shown in table 4.1 overleaf. Of the total circulation of national daily and Sunday newspapers, around 86 per cent is controlled by just four companies, and over half by just two companies (News International and Trinity Mirror). One individual, Rupert Murdoch, is the major force behind News International, which owns the *Sun* and *The Times*, newspapers which make up about 33 per cent of all national daily newspaper sales in the United Kingdom. Rupert Murdoch alone accounted for about 33 per cent of the total daily and Sunday newspaper sales in 2005. As table 4.1 shows, this concentration of ownership extends also to other areas of the media, such as TV and book and magazine publishing. The details of who owns what are continually changing, as concentration of ownership is an on-going process with take-overs

Table 4.1. Who owns what: national newspaper group ownership and some of their interests in publishing and television: United Kingdom, 2005

Company	Share of UK national daily newspaper circulation (%) (June 2005)	National newspapers	Also owns
News International	33	*Sun, The Times, News of the World, Sunday Times*	40% of BSkyB; HarperCollins book publishers
Trinity Mirror	18	*Daily Mirror, Sunday Mirror, Daily Record, People, Sunday Mail*	Over 250 regional newspapers
Daily Mail & General Trust	19	*Daily Mail, Mail on Sunday*	Second-largest regional newspaper owners, with over 100 papers, including London's *Evening Standard*; 90% of Teletext; 20% of ITN; Performance TV
Northern & Shell	14	*Daily Express, Sunday Express, Daily Star, Daily Star Sunday*	*OK!* magazine; various soft porn TV channels
Telegraph Group (part of Press Holdings Limited)	7	*Daily Telegraph, Sunday Telegraph, The Scotsman*	*Spectator*
Pearson	3	*Financial Times*	Longman and Penguin book publishers
Guardian Media Group	3	*Guardian, Observer*	Over 40 local newspapers
Seven companies	97		

Source: Data from Audit Bureau of Circulation; corporate websites.

and mergers occurring, providing a stronger financial base for competition in the international market. The same few companies control a wide range of different media, and therefore a large proportion of what we see and hear in the media. In 2005 Rupert Murdoch, for example, also owned 40 per cent of BskyB, and all of HarperCollins, the world's largest English-language book publisher.

The concentration of media ownership has four distinct features:

- There is concentration of ownership within a single medium; for example, one company owning several newspapers.

Rupert Murdoch of News Corporation is now the world's most powerful media owner, with substantial interests in TV, satellite broadcasting, film, and newspaper, magazine and book publishing across the world. He owns more than 175 titles on three continents, publishes 40 million papers a week and dominates the newspaper markets in Britain, Australia and New Zealand
Photo: News International

- These owners also have interests in a range of media, such as news-papers, magazines, book publishing, television, the film industry and music.
- This ownership is international – the owners have media interests in many different countries of the world.
- Media companies are often part of huge conglomerates – companies that have a range of interests in a wide variety of products besides the media. Virgin, for example, has an airline, a train company, soft drinks, financial products and mobile phones, on top of its wide-spread media interests.

This concentration of ownership gives a lot of power to a small number of companies and individuals who control the media industry. This has given rise to three main and related concerns:

- Are the media simply spreading a limited number of dominant ideas (the dominant ideology) through society, so protecting the interests of the dominant class in society?
- Do the owners of the media control the content of the media?
- What effects do the media have on the audiences they aim at?

Activity

1 Suggest reasons why the concentration of ownership of the mass media might be of some concern in a democracy.
2 Do you think there should be restrictions on the number of media that any one person should be allowed to own? Give reasons for your answer.

The mass media and ideology

The concept of a **dominant ideology** is generally linked with Marxism, which sees the dominant ideology as that of the dominant class in society, being spread through the rest of the population to justify the power of the dominant class. The dominant ideology is mainly about persuading people to accept the way things are presently organized, because persuading them and trying to obtain their consent is a far more effective means of controlling the population than force.

Marxists argue that the media play an important role in spreading this dominant ideology and creating a general consensus or agreement about what constitutes 'reasonable' and 'unreasonable' ways of thinking and behaving. This is because the media have the means to provide incomplete or distorted views of the world, and to ignore, attack, dismiss or present as 'unreasonable' any groups, events or ideas which challenge or threaten the dominant ideology. The media thereby create a climate of conformity among the mass of the population which justifies the rule of the rich and powerful. The following section examines competing views on whether and to what extent the mass media are simply the tools of the dominant class.

> **Ideology** refers to a set of ideas, values and beliefs that represent the outlook, and justify the interests, of a social group. The **dominant ideology** is one which justifies the social advantages of wealthy, powerful and influential groups in society, and justifies the disadvantages of those who lack wealth, power and influence.

Do the owners of the media control their content?

Within sociology, there are three main approaches to the issue of ownership and control of the media. These are known as the manipulative or instrumentalist approach, the dominant ideology or hegemonic approach, and the pluralist approach.

The manipulative or instrumentalist approach

This is a traditional Marxist approach. This suggests that the concentration of ownership of the mass media in the hands of a few media corporations enables the owners to control media output, and serve ruling class interests. The media are seen as an instrument through which the ruling class is able to manipulate media content and media audiences in its own interests.

According to this approach:

- The owners of the media, like newspaper owners, have direct control of the content of the media, and they can and do interfere in media content.
- The owners use the media to spread ideas (the dominant ideology) which justify the power of the dominant class.
- Media managers have little choice other than to run the media within the boundaries set down by the owners.
- Journalists depend for their jobs on supporting the interests of the owners. The reports of journalists are therefore biased (one-sided). Journalists censor their own reports to avoid criticism of the interests of the dominant class. Ideas or groups which threaten the status quo (the existing arrangements in society) are attacked, ridiculed or ignored.
- The audience is assumed to be passive – a mass of unthinking and uncritical 'robots'. This audience is exposed to only a limited range of opinions, and is manipulated through biased reports. It is 'fed' on a dumbed-down mass diet of undemanding, trivial and uncritical content. This stops people focusing on serious issues, or encourages them to interpret serious issues in ways favourable to the dominant class.

Strengths of the manipulative or instrumentalist approach

- There is evidence that, occasionally, media owners do interfere in the content of newspapers, and appoint managers and editors who conform to their views (and sack those who don't). For example, in February 2003, Rupert Murdoch was arguing strongly in interviews for a war with Iraq. It is unlikely to be coincidence that all his 175 newspapers around the world backed him.
- Ownership of the media industry is highly concentrated, as are the news agencies which provide information.
- Journalists do ultimately depend on the owners for their careers, and can't afford to upset their bosses.

Weaknesses of the manipulative or instrumentalist approach

- Pluralists (see below) would argue there is a wide range of opinion in the media, and the media's owners and managers are primarily concerned with making profits. This means attracting large audiences to gain advertisers and the only means of doing this is to provide what the audiences – not the owners – want.

- The state regulates media ownership so no one person or company has too much influence. By law, TV and radio have to report news impartially, and can't therefore simply churn out biased, one-sided reports.
- Audiences are not as gullible and easily manipulated as the manipulative approach suggests – people can accept, reject or interpret media messages, depending on their existing ideas and experiences.

The dominant ideology or hegemonic approach

This is a more recent, neo- (new) Marxist approach. This approach also suggests the mass media spread a dominant ideology justifying or legitimizing the power of the ruling class. It differs from the manipulative approach by suggesting this is not carried out by the direct control of owners and direct manipulation of journalists, media content and the audience. It recognizes the power of owners, but suggests that they rarely interfere in media content, though they do have an influence upon it. Rather, this approach emphasizes the idea of **hegemony**. This is the process whereby the dominant ideology of the ruling class is shared by media managers and journalists, and other social classes are persuaded to accept the values and beliefs in that ideology as reasonable, 'normal' and 'common sense'.

> **Hegemony** means the dominance in society of the ruling class's set of ideas over others, and consent by the rest of society to acceptance of them.

According to this approach:

- The owners of the media, like newspaper owners, rarely have direct control of the content of the media. Day-to-day control and media content are left in the hands of managers and journalists.
- Media managers and journalists, while inevitably influenced by the desire not to upset the owners and to protect their careers, also need to attract audiences and advertisers. Media content critical of the dominant ideology sometimes helps to attract audiences, and some occasional criticism maintains a pretence of objective, unbiased reporting most of the time.
- Nevertheless, journalists do generally support the dominant ideology, not because the owners order them to, but because they share a similar view of the world to that of the dominant class. Most journalists tend to be white, middle-class and male, and are socialized into a set of professional values which share a set of taken-for-granted assumptions in keeping with the dominant ideology. This makes groups, events or ideas threatening the status quo seem unreasonable, extremist, ridiculous, funny or trivial, to be attacked or not taken

seriously. The dominant ideology generates a consensus (a wide agreement) about what is worthy, good and right for all.

- These common-sense assumptions shared by journalists mean the audience is exposed to only a limited range of opinions, mostly within the framework of the dominant ideology. Audiences are therefore, over time, unconsciously persuaded to see the dominant ideology as the only reasonable and sensible view of the world. The hegemony of the ruling ideas is therefore maintained.

Strengths of the dominant ideology or hegemonic approach

- This approach recognizes that owners are often not involved in the day-to-day running of their media businesses.
- It recognizes that media managers, editors and journalists have some professional independence, and are not simply manipulated by media owners.
- It recognizes that there can be a range of media content to attract audiences, some of it critical of the dominant ideology. Nevertheless, journalists are socialized into a culture where the dominant ideology suggests the most 'reasonable' explanation of events and the way they are reported.

Weaknesses of the dominant ideology or hegemonic approach

- The approach underrates the power and influence of the owners. Owners do appoint and dismiss managers and editors who step too far out of line, and journalists' careers are dependent on gaining approval of their stories from editors.
- Agenda-setting and gate-keeping (discussed later in this chapter) mean some items are deliberately excluded from reporting in the media, and audiences are encouraged to think about some events rather than others. Audiences have little real choice of media content, as newspapers and TV programmes are produced within a framework of the dominant ideology. This suggests a direct manipulation of audiences.
- Journalists' news values (discussed later) mean that sometimes journalists do not simply trot out the dominant ideology, but can develop critical, anti-establishment views which strike a chord with their audiences. An example might be campaigns against government corruption or wrongdoing by large companies.

The pluralist approach

Both the manipulative and hegemonic approaches above assume those who own, control and work in the media shape their content, spreading

Agenda-setting refers to the media's influence over the issues that people think about because the agenda, or list of subjects, for public discussion is laid down by the mass media.
Gate-keeping is the power of some people, groups or organizations to limit access to something valuable or useful. For example, the mass media have the power to refuse to cover some issues and therefore not allow the public access to some information.
News values are the values and assumptions held by editors and journalists which guide them in choosing what is 'newsworthy' – what to report and what to leave out, and how what they choose to report should be presented.

the dominant ideology among media audiences and protecting the interests of powerful groups in society. The pluralist approach is very different from these. Pluralists suggest that there is no dominant ruling class, but many competing groups with different interests. All these different interests are represented in the media. The owners do not directly control the content of the media, but rather what appears in the media is driven by the wishes of consumers – audiences will simply not watch TV programmes or buy newspapers which do not reflect their views.

According to the pluralist approach:

- Owners do not have direct control over the content of the media.
- There is no single dominant class, but a wide range of competing groups in society with different interests. These differing interests are reflected in a wide range of media, covering all points of view.
- Media content is driven, not by a dominant ideology or the interests of owners, but by circulation and audience figures and the search for profits. This means the media will serve up whatever is necessary to satisfy audience tastes and wishes.
- The mass media are generally free of any government or direct owner control and can present whatever point of view they want, and audiences are free to choose in a 'pick 'n' mix' approach to whatever interpretation suits them.
- The media are controlled by media managers who allow journalists a great deal of freedom. They have to offer a wide selection of views to satisfy and maintain their audiences. Audiences are not manipulated by the media, but rather have some control over the media by the choices they make about the programmes they watch or the newspapers they buy. Audiences can select what they want from the wide range of media and media content available.
- Journalists write stories using 'news values' (discussed later in this chapter) reflecting the wishes and interests most relevant to their audiences. There is no dominant ideology or ruling class bias being pumped out and manipulating audiences, but journalists provide what the audiences want. Any bias simply reflects what the audiences want, and they have the freedom to accept, reject or ignore media content. The mass media don't manipulate or brainwash audiences, and indeed have little effect on them, as they already have views of their own.

Strengths of the pluralist approach

- There is a wide range of newspapers, magazines, television channels and other media reflecting a huge range of interests and ideas, including those which challenge the dominant ideology.

- Journalists are not simply the pawns of their employers, but have some professional and editorial honesty and independence, and are often critical of the dominant ideology.
- The fight for audiences in competition with other companies means the mass media have to cater for audience tastes – newspapers and TV channels have to be responsive to their audiences, otherwise they'll go out of business.

Weaknesses of the pluralist approach

- While managers, journalists and television producers have some independence, they work within constraints placed on them by the owners. Editors are controlled and appointed by owners. The main sources of information for journalists tend to be from those groups who are the most powerful and influential members of society, and their views are given greater weight than less powerful groups. News is collected by a few news companies and agencies, often paid for by the media owners themselves.
- Media owners strongly influence who is appointed at senior levels of the media, and top managers, editors and owners often share a similar outlook on the world.
- Not all groups in society have equal influence on editors and journalists to get their views across, and only very rich groups will have the resources required to launch major media companies to get their views across independently. It is the rich, powerful and influential who are more likely to be interviewed on TV, to appear on chat shows, to be quoted in newspapers, and so on.
- The owners have on numerous occasions sacked uncooperative editors, and both governments and rich individuals have brought political or legal pressure to bear to stop programmes, newspaper stories and books which threaten their interests.
- The pressure to attract audiences doesn't increase media choice but limits it – the media decline in quality, and news and information get squeezed out or sensationalized, as the media aim for large mass markets with unthreatening, unchallenging and bland content aimed at an undemanding mass audience.
- Hegemonic theorists (see above) would argue that people have been socialized by the media themselves into the belief that they are being provided with what they want. The media themselves may have created their tastes, so that what audiences want is really what the media owners want.

Table 4.2 overleaf summarizes approaches to ownership of the media and media content.

Table 4.2. Ownership of the media and media content: a summary

	Manipulative or instrumentalist approach	*Dominant ideology or hegemonic approach*	*Pluralist approach*
Role of owners	Direct control and manipulation	Influence and persuasion	No direct control, and wide range of competing interests
Media content	Dominant ideology	Dominant ideology, but sometimes critical of it to attract audiences	Need for circulation and audience figures, and profits, means content is what audiences – not owners – want
Role of media managers and journalists	Told what to do by owners, or within framework set by them	Some independence from owners, but share dominant ideology, and so present most stories in that framework, though need to attract audiences and advertisers	Have high level of independence, so long as they attract audiences and therefore profits
View of audience	Passive – audiences manipulated by owners	Passive – audiences persuaded to accept dominant ideology	Active – audiences make choices between media and can accept, reject, reinterpret or ignore media content

Activity

Go through each of the following statements, identifying them as corresponding most closely to the manipulative or instrumentalist approach, or the dominant ideology or hegemonic approach, or the pluralist approach.

1 'I'm in the business of making money, and I'll use the media I own to provide whatever the audience wants.'
2 Generally the media supports the interests of the dominant groups in society, but a bit of criticism every now and then encourages people to believe the media are telling us the truth about society.
3 The concentration of media ownership means that the views expressed in the media reflect little more than the interests of the owners.
4 There is such a wide variety of media to choose from that everyone's views are represented somewhere.
5 The media is controlled and run mainly by white, middle-class males, so they mainly spread the existing dominant ideas in society.
6 Media audiences are exposed to only a limited range of opinions, and so over time people are persuaded to accept only a limited view of the world, mainly that of the most powerful groups in society.

7 The media are owned by a few rich individuals, so the public are fed on a media diet of political propaganda protecting the owners' interests.

8 Journalists are just the tools of the owners, and they can't criticize the interests of the powerful without losing their jobs.

9 If readers aren't attracted, advertisers won't advertise and media companies will go out of business. Survival in the competitive world of newspaper publishing means readers are the ones who decide in the end what they want to see in the media.

10 The media cons people in subtle ways over a period of time that the only reasonable view of the world is that of the most powerful groups in society.

Activity

Answer the following essay question in about one and a half to two sides of A4:
Critically assess the pluralist view of the mass media.

The effects of the mass media: does control of the media matter anyway?

The debate above, particularly the manipulative and dominant ideology approaches, suggests that the content of the media does have some effect on the audience. However, this cannot be taken for granted. People are conscious, thinking human beings, not mindless robots. They might not swallow everything they come across in the media, and they might respond in a variety of ways to what they read or watch on TV. For example, they might dismiss, reject, ignore, criticize, forget or give a different meaning to a media message, and this is likely to be influenced by factors such as their own social experiences, their ethnic group, social class, gender and so on. For example, a black person is likely to reject a racist message in a TV broadcast or newspaper report.

We also need to be aware that the media are only one influence on the way people might think and behave, and there is a wide range of other agencies involved in people's socialization. Families, friends, schools, workplaces and workmates, churches, social class, ethnicity, gender, disability, age and so on may all influence individual and group behaviour and attitudes. It would be somewhat foolhardy to suggest all behaviour can be explained by exposure to the media, so we must constantly situate media influences alongside these other factors.

This section examines the different approaches sociologists have adopted to the question of whether media content does actually have an influence or effect on audiences. There are competing views on this, mainly centred on the issue of whether audiences are passive dopes mindlessly consuming media content, or active interpreters of that content, giving it different meanings and interpretations.

The hypodermic syringe model

This is a very simple model, and most commentators would now regard it as an old-fashioned and inadequate view of the relationship between media content and the audience – readers, listeners and viewers. This model suggests that the media act like a hypodermic syringe, injecting messages and content into the 'veins' of media audiences. Audiences are seen as unthinking, passive robots, who are unable to resist the 'drug' injected by the media. In this view, media messages fill audiences with the dominant ideology, sexist and racist images, scenes of violence or other content, and the audience then immediately acts on these messages. It is like seeing violence on television, and then going out and attacking someone. It is a simple view of the media as causing immediate changes in people's behaviour.

Strengths of the hypodermic syringe model

There are few strengths of the hypodermic syringe model, though there is some evidence that, on rare occasions, people do react quite directly to

The hypodermic syringe model suggests that the media inject messages into the 'veins' of media audiences

what they see in the media. For example, 'copycat' crimes or urban riots. Also, advertisers spend millions of pounds on advertising their products, and we might reasonably assume that these have some effect on consumers and the sale of the goods advertised.

Weaknesses of the hypodermic syringe model

- The model assumes the entire audience is passive and will react in the same way to media content. However, people may well have a range of responses to media content, depending on their own social situation and the experiences they have had. For example, violence in the media could have a variety of effects – people might be appalled and become determined to stamp it out; others might use it to work out their violent fantasies so it doesn't happen in real life; others might simply ignore it.
- It assumes audiences are passive, gullible and easily manipulated – but people are active thinking human beings, who have their own ideas, and who interpret what they see and can give different meanings to it.
- It assumes the media have enormous power and influence, overriding all other agencies of socialization and people's own experiences.
- There is little evidence that media content has the immediate effects on audiences the model suggests.

The two-step flow model

The weaknesses of the hypodermic syringe model are tackled by what is known as the two-step flow model, developed by Katz and Lazarsfeld (1955). This model recognizes that audiences do not simply passively react to media content, and will respond in a variety of ways to it. These responses will be influenced by the beliefs and values they already hold, their own experiences, and the opinions of those in their own family, at work, school or college, or in peer groups.

This model of media influence suggests that people are influenced by 'opinion leaders'. These are those respected members of any social group who get information and form views from the media, who lead opinion and discussion in their social groups, and whom others listen to and take notice of. It might, for example, be an assertive and popular student whose views others tend to take notice of. The two-step flow model suggests that it is these opinion leaders who are influenced by the media (the first step) and they then pass on these opinions, selectively and with their own interpretations, to others in their social groups (the second step). Members of these groups may then, in turn, pass on their opinions to others, in a kind of chain reaction leading from one person or group to another.

Strengths of the two-step flow model

- This model recognizes that the effects of the mass media are not as direct, powerful and influential as the hypodermic syringe model suggests. It suggests that opinion leaders are the ones most subject to media influence, not the whole audience.
- It recognizes that audiences are not completely passive and uncritically accepting of direct media messages, but that 'opinion leaders' select, interpret and filter media messages before they reach mass audiences, and it is this process that influences any effects the media might have.
- It recognizes that media audiences are not a mass of isolated individuals, but that the social groups to which people belong influence the opinions they hold and how they respond to and interpret media content.
- It recognizes that people form their own judgements on media content, although this is influenced by opinion leaders, and they can therefore give meanings other than those intended by the media. For example, a group of Labour Party supporters watching a Conservative Party election broadcast might critically discuss and mock the Conservative views expressed, and reconfirm their own support for Labour – presumably not the intention of those trying to persuade people to vote Conservative.

Weaknesses of the two-step flow model

- There are probably more than two steps in the media's influence. Media content could be selected and interpreted by many different individuals in different groups. For example, parents (as opinion leaders) may have one view, an 'opinion leading' workmate another view, and a sociology teacher still another. This might mean ideas and interpretations of media content get bounced around in discussions in a variety of groups, creating many steps in the flow of media influence.
- It still rests on the basic assumption that the influence of the media flows from the media to the audience, and assumes that media audiences are more or less victims of media content, even if the mass audience is insulated by opinion leaders.
- It suggests that people are very vulnerable to influence and manipulation by opinion leaders. It does not recognize that people may have views, opinions and experiences of their own on which to base their views of media content.
- It suggests the audience is divided into 'active' viewers/readers (the 'opinion leaders') and 'passive' viewers/readers who are influenced

by the opinion leaders. It doesn't explain why opinion leaders are directly influenced by media content when others in the audience are not.

The cultural effects model

Cultural effects theory recognizes that the media are owned and heavily influenced by the dominant and most powerful groups in society, and their interests strongly influence the content of the media. This content is mainly in keeping with the dominant ideology.

Like the hypodermic syringe and two-step flow models, the cultural effects model suggests that the media do have an effect on the audience. However, the media do not have the direct effects of the 'hypodermic' model, or the effects via opinion leaders of the two-step flow model. Rather, the cultural effects model suggests that the media gradually influence the audience over a period of time – a sort of slow, steady, subtle, ever present process of brainwashing which gradually shapes people's taken-for-granted common-sense ideas and assumptions, and their everyday view of the world. For example, if we see minority ethnic groups nearly always portrayed in the context of trouble and crime, or women portrayed only as housewives, mothers, lovers and sex objects, over time this will come to form the stereotypes we hold of these groups, to the exclusion of other aspects of their lives.

However, cultural effects theory suggests the extent of these media effects will be affected by the social characteristics and experiences of audience members. For example, women might well resist gender stereo-typing in the media, and black people (and many white people) may well reject racist stereotypes.

While the cultural effects model suggests the media will generally spread the dominant ideology in society, it implies audiences may respond in different ways depending on their own social situation and their own experiences and beliefs. They might support and agree with the content and 'slant' of TV and newspaper reporting, but they might also be critical of or even reject that content, in line with their own social experiences. For example, white people living in multicultural communities might well have different views of ethnic minorities from those who have no such experience of minority ethnic group life. This could mean that each group might respond differently to images of ethnic minorities presented in the media. The group with their own experiences of ethnic minorities might reject or modify media content because of their own first-hand experiences, while those without such experience may well take for granted the media content, as they have no experiences of their own to judge media content by.

Selective exposure, selective perception and selective retention

Not everyone views the same media content in the same way

Theories of the effects of the media on audiences often assume that people are like blank pieces of paper, with no experiences of their own to interpret what they hear, see or read. People may only watch or read media that fit in with their existing views and interests (*selective exposure*), they will react differently to the same message depending on whether it fits in with their own views and interests (*selective perception*), or they will 'forget' material that is not in line with their views and interests (*selective retention*). An example of this might be the way people respond to party political election broadcasts, depending on which political party they personally support, as suggested in the cartoon above. During the Iraq war of 2003, the *Daily Mirror* passionately opposed the war, yet half its readers were in favour. The *Daily Mail* was a strong supporter of the war – but one-quarter of its readers opposed it. People do seem to have their own views beyond what the media tell them.

Strengths of the cultural effects model

- This model recognizes the power of the dominant class to influence the content of the media. The media transmit a dominant ideology as journalists generally share the worldview and assumptions of that dominant ideology.
- It recognizes that media audiences are not passive absorbers of media messages, but that they can and do respond differently to media content. They actively interpret media content in the light of their own social circumstances and experiences, and their values and beliefs.

- It recognizes that the media, although they generally present a biased, ideological view of the world favouring the dominant class, don't always have the same effect on media audiences.
- It recognizes that the media are likely to be influential as a key shaper of people's view of the world, but these effects are likely to be over a long time period, rather than immediate and short-term. Over this long period, the media gradually persuades most people to accept that media content represents a mainstream, common-sense view of the world, though this in reality reflects the dominant ideology. Long-term media exposure will therefore ultimately influence and shape the way people think and behave.

Weaknesses of the cultural effects model

- The model gives too much emphasis to the active role of media audiences. Those with power in society set the framework for media content, and over the long term socialization by the media limits the ability of audiences to resist media messages.
- It assumes media personnel like journalists work within the framework and assumptions of the dominant ideology. This fails to recognize that journalists have some independence in their work, and can sometimes be very critical of the dominant ideology and the existing arrangements in society.

In general, the hypodermic, two-step flow and cultural effects models see the media, to a greater or lesser extent, as having an influence sooner or later over the way people think and behave. The final model of media effects, the uses and gratifications model, asks not so much what the media do to people as what people do with the media, and recognizes that audiences are not always or simply the unwitting 'victims' of media messages.

The uses and gratifications model

The uses and gratifications model starts with a view that media audiences are thinking, active and creative human beings. In this view, media audiences are active, and *use* the media in various ways for their own various pleasures and interests (*gratifications*). The emphasis changes from the various ways the media influence and manipulate people to an emphasis on the way audiences use the media.

Media audiences are not simply passive robots who are easily manipulated, led by opinion leaders or have their ideas moulded over time by the routine process of constant exposure to the dominant ideology.

Media audiences use the media in a whole variety of ways. For example,

McQuail (1972) and Lull (1990) suggest a variety of uses and gratifications of the media. They may be used for:

- leisure, entertainment and relaxation, as an escape from daily routine
- personal relationships and companionship, through identification with communities like *Coronation Street* or *EastEnders*, or situations and characters in reality TV shows like *Big Brother*, or as a conversation starter in group situations
- personal identity, using the media to explore and confirm their own identities, interests and values, for example keeping up with contemporary trends in cooking, gardening or music, fashion changes and social attitudes
- information, such as keeping up with the news and current affairs
- background 'wallpaper' while doing other things

People will use the media for different uses and gratifications

This variety of uses of the media, providing a range of pleasures, means people make conscious choices, select and interpret what they watch on TV or read in newspapers and magazines, and use them for an array of needs which they themselves decide. These different uses mean the effects of the media are likely to be different in each case, depending on what people are using the media for. We therefore can't assume that the uses and effects even of the same media content will be the same in every case.

Strengths of the uses and gratifications model

- This model recognizes the active role of media audiences.
- It recognizes that audiences make conscious choices about how they

use the media, and media companies therefore have to provide a range of content to satisfy these choices.

● It recognizes that audiences have the power to decide media content: a failure by media companies to satisfy audience pleasures will mean no viewers, listeners or readers, hence no advertisers, and therefore the companies or the particular channel, radio station or newspaper will risk going out of business.

● It recognizes that the uses and gratifications of the media are likely to vary from one individual to the next, and these will be influenced by factors such as their age, gender, social class or ethnicity, and their previous experiences, attitudes and values. For example, a soft porn cable TV channel or a programme about cars is likely to have rather different uses and gratifications for men and women. It therefore becomes very difficult to generalize about the effects of the media, as people will be selective in their exposure to, and perception and retention of, media content.

Weaknesses of the uses and gratifications model

● The model overestimates the power of the audience to influence media content. It also underestimates the power and influence of the media and media companies to shape and influence the choices people make and the 'pleasures' they derive from the media. Media companies set the choices, and the media may create the different pleasures themselves, through devices like advertising.

● It focuses too much on the use of the media by individuals. It doesn't allow for the group aspects of media audiences, unlike the two-step flow and cultural effects models, which recognize that people often relate to the media in social groups, and it is these group settings which will influence their uses and gratifications.

● The focus on individual uses and gratifications ignores the wider social factors affecting the way audiences respond. Common experiences and common values may mean many people will respond in similar ways to media content.

Table 4.3 summarizes approaches to the media's effects on audiences.

Activity

1 Suppose you wanted to study the effects of a TV programme on an audience. Suggest how you might go about researching this.

2 Carry out a short survey finding out what use people make of the mass media in their daily lives (using ideas from the uses and gratifications approach outlined above). You might also ask them about how much and in what ways they think they are influenced by the content of what they see in the media.

TABLE 4.3. The effects of the media on audiences: a summary

	Hypodermic syringe model	*Two-step flow model*	*Cultural effects model*	*Uses and gratifications model*
Effect of media content on audiences	Direct and immediate effect on people's behaviour	Indirect effects, through role of 'opinion leaders' who make interpretations and pass them on to others	Long-term effects through continuous exposure and persuasion into acceptance of the dominant ideology	Effects vary from one individual to the next. Can't generalize about media effects – it depends what people use media for. People will demonstrate *selective exposure, selective perception and selective retention*
View of audience	Passive and easily manipulated	Not completely passive, as influenced only indirectly through 'opinion leaders' and through discussion in social groups	Not completely passive, as people will respond according to their own interpretations, social circumstances and beliefs	Active, and make conscious choices, and select and use media for their own pleasures

---

Activity

1　Suggest three needs that people might satisfy by using the mass media.
2　Suggest three reasons why the media may not affect their audience.
3　Answer the following essay question, in about one and half or two sides of A4 paper:
　Critically examine the 'hypodermic syringe' approach to the effects of the mass media on audiences.

Violence and the media

Violent TV news reports, dramas, films, videos (sometimes including pornography) and computer games are now part of popular culture, and more people are exposed to such violence than ever before. By the time they are 18, estimates suggests American children will have seen around 16,000 real and fictional murders on television and 200,000 acts of violence on television.

Such media violence is often blamed for increasing crime and violence in society. A high profile example of this was the murder in 1993 of 2-year-old James Bulger by two 10-year-old boys. The judge in the case commented: 'I suspect that exposure to violent video films may in part be an explanation.' This view was disputed by the police, who said they could find no evidence that videos viewed by the family could have encouraged the boys to batter a toddler to death.

Nonetheless, such assertions that media violence generates real-life violence are commonplace, and masses of research has been done to investigate whether such a link really exists, particularly in relation to children.

Activity

1 Write an explanation of how each of the four effects models – hypodermic syringe, two-step flow, cultural effects, and uses and gratifications – outlined earlier in the chapter might view the effects of media violence.
2 In the light of the above, suggest reasons why children might be more vulnerable to media violence than adults.

A lot of this research has been carried out in laboratory conditions, and involves exposing people to violent media content to see if they then behave violently. The 'Bobo Doll' experiment is typical of a lot of this experimental research (see box). Although much of this experimental

The Bobo Doll experiments

In one of a range of experiments conducted from the 1960s onwards, Bandura and his colleagues exposed three groups of children to violent scenes involving attacks on a large, self-righting inflatable plastic doll with a mallet. One group was shown the doll being attacked by an adult in real life, another group was shown the same adult attacking the doll in a film, and the third group was shown the same scene involving cartoon characters. A fourth group of children was not exposed to any violent scenes. When the first three groups were later placed in a room with a similar doll, they acted in the same violent ways they had observed earlier. The fourth group of children who had not been exposed to any violent scenes displayed no violent behaviour. The conclusion drawn was that exposure to scenes of violence causes violence among those who see it.

work claims to have established some links between violent TV viewing and violent behaviour, a review by Newburn and Hagell (1995) of over 1,000 studies concluded the link between media violence and violent behaviour was 'not proven'. Evidence suggests it may be true around 10 per cent of the time, but such children may have had tendencies to violence regardless of television viewing. A 2003 report by the Broadcasting Standards Commission found that children are fully aware that television production is a process and that they are not watching reality, with the report concluding: 'They are able to make judgements . . . they are not blank sheets of paper on whom messages can be imprinted.' Despite all the research, there is therefore little reliable and undisputed evidence about whether violence in the media leads to an increase in aggressive behaviour.

Problems of researching media violence

Research into the area of whether violence in the media generates real-life violence is fraught with difficulty:

- How is such violence to be defined in the first place? Boxing and wrestling, fights in TV dramas, parents hitting children, police attacking protesters, shooting, and news film of warfare all depict violent scenes, but are they seen by researchers in the same way?
- Is there a difference between scenes showing real-life violence, fictional violence and cartoon violence? Can people distinguish between them?
- Even if agreement is reached on what violence is, how can the effects be measured?
- Much of the research has been conducted on small samples in artificial laboratory conditions. This raises questions about whether

people will react in the same way in real life as they do in laboratory conditions, and whether the results can be applied to, or generalized to, the whole population.

Giddens (2001) summarizes the problems of much of the research on media violence in the following way:

> The studies . . . differ widely in the methods used, the strength of the association [between violent media and behaviour] supposedly revealed, and the definition of 'aggressive behaviour'. In crime dramas featuring violence (and in many children's cartoons) there are underlying themes of justice and retribution. A far higher proportion of miscreants are brought to justice in crime dramas than happens with police investigations in real life, and in cartoons harmful or threatening characters usually tend to get their 'just deserts'. It does not necessarily follow that high levels of the portrayal of violence create directly imitative patterns among those watching . . . In general, research on the 'effects' of television on audiences has tended to treat viewers – children and adults – as passive and undiscriminating in their reactions to what they see.

Much of the research has therefore been based on a hypodermic syringe model of media effects, and doesn't deal with how people interpret what they see, the context in which they view the violence (such as discussing with others or the uses they are making of the media), or with the wider range of influences on people's behaviour apart from the media.

Activity

1 Suggest a range of ways that people might interpret and respond to seeing violent content in the media – for example, switching the television off, or going out and beating someone up. Try to link some or all of these responses to the various media effects models (hypodermic, uses and gratifications, two-step flow, etc.)
2 The following table shows five claims about the effects of violence in the mass media. Look at each of them, and try to criticize them in as many ways as you can. The first is done for you.

Effects of violent media content	Criticism
'It desensitizes the audience to violence – people become less sensitive to it and they become more tolerant of it in real life. For example, showing sexually violent scenes and violence against women makes people accept it more in real life.'	Violent media content might so horrify and sensitize people to it that they become opposed to it in real life.

Effects of violent media content	Criticism
'It removes people's inhibitions to violence.' 'If violence on television and film is seen as commonplace, then people will feel less inhibited from using violence to resolve problems in real life.' 'Watching violent videos, films and TV programmes makes people violent.' 'People learn to imitate the violence they see in the media.'	

3   On about one and a half sides of A4 paper, write an essay answering the following question:
    Assess the extent to which exposure to the mass media might make people behave in a more violent manner.

What affects the content of the media? Bias in the media

Bias means that a subject is presented in a one-sided way, favouring one point of view over others, or ignoring, distorting or misrepresenting issues.

The mass media obviously cannot report all events and issues happening every day in the world, nor cover every interest in the world. Of all the happenings that occur, how is media content selected? Who decides which of these events or interests is worthy of media coverage? The content of the media, like any other product for sale, is manufactured. Journalists decide which issues to report or ignore, and how to present what they select. What factors affect the production and 'packaging' of this product? Is media content biased or does it present a balanced and truthful view? What decides the content of the mass media?

The owners

Although the manipulative view discussed earlier in this chapter, with the owners controlling media content, is rather oversimplified, sometimes the private owners of the mass media will impose their own views on their editors. However, even when the owners don't directly impose their own views, it is unlikely that those who work for them will produce stories which actively oppose their owners' prejudices and interests, if they want to keep their jobs. The political leanings of the owners and editors are overwhelmingly conservative.

Making a profit

The mass media are predominantly run by large business corporations with the aim of making money, and the source of much of this profit is advertising, particularly in newspapers and commercial television. It is this dependence on advertising which explains why so much concern is expressed about 'ratings' for television programmes, the circulation figures of newspapers, and the social class of their readers. Advertisers will usually advertise only if they know that there is a large audience for their advertisements, or, if the audience is small, that it is well off and likely to buy their products or services.

Advertising and media content

The importance of advertising affects the content of the media in the following ways:

- Audiences or readers must be attracted. If they are not, then circulation figures or TV ratings will fall, advertisers will not advertise, and the particular channel or newspaper may go out of business. The *Sunday Correspondent, Today, News on Sunday* and the *London Daily News* are all newspapers which have collapsed in the last twenty years for this reason. This means that what becomes 'news' is partly a result of commercial pressures to attract audiences by selecting and presenting the more colourful and 'interesting' events in society.

- In order to attract the widest possible audience or readership, it becomes important to appeal to everyone and offend no one (unless offending a few helps to generate a larger audience). This leads to conservatism in the media, which tries to avoid too much criticism of the way society is organized in case it offends the readers or viewers. This often means that minority or unpopular points of view go unrepresented in the mass media, and this helps to maintain the hegemony of the dominant ideas in society.

- It may lead to a distortion of the 'news' by concentrating on sensational stories, conflict, gossip and scandal, which are more likely to attract a mass audience than more serious issues are. Alternatively, for those media which aim at a 'select' readership from the upper and upper middle classes, it is important that the stories chosen should generally be treated in a conservative way, so as not to offend an audience which has little to gain (and everything to lose) by changes in the existing arrangements in society.

Organizational constraints

Newspapers and TV programmes tend to work within quite tight time schedules – this is often a 24-hour, or shorter, cycle, as newspapers and TV news programmes report news on a daily or more frequent basis. This means that short cuts to news gathering may need to be taken, that inadequate evidence is collected to justify any conclusions drawn, and that stories aren't checked as carefully as they should be.

Agenda-setting

Agenda-setting refers to the media's influence in laying down the list of subjects, or agenda, for public discussion.

Obviously, people can only discuss and form opinions about things they have been informed about, and it is the mass media which provide this information in most cases. This gives those who own, control and work in the mass media a great deal of power in society, for what they choose to include or leave out of their newspapers or television programmes will influence the main topics of public discussion and public concern. This may mean that the public never discuss some subjects because they are not informed about them.

Gate-keeping

The media's power to refuse to cover some issues and to let others through is called gate-keeping. The issues which are not aired are frequently those most damaging to the values and interests of the upper class. Sometimes the media do not cover issues either because journalists and editors think they lack interest to readers and viewers, or because they regard them as too offensive, controversial or threatening to existing society. For example, strikes are widely reported (nearly always unfavourably), while industrial injuries and diseases, which lead to a much greater loss of working hours (and life), hardly ever get reported. This means that there is more public concern with stopping strikes than there is with improving health and safety laws. Similarly, crime committed by black people gets widely reported in the media, but little attention is paid to attacks on black people by white racists. A final example of gate-keeping is the way welfare benefit 'fiddles' are widely reported, but not tax evasion, with the result that there are calls for tightening up benefit claim procedures, rather than strengthening those agencies concerned with chasing tax evaders.

Norm-setting

Norm-setting describes the way the mass media emphasize and reinforce conformity to social norms, and seek to isolate those who do not conform by making them the victims of unfavourable media reports.

Norm-setting is achieved in two main ways:

- Encouraging conformist behaviour, such as not going on strike, obeying the law, being brave, helping people and so on. Advertising, for example, often reinforces the gender role stereotypes of men and women.

- Discouraging non-conformist behaviour. The mass media often give extensive and sensational treatment to stories about murder and other crimes of violence, riots, social security 'fiddles', football hooliganism, illegal immigrants, and so on. Such stories, by emphasizing the serious consequences which follow for those who break social norms, are giving 'lessons' in how people are expected *not* to behave. For example, the early media treatment of AIDS nearly always suggested it was a disease only gay men could catch. This was presented as a warning to those who strayed from the paths of monogamy and heterosexuality – both core values within the dominant ideology.

Activity

1 Study the main newspaper headlines or major television or radio news stories for a week. Draw up a list of the key stories, perhaps under the headings of 'popular newspapers' (like the *Sun* and the *Mirror*), 'quality newspapers' (like the *Guardian*, the *Daily Telegraph* and *The Times*), 'ITN news', 'BBC TV news' and 'radio news' (this is easiest to do if a group of people divide up the work). You might also research these on the web, using the following sites:

   www.bbc.co.uk
   www.itn.co.uk
   www.guardian.co.uk
   www.timesonline.co.uk
   www.thesun.co.uk
   www.mirror.co.uk

2 Compare your lists, and see if there is any evidence of agreement on the 'agenda' of news items for that week. If there are differences between the lists, suggest reasons for them.

3 Try to find examples of norm-setting in the headlines and stories you have identified. Explain in each case what types of behaviour are being encouraged or discouraged.

These processes of agenda-setting, gate-keeping and norm-setting mean some events are simply not reported and brought to public attention. Some of those that are reported may be singled out for particularly unfavourable treatment. In these ways, the mass media can define what the important issues are, what 'news' is, what the public should and should not be thinking about, and what should or should not be regarded as 'normal' behaviour in society.

The presentation and social construction of the news

The discussion above suggests that what counts as 'the news' is heavily influenced by the processes of agenda-setting, gate-keeping and norm-setting, and the need to attract audiences. In other words, the news is 'constructed' by a range of social influences, rather than simply being 'out there' waiting to be collected.

Activity

1 Carry out a short survey asking people which of the mass media they use as their main source of news, and which they see as the most believable, truthful and reliable source of news, and why.
2 Analyse your results, and try to explain any differences you find.

The way news items are presented may be important in influencing the way people are encouraged to view stories. For example the physical position of a news story in a newspaper (front page or small inside column), the order of importance given to stories in TV news bulletins, the choice of headlines, and whether there is accompanying film or photographs will all influence the attention given to particular issues.

Some issues may not be covered at all if journalists or camera crews are not available, especially in international news reporting, and the space available in a newspaper or TV programme will influence whether an event is reported or not. A story may be treated sensationally, and it may even be considered of such importance as to justify a TV or radio 'newsflash'. Where film is used, the pictures shown are always selected from the total footage shot, and may not accurately reflect the event. The actual images used in news films may themselves have a hidden bias. For example, the Glasgow University Media Group has shown how, in the reporting of industrial disputes, employers are often filmed in the peace and quiet of their offices, while workers are seen shouting on the picket lines or trying to be interviewed against a background of traffic noise. This gives the impression that employers are more calm and reasonable people and have a better case than the workers.

The media can also create false or biased impressions by the sort of language used in news reporting, such as words like 'troublemakers', 'rioters' or 'pointless'.

Inaccurate and false reporting

Other sources of bias lie in inaccurate reporting, because important details of a story may be incorrect. Politicians are always complaining that they have been inaccurately quoted in the press. False reporting, through either completely making up stories or inventing a few details, and the media's tendency to exaggerate and dramatize events out of all proportion to their actual significance in society, typical of much reporting of the royal family, are devices used to make a story 'more interesting' and sell newspapers or attract viewers – this is particularly common in the mass circulation tabloid press. Such methods mean the media can be accused of manipulating their audiences.

News values and 'newsworthiness'

Journalists obviously play an important role in deciding the content of the mass media, as it is journalists who basically select what 'the news' is and decide on its style of presentation. Research has shown that journalists operate with values and assumptions about which events they regard as 'newsworthy'. These assumptions are called news values, and they guide journalists in deciding what to report and what to leave out, and how what they choose to report should be presented. So news doesn't just happen, but is *made* by journalists. In this sense, it is socially constructed.

Events or issues that are newsworthy include:

- issues that are easily understood
- events that occur quickly or unexpectedly, such as disasters
- events that involve drama, conflict, excitement and action
- events that are in some way out of the ordinary
- events that have some human drama or interest to them, such as the activities of famous personalities, scandal, natural disasters or terrorist attacks
- events that are considered important – events in Britain are generally considered more important than those happening in the rest of the world, and national events are generally considered more important than local ones

- stories that fit the style of a paper, the balance of items (human-interest stories, political news, domestic and foreign news, crime stories etc.), its political slant and the values of the journalists

- stories which it is assumed will be of interest to the newspaper's readership or TV audience – giving the readers and viewers what journalists and producers think they want; this is of great importance if the audience or readership is to continue to be attracted and viewing figures kept up or papers sold

The idea of news values means that journalists tend to play up those elements of a story which make it more newsworthy, and the stories that are most likely to be reported are those which include many newsworthy aspects.

Activity

Photo: Ted Fussey

The sudden death in a car accident of Diana, Princess of Wales, on 31 August 1997 dominated world newspaper and TV headlines for many days, and newspaper sales increased by up to 50 per cent. More than 31 million people watched the funeral on television in Britain – three-quarters of the adult population – and an estimated one billion around the world, making it the biggest single televised event in history.

The 'twin towers' of New York's World Trade Center before their destruction

The terrorist attack on the 'twin towers' of the World Trade Center in New York on 11 September 2001 (9/11) was another massive international news story. Two passenger aircraft were hijacked, and deliberately crashed into the twin towers, causing both towers to collapse, and killing around 3,000 people. This dominated world news for weeks and months afterwards.

On 26 December 2004, the most powerful undersea earthquake in forty years triggered tidal waves, or tsunami, that travelled thousands of miles to crash on to the coastlines of at least five Asian countries. More than 300,000 people were killed, missing or unaccounted for, and millions of others were affected.

1　Refer to the three news stories here, or any major news stories currently receiving wide coverage in the mass media. List the features of these stories which you think make them 'newsworthy'.

2　Imagine you wanted to run a campaign to prevent a waste incinerator being built in your neighbourhood (or choose any topic of interest to you). In the light of the issues identified in this chapter relating to the social construction of news, suggest ways you might get the attention of journalists and activities you might undertake to achieve media coverage of your campaign. Explain why you think the activities you identify might be considered newsworthy.

The assumptions and activities of journalists

The Glasgow University Media Group, who generally support a Marxist-oriented dominant ideology/hegemonic approach to the media, and a cultural effects approach to media effects, emphasize the importance of the assumptions of journalists in forming media content and suggesting interpretations of issues to media audiences.

- Journalists are likely to give greater importance to the views of powerful people, since these people have more access to the media and their views appear more 'reasonable' to journalists.
- Journalists tend to be somewhere in the moderate centre ground of politics, and so ignore or treat unfavourably what they regard as 'extremist' or 'radical' views.
- Journalists tend to be mainly white, male and middle class, and they broadly share the interests and values of the dominant ideology. This influences whose opinions they seek for comment, what issues they see as important, and how issues should be presented and explained to audiences (this is also linked to the news values discussed above). The Glasgow University Media Group has shown how the explanations given in the media often favour the views of dominant and powerful groups in society, such as managers over workers, or police over protesters.
- Journalists are doing a job of work, and they like to keep their work as simple as possible. This means they often obtain information from news agencies, government press releases, 'spin doctors', public relations consultants and so on. This means powerful and influential groups like businesses, the government, political parties, and those with power and wealth are more likely to be able to influence journalists.

These features affecting the content of the media suggest that the mass media generally present, at best, only a partial and biased view of the world, which often favours the dominant ideology in society. However, it must also be recognized that journalists do occasionally expose injustice, corruption in government and business, and therefore are not always or simply in the pockets of the powerful.

Figure 4.1 overleaf sums up all the main influences on the content of the mass media.

Activity

1 Explain, with examples, what is meant by 'news values'
2 Suggest three reasons why journalists might be reluctant to write articles critical of the most powerful groups in society.
3 Write an essay of about one and a half to two sides of A4 answering the following question:
   Evaluate the view that the mass media may not tell us what to think, but they do tell us what to think about.

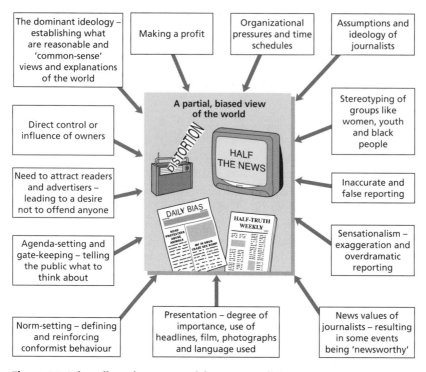

The dominant ideology – establishing what are reasonable and 'common-sense' views and explanations of the world

Making a profit

Organizational pressures and time schedules

Assumptions and ideology of journalists

Direct control or influence of owners

Need to attract readers and advertisers – leading to a desire not to offend anyone

Agenda-setting and gate-keeping – telling the public what to think about

A partial, biased view of the world

DISTORTION

HALF THE NEWS

DAILY BIAS

HALF-TRUTH WEEKLY

Stereotyping of groups like women, youth and black people

Inaccurate and false reporting

Sensationalism – exaggeration and overdramatic reporting

Norm-setting – defining and reinforcing conformist behaviour

Presentation – degree of importance, use of headlines, film, photographs and language used

News values of journalists – resulting in some events being 'newsworthy'

Figure 4.1 What affects the content of the mass media?

The media, crime and deviance

The mass media provide knowledge about crime and deviance for most people in society, including politicians, the police, social workers and the public at large. The mass media tend to be very selective in their coverage of crime, exploiting the possibilities for a 'good story' by dramatizing, exaggerating and sensationalizing some crimes out of all proportion to their actual extent in society. For example, attacks on old people and other crimes of violence – which are quite rare – are massively overreported, giving a false and misleading impression of the real pattern and extent of such crimes. This process can create many unnecessary fears among people, particularly among the housebound elderly, by suggesting that violence is a normal and common feature of everyday life.

This process of exaggerating, distorting and sensationalizing crime also applies to the media treatment of deviant (non-conformist) behaviour in general. The media have the power to label and stereotype certain groups and activities as deviant, and present them as acting irrationally, outside the boundaries of 'normal' behaviour, and as a threat to society which

Activity

1 How do you think your views about the levels and seriousness of crime in society are influenced by media reporting?
2 Draw up a stereotype of a 'typical criminal', and explain where you got your ideas from.

should be condemned. Those they define as deviants are frequently used as scapegoats for social problems. Those who support the hegemonic approach to the media see this as part of the process of strengthening the status quo and marginalizing those who challenge or threaten it.

Even if much of what is reported is untrue or exaggerated, it may be enough to whip up a **moral panic**, generating growing public anxiety and concern about the alleged deviance. The deviants themselves, who are seen as presenting this threat to society, become labelled as **folk devils** – visible reminders of what we should not be. In this view, some deviant groups play much the same role as witches in the past – an easy scapegoat to blame for all of society's problems.

This can raise demands for action by the agencies of social control to stop the alleged deviance. Often these agencies, such as newspaper editors, the churches, politicians, schools, social services, the police and magistrates, will respond to the exaggerated threat presented in the media by 'pulling together' to overcome this imagined or exaggerated threat to society by taking harsher measures against the apparent 'troublemakers'. Such action, particularly by the police, can often make what was a minor issue much worse, for example by causing more arrests, and amplify (or make worse) the original deviance. It's possible that it might even create deviance where there was none before, as people get swept away by the excitement of events, and the presence of reporters and TV cameras. The way the media may actually create or make worse the very problems they condemn is known as **deviancy amplification**.

Groups which have fitted this pattern include mods and rockers in the 1960s and other youth subcultures, glue-sniffers and football 'hooligans'. Figure 4.2 illustrates the way the media can amplify deviance and generate a moral panic. Figure 4.3 shows a range of moral panics which have arisen in Britain since the 1950s.

The work of Stan Cohen

In his book *Folk Devils and Moral Panics* (1972), Stan Cohen showed how the media helped to create two opposing youth groups in the 1960s – the mods (who drove scooters and wore parkas) and the rockers (who drove motorbikes and wore leather gear).

A **moral panic** is a wave of public concern about some exaggerated or imaginary threat to society, stirred up by exaggerated and sensationalized reporting in the mass media.
Folk devils are individuals or groups posing an imagined or exaggerated threat to society.

Deviancy amplification is the way the media may actually make worse or create the very deviance they condemn by their exaggerated, sensationalized and distorted reporting of events and their presence at them.

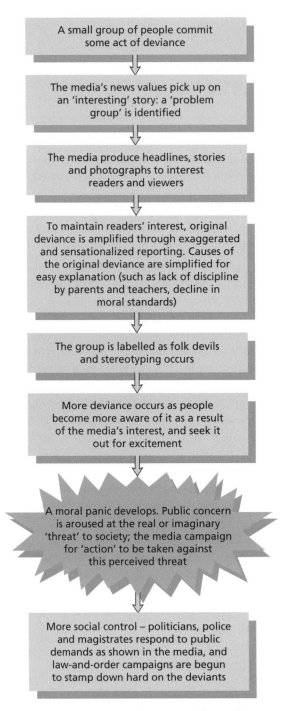

Figure 4.2 Deviancy amplification, moral panics and the media

Figure 4.3 Folk devils and moral panics: Great Britain, 1950s–2000s

In 1964, at Easter bank holiday weekend in Clacton and other seaside resorts, there were some minor acts of vandalism and a few scuffles between some mods and rockers, though the level of violence was little different from that occurring anywhere else in the country. However, the media carried hugely exaggerated reports of what had occurred (there was not much other news that day as it was a bank holiday weekend), and front-page headlines gave the misleading impression that Clacton had been terrorized and torn apart by pitched battles between rival gangs.

This generated a moral panic, with widespread public fear of and hostility towards the mods and rockers, and they came to be seen in the period after this as folk devils posing major threats to public order. The police were therefore forced to stamp down hard on the mods and rockers to respond to the alleged deviant behaviour which had been so exaggerated by the media. This resulted in growing numbers of arrests, and encouraged more young people to identify with one of the two groups in ways they had not done before the media's reporting of the events.

Before these events, the mods and rockers did not see themselves as rival groups, and most young people did not identify with either of them. However, the publicity created by the media's exaggerated, distorted and sensationalized reporting encouraged more young people to identify with the two groups, and adopt their styles as fashionable and exciting lifestyle choices. This raised public fears to even greater heights. The example of the mods and rockers shows how the media's reporting of deviance can actually create the very problems they are allegedly concerned about, and generate public concerns about a problem that only existed because the media created it.

Activity

Read carefully the previous sections on 'What affects the content of the media', 'The presentation and social construction of the news' and 'The media, crime and deviance', and then answer the following questions:

1 Identify and explain three reasons why the mass media might distort, exaggerate and sensationalize the extent of deviance and crime in society.

2 How does the concept of 'news values' help to explain sensationalism in the mass media? Give as many examples as you can, drawing on current TV or newspaper reports to illustrate your answer.

3 Refer to figures 4.2 and 4.3 on pp. 204–5 and try to fill in each of the stages of any current moral panic in society.

4 With reference to figures 4.1 (p. 202), 4.2 and 4.3, suggest reasons why the lifestyles and activities of young people are often the focus of media amplification of deviance and why it is young people who are often portrayed as 'folk devils'.

Media representations and stereotyping

One of the concerns of many media sociologists has been with the way social groups are portrayed in the mass media. These portrayals are known as **media representations**. Media representations very often conform to and create stereotypes – generalized, oversimplified views of the features of a social group, allowing for few individual differences between members of the group. The following sections examine these representations in the media.

> **Media representations** are the categories and images that are used to present groups and activities to media audiences, which influence the way we think about these activities and groups.

Media representations of age

Different age groups tend to be represented in different ways in the mass media. Children (up to the age of about 14) are often presented as consumers of toys and games, and are generally presented in a positive light.

Youth

Youth (from around age 15 to the early twenties) are often portrayed as a 'problem group' in society, and as a major source of anti-social behaviour, particularly young working-class males. Exciting stories and sensational headlines help to sell newspapers and attract TV viewers. The mass media often generate this excitement by creating stereotypes of young people as troublemakers, layabouts and vandals, and by exaggerating the occasional deviant behaviour of a few young people out of proportion to its real significance in society. This was seen earlier in this chapter in Stan Cohen's research into the mods and rockers. The mass media provide for many people the only source of information about events, and therefore distort people's attitudes and give a misleading impression of young people as a whole. Old people, who tend to be more home based, are particularly vulnerable to believing such stereotypes, as their impressions are likely to be formed strongly by the media.

Cohen argues that young people are relatively powerless, and an easily identifiable group to blame for all of society's ills. Consequently, young people have often been used as scapegoats by the media to create a sense of unity in society, by whipping up a moral panic against the folk devils who pose a threat to society, and uniting the public against a common 'enemy'. As a result of these media-generated moral panics, all young people may then get labelled and stereotyped as potentially troublesome or as an anti-social 'problem group'.

Older people

Older people, say in the late fifties onwards, are often presented in the media in quite negative ways. Being poor, in ill-health, forgetful, and

personally difficult and grumpy are typical stereotypes. There are sometimes different stereotypes for men and women. Sometimes older men are
presented in a positive light, with an image of distinguished, experienced
and informed 'wise old age', as political leaders, successful business
people and so on. By contrast, there are few positive images of older
women, as women are, in media imagery, to be forever young and youth-
ful, and there are not many positive roles for them as they get older.
However, both the changing role of women in society, and the growing
numbers of older people in the population, mean we might come to
expect more positive images of ageing emerging in the media.

Media representations of social class

The working class

The working class is often presented in the context of traditional working-
class communities, such as those portrayed in soaps like *EastEnders* or
Coronation Street. These community values are often praised, but they
have little relation to reality, as such working-class communities have
declined and disappeared with the decline of traditional industries like
coal mining, shipbuilding, the steel industry and docking.

   In a further stereotype, working-class people are presented, like working-
class youth, in the context of trouble, for example as strikers in industrial
disputes, undesirable welfare scroungers, and inadequates unable to cope
with life's difficulties. A similarly negative image is that of the 'couch potato',
who sits around doing nothing but watching television all day. The working
class is also linked to masculinity and physically hard work, and this is often
the representation found in advertising, for products such as jeans and beer.

The middle class

In contrast to the representation of the working class, the middle class is
generally presented as successful, and coping with problems. The middle
class is often overrepresented in media content – there is more exposure of
middle-class lifestyles than is justified by their proportion in the population as a whole. This fits in neatly with the dominant ideology/hegemonic
and cultural effects models of media control and influence, as positive
representations of the middle class, and negative ones of the working
class, help to reinforce the dominant ideology and the 'normality' of
middle-class life.

Media representations of ethnicity

Minority ethnic viewers, especially Asian viewers, rarely see their lives or
the issues that concern them reflected on TV channels. However, it seems

likely that this representation will improve, as black and Asian people extend the range of programmes they can receive by moving to satellite and cable TV – something they are doing faster than any other ethnic groups. This is particularly true among younger people, who are the fastest growing section of these minority ethnic groups. This change is one TV networks need to take account of if they are to retain viewers and therefore justify the licence fee (in the case of the BBC) or retain advertisers (in the case of commercial channels).

To improve diversity in British television and promote minority ethnic groups both among media company employees and among those portrayed in programmes, the Cultural Diversity Network was established by UK broadcasters in 2000. Nevertheless, it is still the case that only Channel 4 has a requirement under its licence to produce at least three hours a week, on average, of multicultural programming, with no other channel having such an obligation.

Although there is a high proportion of black and Asian TV presenters, ethnic minorities are underrepresented in senior management of the media companies, including the BBC.

Black and Asian people are frequently stereotyped and used as scapegoats in the media. Black and Asian people make up only about 8 per cent of the population of Britain, yet frequently this small minority are presented in quite negative ways in the media, as if they were major causes of conflict and social problems that otherwise wouldn't exist. These images often reflect the news values and ideology of journalists.

These minority ethnic groups often only appear in the media as scapegoats on which to blame a range of social problems, and in a limited range of degrading, negative and unsympathetic stereotypes, such as:

- law breakers, involved in drug dealing, welfare fraud and 'mugging' (street robbery with violence)
- low paid workers
- people with a culture which is seen as 'alien' and a threat to British culture – a kind of 'enemy within', with immigration seen as a threat to the British way of life and the jobs of white workers
- people causing conflict and trouble, as in stories portraying racial problems
- people causing social problems, such as asylum seekers, illegal immigrants, rioters, welfare scroungers, lone parents and so on, rather than as people with social problems like persecution in the countries they have fled from, poverty, racial discrimination, poor housing, and racist attacks by white people
- people who often do well in sport and music, but are rarely portrayed as academic or professional successes

- people who have problems internationally – for example, who run their own countries chaotically, who live in famine conditions (images of starving babies), who are always having tribal conflicts, military coups and so on, who need the white Western populations to help solve their problems for them

These stereotypes, some of which have in recent years also been applied to white people from Eastern Europe and countries close to Russia, like the Ukraine and Latvia, may well have a negative influence on audiences, creating, confirming and reinforcing the public's racial prejudices, and putting the blame on black people and other minority ethnic groups for problems that are not created by them at all. Such stereotypes may further racial discrimination and racist attacks on minority ethnic groups, and add further to the problems and disadvantages that many people from minority ethnic groups face in contemporary Britain.

These effects are more likely among those who have no experience themselves of minority ethnic life to draw on to offset the impact of these stereotypes. Any effects are likely to be influenced by these experiences and, of course, by the ethnic origin of the audience itself.

However, media stereotypes of black and minority ethnic group people are changing. We are seeing black and Asian actors moving into more popular dramas and soaps, and there are more programmes, TV channels, videos and magazines being targeted at black and Asian audiences. The Cultural Diversity Network aims to encourage more black and minority ethnic group people into senior positions in managing media companies and producing programmes, and to promote the writing of more roles for actors and actresses from minority ethnic groups. This may mean that more positive representations of minority ethnic groups will appear, with greater attention focused on their perspective.

Media representations of gender

Women are underrepresented in positions of power and influence in the management of the media industry, and among editors, journalists and TV producers. Women also appear less than men on TV, and in a narrower range of roles. These roles are often associated with the stereotypes listed below. This means that the mass media tend to be patriarchal – both controlled mainly by men and presenting a male view of women and 'femininity' in the interests of men. This patriarchal control and the spreading of a patriarchal ideology means that women are often presented in a limited number of stereotyped roles. Women are mostly portrayed:

- as concerned with beauty, childrearing, housework, cooking, love and relationships
- as housewives, mothers or lovers
- in their relation to men, whether they be brothers, husbands, bosses, fathers or lovers
- as young, pretty and sexually attractive
- as more likely to be indoors rather than outdoors
- as sex objects – the image of the slim, sexually seductive, scantily clad figure typically found on page three of the *Sun* newspaper, or in advertising aimed at men; or as objects of male fantasy in pornography
- as emotional and unpredictable
- as concerned with getting and keeping a man, being a good partner, keeping the family together and being a source of and managing family emotions
- as either good (little sexuality, sensitive, domesticated, supporting their men) or bad (sexually active, strong, selfish, independent minded and not dependent on men)
- as mainly concerned with romance
- as victims, as in many horror films and TV programmes, with men as their 'saviours'

The 'cult of femininity'

Ferguson (1983) argued that teenage girls' magazines prepared girls for feminized adult roles, and generated a 'cult of femininity'. This 'cult of femininity' included themes like getting and keeping a partner, being a good wife/partner, keeping a happy family, what to wear, how to be a good cook and so on. These socialized young girls into the stereotyped values and roles of femininity as established in our society, and these themes are often reflected in adult women's magazines, with their concerns with personal and emotional relationships, family, beauty, health and fashion.

Representations of men and patriarchy in the media

In contrast to women, men appear in a much wider range of roles, most often outside the home, and are generally portrayed both in a wider range of occupations and in those carrying higher status, for example as the 'boss' rather than the secretary. The stereotype of the tough, assertive, dominant and rational male often appears, but not as exclusively as the stereotypes of women.

Male voices are more likely to be used in 'voice-overs' in advertising (voice-overs are the commentaries you get during TV adverts). This reinforces the idea of men as authority figures, giving advice to consumers. Men are also often portrayed as strong, rational and unemotional. In

These images in the *Sun* and the *Daily Star*, which between them sell over four million copies every day, are typical of the representation of women in much of the mass circulation 'red top' tabloid press

addition, growing old is less of a problem for men in the world of television, but women are often expected to be young and attractive, whether as actresses, presenters or even media personnel.

News values, discussed above, are often influenced by patriarchal ideology, with women's interests being ignored or given trivial treatment. The women's pages of newspapers are often filled with articles that 'speak to' the male media stereotype of what women are thought to be interested in.

While some or many women may reject these stereotypes (in keeping with the uses and gratifications approach discussed earlier), these representations of women and men in the media may have a long-term influence (as the cultural effects model suggests) on the way both men and women come to see their respective positions in society as inevitable and unchangeable. At present, these stereotypes are clearly to the benefit of men, with women presented as no threat to male dominance.

Harmful consequences of media stereotyping

These gender stereotypes may well have long-term harmful effects and consequences. For example, the reinforcement of gender roles, through socialization via the media, may encourage discrimination against women or limit the self-confidence, outlooks and ambitions of young women. There may be particularly harmful effects in those cases where the reality of women's lives does not conform to the media stereotypes. Stereotyping may succeed in inducing feelings of guilt, inadequacy and lack of self-confidence among the majority of women who do not match up to the 'sex object' or the 'happy housewife' images.

That these issues do matter was demonstrated by a 2000 report published by the British Medical Association on mental health and eating disorders, which concluded that 'the gap between the ideal body shape and the reality is wider than ever. There is a need for more realistic body shapes to be shown on television and in fashion magazines.' Research in 2001 from Glasgow University found women were up to ten times more likely to be worried about their weight than men, even when they were not overweight. A 2005 survey for *Bliss* magazine, aimed at girls aged 13–18, found teenage girls were obsessed with body image and the desire to acquire a 'perfect' celebrity body, with just 8 per cent claiming to be happy with their body. Over half were unhappy with their faces, teeth, skin, breasts, tummies, bottoms, thighs and legs. Media stereotyping and the growing exposure to images of 'perfection' in magazines, on TV, in films, music videos and advertisements may contribute to explaining why so many women are so concerned with slimming and dieting, why anorexia and other eating disorders are illnesses affecting mainly teenage girls, and why many housewives in this country are on tranquillizers.

Despite these traditional stereotypes, women's position in society is changing rapidly, and women are now becoming more successful than men in education and in the job market. As the pluralist model predicts, there are new magazines catering for working women, and it may well be that in time gender stereotyping will diminish, as women demand more from the media than increasingly outdated and patriarchal stereotypes. In a world where advertising revenue and profits are driving forces of the media, such demands by half the population cannot be ignored forever.

Media representations of disability

White, middle-class and able-bodied men often form media representations of disability. Disability is nearly always presented as a problem of disabled individuals themselves, rather than something that is created by society. For example, it is not being in a wheelchair which creates all the difficulties, but the fact that buildings and roads are not designed for wheelchair access.

Disabled people are rarely featured in the media, and when they are, they are nearly always in roles defined by their disability – playing a disabled person – rather than as characters whose main role is doing something else, but who happen to have a disability as well.

Media stereotypes of disability include ideas that disabled people are dependent on others, less than human, are monsters or wicked people, or have maladjusted personalities and aren't like other people. Alternatively, they may be seen as people to be made fun of or pitied, or praised for their courage in coping with their disability. Only rarely do the media treat disability as a perfectly normal part of everyday life.

While disabled people and those who have some personal experience of disability may be able to resist or reinterpret these general stereotypes, for the many who lack such experience the media may play an important role in forming distorted views of disability.

Activity

1   Applying the media effects theories discussed earlier in this chapter, explain how each theory might view the effects of media representations on audience perceptions of young people, women, the disabled and minority ethnic groups.

2   Write an essay on about one and a half sides of A4 paper answering the following question:
    Explain what is meant by media representations, and examine the ways the media represent both gender and ethnicity.

Activity

Keep a diary for one week of your media viewing. While watching your favourite television programmes and television advertising, make a note of examples of stereotypes of family life, young and old people, men and women, different social classes, minority ethnic groups and disabled people. Explain what these stereotypes are.

The mass media and mass culture

Mass culture

Mass culture, sometimes called popular culture, refers to cultural products which are produced as entertainment for sale to the mass of ordinary people. These involve mass-produced, standardized, short-lived products of no lasting value, which are seen to demand little critical thought, analysis or discussion.

Mass culture is highly commercialized, involving mass-produced, standardized and short-lived products, sometimes of trivial content and seen by some as of no lasting 'artistic' value. These cultural products are designed to be sold on the global mass market to make profits for the 'culture industry' that produces them.

Mass or popular culture is everyday culture – simple, undemanding, easy-to-understand entertainment, rather than something 'set apart' and 'special'. Such products aimed at popular tastes might include mass-circulation magazines, 'red top' tabloid newspapers like the *Sun* or the *Mirror*, television 'soaps' and reality TV shows, films, dramas and thrillers, rock and pop music, feature films for the mass market, and thrillers bought for reading on the beach. Mass culture is largely linked to passive and unchallenging entertainment, designed to be sold to the largest number of people possible. Such products demand little critical thought, analysis or discussion, and rarely provide any challenge to the existing social structure or dominant cultural ideas.

'High culture'

High culture refers to specialist cultural products, seen as of lasting artistic or literary value, aimed at small, intellectual, predominantly upper-class and middle-class audiences, interested in new ideas, critical discussion and analysis.

Mass culture is generally contrasted with 'high culture'. High culture is seen as something set apart from everyday life, something 'special' to be treated with respect and reverence. High culture products, aimed at mainly middle-class and upper-class audiences with what might be viewed as 'good taste', might include 'serious' news programmes and documentaries, involving comprehensive detail, social and political analysis and discussion. Other products include classical music like that of Mozart or Beethoven, opera, jazz, foreign language or specialist 'art' films, and what has become established 'literature', such as the work of Dickens, Jane Austen or Shakespeare, and visual art like that of Monet, Gauguin, Picasso or Van Gogh.

Mass culture is seen by many as inferior to or not as worthwhile as high culture. Mass culture is seen as short-lived and disposable, while high culture is seen as involving things of lasting value and as part of a heritage which is worth preserving. Contrasts might be made between the products on display at the local multiscreen leisure/cinema complex, and the Tate Modern in London, or between a Virgin Megastore and a select local art gallery.

The mass media have played an important role in the development of this mass culture, which has become an aspect of the globalization process. This refers to the growing interdependence of societies across the world, sharing increasingly similar consumer products inspired by media advertising and a shared mass culture spread through a media-generated culture industry, with the same cultural products sold across the globe. Television companies sell their programmes and programme formats like *Big Brother* and *Who Wants to be a Millionaire?* globally. For example, in 2004 *Who Wants to be a Millionaire?* was distributed to 106 countries, *The Weakest Link* to 98, and *Pop Idol* to 30 countries. It is the media that have made some American and British film and music stars known across the world (and made English the internationally dominant language), with huge success in marketing their merchandise in global markets. The Beatles, for example, had sold 12 million copies of their *Beatles1* hits compilation CD in two months by the end of 2000, and Elvis Presley had sold an estimated one billion records and CDs worldwide by 2005 – including two UK number one singles in 2005 – despite being dead since 1977.

The media are an industry as well as a cultural product. It is mainly the media that create, promote and sell both their own products (TV programmes, 'soaps', CDs, DVDs, etc.) and, through advertising, other popular cultural ideas and products such as designer clothes, fashions, home cinema televisions, DVD and MP3 players, styles of furniture and so on to mass audiences.

A Marxist view of mass culture

Such a mass culture is of great advantage to the media owners, who gain colossal profits from exporting and advertising these products across the globe, along with promoting the identities and lifestyles that encourage people to consume them. Mass culture has also spawned a mass counterfeiting industry, producing fake designer clothes, perfumes, watches, CDs, computer programs and videos/DVDs, catering for those who can't afford the 'real thing'.

Some Marxists argue that mass culture maintains the ideological hegemony (or the dominance of a set of ideas) and the power of the dominant social class in society. This is because the consumers of mass culture are lulled into an uncritical, undemanding passivity, making them less likely to challenge the dominant ideas, groups and interests in society.

However, high culture at the same time faces threats from mass culture. High culture 'art forms' are themselves increasingly being turned into products for sale in the mass market. Classical music is used as a marketing tune by advertisers: for example, Verdi was used as a British Airways television advertisement theme, and Puccini's *Nessun Dorma* for football. They are then released on best-selling CDs. Leonardo da Vinci's *Mona Lisa* is replicated on everything from socks and T-shirts to chocolates and can lids (visit www.studiolo.org/Mona for some other bizarre images and uses of the *Mona Lisa*), and 'great works' of 'high culture' literature are made into feature films. Shakespeare's *Romeo and Juliet* is transformed into the popular romp of the commercial *Shakespeare in Love*, and complex characters and stories in literature are simplified for mass television and cinema audiences.

Activity

1 In a group, discuss the differences between 'high culture' and 'mass culture'. Identify as many named examples as you can (at least six) of items you regard as part of 'high culture' and a similar number of items you regard as part of popular culture. Explain why you have selected the items you have for each category.

2 Try to think of examples of 'high culture' items which have been included in and become a part of popular culture.

3 Do you think it is really possible to clearly identify differences between 'high culture' and 'mass culture'? Is there more than one mass culture? Are there any ways you think 'high culture' is superior to popular culture, or do you think they are just as good as each other? Is it just a matter of opinion or are these value judgements? Give reasons for your answer, with actual examples drawn from your own everyday cultural experiences, like television programmes, books, magazines, advertisements, music or cinema films.

4 To what extent do you think that the mass media might be creating a mass culture of undemanding and uncritical consumers? Explain the reasons for your answer.

Criticisms of the idea of a 'mass culture'

Pluralists argue that there is no such thing as mass, popular culture. The internet, cable, satellite and digital television, and the global reach of modern mass media technology offer a huge range of media products, giving consumers a wide diversity of cultural choices. Rather than being

Fake Levi label

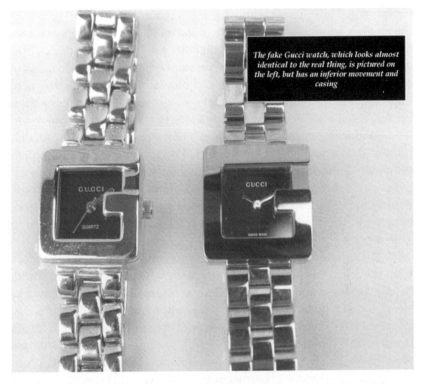

The fake Gucci watch, which looks almost identical to the real thing, is pictured on the left, but has an inferior movement and casing

Mass culture has also spawned a mass counterfeiting industry, producing fake designer goods of all kinds, which manufacturers are very keen to stop – as shown by the counterfeit CDs being crushed (opposite, top); the Levi's label shown is a fake (opposite, bottom), as is the Gucci watch on the left of its picture (above), compared with the real thing alongside it

doped into passivity, consumers and audiences now have more choices and knowledge available to them than ever before in history. This, they claim, makes it ever more difficult for any one set of ideas to dominate in society through the mass media.

Into the future

We now live in a society where much of our view of the world is influenced to some extent by the mass media. In many ways, our view of reality is formed through media imagery rather than personal experience, and we are subjected daily to media interpretations. The twenty-first century is likely to see an enormous increase in the power and influence of already powerful media companies.

With global satellite, cable and digital television, and the huge growth of the internet, postmodernists argue that the media no longer reflect reality but actively create reality. Many of us actually define our identities – how we see and define ourselves and how we want others to see us – in terms of media imagery, where colour, form and media-induced trends are more important than the content of products. It is not the quality of the clothes, drink or mobile phones we buy that matters, but whether they conform to media-induced images, styles, brand names and trends. The media-promoted designer labels of mass culture become more important than the quality of the products. In films, it is not the story that matters so much as how good the special visual and sound effects are; not the script or the writing, more the icon and the big-name 'stars'. There are any number of people who are famous for no reason at all except for being made into 'celebrities' by the media.

We are now bombarded with so much information, imagery and ideas from the mass media that there is increasing uncertainty in the world: people no longer know what to believe as international media networks steadily loosen our grip on, and challenge our notions of 'the truth'. Some argue this has meant we inhabit a world shaped by the media. Media imagery and representations themselves become our reality, until we identify more with them than we do with our own daily experiences, and increasingly live media-led virtual lives rather than real ones. We are more likely to identify with the lives and communities of television soap charac-ters than we are with our next-door neighbours and the communities we actually live in.

Such views are controversial, and assume that people approach the media without any prior experiences of their own, and that they do not discuss, interpret, ignore or reject media imagery and messages. The mass media are only one element – albeit an important one – in shaping our lives. For many of us, our gender, ethnicity, sexuality, age, social class, whether we are able-bodied or disabled, our experiences of school, college, work, friends and family, our political or religious beliefs – all these are likely to influence how we select, interpret and respond to the mass media.

Activity

1   Identify all the changes you can imagine might occur in the mass media over the next century. How do you think the relationship between the media and audiences might change?
2   How do you think the changes you imagine might affect our daily lives?

Chapter summary

After studying this chapter, you should be able to:

- identify formal controls on the mass media
- critically discuss the issue of how media ownership influences the content of the media, including the strengths and weaknesses of the manipulative or instrumentalist approach, the dominant ideology or hegemonic approach, and the pluralist approach
- critically discuss the effects of the mass media, including the strengths and weaknesses of the hypodermic syringe, the two-step flow, the cultural effects and the uses and gratifications models
- discuss the effects of violence in the media, and the problems of researching it
- identify and discuss the influences on the content of the mass media, and the issue of media bias
- discuss the way 'the news' is socially constructed
- identify the factors that make stories newsworthy
- discuss the media's portrayal of crime and deviance, including how the media can amplify deviance and generate moral panics
- critically discuss a range of media representations and stereotypes, including age, social class, ethnicity, gender, and disability
- consider the role of the mass media in relation to mass or popular culture

Key terms

- agenda-setting
- bias
- deviancy amplification
- dominant ideology
- folk devils
- gate-keeping
- globalization
- hegemony
- high culture
- ideology
- mass culture/popular culture
- media representations
- moral panic
- news values
- norm-setting

Coursework suggestions

1 Carry out an investigation into stereotyped representations in television, advertising, magazines, etc., of age, gender, social class, minority ethnic groups or disability. Link your study to theories of media effects.

2 Study some of the 'quality' and 'popular' newspapers over a period of time, and examine the news values which seem to influence what is reported and how these items are presented

3 Carry out unstructured interviews with the editor and journalists of a local newspaper, and give an in-depth account of how they decide what to print and what not to, and what they think makes a story 'newsworthy'.

4 Carry out a survey to find out which of the news media (newspapers, television or radio) people see as the most reliable and trustworthy in presenting the news. Try to include in your survey the reasons people give for their answers.

A number of the activities in this chapter could easily be adapted to make up a suitable coursework proposal.

Exam Questions

MASS MEDIA

Time allowed: 1 hour 15 minutes   **Total for this Question:** *60 marks*

Item A

There has long been a concern among the public, politicians and some researchers about the possible effects of exposure to violent messages or images in the mass media. One approach by researchers has been to conduct laboratory-style experiments to try to discover if there are such effects. This is usually done by taking two groups with identical characteristics (for example, the same age, sex, etc) and then exposing one group to a violent sequence of film, while the other group is shown a 'neutral' sequence.   5
The responses of the two groups are then observed to see if one group shows more aggressive behaviour than the other immediately after viewing the film. Many studies using this approach, such as Eysenck and Nias, have found that exposure to media depictions of violence has a direct and powerful effect on the audience.

Item B

A major interest of researchers is whether the mass media are biased in their selection and presentation of the news. For example, some sociologists argue that the media reproduce the views of the ruling class and portray subordinate groups in stereotypes. Studies by the Glasgow University Media Group have shown that the language and 'visuals' used in TV news broadcasts are biased against particular groups; that stories are selectively reported (for instance, the effects of strikes are given more coverage than their   5
causes) and that there is a hierarchy of access to the media, in which more powerful groups find it easier to get their views heard. Sociologists have also examined how news values – that is, the criteria that journalists and editors use in deciding whether an event is 'newsworthy' – produce systematic biases in the news.

(a) Explain what is meant by a stereotype (**Item B**, line 3).   *(2 marks)*
(b) Suggest **two** reasons why exposure to mass media depictions of violence might **not**
    produce violent behaviour in the audience (**Item A**).   *(4 marks)*
(c) Give **three** example of 'news values' (**Item B**, line 7).   *(6 marks)*
(d) Identify and briefly explain **two** problems of using the method described in **Item A** to
    measure the effects of the media on their audiences.   *(8 marks)*
(e) Examine the ways in which the mass media portray any **two** of the following: age;
    ethnicity; sexuality; disability.   *(20 marks)*
(f) Using material from **Item B** and elsewhere, assess the view that the selection and
    presentation of the news by the mass media are biased.   *(20 marks)*

(AQA AS Unit 1 January 2003)

MASS MEDIA

Time allowed: 1 hour 15 minutes   **Total for this Question:** *60 marks*

Item A

Over the years, many studies have focused on the effects of the media on their audiences. For example, the effects of viewing violence on television have been widely studied and researchers have suggested an equally wide range of effects that this might have on viewers. Much of this research has been influenced by the hypodermic syringe model.

A different approach to the media–audience relationship is the uses and gratifications model. This model   5
sees people as using the media in various ways to fulfil their needs. It sees audiences as being in control – as active interpreters of media output, using the media consciously and rationally as a way of satisfying their various needs.

The method generally used to investigate uses and gratifications is to compile a questionnaire listing different reasons for viewing and to give this to a cross-section of the audience. The researchers then   10
analyse and categorise the responses into the different uses that the audience make of the media.

Item B

Pluralists argue that society is made up of many competing sections, each with more or less equal access to resources and influence. Different parts of the media cater to these various sections of society. The media reflect society: just as there is diversity within society, so there is diversity in media content.

Pluralism appears in the work of many media commentators, particularly in the ideas of media workers themselves. Indeed, many of the pluralist studies of media content and effects, such as Martin Harrison's   5
highly critical study of the Glasgow Media Group's work, were funded by the media industry. One plural-ist author, who is also a media professional, is the BBC radio news correspondent, Nicholas Jones. Jones argues that radio news is neutral, fair and balanced. He examined media reporting of industrial disputes and claimed that any *apparent* bias depends on how successful workers and management are in obtain-ing suitable media coverage of their positions.   10

Source: Adapted from M. Haralambos and M. Holborn, *Sociology: Themes and Perspectives*
(Collins) 5th edition 2000

(a) Explain briefly what is meant by 'the hypodermic syringe model' (**Item A**, line 4).   *(2 marks)*
(b) Identify **two** possible effects that viewing violence on television may have upon audiences (**Item A**, lines 2–3).   *(4 marks)*
(c) Suggest **three** needs that audiences might fulfil by using the mass media (**Item A**, line 6).   *(6 marks)*
(d) Identify and briefly explain **two** criticisms of the uses and gratifications approach (**Item A**).   *(8 marks)*
(e) Examine the ways in which gender and sexuality are portrayed in the mass media.   *(20 marks)*
(f) Using material from **Item B** and elsewhere, assess the pluralist view of the mass media.   *(20 marks)*

(AQA AS Unit 1 January 2004)

Education

EDUCATION is a major social institution, and schools in Britain command a captive audience of virtually all children between the ages of 5 and 16. During this period of compulsory schooling, children spend about half of the time they are awake at school during term time – about 15,000 hours of their lives. School is therefore a major agency of secondary socialization in advanced industrial societies.

Education in Britain before the 1970s

The 1944 Education Act established three types of secondary school – grammar, technical, and secondary modern schools. These three types of secondary school became known as the tripartite system. It was thought that children had three different sorts of ability, which were fixed by the age of 11, were unlikely to change, and could be reliably and accurately measured at age 11 by a special intelligence quotient test (IQ test). This became known as the 11+ exam. Until the 1960s, all children went first to primary schools (as they do now) but then were selected by the 11+ examination to go to one of the three types of secondary school, according to their performance in the exam. The 15–20 per cent of children with the best 11+ exam results went to grammar schools, with most children going to secondary modern schools. There were hardly any technical schools established.

During the 1960s the tripartite system came under increasing attack. The 11+ exam was seen as an unfair, unreliable and inaccurate selection test, which disadvantaged children from working-class homes and damaged the self-esteem and educational opportunities of children who failed to win a place at a grammar school. Secondary modern schools were seen as inferior, second-rate schools, with grammar schools having higher status and offering better life chances to their pupils. Figure 5.1 shows the

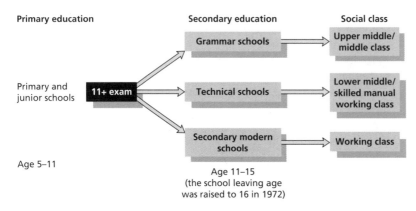

Figure 5.1 The tripartite system after the 1944 Education Act

tripartite system, and the social classes young people were being prepared for as adults.

Research in the 1950s and 1960s suggested that the talent, ability and potential of many children in the secondary modern schools were being wasted. It was felt that this wasted talent could be better developed in comprehensive schools, which accept pupils of all abilities. As a result, in the 1960s the tripartite system was abolished in most of the country, and by the 1970s most children attended comprehensive schools.

Comprehensive schools and selection

Comprehensive education abolished both selection at age 11 by the 11+ exam and the three types of secondary school. Children in most areas now, regardless of their ability, generally transfer to the same type of school at the age of 11, with no selection by examination. Around nine out of ten young people in 2005 were attending some form of comprehensive school, with just 164 grammar schools remaining.

'True' comprehensive schools have no selection by ability at all, and children of all abilities are admitted to the same types of school and taught in mixed ability classes. While most schools are now comprehensive schools in that they do not select the majority of the pupils they admit by ability, there are different types of comprehensive school, and some selection by ability does continue in the education system and, through streaming, in many comprehensive schools as well.

The issue of selection by ability for secondary education, and whether this is necessary to give young people the most suitable form of secondary education, are still hotly disputed matters. In 2005, secondary 'specialist' schools were allowed to select up to 10 per cent of their pupils by ability, and there has been a return to streaming and a move away from mixed ability teaching. Policy-makers of all political parties in the early years of the twenty-first century were increasingly talking of a return to selection for secondary education, based on student attitudes, aptitudes, interests, capabilities and skills.

School and college 'league tables' and the judging of schools and colleges on their results (see later in this chapter) constantly raise the issue of whether students should be selected by ability so some schools get the best, most able students in an area.

The case against selection: the advantages of comprehensive education

Opportunities remain open

In comprehensive schools, the possibility of educational success and obtaining qualifications remains open throughout a child's school career, since moving between streams and classes within one school is easier and more likely to happen than moving between different types of school in a selective system.

Late developers benefit

Late developers, whose intelligence and ability improve later in life, can be catered for better in the comprehensive system, rather than having their opportunities limited at an early age.

More get better qualifications

Fewer students leave school without any qualifications in the comprehensive system, and more obtain higher standards than under selective systems, such as where grammar schools continue to exist or where there are other forms of selection by ability.

More social mixing and fewer social divisions

As all children attend the same type of school, there is more social mixing between students from homes of different social class and ethnic backgrounds, and this helps to overcome divisions between different social groups. Selection by ability in education often benefits the middle class, which dominates selective schools and the top streams in streamed comprehensive schools. The reasons for this are discussed later in this chapter.

Reduced risk of the self-fulfilling prophecy

Children are less likely to be branded as 'failures' at an early age, lowering their self-esteem (how they feel about themselves and their ability) and avoiding the damaging effects of the **self-fulfilling prophecy**. This is discussed later in this chapter.

Benefits of mixed ability teaching

Where all pupils of the same age, regardless of their ability, are taught in the same type of school and in the same classroom (mixed ability teaching) the more intelligent pupils can have a stimulating influence on the less able, and the problems created by the self-fulfilling prophecy are easier to avoid. Recent research has shown that mixed ability teaching has

The **self-fulfilling prophecy** is the process whereby people act in response to predictions of the way they will behave, thereby making the prediction come true. In education, this means that when testing and selection by ability predicts that a student won't do well, the prediction actually comes true, because of the low expectations of teachers, and the consequent poor image students have of their own ability.

no negative effect on the 'high flyers', improves the performance of the 'less able', and makes no difference to a school's overall examination performance.

More choice and opportunity

The large size of many comprehensive schools, designed to contain all pupils in an area, means there are more teachers teaching a wider range of subjects to meet the needs of pupils of all abilities, with a great variety of equipment and facilities. This benefits all pupils and gives them greater choices and opportunities to develop their talents, to reach their full potential and gain some educational qualifications.

Benefits for working-class students

Selective schools and streamed comprehensives can be much like the tripartite system, with working-class students less likely to gain places in selective schools, and more likely to be placed in the bottom streams.

The case for selection: criticisms of comprehensive education

'Creaming off'

Where selective (grammar) schools continue to exist, they 'cream off' the most able students, so the so-called comprehensives are not true comprehensives at all, and little different from the secondary moderns of the tripartite system.

'High flyers' are held back

Because comprehensive schools contain pupils of all abilities, brighter children are held back by the slower pace of learning of the less able. Critics argue this wouldn't happen with selection, as 'high flyers' are taught in the same school or streams within a school.

Overlooked talents and discipline problems

The large size of some comprehensives, containing all students in an area, may make it impossible for staff to know all pupils personally, and this may create discipline problems and the talents of individuals may not be noticed and developed.

Stretching the most able

Selection by ability through streaming or setting (rather than mixed ability teaching) in the same school means brighter students can be 'stretched', rather than being held back by slower learners who take up the teacher's

Selection by ability can have harmful effects on the self-esteem of students, and create a self-fulfilling prophecy

time, and who may be disruptive because they are unable to cope with the work. Many so-called comprehensive schools are not true comprehensives, as they stream or set pupils, and this is really a form of selection in the same school.

Activity

1 Do you think young people should be selected by ability for secondary schools? What arguments would you put forward both for and against the idea of selection by ability?
2 Do some people develop their talents and abilities later in life? Can you think of examples from your own experience of people who seem to have become 'more intelligent' as they grew older?

Education from 1988 onwards: the free market in education and increased state intervention

While the comprehensive system has succeeded in improving overall educational standards, the comprehensive system came under increasing criticism in the 1980s and 1990s for not meeting the needs of employers and industry closely enough, for not reaching high enough standards, and for failing to benefit the most disadvantaged, poorest groups in society. As a result, attempts have been made to tie all parts of the education system more closely to the needs of industry and business, to raise standards, and to target the most disadvantaged groups.

The 1988 Education Reform Act was the most important piece of educational legislation since the 1944 Education Act. Many of the changes it introduced reduced local control of the education system, for example by teachers and local education authorities, and increased control by the state, school governors, headteachers and parents.

These changes were based on free market principles. It was thought that by introducing competition between schools and colleges, and by giving parents a choice as 'consumers' of education – rejecting some schools in favour of others, as people choose between competing products in a supermarket – education standards would rise, and poorly performing schools would risk losing money as pupil numbers fell, and might face closure.

There has been a rapid and bewildering number of changes in education since 1988. This section aims to examine some of the main changes, and some will be referred to during the course of this chapter.

The key aims of educational change

The move to comprehensive schooling, and more recent changes in the education system, have been driven by four main aims:

Equality of educational opportunity is the idea that every child, regardless of his or her social class background, ability to pay school fees, ethnic background, gender or disability, should have an equal chance of doing as well as his or her ability will allow.

A **meritocracy** (or meritocratic society) is a society where occupational positions (jobs) and pay are allocated on the basis purely of people's individual talents, abilities, qualifications and skills – their individual merits. In Britain today, this nearly always means educational qualifications.

- Economic efficiency: developing the talents of young people to improve the skills of the labour force so Britain maintains a successful position in the world economy.
- Making the education system meet the needs of industry and employers through more emphasis on vocational education.
- Raising educational standards.
- Creating equality of educational opportunity in a meritocratic society, and establishing a fairer society by opening up opportunities for secondary and further/higher education to the working class and other disadvantaged groups.

Vocational education

The emphasis on making education meet the needs of industry, and preparing young people for work, is known as vocational education. A key feature of this has been on improving the quality of the basic skills of the workforce, with a particular focus on the 14–18 age group. The aim has been to develop the talents of young people to improve the skills of the labour force so Britain maintains a successful position in the world economy, and to produce a more flexible labour force, fitting education more to the needs of employers. Measures to achieve this have included:

- Work experience programmes for pupils in school years 10 and 11 to ease the transition from school to work, and help/encourage them to get jobs successfully and carry them out well, with a better understanding of work and the economy.
- More educational courses, and government training schemes for those leaving school, which are more closely related to the world of work, and concerned more with learning work-related skills. For example, work-based NVQs (National Vocational Qualifications) and school/college-based GNVQs (General National Vocational Qualifications) were developed to provide nationally approved and recognized qualifications for vocational courses. Vocational GCSEs and applied GCEs (vocational 'A' levels) were intended as vocational alternatives to academic GCSEs and A levels.
- An expansion of post-16 education and training, with coordination and funding through business-dominated Learning and Skills Councils.
- A stronger emphasis on key skills in the use and application of number, and in communication and information technology. These are the skills that most employers find that school leavers lack, with poor communication skills mentioned by almost two-thirds of employers in 2004 as one of the most frequent problems they face in recruiting staff.

All these changes were designed to produce a more flexible labour force, fitting education to the needs of employers.

Raising standards

More money for schools, more nursery education, and smaller primary school classes

The Labour government, first elected in 1997, established a national maximum class size of thirty for all 5, 6 and 7 year olds, and allocated huge amounts of extra money to schools to enable them to provide the staff, materials, buildings and facilities to enable them to provide a high quality learning environment for children, and thereby improve standards. All children aged 3 and 4 now get a guarantee of five half-days of nursery education a week.

Activity-based learning

Teaching has become more student centred and activity based, with the aim of developing students' skills and understanding. GCSE, AS and

A levels, GNVQ and applied GCEs have become more activity and skills based exams, and involve students doing more coursework. This has led to much better exam results among 16–18 year olds. Modular exams (which students can take in parts) aim to ensure that all students can obtain some qualifications by allowing them to resit parts of a course. AS levels aim to encourage 16–18 year-olds to study a broader range of subjects, and make them more flexible and less specialized.

The National Curriculum, national testing, target-setting and the literacy and numeracy hours

To improve standards across the country, and ensure all students had access to the same high quality curriculum, the 1988 Education Reform Act set up the National Curriculum, a range of subjects and set 'programmes of study' that must be followed by all school students. There are 'attainment targets' (goals which all teachers are expected to enable students to reach), with testing (the Standard Assessment Tests or SATs) at ages 7, 11 and 14 (Key Stages 1, 2 and 3) to ensure these targets are met. In addition, all primary schools (Key Stages 1 and 2) must have a literacy hour and a numeracy hour each week, to improve basic skills in these areas.

National 'league tables'

Schools and colleges are now required to publish tables of testing (SATs) and exam results (GCSE, AS level, A level, applied GCE and GNVQ). These have become known as 'league tables' and are designed to give parents and students an idea of how well schools and colleges are doing so they can choose the best. By encouraging competition for students between schools and colleges, these league tables aim to raise overall standards.

Local management of schools (LMS)

Local management of schools (LMS) gives schools (rather than the local education authority – county and city councils in most areas) much greater control of their budgets, and of a wide range of other aspects of the school. Further education and sixth form colleges have also become completely independent of the local education authority. This is designed to make schools and colleges more responsive to local needs and the wishes of parents. These changes aimed to encourage schools and colleges to run on market principles, where they compete with one another for students and therefore funds.

Formula funding

Schools and colleges are funded by a formula which is largely based on the number of students they attract. It was thought this would drive up stand-ards by rewarding 'successful' schools and colleges that attracted students (and hence money), giving less successful schools and colleges the incentive to improve.

Open enrolment and parental preference

Parents are now allowed to express a preference for the school of their choice, and a school cannot refuse a pupil a place if it has vacancies. This was designed to raise the quality of teaching and exam results by encouraging competition between schools. Unpopular schools run the risk of losing pupils and therefore money, and the government has taken steps to close what it sees as 'failing' schools which are unpopular with parents and where exam and test results, and standards of behaviour, are poor. In most cases, parents don't really have much choice of school, as places are usually filled up by those living in the school's 'priority area' (the area from which children are admitted first).

More information for parents

To help parents to choose the 'best' schools and encourage schools to improve their standards and performance, schools now have to provide, by law, a wide range of information for parents, including the standards achieved, examination and National Curriculum test results, details of the school budget, the amount of authorized and unauthorized absence, and what school leavers do after they leave school.

Specialist schools and selection by ability

Since the early 2000s there has been a huge growth in the number of 'specialist schools', those with the highest status being the city academies. These schools have a special focus on their chosen subject area, such as technology, languages, business and enterprise, or music. These are an attempt to move away from what were called 'bog standard' comprehensives. These schools have to raise money from private business, but they then get extra money from the government and are allowed to select up to 10 per cent of their pupils by 'aptitude' (ability). It is thought that by specializing these schools will raise standards in their specialist subjects, and that selection by ability will raise standards, not just in the specialist subjects, but across the whole school curriculum.

The Office for Standards in Education (Ofsted)

The Office for Standards in Education (Ofsted) was established to conduct inspections of all state schools, further education colleges and local education authorities at least once every six years. This aimed to ensure schools, colleges and local education authorities were doing a good job, by publishing their inspection reports and requiring action to be taken on any weaknesses identified.

Equality of educational opportunity and helping the most disadvantaged groups

The Labour government, first elected in 1997, emphasized the need to create equality of educational opportunity for all, particularly focusing on the most deprived and most disadvantaged areas where educational results were poor. This was carried out through a number of measures, including schemes such as SureStart to ensure children in disadvantaged areas had the best start in life, and more money and better-paid teachers were provided for schools in the poorest areas through schemes such as Excellence in Cities and Education Action Zones. According to a 2003 Ofsted report, these schemes had only mixed success, and seemed more successful in improving standards among primary, rather than secondary school students. These measures are considered a little more later in this chapter.

Activity

1 Identify and explain the various ways in which the educational reforms from the 1980s to the 2000s have increased national control of the education system.
2 Is competition between schools and colleges a good thing? Identify and explain its advantages and disadvantages.
3 Do you think the recent changes in education will succeed in raising standards? Go through each of the changes since the 1980s, and explain why they might or might not improve standards.
4 Do you think schools alone can be held responsible for exam results and truancy rates? What other factors might influence how good a school's exam results are, and whether pupils play truant or not?
5 What should the aims of schooling be? Do you think schools and colleges should be mainly concerned with meeting the needs of business and industry, and fitting people into the job market? Or should they be concerned mainly with the development of individuals' talents and interests? Give reasons for your answer.

Criticisms of the free market in education, vocational education and other recent changes

While the changes in education may have given individual schools more control of their affairs, and made them more responsive to parents, this has been at the expense of greater central government control, such as through the National Curriculum, and cooperation between schools has been replaced with competition. The development of the free market in education, increased intervention by central government, the attempt to raise standards and the more vocational emphasis in education have been very controversial, and these changes have been criticized in a number of ways. The main criticisms are outlined below.

The middle class has gained the most

Middle-class parents have been able to make the greatest use of parental choice and open enrolment, and it is they who are better placed to make the most effective use of the education system and exploit the new system to their children's advantage. The educational system remains socially selective, and the higher the social class of the parents, the better are the schools to which they send their children. Because of their own higher levels of income and education, they are better placed than many working-class parents to:

- shop around and find the best schools
- understand and compare schools in the league tables
- know more about how to assess school Ofsted inspection reports and what constitutes a 'good school'
- afford more easily to move into the priority areas of the 'best' schools
- afford higher transport costs, giving their children a wider choice of schools
- make more effective use of appeals procedures should they be refused a place at their chosen school

This means that those who have already benefited from education the most will gain more, while those who are more disadvantaged may become further disadvantaged.

Student needs at risk and social divisions increased

The free market may open up further the gap between the educational achievements of working-class and middle-class young people. The traditional pursuit of equality of educational opportunity, so all do as well as they are able, has been replaced with the need to demonstrate high results to keep up the image of the school or college in the 'league tables' of results. Weaker students, who are more likely to come from working-class backgrounds (as is explained later in this chapter), may find their needs are neglected because of the risk of them getting poorer results and therefore undermining the position of the school/college in the league tables.

Because of the competitive climate, brighter students, or those, for example, on the C/D grade borderline at GCSE, are likely to get more resources spent on them, disadvantaging weaker students who are less likely to deliver the prestige results.

As a result, social divisions between the middle class and the working class are widened.

Specialist schools and selection by ability

As seen earlier, and later in this chapter, selection by ability can lead to a lowering of the self-esteem of those not selected, and may lead to lower expectations by teachers and the self-fulfilling prophecy. Specialist schools are often seen as being 'better' schools, and therefore given higher status by parents and pupils than other schools, and are given extra resources. As pupils compete for places, specialist schools may increasingly select their pupils by ability (up to 10 per cent of their intake). This will create unfair competition between schools, and increase inequality between them. Middle-class parents are likely to gain most from this, and the working class to lose out, adding further to social divisions between social classes.

The unfairness of league tables

League tables of test and exam results don't really reveal how well a school or college is doing. This is because, as later parts of this chapter show, the social class, ethnic and gender backgrounds of students can affect how well they perform in education. Schools and colleges in more deprived working-class areas may produce results which are not as good as those in middle-class areas, yet their students have actually made much more progress than middle-class students compared to what they started school with. For example, a sixth form or college where students enter with four GCSEs grade C cannot normally be expected to get results at AS and A level as good as one where students enter with seven GCSEs grades *A, A and B. The latter sixth form or college might get better results and a higher league table position than the first one, but the scale of achievement of the students in the first one might in reality have been greater.

League tables therefore do not show how much value has been added by the educational institution (the 'value-added' approach). They may conceal underperforming schools or colleges in advantaged middle-class areas, where results should be much better given their social class intake, and successful schools and colleges in more deprived working-class areas.

Difficulties in improving schools and colleges

Competition between schools and colleges for students, and therefore for money, the emphasis on exam results, and presenting a good 'image' to parents in the free market may make it harder for poorer schools and colleges to improve, as students go elsewhere. Such schools and colleges may therefore lack the resources to improve their performance – the opposite of what was intended by the reforms.

'Dumbing down'

As school students, and particularly post-16 further education and sixth form students, now have a choice of institutions, this may lead to a 'dumbing down' of teaching and subject content. The need for schools and colleges to retain students – and the money they bring with them – means that if students have too much work to do or find the work difficult, they may go to another course or educational institution where things seem 'easier' and less demanding. Retaining (keeping) students may mean not pushing students too hard for fear of losing them.

Problems with the National Curriculum and testing

The National Curriculum has been criticized for not giving teachers enough opportunity to respond to the needs of their pupils, as teachers are told what they have to teach and when they have to teach it. Testing (the SATs) has been criticized, particularly at Key Stage 1 (age 7), for putting too much pressure on young children, and possibly giving them a sense of failure early in their schooling. More generally, teaching may become too focused on the content of the tests as a way to get the good test results needed for a high position in the league tables, at the expense of the wider school curriculum.

Inadequate vocational education

Work experience is often seen by school students as boring and repetitive, involving little development of their skills and little to do with their future ambitions. Post-school training schemes are often criticized for providing little development of skills, for being used as a source of cheap labour by employers, and for not leading to 'proper' jobs at the end of the training. Such schemes are sometimes seen as having more to do with reducing politically embarrassing unemployment statistics, and keeping young people away from crime and other forms of deviance than producing a skilled labour force. Vocational education and qualifications, like GNVQ and vocational GCSEs and applied GCEs (vocational A levels), are often seen as having lower status than more traditional academic subjects and courses. Vocational qualifications are, in general, less likely to lead to university entry, and are more likely to lead to lower status, lower paid jobs as adults.

University qualifications generally lead to better paid jobs and higher social class positions. Parents, teachers and students themselves therefore often see vocational qualifications as 'inferior' or a second-rate option compared to more traditional academic subjects and courses. Those from working-class backgrounds are more likely to find themselves taking vocational subjects and courses, reinforcing divisions between social classes.

Activity

1 Think back over your school work experience programmes. Were they very useful to you? Give reasons for your answer.

2 Do you think AS and A levels have the same status as vocational qualifications, such as GNVQs and applied GCEs?

3 Do you think there is any evidence of 'dumbing down' in standards, or do you think standards are going up? Ask a few of your teachers or lecturers what they think.

4 Is offering the option of vocational GCSEs at age 14 a sensible idea? How might this affect the future career prospects of young people compared to those doing traditional academic GCSEs? Do you think this might have any effect on equal opportunities for all in education?

Activity

1 Explain what is meant by a meritocracy.

2 Suggest three educational policies that have attempted to improve standards in education in the last twenty years.

3 Identify and explain two reasons why league tables of test and exam results may not give a fair impression of how effective a school or college is.

4 Explain what is meant by the self-fulfilling prophecy.

5 Explain why middle-class parents might be more effective in achieving better schooling for their children than those from working-class backgrounds.

6 Suggest two reasons why selection by ability in education may have harmful effects on some children.

7 On about two sides of A4 paper, answer the following question:
Examine the view that recent reforms in education have not benefited all children equally.

Sociological perspectives on education

This section is concerned with the different explanations of the role of the education system in society. The focus here is on two structural or 'macro' approaches, functionalism and Marxism, which try to understand the role of education in relation to other social institutions, such as the economy (the world of work and production).

The functionalist perspective on education

The functionalist perspective on education follows the same principles as all functionalist approaches to the study of society. It is concerned with the functions or role of education for society as a whole, in particular its contribution to maintaining social stability through the development of value consensus, social harmony and cohesion. It examines the links between education and other social institutions, such as the family and the workplace. The two most important writers on education from a functionalist perspective have been Émile Durkheim (1858–1917) and the American functionalist Talcott Parsons. They identified four basic functions of education:

1   Passing on society's culture

Education meets a key **functional prerequisite** by passing on to new generations the 'central' or 'core' values and culture of a society. This is achieved by both the '**hidden curriculum**' and the actual subjects learnt at school (the curriculum), for example through subjects like Citizenship and Personal, Social and Health Education (PSHE). This unites or 'glues' people together by giving them shared values (a value consensus) and a shared culture.

2   Providing a bridge between the particularistic values and ascribed status of the family and the universalistic values and achieved status of industrial society

Durkheim argued that schools are a 'society in miniature' – a small-scale version of society as a whole that prepares young people for life in the wider adult society.

Parsons sees school as an important unit of secondary socialization, increasingly taking over from the family as children grow older. He argues schools provide a bridge between the 'particularistic' values and ascribed status of the family, and the 'universalistic', meritocratic values and achieved status of contemporary industrial societies.

Children's status in the family is ascribed and they are judged in terms of **particularistic values**. For example, their status is ascribed as a child and not an adult, or as a younger rather than an older brother or sister, and they are treated as special individuals and judged differently from everyone else outside the family. However, wider adult industrial society is meritocratic. People have to earn their status positions according to their individual achievements, such as talent, skill, or educational qualifications.

In this situation of achieved status, the same universalistic rules apply to everyone, regardless of who they are. For example, a teacher marking

Functional prerequisites refer to the basic needs that must be met if society is to survive.

The curriculum of a school or college is the formal content of subject lessons and examinations. The **hidden curriculum** concerns not so much the content of lessons as the way teaching and learning are organized. This includes the general routines of school life which influence and mould the attitudes and behaviour of students, such as the school rules, dress codes, obeying the authority of teachers, and so on.

Particularistic values are rules and values that give a priority to personal relationships.

Universalistic values are rules and values that apply equally to all members of society, regardless of who they are.

student essays might reasonably be expected to mark every essay by the same criteria (universalistic values), not give different marks depending on whether they liked the student or not (particularistic values), and those same students might be expected to achieve a place at university because of their exam grades, not because they knew someone who worked there.

Activity

1 Identify those features which make school life like a 'society in miniature', preparing people for wider society.
2 Parsons suggests that schooling provides a bridge between the family and wider adult society. Think about your own schooling, and the way that, as you moved from infant school through to the end of secondary schooling, teacher attitudes and the experience of schooling changed. Can you identify any evidence of a move from particularism to universalism?
3 Identify all the features of both the formal curriculum and the hidden curriculum, with examples, which transmit values and culture from one generation to the next. To what extent do you think those things learnt in school actually unite people in society?

---

3   Providing a trained and qualified labour force

The **division of labour** is the division of work or occupations into a large number of specialized tasks, each of which is carried out by one worker or a group of workers.

Functionalists see the expansion of schooling and higher education as necessary to provide a properly trained, qualified and flexible labour force to undertake the wide range of different jobs which arise from the specialized division of labour in a modern industrialized society. They argue the education system prepares this labour force, and makes sure the best and most qualified people end up in the jobs requiring the greatest skills and responsibilities.

4   Selecting and allocating people to roles in a meritocratic society, and legitimizing social inequality

For functionalists, like Davis and Moore (1945), the education system is a means of selecting or sifting people for different levels of the job market, and ensuring the most talented and qualified individuals are allocated to the most important jobs. By grading people through streaming and test and exam results, the education system is a major method of role allocation – fitting the most suitable people into the hierarchy of unequal positions in society.

In a meritocratic society, access to jobs, and the inequalities of wealth, status and power, depend mainly on educational qualifications and other skills and talents. Davis and Moore suggest that in this educational race for success there is equality of educational opportunity, and everyone who has the ability and talent and puts in the effort has an equal chance of coming out ahead. Inequalities in society are therefore legitimized – made to seem fair and just. Those who succeed deserve their success, and those who fail have only themselves to blame.

Table 5.1 summarizes some criticisms of the functionalist view of education.

Activity

To what extent do you think the school work you are doing, or did, and the qualifications you obtain(ed) at school might be preparing, or did prepare you, for doing a job? Identify, with examples, the links between your school subjects and exams and earning a living.

Marxist perspectives on education

Marxist perspectives on education emphasize the way the education system reproduces *existing* social class inequalities, and passes them on from one generation to the next. At the same time, it does this by giving the impression that those who fail in education do so because of their lack of ability and effort, and have only themselves to blame. In this way, people are encouraged to accept the positions they find themselves in after schooling, even though it is disadvantages arising from social class background that create inequalities in educational success.

The work of Althusser: education as an ideological state apparatus

The French Marxist Althusser (1971) saw the main role of education in a capitalist society as the reproduction of an efficient and obedient labour force. This involves two aspects:

- the reproduction of the necessary technical skills
- the reproduction of ruling class ideology (the dominant beliefs and values) and the socialization of workers into accepting this dominant ideology (this is known as false consciousness)

Althusser argues that to prevent the working class rebelling against their exploitation, the ruling class must try to win their hearts and minds by persuading them to accept ruling class ideology. This process of persuasion is carried out by a number of ideological state apparatuses, such as the family, the mass media, the law, religion and the education system. Althusser argues that in contemporary Western societies the main ideological state apparatus is the education system. The education system:

Ideological state apparatuses are agencies of the state which serve to spread the dominant ideology and justify the power of the dominant social class.

Table 5.1. Criticisms of the functionalist view of education

Functionalist view	Criticism
Education passes on society's culture from one generation to the next, including shared norms and values. These provide the 'social glue' which creates social solidarity and social cohesion.	*Marxists* would argue that this view ignores the inequalities in power in society. There is no value consensus, and the culture and values passed on by the school are those of the dominant or ruling class. *Feminists* might argue the school passes on patriarchal values, and disadvantages girls and women
Education provides a bridge between the particularistic values and ascribed status of the family and the universalistic values and achieved status of wider industrial society	There is some doubt about how far contemporary industrial society is really based on universalistic values and achieved status. Many in the upper class inherit wealth, and there are many 'elite' jobs where ascribed status characteristics such as social class, gender and ethnic background still have a very important influence
Education provides a trained and qualified labour force	The link between educational qualifications and pay and job status is a weak one, and certainly much weaker than functionalists assume. The content of what people learn in schools often has very little to do directly with what they actually do in their jobs. Collins (1972) argues most occupational skills are learned 'on the job' or through firms' own training schemes. The demand for educational qualifications for many occupations is simply an attempt to raise the status of the occupation, rather than providing the knowledge and skill requirements necessary for performing the job
Effective role selection and allocation. Education selects the 'right' people for the most suitable jobs in a meritocratic society	The education system does not act as a neutral 'sieve', simply grading and selecting students according to their ability. Social class, ethnicity and gender seem to be the major factors influencing success or failure in education. There is no equality of opportunity in education – everyone does not start at the same point, and not everyone has the same chance of success in education, even when they have the same ability
Education legitimizes social inequality	Bowles and Gintis (1976) (discussed later) argue that the education system simply disguises the fact that there is no equality of opportunity in education, and that it is social class, ethnicity and gender that are the main influences on educational success

- passes on ruling class ideology justifying the capitalist system
- selects people for the different social classes as adults, with the right attitudes and behaviour; for example, workers are persuaded to accept and submit to exploitation, and managers and administrators to rule

---

Activity

1 Refer to figure 5.2. Suggest the attitudes and values that might be required by those leaving the education system at different stages for different levels of employment.

2 Can you think of values or ideas that are passed on through the education system which might be in the interests of the dominant groups in society rather than in the interests of all?

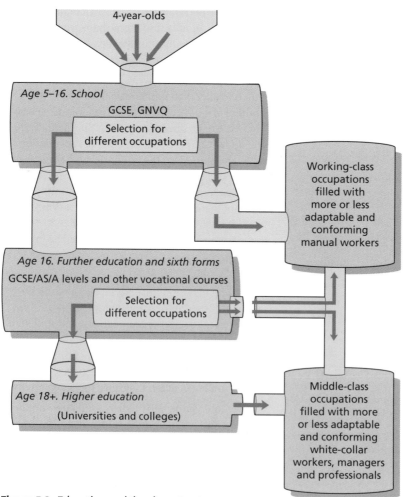

Figure 5.2 Education and the class structure

Bowles and Gintis: schooling and the 'long shadow of work'

In *Schooling in Capitalist America* Bowles and Gintis argue, like Althusser, that the major role of education in capitalist societies is the reproduction of labour power – a hard-working, and disciplined workforce. Bowles and Gintis argue that such a workforce is reproduced in two main ways:

1   Through the hidden curriculum of schooling and the correspondence, or very close similarity, between the social relationships at school and at work – in particular, the way schooling operates in the 'long shadow of work'.
2   Through the role of the education system in legitimizing or justifying inequality.

Schooling and the 'long shadow of work'   Bowles and Gintis argue that the hidden curriculum in schools corresponds closely to many features of the workplace. Table 5.2 illustrates some elements of this correspondence between the hidden curriculum at school and its links with relations at the workplace.

Table 5.2. The hidden curriculum

Features of the hidden curriculum	*What is being taught*
Privileges and responsibilities given to sixth formers	Respect for elders
School rules, detentions and exclusions, rewards like merit badges, prizes, good marks, etc.	Conformity to society's rules and laws, whether you agree with them or not
School assemblies	Respect for religious beliefs and the dominant moral values
Males and females often playing different sports, having different dress rules, and being counselled into different subjects, further education courses, and careers; many teachers having different expectations of boys and girls	Males and females being encouraged to conform to gender stereotypes and work in different jobs; for example, women being encouraged into taking primary responsibility for housework and childcare
Competitive sports and competition against each other in class rather than cooperating together; students being tested individually – being encouraged to rely on themselves rather than others	Workers having to compete for jobs and wages, and individuals having to stand on their own two feet – not joining with other workers to take action
Respecting authority of teachers regardless of what they say or do; pupils always having to justify where they're going and why, and do as they're told	Respect for those in authority, such as bosses at work and the police
Punctuality/being on time – time belonging to the school, not the pupil	Good time-keeping at work – the employer pays for the worker's time, so it belongs to the firm, not the worker

Table 5.2. (continued)

Features of the hidden curriculum	What is being taught
Concentrating on schoolwork, whether or not it's boring and whether or not you want to do it	Workers having to accept boring, menial and repetitive jobs
Value being placed on hard work and getting on	Everyone being able to make it to the top if she or he tries hard enough
Grading by ability, and exam success/failure	The differences in pay and status between social classes being natural and justified – those higher up are more intelligent and better qualified
Rewarding (by high grades) qualities of dependability, punctuality and acceptance of authority	Workers' duty to be dependable, be punctual and accept bosses' authority
Different streams and bands	Getting used to accepting the different levels of the job market, such as professional, managerial, skilled, semi-skilled and unskilled manual occupations, which are seen to be based on ability
Pupils lack power and control about the subjects taught or how the school is run or the school day organized	Workers' lack of power and control at work
The authority hierarchy of the school, involving pupils fitting into a complex organization of heads, deputies, heads of department, year heads, etc.	Messages about being placed in the hierarchies of power and control in society and accepting it – for example, in the authority hierarchy at work
The school curriculum being broken up into separate subjects which are clearly separated from one another	Work is divided into many separate jobs (the division of labour) which keeps the workforce from having knowledge of the whole process
Schools aim to motivate pupils by marks, grades and qualifications	Working for pay in unfulfilling and powerless jobs

---

Activity

1 Describe in detail five features of the hidden curriculum found in your school, or the one you once attended, which reflect the expectations of employers and the demands of the workplace after school.
2 Drawing on your own experiences at school, what features of your education do you think prepared/will prepare you most for life after school? Think of particular subjects studied and activities undertaken, and the features of the hidden curriculum in table 5.2 which were/are found in your school.
3 Using examples from your own school life, to what extent do you agree with Bowles and Gintis that 'schooling operates in the long shadow of work'?
4 The features of the hidden curriculum shown in table 5.2 are mainly influenced by Bowles and Gintis's Marxist approach. The functionalists also

> see the hidden curriculum as an important means of students being taught the culture and values of society so that a value consensus can be built and society can be kept stable and harmonious. Suggest ways that functionalist writers might alter the second column above ('What is being taught') to give it more of a functionalist than a Marxist 'flavour'.

The legitimation of inequality Bowles and Gintis argue that the educational system:

- helps to maintain, justify and explain (legitimate or legitimize) the system of social inequality of capitalist society
- helps people to come to terms with their own position in it
- and therefore helps to reduce discontent and opposition to inequality

Bowles and Gintis reject the functionalist view that social class inequalities in capitalist society arise from fair competition in education, in which everyone stands an equal chance. In contrast, they argue that social class background, ethnicity and sex are the main factors related to success or failure in education and the job market. People from upper and upper middle-class backgrounds (and who are white and male) tend to obtain higher qualifications and jobs than working-class children of similar ability. Bowles and Gintis see both equality of opportunity and meritocracy as myths that promote the idea that failure in education arises from lack of ability or hard work, when in most cases it arises because of social class and family background. Education is therefore seen as a kind of 'con trick' that hides the fact that it maintains and reproduces the existing pattern of social class inequalities between generations, and in most cases simply confirms individuals' class of origin (the one they were born into) as their class of destination (the one they end up in as adults).

Criticisms of Althusser and Bowles and Gintis

Althusser and Bowles and Gintis have been criticized on two main fronts:

- There is a lack of detailed research into schools. Althusser and Bowles and Gintis assume the hidden curriculum is actually influencing pupils, but pupils are often not passive recipients of education, and often have little regard for teachers' authority and school rules and discipline (as Willis's research below shows).
- Bowles and Gintis ignore the influence of the formal curriculum. This does not seem designed to promote the ideal employee for capitalism, and develop uncritical, passive behaviour. The humanities and subjects like sociology produce critical thinkers, while work-related courses remain of relatively low status. Employers often complain that

the education system does not produce well-qualified workers with suitable skills.

The work of Willis

Paul Willis's work, *Learning to Labour: How Working Class Kids Get Working Class Jobs* (1977), helps to overcome some of the weaknesses of more traditional Marxist approaches like those of Althusser and Bowles and Gintis. Willis adopts a Marxist approach, but also draws on the interactionist perspective.

Willis recognizes that schools do not produce a willing and obedient workforce – a quick glance at almost any secondary school provides evidence that students do not always obey teachers, that they can be disruptive and challenge the school. Willis says it is easy to understand why middle-class young people willingly go into secure and well-paid middle-class career jobs, but what is more difficult to explain is why working-class young people go so willingly into dead-end, low paid and boring manual working-class jobs.

Willis studied a group of twelve working-class male pupils he referred to as 'the lads' in a school on a working-class housing estate in Wolverhampton in the 1970s. The 'lads' developed an **anti-school** or **counter-school subculture** opposed both to the main aims of the school, and to the 'ear 'oles' – conformist pupils who generally conformed to school values. 'The lads' attached little value to the aims of the school, such as gaining qualifications, and their main priority was to free themselves from control by the school, to avoid or disrupt lessons, to have a 'laff' and to get into the world of work as soon as possible.

> An **anti-school** or **counter-school subculture** is a group organized around a set of values, attitudes and behaviour in opposition to the main aims of a school.

Rejecting schooling and wanting to leave school as soon as they could and escape from the 'pen-pushing' of the 'ear 'oles', the 'lads' did not see school as relevant to them. Their priorities were to get their hands on money, to impress their mates, to keep up with older drinkers in the pub, to impress the girls, and to show they could 'graft' in male manual jobs as well as the next man.

In this context, school was boring, pointless and irrelevant to their lives, and stopped them smoking, drinking, going out at night, getting a job and cash, and involving themselves in the 'real' world of male, manual work.

Willis found a similarity between the counter-school culture and the workplace culture of male lower working-class jobs, such as **sexism**, a lack of respect for authority and an emphasis on 'having a laff' to escape the boring and oppressive nature of both school and work.

> **Sexism** refers to prejudice or discrimination against people, especially women, because of their sex.

Willis's research suggests that schools are not directly preparing the sort of obedient and docile labour force required by capitalism which Althusser and Bowles and Gintis suggest. Young, working-class males are not forced or persuaded by the school to leave and look for manual jobs, but actively *reject* school through the counter-school culture and willingly enter male semi-skilled and unskilled work the minute they leave school.

Activity

1   To what extent do you think Willis's research might be true of all schools? Do you think there are any reasons why there might be uncertainty about this given the size of Willis's study?
2   What evidence is/was there at your own school of an anti-school or counter-school subculture like that of 'the lads'? Give examples of the types of behaviour displayed by such students, and suggest reasons for it.

A comparison of functionalist and Marxist perspectives on education

Similarities and differences

The functionalist and Marxist views of education have a number of similarities:

- Both see schools playing a role in legitimizing (justifying and explaining) social inequality.
- Both are 'macro' (large-scale) theories concerned with the structural relationship between education and other parts of the social system, such as the economy and social inequality.
- Both see education as serving the 'needs' of industrial and/or capitalist society.
- Both see the education system as a powerful influence on students, ensuring they conform to existing social values and norms.

But they have differences too, summarized in table 5.3 overleaf.

Criticisms of both perspectives

- They both give too much emphasis to the role of education in forming students' identity, and they pay too little attention to the influences of other agencies of socialization, such as the family, the mass media and work.
- They don't fully consider the way students react to schooling in ways that aren't necessarily 'functional' for the social system or capitalism. For example, pupils disrupt schools, play truant and don't learn, and workers go on strike. (However, note the exception of Willis's work here.)
- They both see too tight a link between education and the economy, and exaggerate the extent to which schools provide a ready, willing

Table 5.3. Differences between the functionalist and Marxist perspectives on education

Functionalism	*Marxism*
Education serves the needs of an *industrial* society with an advanced division of labour	Education serves the needs of a capitalist society divided into social classes
Education serves the 'needs' of the social system by socializing new generations into society's culture and shared norms and values, leading to social harmony, stability and social integration	Education serves the 'needs' of capitalism by socializing children into the dominant ideology (ruling class norms and values), leading to an obedient workforce and the stability of capitalism
The hidden curriculum helps to prepare society's future citizens for participation in a society based on value consensus	The hidden curriculum helps to persuade society's future citizens to accept the dominant ideology and their position in a society based on inequality, exploitation and conflict
Education provides a means for upward social mobility for those who have the ability	With the exception of a few individuals, education confirms individuals' class of origin (the one they were born into) as their class of destination (the one they end up in as adults). Education therefore contributes to the reproduction of present class inequalities between generations, and does not provide a means of upward social mobility for most people
Education justifies and explains (legitimizes) social inequality, as roles are allocated according to meritocratic criteria such as educational qualifications, in a society in which all have equality of opportunity	Education legitimizes social class inequality by persuading working-class individuals to accept that their lack of power and control at work and in society generally is due to their lack of academic ability, effort and achievement, when in fact they do not have the same opportunities as those who are more advantaged

and qualified labour force. The new emphasis on vocational education and pressure to drive up school standards is a direct response to employers who criticized schools for *not* providing a suitably disciplined and qualified labour force.

Interactionist perspectives on education

Interactionist perspectives study small-scale activities and focus more on what actually happens within schools and classrooms. They are interested in how students come to be defined in particular ways, for example as 'good' or 'bad' students, and the consequences that arise from these definitions. These approaches will be discussed later in this chapter, but it is worth noting that these micro or small-scale detailed studies are a contrast to the macro or large-scale structuralist approaches of functionalism and Marxism.

Activity

1   Suggest three ways in which schooling prepares young people for the world of work.
2   Explain what is meant by the legitimization of social class inequality, and suggest two ways in which schooling might do this.
3   Identify and explain two ways in which the educational system contributes to the economy.
4   Explain what is meant by the 'hidden curriculum', and suggest two ways this might prepare children for adult life.
5   In about two sides of A4 paper, answer the following question:
    Assess the view that the main role of education is the reproduction of social class inequalities from one generation to the next.

Is contemporary Britain a meritocracy?

Functionalist writers like Parsons have suggested the education system and society as a whole are based on the principles of meritocracy and equality of opportunity.

In a meritocracy, educational achievements and qualifications should be based only on the ability, skills and hard work of individuals, and everyone should have an equal opportunity to develop whatever skills and talents she or he may have. Factors like social class background, ethnicity, gender or disability should present no obstacle to an individual in developing to the full whatever talents they have.

There is evidence, however, that Britain is not meritocratic, and that social inequality is not based simply on different levels of educational achievement. For example, people with the same educational qualifications often earn vastly different amounts, and the link between educational qualifications and pay levels is relatively weak. Marxists like Bowles and Gintis and many non-Marxists argue that there is no real equality of opportunity in education, and that what the education system really does is to maintain and reproduce existing social class, ethnic and gender inequalities from one generation to the next.

The evidence for this lack of equality of opportunity in education is that, even for students of the same ability, there are wide differences in educational achievement which are closely linked to the social class origins of students, and their gender and ethnic characteristics.

The following sections look at the evidence for these inequalities in educational opportunity and achievement, and seek explanations for them.

Natural intelligence or IQ

Some argue that some people are simply born more 'intelligent' than others – they have more innate (inborn) natural intelligence and this explains the underachievement in education of some social groups.

However, sociologists have generally been very critical of the notion of innate intelligence and the accuracy of the IQ (intelligence quotient) tests used to measure this. This is because there is a social pattern of underachievement along the lines of social class, ethnicity and gender, and a far more random pattern would be expected if intelligence was simply a product of biological differences. Biological explanations underestimate the importance of material and cultural factors both in forming intelligence and in the patterns of educational achievement. Table 5.4 summarizes the

> **Underachievement** is the failure of people to fulfil their potential – they do not do as well in education (or other areas) as their talents and abilities suggest they should.

Table 5.4. Arguments for and against the view that natural intelligence explains differences in educational achievement

For	Against
Intelligence is inborn, and is inherited from parents	It is impossible to separate inborn intelligence from environmental factors, and the intellectual development of even very young children will be affected by the stimuli they are exposed to, such as space to play, diet, toys, family income, housing, and interaction with parents, which will influence the way intelligence develops
Intelligence can be measured by IQ tests	IQ tests are bound to be affected by the culture in which people grow up – for example, whether they are used to working individually, or under timed test conditions. Performance in IQ tests can be affected by factors other than intelligence, such as how people react in a test situation, whether they care or not, how they're feeling at the time, their state of health, whether they've had practice or not, and so on. IQ tests are simply testing how good people are at doing them, and this is influenced by early learning and socialization
Intelligence is fixed and can't be changed	IQ tests tell us nothing about people's potential. A stimulating environment, early years education in a playgroup or nursery, and formal education, or a lack of it, can improve or diminish intelligence. There are many instances where people with a low early IQ score go on to achieve educational success, and where people with a high IQ score do not achieve success
High measured intelligence leads to high levels of educational achievement and occupational success	People with similar IQ scores from different backgrounds do not show similar levels of educational and occupational success. Material and cultural factors, and the ways teachers treat pupils with a high IQ score differently from those with a low score, explain these differences, not innate ability

arguments for and against the notion that inborn intelligence explains differences in educational achievement.

Social class differences in educational achievement

Social class is the key factor influencing whether a child does well or badly at school. There are major differences between the levels of achievement of the working class and middle class and, in general, the higher the social class of the parents, the more successful a child will be in education. The degree of social class inequality in education begins in the primary school and becomes greater as children move upward through the education system, with the higher levels of the education system dominated by middle-class and upper-class students.

A comparison of social class differences in educational achievement

When students from the lower working class have been compared to middle-class children of the same ability, it has been found that:

- They are more likely to start school unable to read.
- They do less well in tests like the National Curriculum SATs.
- They are less likely to get places in the best state schools. In 2005, only 3 per cent of those attending state schools which were in the top 200 for performance received free school meals – the standard poverty indicator used in schools – compared to 17 per cent nationally.
- They are more likely to be placed in lower streams.
- They generally get poorer exam results. For example, around three-quarters of young people from upper middle-class backgrounds get five or more GCSEs *A–C, compared to less than a third from lower working-class backgrounds.
- They are more likely to leave school at the minimum leaving age of 16, many of them with few or no qualifications of any kind. Only about half of young people from unskilled manual families stay on in post-16 full-time education, compared to about nine in every ten from managerial and professional families.
- They are more likely to undertake vocational or training courses if they stay in education after 16, rather than the more academic AS- and A-level courses, which are more likely to be taken by middle-class students.
- They are less likely to go into higher education. In 2002 about 77 per cent of university students came from middle-class backgrounds, even though only just over half of the population was middle class. Young people from unskilled backgrounds are less than a quarter as likely to enter higher education as those from upper middle-class professional backgrounds.

Explaining social class differences in educational achievement

There is a range of factors that sociologists have identified in explaining the pattern of differences in educational achievement (figure 5.3). These can be grouped into three main categories:

- material explanations, which put the emphasis on social and economic conditions
- cultural explanations, which focus on values, attitudes and lifestyles
- factors within the school itself

The following sections mainly focus on social class differences, though some of these differences will also be referred to later in discussing gender and ethnic group differences.

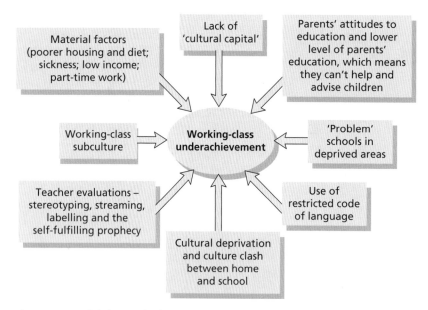

Figure 5.3 Social class and educational achievement

Material explanations

Although schooling and further education are free (though there are fees for higher education), material factors like poverty and low wages, diet, health and housing can all have important direct effects on how well individuals do at school. Indicators of social deprivation like these make an important contribution to explaining the pattern of working-class underachievement in education.

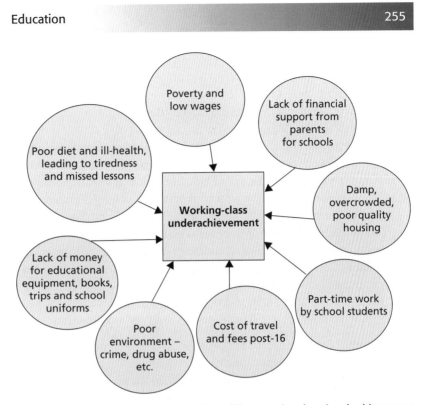

Figure 5.4 Material factors explaining class differences in educational achievement

Poverty and home circumstances   These are some of the factors in a child's background that can affect their chances in education:

- Douglas found in early research in *The Home and the School* (1964) that poor housing conditions such as overcrowding and insufficient space and quiet can make study at home difficult.
- Poorer diets and higher levels of sickness in disadvantaged homes may mean tiredness at school, making learning more difficult, and more absence and falling behind with lessons.
- Low income or unemployment may mean that educational books and toys are not bought, and computers are not available in the home. This may affect a child's educational progress before or during her or his time at school. There may also be a lack of money for out-of-school trips, sports equipment, calculators and other 'hidden costs' of free state education.
- It may be financially difficult for parents on a low income to support students in education after school-leaving age. This is particularly the case in further education, where there are few grants available and there may be travel costs involved. In higher education, student grants have been replaced by student loans, and tuition fees are

payable, and these are likely to be a source of anxiety to those from poorer backgrounds, deterring them from going to university.

- Poorer parents are less likely to have access to pre-school or nursery facilities, which may affect their children's development compared to those who have such access.
- Young people from poorer families are more likely to have part-time jobs, such as paper rounds, babysitting or shop work. This becomes more pronounced after the age of 16, when students may be combining part- or full-time work with school or college work. This may create a conflict between the competing demands of study and paid work.
- Schools themselves in poorer areas may suffer disadvantages compared to those in more affluent middle-class areas. For example, many schools today rely on support from parents to finance extra resources for the school, and parents in poorer areas are less likely to be able to raise as much as those in more middle-class areas. This will mean schools in poorer areas will have less to spend on pupil activities.

The effects of these material factors tend to be cumulative, in the sense that one aspect of social deprivation can lead to others. For example, poverty may mean overcrowding at home *and* ill-health *and* having to find part-time work, making all the problems worse. The cartoon illustrates this.

The catchment area   Catchment areas (or priority areas) are the areas from which primary and secondary schools draw their pupils. In deprived areas, where there may be a range of social problems such as high unemployment, poverty, juvenile delinquency, crime, and drug abuse, there are often poor role models for young people to imitate. The accumulated effects of the environment on children's behaviour mean schools in such areas are more likely to have discipline problems that prevent students

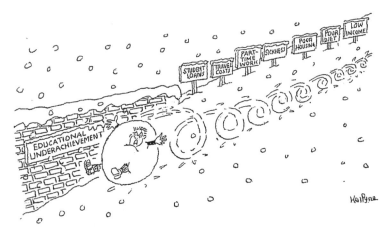

The effects of social deprivation on educational achievement are cumulative

from learning, and a higher turnover of teachers. This may mean children from the most disadvantaged backgrounds have the 'worst' schools. In contrast, schools in middle-class neighbourhoods will probably have stronger and more conformist role models for young people, have fewer discipline problems and therefore offer a better learning environment.

Material explanations therefore have a major impact in explaining the underachievement of many children from poorer backgrounds. This was confirmed by research by Gibson and Asthana (1999), which found that the greater the level of family disadvantage, measured in terms of lack of parents' qualifications, unemployment, and not owning a car or house, the smaller the percentage of students gaining five or more GCSEs at grades *A to C.

Cultural explanations – cultural deprivation

Cultural explanations of underachievement in education suggest that the values, attitudes, language, and other aspects of the life of some social groups is deficient or deprived in various ways in relation to the white, middle-class culture of the education system. This is known as **cultural deprivation**, and places the blame for educational underachievement on young people's socialization in the family and community, and on the cultural values with which they are raised.

> **Cultural deprivation** is the idea that some young people fail in education because of supposed deficiencies in their home and family background, such as inadequate socialization, failings in pre-school learning, inadequate language skills and inappropriate attitudes and values.

Parents' attitudes to education   Douglas found the single most important factor explaining educational success and failure was the degree of parental

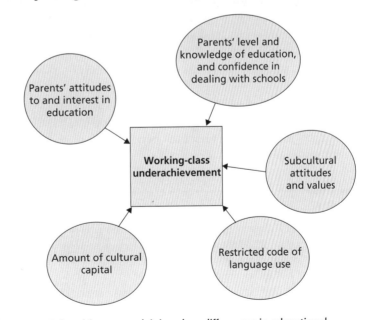

Figure 5.5 Cultural factors explaining class differences in educational achievement

interest and encouragement in their children's education. He found that middle-class parents, compared to working-class parents, on the whole:

- took more interest in their children's progress at school, as indicated by more frequent visits to the school to discuss their children's progress
- became relatively more interested and encouraging as the children grew older, when exam options are selected and career choices loom
- were more likely to want their children to stay at school beyond the minimum leaving age and to encourage them to do so

Parents' level of education   Because they are generally themselves better educated, middle-class parents tend to understand the school system better than working-class parents. Lower working-class parents may feel less confident in dealing with teachers at parents' evenings, and in dealing with subject options and exam choices. Middle-class parents know more about schools, the examination system and careers and so are more able to advise and counsel their children on getting into the most appropriate subjects and courses. They can 'hold their own' more in disagreements with teachers (who are also middle-class) about the treatment and educational progress of their child; they know more about complaints procedures, and fighting sex discrimination against their daughters; they know which educational toys, games and books to buy, or 'cultural' events to go to, to stimulate their children's educational development both before and during schooling (and they have the money to pay for them); and they can help their children with school work generally. As a consequence, even before they get to school middle-class children may have learned more as a result of their socialization in the family. These advantages of a middle-class home may be reinforced throughout a child's career in the education system.

Sub-cultural explanations   These explanations suggest that different social classes have some different values, attitudes and lifestyles, or different subcultures, and that these affect the performance of children in the educational system.

> A **subculture** is a smaller culture held by a group or class of people within the main culture of a society, in some ways different from the main culture, but with many aspects in common.

Activity

1 Identify some subcultures in contemporary Britain, and describe the ways you think their values, attitudes and lifestyles might differ from 'mainstream' culture. An example of such a subculture might be that of travellers (but think of your own examples too).
2 Do you think working-class people and middle-class people have different subcultures? Suggest ways in which the attitudes and values of these two social classes might differ.

Table 5.5. Class subcultures and educational achievement

Class	Subculture	Effects on educational achievement
Middle class	In middle-class jobs, the promise of career progress through individual effort and educational qualifications leads to a *future orientation* (planning for the future) and *deferred gratification* (putting off today's pleasures for future gains). *Individual effort* and intelligence are seen as the key to success	Children are socialized into values and attitudes which encourage ambition and educational success. A *future orientation* and *deferred gratification* creates a recognition of the need for individual hard work, staying in and doing homework, and staying on in further/ higher education in order to get the qualifications needed for career success. *Individual effort* is seen as providing the key to educational success
Working class	In working-class jobs, educational qualifications are often not very important for work. The lack of promotion opportunities leads to a *present-time orientation* (a lack of emphasis on long-term goals and future planning), *immediate gratification* (getting pleasures now, rather than putting them off for the future), and *fatalism* (an acceptance of the situation rather than attempts to improve it). Working together (*collectivism* through trade unions) provides more gains than individual effort	Children are socialized into general sets of values and attitudes which don't encourage ambition and educational success. *Immediate gratification*, a *present-time orientation* and *fatalism* discourage effort for future rewards, such as exam success. Leaving school and obtaining a skill/getting a job and money are seen as more important than educational qualifications. *Loyalty to the group* (collectivism) discourages the individual effort and achievement which success at school demands

Two main researchers have developed these subcultural explanations: the British sociologist Sugarman (1970) and the American H.H. Hyman (1967). Table 5.5, based on the work of Hyman and Sugarman, shows how the different values and attitudes of the middle class and working class might influence children's progress in school.

Language use and educational achievement: Bernstein and the restricted and elaborated codes   Success in education depends very heavily on language – for reading, writing, speaking and understanding. The ability to read and understand books, to write clearly, and to be able to explain yourself fully in both speech and writing are key language skills required for success in education. If these skills are not developed through discussion, negotiation and explanation in the family, then such children will be disadvantaged in education.

Bernstein (1971) has argued that there are two types of language use, which he calls the 'elaborated code' and the 'restricted code'. It is middle-class children's familiarity with the elaborated code that gives them a better chance of success in education.

- The restricted code is the sort of language which is used between friends or family members – informal, simple, everyday language (such as slang), sometimes ungrammatical and with limited explanation and vocabulary. The restricted code is quite adequate for everyday use with family or friends because they know what the speaker is referring to – the context is understood by both speakers and so detailed explanation is not required. The restricted code is used by both middle-class and working-class people, but Bernstein argues lower working-class people are mainly limited to this form of language use.

- The elaborated code is the sort of language which is used by strangers and individuals in some formal context, where explanation and detail are required, such as that used by teachers in the classroom when they are explaining things, or in an interview for a job, writing a business letter, writing an essay or an examination answer, or in a school lesson or textbook. It has a much wider vocabulary than the restricted code. According to Bernstein, the elaborated code is used mainly by middle-class people.

Bernstein argues that the language used in schools is the elaborated code of the middle class. It is this that gives the middle-class student an advantage at school over working-class children, since understanding textbooks, writing essays and examination questions, and class discussions

> The **restricted code** is the informal, simple, everyday language, sometimes ungrammatical and with limited explanations and vocabulary, which is used between friends or family members.

> The **elaborated code** is the sort of formal language used by strangers and individuals in some formal contexts where explanation and detail are required, and uses a much wider vocabulary than the restricted code.

require the detail and explanation which is found mainly in the formal language of the elaborated code. Middle-class children who are used to using the elaborated code at home will therefore find school work easier and learn more than those working-class children whose language experience is limited only to the restricted code. The cartoon illustrates these two different types of language use.

Bernstein's work has been subject to a number of criticisms:

- Bernstein tends to put all the middle class together as having equal use of the elaborated code, but there are wide differences between the higher and lower sections of the middle class. A similar point can be made about higher and lower sections of the working class and the use of the restricted code. It is difficult to generalize about all working-class and middle-class families, and there is likely to be a diversity of arrangements in the way language is used in the family.
- Rosen argues that Bernstein gives few examples to back up his claims of the existence of restricted and elaborated codes. He accuses Bernstein of creating a myth of the superiority of middle-class speech.
- Labov (1973) is very critical of the notion that working-class speech is in any way inferior to that of the middle class. Based on his research in Harlem, in New York, Labov claims they are simply different.

Bourdieu's theory of cultural capital   Bourdieu (1971) was a French Marxist, who saw the culture of the school as giving an inbuilt advantage to middle-class children.

Bourdieu argues that each social class possesses its own cultural framework or set of ideas, which he calls a habitus.

> A **habitus** is the cultural framework and set of ideas possessed by a social class, into which people are socialized and which influences their cultural tastes and choices.

This cultural framework contains ideas about what counts as 'good' and 'bad' taste, 'good' books, newspapers, TV programmes and so on. This habitus is picked up through socialization in the family. The dominant class has the power to impose its own habitus in the education system, so what counts as educational knowledge is not the 'culture of society as a whole', but that of the dominant social class.

Those who come from better-off middle- and upper-class backgrounds have more access to the culture of the dominant class. Bourdieu calls this advantage cultural capital.

> **Cultural capital** is the knowledge, language, manners and forms of behaviour, attitudes and values, taste and lifestyle which gives middle-class and upper-class students who possess them an inbuilt advantage in a middle-class controlled education system.

Possession of cultural capital gives greatly improved chances of success in education, and can be turned into educational capital (educational qualifications), and this can in turn lead to possession of economic capital (material advantages like a high income).

Upper- and middle-class children are more successful in education because they possess more cultural capital. Those from the working class are more likely to fail exams, to be pushed into lower status educational

Cultural capital in action

streams or courses, or to drop out or be pushed out of the educational system, because they lack cultural capital.

Bourdieu therefore suggests that, while the schooling process appears to be 'neutral' and fair, because schools measure all pupils against the same culture and knowledge, it is not really neutral at all because the culture of the educational system is that of the dominant class, which middle-class children already possess – and working-class children lack – through socialization in the family.

Activity

1 How do you think your family background helped or didn't help you in making progress in education?
2 Refer to the cartoon. Identify all the cultural features you can which might encourage success in education, and explain how the cartoon illustrates the concept of cultural capital.
3 What 'cultural capital' and skills do you think are important for success in education? Draw up a list of these, and explain in each case how they might help in schooling.

Criticisms of cultural explanations

Cultural explanations place the blame for educational underachievement on the home and family background, with the culture of the lower working class seen as deficient or deprived in various ways compared to that of the middle class. For example, the working class lacks the attitudes and values, the necessary language skills or the cultural capital which are important

---

The culture clash

Cultural explanations suggest that schools are mainly middle-class institutions, and they stress the value of many features of the middle-class way of life, such as the importance of hard work and study, making sacrifices now for future rewards (deferred gratification), the elaborated code of language, 'good' books, good TV programmes, 'quality' newspapers and so on. School for the middle-class child often represents an extension of earlier home experiences, while for the working-class child there may be a clash between home and school. Middle-class children therefore arrive at school with the cultural capital enabling them to be more 'tuned in' to the demands of schooling, such as the subjects that will be explored there, seeking good marks, doing homework, showing good behaviour and a cooperative attitude to teachers, and other features of middle-class culture. Consequently, they may appear to teachers as 'more intelligent' and more sophisticated, promising students. By contrast, working-class children may face a difference and conflict between the values of the home and those of school. This is known as the culture clash.

---

for educational success. However, there have been a number of criticisms of these cultural explanations of working-class underachievement:

Exaggeration   They tend to exaggerate the differences and downplay the similarities between the attitudes and beliefs of the different social classes.

Overlooking practical difficulties and lack of self-confidence   Many working-class parents are very concerned and ambitious for their children's success in education. Douglas, for example, used measures of 'parental interest' based on teachers' comments about parents' attitudes, and the number of times parents visited schools. However, manual workers work longer hours, have less flexibility and choice in their working hours, do more shift work, get less time off with pay, and are less educated than teachers and many other members of the middle class. Not visiting a school may not be evidence of a lack of interest or encouragement by working-class parents, but of the material constraints of their jobs, and a lack of confidence arising from their own lack of education, which prevent them turning parental interest into *practical* support in the way middle-class parents can.

Ignoring the role played by schools themselves   Schools do not simply 'process' children whose attitudes and ambitions are pre-formed in the family, but play an active part in forming those attitudes and ambitions. Middle-class students may perform better because they receive more praise and encouragement from teachers, as they are more 'in tune' with teachers. Blaming the family and social class background can lead to low expectations by teachers and may encourage some teachers and schools to label lower working-class children as 'born to fail', and therefore to neglect their needs. This 'not worth bothering' approach and the resulting self-fulfilling prophecy, rather than so-called cultural deprivation, may lead to the poor performance of some children in school. These issues are discussed shortly.

The need for schools to change　If there is a 'culture clash' for working-class children going to school, then rather than blaming their family and social class background, schools should be pressed to improve the situation. Keddie in *Tinker, Tailor . . . the Myth of Cultural Deprivation* (1973) argues that there is no cultural deprivation, but merely a cultural difference. She suggests that the idea of cultural deprivation fails to recognize the cultural strengths of those said to be deprived. The problem arises because education is based on white middle-class culture, which disadvantages those from other backgrounds. It is not that the working class is in some ways 'deficient', but that the school is failing to meet the needs of working-class children and to recognize their culture as worthwhile. Explanations for class differences in educational achievement should therefore focus more on the nature of what happens inside the school, and the cultural values it promotes.

Compensatory education and positive discrimination

Cultural deprivation theories suggest that for all young people to have an equal chance in the educational system, those from culturally deprived backgrounds need extra help and resources to help them compete on equal terms with other children. This idea of extra help is known as compensatory education, and involves positive discrimination.

Schools in disadvantaged areas, where home and social class background are seen as obstacles to success in education, are singled out for extra favourable treatment, such as more, and better-paid teachers and more money to spend on buildings and equipment, to help the most disadvantaged succeed in education.

The idea of positive discrimination is based on the idea of equality of educational opportunity. In this view, children from disadvantaged backgrounds and poor homes can only get an opportunity in education equal to those who come from non-disadvantaged backgrounds if they get unequal and more generous treatment to compensate.

Compensatory education is extra educational help for those coming from disadvantaged groups to help them overcome the disadvantages they face in the education system and the wider society.
Positive discrimination involves giving disadvantaged groups more favourable treatment than others to make up for the disadvantages they face.

Educational Priority Areas and Education Action Zones　In Britain, compensatory education first began in the 1970s with the setting up of

Educational Priority Areas in socially disadvantaged areas. These were discontinued in the early 1980s, but re-emerged in a modified form in the late 1990s in the form of Education Action Zones.

Educational Priority Areas were abandoned in the 1980s because compensatory education didn't really succeed in improving educational achievement. An Ofsted report in 2003 found that Education Action Zone schools were succeeding in improving schools in disadvantaged areas, with better attendance and fewer exclusions, and rising levels of educational achievement. There were more opportunities for young people, who had higher aspirations, confidence and self-esteem. However, improvements in educational achievement were much greater in primary schools, and Ofsted said educational achievements in some Education Action Zone secondary schools 'often remain very low and give cause for continuing concern'.

Education Action Zones became Excellence in Cities Action Zones (EiCAZs) in 2005.

There are many attempts being made to overcome the disadvantages that young people from deprived communities face in achieving success in education. Material and cultural disadvantages have many complex causes, and solutions are likely to take a number of years, and involve a wide range of social policies to reduce the poverty, low income and ill-health that underlie much educational failure. It still remains to be seen how successful these programmes of compensatory education will be, but previous experience would suggest that schools alone cannot compensate for inequalities of educational opportunity arising from inequalities in society as a whole.

Activity

1 Go to the following websites, www.standards.dfes.gov.uk/sie/eic and www.standards.dfes.gov.uk and identify three policies which are currently being followed to improve educational opportunities in the most disadvantaged communities. Explain in each case how these might improve educational opportunities.

2 Suggest three *material* factors in pupils' home and family background that may affect how successful they are in education.

3 Explain what is meant by 'immediate gratification' and 'fatalism', and how these might affect working-class pupils' educational achievements.

4 Explain, with examples, what is meant by a 'culture clash' between the home and the school.

5 Identify three *cultural* factors that may affect pupils' educational achievements.

6 Identify two ways in which a school's catchment area might influence the education of pupils from the area.

7 Suggest three criticisms of cultural explanations for underachievement in education.

Factors inside the school – the interactionist perspective

The explanations of working-class underachievement discussed so far have centred largely on the structural material and cultural factors outside the school that shape children before and during schooling. It is almost as if those from upper- and middle-class backgrounds are born to succeed in education, while those from the most disadvantaged, poor backgrounds are born to fail.

However, many would argue that schools can make a difference to the life chances of students whatever their backgrounds, as for example Rutter's work has suggested (see the box on 'Do schools make a difference?').

Much research has suggested that social patterns of underachievement in education are affected by what goes on in school classrooms, and how the meanings constructed there – how teachers and students come to see each other – affect student progress. For example, it is possible that socio-logical evidence demonstrating a link between working-class origin and

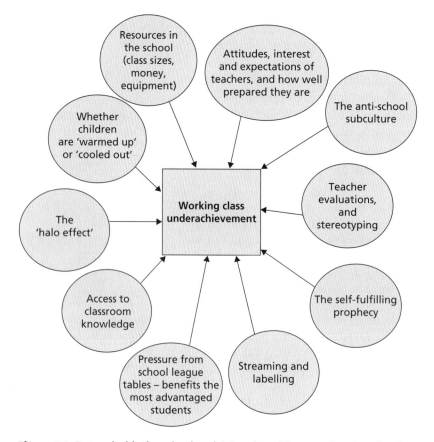

Figure 5.6 Factors inside the school explaining class differences in educational achievement

underachievement may have led teachers to expect working-class pupils to perform poorly, and these low expectations may actually be an important factor contributing to their failure.

Do schools make a difference?

Michael Rutter and his colleagues in *Fifteen Thousand Hours: Secondary Schools and their Effects on Children* (1979) reported research that showed, in the face of much previous research suggesting the opposite, that 'good' schools can make a difference to the life chances of all pupils. Rutter suggested that it is features of the school's organization which make this difference. These positive features are summarized below:

- Teachers are well prepared for lessons.
- Teachers have high expectations of pupils' academic performance, and set and mark classwork and homework regularly.
- Teachers set examples of behaviour; for example, they are on time and they use only officially approved forms of discipline.
- Teachers place more emphasis on praise and reward than on blame and punishment.
- Teachers treat pupils as responsible people, for example by giving them positions of responsibility looking after school books and property.
- Teachers show an interest in the pupils and encourage them to do well.
- There is an atmosphere or ethos in the school which reflects the above points, with all teachers sharing a commitment to the aims and values of the school.
- There is a mixture of abilities in the school, as the presence of high ability pupils benefits the academic performance and behaviour of pupils of all abilities.

Activity

Refer to the box above.

1 Explain how you think each of the features of a 'good' school which Rutter and his colleagues describe might or might not help pupils of all backgrounds and abilities to make more progress.
2 Do you agree or disagree with Rutter's features of a 'good' school? Are there any other features that you would expect to find in a 'good' school or college? Give reasons for your answer.
3 List at least six characteristics, based on your own opinions and reading, of a 'good teacher'.
4 How important do you think the role of the school and teachers is in the educational progress of pupils compared to the material and cultural factors discussed earlier in this chapter?

Much of the research in this area is based on the Interactionist perspective. From this perspective, pupils are not seen simply as passive 'victims' of structural material or cultural forces outside the school which cause underachievement. On the contrary, the emphasis is on the way, through interaction with others, teachers or pupils come to interpret and define situations, and develop meanings which influence the way they behave.

Teacher evaluations, stereotyping, labelling and the self-fulfilling prophecy   Teachers are constantly involved in judging and classifying pupils in various ways, such as 'bright' or 'slow', as 'troublemakers' or ideal pupils, or as hardworking or lazy. This process of classification or *labelling* by teachers has been shown to affect the performance of students. The stereotype held by the teacher (good/bad or thick/bright student and so on) can produce a 'halo effect'.

> A **halo effect** is when pupils become stereotyped on the basis of earlier impressions, and these impressions colour future teacher–student relations.

Writers such as Hargreaves (1976), Cicourel and Kitsuse (1971), Becker (1971) and Keddie (1971) found teachers initially evaluate pupils in relation to their stereotypes of the 'ideal pupil'. A whole range of non-academic factors such as speech, dress, personality (how cooperative, polite and so on), enthusiasm for work, conduct and appearance make up this stereotype of the 'ideal pupil', and influence teachers' assessments of students' ability. The social class of the student has an important influence on this evaluation. Students from working-class homes are often seen as being poorly motivated and lacking support from the home, and showing disruptive behaviour in the classroom. This may mean they are perceived by teachers as lacking ability, even if they are very able. By contrast, those from middle-class backgrounds most closely fit the teacher's 'ideal pupil' stereotype, and teachers may assume that children who enter school already confident, fluent and familiar with learning, who are more likely to be from middle-class homes, have greater potential and will push them to achieve accordingly.

The way teachers assess and evaluate students affects achievement levels, as pupils may gradually bring their own self-image in line with the one the teacher holds of them ('what's the point in trying – the teacher thinks I'm thick'). Those labelled as 'bright' and likely to be successful in education are more likely to perform in line with the teachers' expectations and predictions, while those labelled as 'slow', 'difficult' or of 'low ability' and unlikely to succeed are persuaded not to bother. In both cases, the teachers' predictions may come true. This suggests the difference between 'bright' and 'slow' or 'good' and 'bad' students, and the progress they make in school, are created by the processes of typing and labelling. This is the self-fulfilling prophecy, which is illustrated in figure 5.7.

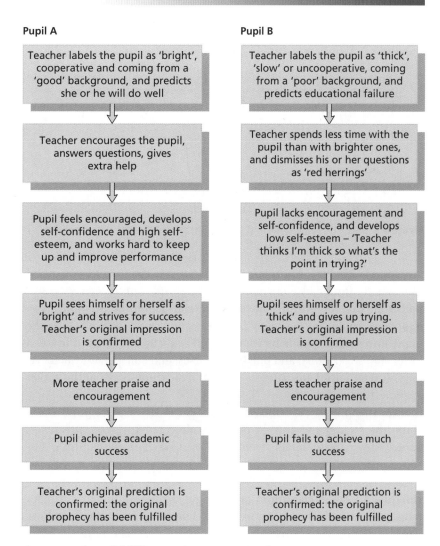

Pupil A

Teacher labels the pupil as 'bright', cooperative and coming from a 'good' background, and predicts she or he will do well

⬇

Teacher encourages the pupil, answers questions, gives extra help

⬇

Pupil feels encouraged, develops self-confidence and high self-esteem, and works hard to keep up and improve performance

⬇

Pupil sees himself or herself as 'bright' and strives for success. Teacher's original impression is confirmed

⬇

More teacher praise and encouragement

⬇

Pupil achieves academic success

⬇

Teacher's original prediction is confirmed: the original prophecy has been fulfilled

Pupil B

Teacher labels the pupil as 'thick', 'slow' or uncooperative, coming from a 'poor' background, and predicts educational failure

⬇

Teacher spends less time with the pupil than with brighter ones, and dismisses his or her questions as 'red herrings'

⬇

Pupil lacks encouragement and self-confidence, and develops low self-esteem – 'Teacher thinks I'm thick so what's the point in trying?'

⬇

Pupil sees himself or herself as 'thick' and gives up trying. Teacher's original impression is confirmed

⬇

Less teacher praise and encouragement

⬇

Pupil fails to achieve much success

⬇

Teacher's original prediction is confirmed: the original prophecy has been fulfilled

Figure 5.7 The self-fulfilling prophecy: two examples

Research by Rosenthal and Jacobson (1968) in California provided useful evidence of the self-fulfilling prophecy. They found that a randomly chosen group of students whom teachers were told were bright and could be expected to make good progress, even though they were no different from other students in terms of ability, did in fact make greater progress than students not so labelled.

Banding and streaming Banding and streaming are ways of grouping students according to their predicted ability.

Being placed in a low stream or band may undermine pupils' confidence and discourage them from trying, and teachers may be less ambitious and

> **Banding** is where whole classes of pupils are put into different groups or bands for particular subjects, while **streaming** involves grouping them for all subjects.

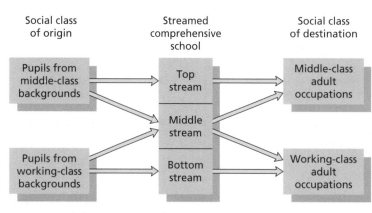

Figure 5.8 Social class divisions and streaming

give less knowledge to lower-stream children than they would with others. This was confirmed by Ball's research in *Beachside Comprehensive* (1981). Ball found that top-stream students were 'warmed up' by encouragement to achieve highly and to follow academic courses of study. On the other hand, lower-stream students were 'cooled out' and encouraged to follow lower status vocational and practical courses, and consequently achieved lower levels of academic success, frequently leaving school at the earliest opportunity.

Since streaming is often linked to social class – the higher a pupil's social class, the greater the chance of being allocated to a top stream – it contributes to the underachievement of working-class pupils. This is illustrated in figure 5.8.

Unequal access to classroom knowledge   Keddie found that teachers taught those in higher-stream classes differently from those in lower streams. Pupils were expected to behave better and do more work, and teachers gave them more, and different types of, educational knowledge, which gave them greater opportunities for educational success. Lower-stream working-class pupils might therefore underachieve in education partly because they have not been given access to the knowledge required for educational success.

The anti-school (counter-school) subculture   Most schools generally place a high value on things such as hard work, good behaviour and exam success. One of the effects of streaming and labelling is to divide students into those in the top streams who achieve highly, who more or less conform to these aims and therefore achieve high status in the school, and those in the bottom streams who are labelled as 'failures' by the school and are therefore deprived of status. In response to this, as studies by Hargreaves in

The anti-school, or counter-school, subculture

Social Relations in a Secondary School and Ball in *Beachside Comprehensive* have shown, bottom-stream pupils often rebel against the school and develop an alternative set of values, attitudes and behaviour in opposition to the academic aims of the school. This is the anti-school or counter-school subculture, as Willis found among 'the lads' discussed earlier in this chapter.

The anti-school subculture provides a means for bottom-stream pupils to improve their own self-esteem, by giving them status in the eyes of their peer group which has been denied them by the school. In this subculture, truancy, playing up teachers, messing about, breaking the school rules, copying work (or not doing any) and generally disrupting the smooth running of the school become a way of getting back at the system and resisting a schooling which has labelled them as 'failures' and denied them status. These are responses to the labels which have been placed on pupils by the school, and as bottom-stream pupils are more likely to be from working-class backgrounds, this contributes further to poor educational performance.

An evaluation of interactionist approaches to education

Interactionist approaches recognize the importance of what happens inside schools Interactionists emphasize the importance of what happens in schools and classrooms, rather than putting the whole blame for educational failure on deficiencies in the pupil, their family, their cultural values

Activity

1   List all the reasons you can think of to explain why pupils from lower working-class homes are more likely to be placed in lower streams than those from middle-class backgrounds.

2   Have you had any experience of the self-fulfilling prophecy in your own schooling? How do teachers communicate impressions of whether they think you are 'bright' or not, and how do you think this might have affected your progress?

3   In what ways do you think students in lower streams are treated differently and given different knowledge from those in higher streams? Give examples to illustrate your answer.

4   How do you think schools and teachers 'warm up' or 'cool out' students?

5   Is there any evidence of an anti-school subculture in your own school, or the school you once attended? What do you think membership of an anti-school subculture might mean to those who belong to it? Draw on examples from your own schooling.

and attitudes, or material circumstances arising from their social class background.

They are too deterministic   Interactionist theories can be too deterministic, in the sense that they suggest that once a negative label is applied, it will always have a negative effect, with the self-fulfilling prophecy coming into effect. In fact, a negative label like 'thick' or 'waster' may have the opposite effect, and encourage those so labelled to prove the label wrong via hard work and academic success.

They do not pay enough attention to the distribution of power in society
Interactionist theories do not explain why so many teachers seem to hold similar views on what counts as an 'ideal pupil', what constitutes 'proper' educational knowledge and ability, and why these appear to be related to social class. They therefore do not take enough account of the distribution of power in society, which means some definitions of knowledge, culture and ability are given more importance than others (as Bourdieu's theory of cultural capital and habitus suggests).

They do not pay enough attention to factors outside the school   Interactionists do not take enough account of the structural, material and cultural factors outside the school, discussed earlier, which influence what happens inside the school. Teachers and schools cannot be held solely responsible for what happens in schools, and they certainly cannot be blamed for problems which have their roots outside the school in the structure of inequality in the wider society.

They do not pay enough attention to other factors inside the school
Interactionists do not take sufficient account of other factors inside the
school, apart from the labelling process, which have an influence on the
achievement levels of students, and are often beyond the control of teachers themselves. These include:

- class sizes
- the financial resources given to education
- the demand to publish 'league tables' of exam results (which may
  influence who gets entered, and whether pupils – and therefore
  money – are attracted to the school or not)
- teacher morale (partly arising from pay and conditions issues, and
  how much upheaval they are expected to deal with as a result of
  government changes in schools)
- the need for teachers, regardless of their philosophy or beliefs, to
  classify/stratify pupils at an early age for different exams and
  occupational routes

They do not provide full explanations   The interactionist approach is
very helpful in drawing attention to the factors inside schools which
explain working-class underachievement. However, a full explanation of
underachievement in education needs to take account of factors both
outside the school and inside the school, both material and cultural
factors and interaction in the classroom. In other words, a full account of
working-class underachievement needs to look at both structural *and*
interactionist explanations.

The double test for working-class children

Taken together, the factors in the home, social class background and the school
discussed above help to explain why working-class young people do less well at
school than their middle-class peers of the same ability. Schools test all pupils
when doing subjects like mathematics, English or science. However, for the
working-class student there is a double test. At the same time as coping with the
academic difficulties of school work which all pupils face, working-class students
must also cope with a wide range of other disadvantages and difficulties.

These problems, on top of the demands of academic work, explain working-
class underachievement in schools. These disadvantages start in the primary
school and become more and more emphasized as young people grow older,
as they fall further and further behind and become more disillusioned with
school. In this context, it is perhaps not surprising that a large majority of those
who leave school at age 16 every year, with few or no qualifications, come from
lower working-class backgrounds.

Activity

Complete the following summary of explanations for social class differences in educational achievement, filling in the gaps from the word list below. Each dash represents one word.

'cooled out'	ability	Bourdieu
meritocratic	dominant class	deprivation
anti-school	poverty	functionalist
streaming	Marxist	legitimize
material circumstances	deficient	interactionist
'warmed up'	self-fulfilling prophecy	evaluations
compensatory	social class stereotypes	restricted
intelligence		educational qualifications

___ theories argue that education selects and allocates the most talented people to the most functionally important roles according to ___ criteria like ability, talents and skills as shown by ___ ___ and achievement. Achievement reflects ___, and middle-class children are more intelligent and harder working than working-class children.

___ theories argue that schools ___ social class inequality by making it *appear* that working-class children fail because of their lack of ___ , when in fact it is a consequence of their home and social class background, and the culture and ideology of the school.

___ explains working-class underachievement as a consequence of the lack of cultural capital, and the fact that the culture of the school is the culture of the ___ ___.

___ ___ of the home affect educational achievement, with factors such as ___ and low wages, poor housing and overcrowding, poorer health and more sickness all contributing to the underachievement of working-class pupils.

Cultural ___ theories suggest that the culture of the lower working class is ___ or deprived. Their different values and attitudes, the lack of parental interest and encouragement, their use of the ___ code of language and their lack of cultural capital undermine their chances of success in education, though positive discrimination and ___ education might help.

___ theories emphasize the importance of what goes on inside schools and classrooms. Teachers' ___ through typing, labelling, banding and ___ generate the ___-___ ___. Middle-class pupils are ___ ___ to succeed, and working-class pupils are ___ ___ to fail. Teachers give different knowledge to, and make different demands on, pupils depending on the stream the students are in. Streaming often reflects ___ ___ ___. These factors can lead to the formation of ___-___ subcultures with opposition to and rejection of educational success.

Activity

1   Identify and explain three factors inside schools which may explain the underachievement of pupils from disadvantaged backgrounds.
2   Explain what is meant by 'labelling', and how it might influence the educational achievements of pupils.
3   Answer the following essay question, in about one and a half to two sides of A4 paper:

Evaluate the arguments and evidence for the view that poverty and material circumstances are the most important reasons for educational underachievement.

(Hint: remember there is a range of explanations apart from poverty and material circumstances.)

Gender differences in educational achievement: the underachievement of boys

While the educational achievements of both males and females have improved in recent years, there are still big differences between them. Until the 1980s, the major concern was with the underachievement of girls. This was because, while girls used to perform better than boys in the earlier stages of their education, up to GCSE, after this they tended to fall behind, being less likely than boys to get the three A levels required for university entry, and less likely to go into higher education. However, in

Facts on gender differences in educational achievement

- Girls do better than boys at every stage in National Curriculum SAT (Standard Assessment Test) results in English, maths and science.
- Girls are now more successful than boys at every level in GCSE, outperforming boys in every major subject (including traditional boys' subjects like design, technology, maths and chemistry) except physics. In English at GCSE, the gender gap is huge, with more than two-thirds of girls getting grades *A–C, compared to about half of boys.
- A higher proportion of females stays on in post-16 sixth form and further education, and post-18 higher education.
- Female school leavers are now more likely than males to get three or more A-level passes.
- More women than men get accepted for university. In 2004, women made up about 56 per cent of top-graded entrants (with the best A-level scores). Over half (54 per cent) of those accepted on degree courses were female, and women now make up a larger proportion of graduates with upper-second and first-class university degrees.

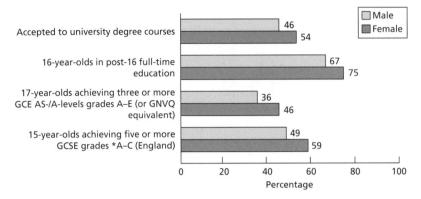

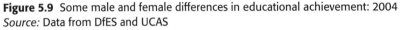

Figure 5.9 Some male and female differences in educational achievement: 2004
Source: Data from DfES and UCAS

the early 1990s girls began to outperform boys, particularly working-class boys, in all areas and at all levels of the education system. The main problem today is with the underachievement of boys, although there are still concerns about the different subjects studied by boys and girls. There are also concerns that girls could do even better if teachers spent as much time with girls as they are obliged to do with boys.

Problems remaining for girls

Despite the general pattern of girls outperforming boys, problems do still remain for girls. Girls still tend to do different subjects from boys, which influences future career choices. Broadly, arts subjects are 'female', science and technology subjects 'male'. This exists at GCSE, but becomes even more pronounced at A level and above. Girls are therefore less likely to participate after 16 in subjects leading to careers in science, engineering and technology.

Girls tend to slip back between GCSE and A level, with girls achieving fewer high-grade A levels than boys with the same GCSE results. There is little evidence that the generally better results of girls at 16 and above lead to improved post-school opportunities in terms of training and employment. Women are still less likely than men with similar qualifications to achieve similar levels of success in paid employment and men still hold the majority of the positions of power in society. Among people in the 16–59 age group in the population as a whole who are in employment or unemployed, men tend to be better qualified than women. However, this gap has decreased among younger age groups, and can be expected to disappear if females keep on outperforming males in education.

Explaining gender differences in education

What follows are some suggested hypotheses and explanations, based on further research, including updated research by Eirene Mitsos and Ken Browne (1998), for the huge improvement in the performance of girls, the underperformance of boys and the subject choices that continue to separate males and females. The explanations are summarized in figure 5.10.

Why do females now do better than males?

The women's movement and feminism The women's movement and feminism have achieved considerable success in improving the rights and raising the expectations and self-esteem of women. They have challenged the traditional stereotype of women's roles as housewives and mothers, and this means many women now look beyond being a housewife/mother as their main role in life.

Equal opportunities The work of sociologists in highlighting the educational underperformance of girls in the past led to a greater emphasis in schools on equal opportunities, in order to enable girls to fulfil their potential more easily. These policies included, among others, monitoring teaching and teaching materials for gender bias to help schools to meet the needs of girls better, encouraging 'girl-friendliness' not only in male-dominated subjects but across the whole range of the experience of girls in schools. Teachers are now much more sensitive about avoiding gender

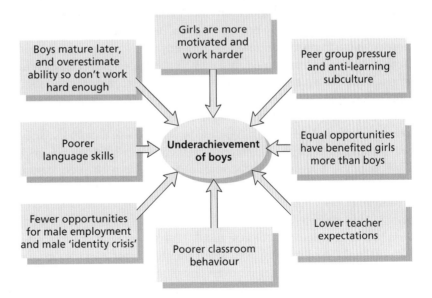

Figure 5.10 Gender and educational underachievement

stereotyping in the classroom, and this may have overcome many of the former academic problems which girls faced in schools.

Growing ambition, more positive role models and more employment opportunities for women   The number of 'male' jobs, particularly in semi- and unskilled manual work, has declined in recent years, while there are growing employment opportunities for women in the service sector. As a consequence, girls have become more ambitious, and they are less likely to see having a home and family as their main role in life. Many girls growing up today have mothers working in paid employment, who provide positive role models for them. Many girls now recognize that the future involves paid employment, often combined with family responsibilities. Sue Sharpe found in *Just Like a Girl* in 1976 that girls' priorities were 'love, marriage, husbands, children, jobs, and careers, more or less in that order'. When she repeated her research in 1994, she found these priorities had changed to 'job, career and being able to support themselves'. Becky Francis (2000) carried out research involving observation of twelve classes of 14–16 year olds and interviews with students in three London secondary schools in 1998–9. Her interviews with girls confirmed Sharpe's findings, and she found many girls were very ambitious, aiming for higher professional occupations like doctors and solicitors, rather than the traditional female occupations like clerical work, hairdressing or beauty therapy. These factors may all have provided more incentives for girls to gain qualifications.

Girls work harder and are better motivated   There is mounting evidence that girls work harder, are more conscientious and are better motivated than boys. Girls put more effort into their work, and spend more time on doing their homework properly. They take more care with the way their work is presented, and they concentrate more in class (some research has shown the typical 14-year-old girl concentrating for about three to four times as long as her fellow male students). Girls are generally better organized: they are more likely to bring the right equipment to school and meet deadlines for handing in work. These factors may have helped girls to take more advantage of the increasing use of coursework in GCSE, and AS-/A-level and vocational courses. Such work often requires good organization and sustained application, and girls do better than boys in these respects.

Girls mature earlier   By the age of 16, girls are estimated to be more mature than boys by up to two years. Put simply, this means girls are more likely to view exams in a far more responsible way, and recognize their seriousness and the importance of the academic and career choices that lie ahead of them.

Why do boys underachieve?

Many of the reasons given above also suggest why boys may be under-achieving. However, there are some additional explanations.

Lower expectations   There is some evidence that staff are not as strict with boys as with girls. They are more likely to extend deadlines for work, to have lower expectations of boys, to be more tolerant of disruptive, unruly behaviour from boys in the classroom and to accept more poorly presented work. This will mean boys perform less well than they otherwise might.

Boys are more disruptive   Boys are generally more disruptive in class-rooms than girls. They may lose classroom learning time because they are sent out of the room or sent home. Four out of every five permanent exclu-sions from schools are of boys; most of these are for disobedience of vari-ous kinds, and usually come at the end of a series of incidents.

The anti-learning subculture   Boys, especially working-class boys, appear to gain 'street cred' and peer group status by not working, and some develop almost an anti-education, anti-learning subculture, where schoolwork is seen as 'girly' and 'unmacho'. This may explain why they are less conscientious and lack the persistence and application required for exam success, particularly where the emphasis is on coursework styles of assessment. This is the sort of subculture adopted by 'the lads' in Paul Willis's *Learning to Labour*, discussed earlier in this chapter. This was rediscovered by Stephen Byers, the former schools minister, in January 1998 when he said, 'We must challenge the laddish, anti-learning culture which has been allowed to develop over recent years and should not simply accept with a shrug of the shoulders that boys will be boys.' Fran-cis's research referred to above confirmed this view that boys achieved more peer group 'macho' status by resisting teachers and schools, through 'laddish' behaviour like messing about in class and not getting on with their work, contributing to their underachievement.

Teaching is often seen as a mainly female profession, and there is a lack of positive male role models, especially in primary schools. This may be a further reason why learning comes to be seen by some boys, from an early age, as a 'feminine' and 'girly' activity. This may further contribute to a negative attitude to schools and schooling.

Declining male employment opportunities and the male 'identity crisis'
The decline in traditional male jobs is also a factor in explaining why many boys are underperforming in education. They may lack motivation and ambition because they may feel that they have only limited prospects, and

getting qualifications won't get them anywhere anyway, so what's the point in bothering? These changing employment patterns have resulted in a number of (predominantly white and working-class) boys and men having lowered expectations, a low self-image and a lack of self-esteem, and have brought about an identity crisis for men, who feel unsure about their role and position. This insecurity is reflected in schools, where boys don't see the point in working hard and trying to achieve. The future looks bleak to them and without clear purpose. This leads boys to attempt to construct a positive self-image away from achievement and towards 'laddish behaviour' and aggressive 'macho' posturing in attempts to draw attention to themselves.

Feeling and behaving differently   Boys and girls feel differently about their own ability, with most boys overestimating their ability, and girls underestimating theirs. Research by Michael Barber (1996) at Keele University's Centre for Successful Schools showed 'that more boys than girls think that they are able or very able, and fewer boys than girls think they are "below average"'. Yet GCSE results show these perceptions to be the reverse of the truth. Boys feel that they are bright and capable but at the same time they say they don't like school and they don't work hard enough to get the results they think they're capable of. This was confirmed by Francis's research in three London secondary schools in 1998–9 , which found that some boys thought it would be easy to do well in exams without having to put in much effort. When they do fail, boys tend to blame either the teachers or their own lack of effort – not their ability. Girls on the other hand lack confidence in and underestimate their ability, and feel undervalued, as researchers such as Licht and Dweck (1987) and Michelle Stanworth (1983) found.

Different leisure – doing not talking   More research is coming to the conclusion that the differences in the achievement of girls and boys is due to the differing ways in which the genders behave and spend their leisure time. To simplify and generalize: while boys run around kicking footballs, playing sports or computer games, and engaging in other aspects of 'laddish' behaviour, girls are more likely to read or to stand around talking. Girls relate to one another by *talking*, while boys often relate to their peers by *doing*. The value of talking, even if it is about the heartthrob of Year 11, is that it tends to develop the linguistic and reasoning skills needed at school and in many non-manual service sector jobs. Peter Douglas argues that 'school is essentially a linguistic experience and most subjects require good levels of comprehension and writing skills'. Further research is revealing an emerging picture of boys viewing the crucial reading and linguistic skills as 'sissy'.

Boys don't like reading   Girls like reading while boys don't: boys see read-ing as a predominantly feminine activity, which is boring, not real work, a waste of time and to be avoided at all costs. Reading is 'feminized' in our culture: women are not only the main consumers of reading in our society, but they are also the ones who read, talk about and 'spread the word' about books, and they are more likely to be the ones who read to their children. Girls are therefore more likely to have positive role models of their own sex than boys. Research has shown that boys tend to stop being interested in reading at about 8 years old.

Girls and boys also tend to read different things: girls read fiction while boys read for information. Schools tend to reproduce this gendered divide: fiction tends to be the main means of learning to read in the primary school years and this puts girls at an early advantage in education.

Activity

Drawing on your own experience, and giving examples, do you think:
- Boys overestimate their ability, while girls underestimate theirs?
- Boys and girls behave differently in school, particularly in relation to how they behave with their peer group?
- Boys don't read as much as girls, and when they do, read different things?
- Boys are more likely to show an anti-education, anti-learning subculture than girls?
- Girls work harder than boys?

Why do males and females still tend to study different subjects?

There is still a difference between the subjects that males and females do at GCSE and above, as figure 5.11 on page 283 shows.

Females are still more likely to take arts and humanities subjects, like English literature, foreign languages and sociology, and males are more likely to take scientific and technological subjects – particularly at A level and above (even though girls generally get better results when they do take them). This is despite the National Curriculum, which makes maths, English and science compulsory for all students. However, even within the National Curriculum, there are gender differences in option choices. For example, girls are more likely to take home economics, textiles and food technology, while boys are more likely to opt for electronics, woodwork or graphics. How can we explain these differences?

Gender socialization   From an early age boys and girls are encouraged to play with different toys and do different activities at home, and they very

Activity

Refer to figure 5.11:

1   In which three A-level subjects was the gap between the percentages of male and female entries the greatest?

2   In which three GCSE subjects was the gap between the percentages of male and female entries the greatest?

3   In which A-level subjects were there more male than female entries in 2004?

4   Which subject showed the greatest gap between the percentages of male and female entries at both GCSE and A level?

5   Which subject had more male entries at GCSE, but more female entries at A level?

6   Why do you think the gap in subject entries between males and females tends, in general, to be smaller at GCSE than at A level?

7   Drawing on the data in figure 5.11, outline the main gender differences in subject choices at GCSE and A level, and suggest reasons for them, with reference to specific subjects.

often grow up seeing their parents playing different roles around the house. Research in 1974 by Lobban found evidence of gender stereotyping in children's books, with women more clearly linked to traditional domestic roles. Research by Best in 1993 found that little had changed since Lobban conducted her research. Such socialization may encourage boys to develop more interest in technical and scientific subjects, and discourage girls from taking them. In giving subject and career advice, teachers may be reflecting their own socialization and expectations, and reinforcing the different experiences of boys and girls by counselling them into different subject options, according to their own gender stereotypes of 'suitable subjects'.

Science and the science classroom are still seen as mainly 'masculine'
As Kelly (1987) found, boys tend to dominate science classrooms – grabbing apparatus first, answering questions aimed at girls and so on, which all undermine girls' confidence and intimidate them from taking up these subjects. Gender stereotyping is still found in science, with the 'invisibility' of females particularly obvious in maths and science textbooks, where examples are often more relevant to the experience of males than females. This reinforces the view that these are 'male' subjects. Research by Colley (1998) suggested that the gender perceptions of different subjects are important influences on subject choice, with the arts and humanities seen by students as feminine, and science and technology as masculine. Colley suggested that the changing content of the curriculum of some subjects can change its gender identity. For example, she found that music, which has traditionally been seen as a feminine subject, is becoming more

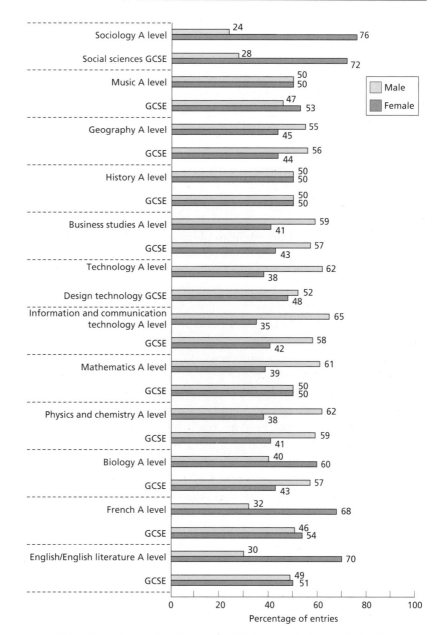

Figure 5.11 Percentages of male compared to female students entering for different subjects at GCSE and A level: UK, 2004
Source: Joint Council for Qualifications, 2005

popular with boys. This is borne out by recent figures. For example, in 2001, boys made up 42 per cent of GCSE music entries, 47 per cent of AS entries, and 43 per cent of A-level entries. By 2004, this had increased to 47 per cent at GCSE, 54 per cent at AS, and 50 per cent at A level. The entry of boys for music GCSE increased in this period by 38 per cent (compared to 13 per cent for girls), by 84 per cent for AS (36 per cent for girls) and by 61 per cent for A-level music, compared to 21 per cent for girls. Colley's research suggested that this change may largely be because the subject has become more computer and electronics based. This application of technology to music production has contributed to the 'masculinization' of the subject's content, making it more appealing as a subject option for boys.

Some concluding comments on gender and underachievement

Educational research, such as that of Spender (1982), has shown that teachers' time is spent mostly on the troublesome boys, rather than on the girls who are keen to learn and to get on with their schooling. Stanworth found students themselves thought boys got more than twice the amount of attention from teachers than girls, in terms of getting help, being asked questions and being encouraged to get involved in class discussions. Francis's research in 1998–9 found classrooms were still dominated by boys, and girls were getting less attention. Girls therefore see teachers spending more time with the boys than with them.

In the face of girls' marked disadvantages, such as underrating themselves and a lack of confidence in their ability, getting less of teachers' time, and having to tolerate the dominance of boys in the classroom, it is perhaps surprising that they tend to do much better at school than boys. This suggests that girls may still be underachieving, even if they are not doing so in relation to the boys.

It is still men who hold most of the highly paid, powerful positions in society – it is still mainly men who pull the strings and 'run' our society.

Activity

The following comments are from Year 11 boys talking about doing English and science:

'I hate it! I don't want to read books.'

'Science is straightforward. You don't have to think about it. There are definite answers. There are no shades to it.'

'In science, everything is set out as a formula, and you have the facts. All you have to do is apply them to the situation.'

'When you read a book, it's like delving into people's lives. It's being nosey.'

'English is about understanding, interpreting … you have to think more. There's no definite answer … the answer depends of your view of things.'

'I don't like having discussions – I feel wrong . . . I think that people will jump down my throat.'

'That's why girls do English, because they don't mind getting something wrong. They're more open about issues, they're more understanding . . . they find it easier to comprehend other people's views and feelings.'

'You feel safe in science.'

(Adapted from Eirene Mitsos, 'Boys and English: classroom voices', *English and Media Magazine*, nos 33 and 34 (1995 and 1996))

1 What points are being made above about why females are more likely to choose to study English than males?
2 Identify all the ways you can think of that gender differences in subject choices might be linked to gender role socialization in society as a whole.
3 Go through the reasons suggested in the sections above for why girls outperform boys in education. List the explanations in what you think is their order of importance, and explain/justify your reasons.
4 Using your answer to question 3, suggest measures that might be taken to improve the educational performance of boys.
5 Drawing on your own experience of schooling, can you identify ways in which boys and girls are treated differently by teachers? Do boys behave differently in class to girls? Are they more disruptive in the classroom? Do boys have a different attitude to school work and to different subjects? Were/are there some subjects in your school which attracted more of one sex than another? Why do you think this might be?
6 Do you think girls, even though they are doing better than boys, are still underachieving in education?
7 Go to the following website, www.standards.dfes.gov.uk/genderandachievement, and identify and explain three policies which are currently being followed to try to improve the educational performance of boys.

Women go out to work more than they used to, and they now make up about half the workforce. However, as seen in chapter 2, research has shown that in the home gender roles have not changed that much: women now not only go out to paid work a lot more, but they still have the majority of the burden of housework, childcare and managing family emotions.

Activity

1   Identify and explain 3 reasons why girls outperform boys in education.
2   Explain what is meant by an 'anti-learning subculture'.
3   Explain how equal opportunity policies may have contributed to the improved educational performance of girls in recent years.
4   Identify and explain 2 reasons why girls and boys often choose to study different subjects.
5   On about two sides of A4 paper, answer the following question:
    Examine sociological explanations for the difference in the performance of boys and girls in the education system.

Ethnicity and educational achievement

While individuals from all ethnic minorities may do outstandingly well, there is concern about the performance of some groups taken overall (see box). The key research in Britain on the underachievement of some ethnic minorities comes from the Swann Report of 1985, two Ofsted (Office for

Achievement and underachievement among ethnic groups

Many children from minority ethnic groups tend to do as well as, and often better than, many white children. For example, Indian Asians are more likely to get better GCSE and A-level results, to stay in education after the age of 16, and to enter university than white students. However, those of Pakistani and Bangladeshi origin, and particularly males from African-Caribbean backgrounds, tend to do less well than they should given their ability:

● Taken overall, they appear to have below average reading skills.
● African-Caribbean, Pakistani and Bangladeshi pupils are less likely to attain higher grade (*A–C) GCSE results than children of white or Indian origin.
● Male African-Caribbeans are overrepresented (there are more than there should be given their numbers in the population as a whole) in special schools for those with learning difficulties. They are twice as likely to be categorized as having emotional, behavioural or social difficulties as white British boys.
● The performance of African-Caribbean pupils worsens as they go through the schooling system, deteriorating between Key Stage 1 and Key Stage 4.
● Despite rising standards of achievement for all ethnic groups, the gap between African-Caribbean and Pakistani pupils and their white peers is now larger than it was ten years ago.
● African-Caribbean school students are between three and six times more likely to be permanently excluded from schools than white students of the same sex, and to be excluded for longer periods than white students for the same offences.

- Where schools are streamed by ability, they are overrepresented in the lower streams. Evidence suggests they are placed in lower streams even when they get better results than some students placed in higher streams.
- They are more likely than other groups to leave school without any qualifications.
- They are less likely to stay on in education post-16, and when they do, they are more likely to follow vocational courses rather than the higher status academic courses, like AS and A levels.

Standards in Education) reports, *Recent Research on the Achievements of Ethnic Minority Pupils* (Gillborn and Gipps, 1996) and *Mapping Race, Class and Gender* (Gillborn and Mirza, 2000), and two DfES (Department for Education and Skills) reports, *Minority Ethnic Attainment and Participation in Education and Training: The Evidence* (2004) and *Ethnicity and Education: The Evidence on Minority Ethnic Pupils* (2005).

Overall, minority ethnic groups tend to do less well than other members of the population, although there are important differences between minority ethnic groups, and the overall statistics disguise wide variations between individuals – some minority ethnic group children are very successful in the education system.

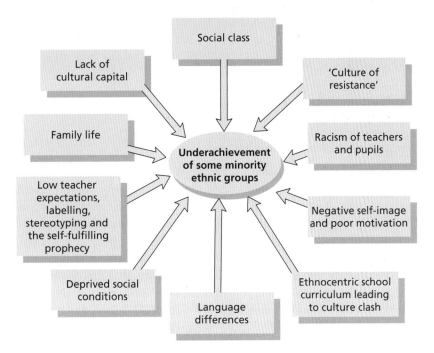

Figure 5.12 Ethnicity and educational achievement

Explanations for ethnic group differences in education

There is no single factor that explains the differences between ethnic groups – a range of factors work together to produce the lower levels of achievement of some minority ethnic groups.

Social class, gender and ethnicity

It is important to remember that social class and gender differences in education can also contribute to explaining differential achievement in terms of ethnicity. The variety of explanations already considered in relation to class and gender should always be born in mind when attempting to explain differences between minority ethnic groups. For example, one explanation for the high attainment of children from Indian Asian minority backgrounds is that they come from a relatively middle-class group, with the underachievement of African-Caribbeans, Pakistanis and Bangladeshis explained by reference to their predominantly working-class backgrounds. All the explanations discussed above surrounding material deprivation, language differences, cultural deprivation, lack of cultural capital, teacher attitudes, teacher expectations/labelling and the self-fulfilling prophecy may then contribute to explaining the differences between ethnic groups.

However, while these factors have an impact, social class differences alone cannot explain differences in achievement between ethnic groups. Gillborn and Mirza (2000) noted: 'Social class factors do not override the influence of ethnic inequality: when comparing pupils with similar class backgrounds there are still marked inequalities of attainment between different ethnic groups.' In other words, black pupils from middle-class backgrounds are little better placed to succeed in education than white pupils from working-class backgrounds.

Social class and material factors

Disadvantaged backgrounds   Minority ethnic children are more likely to live in low income households, and to be in the poorer sections of the working class. Around two-thirds of Pakistani and Bangladeshi households are living below the poverty line. African-Caribbean and Pakistani and Bangladeshi people are around three times more likely to be unemployed as white people. In 2004, 18 per cent of white households were low income households, compared with 27 per cent of African-Caribbean households, and 65 per cent of Pakistani or Bangladeshi households. This means many face problems like poor quality housing, overcrowding, higher levels of unemployment (partly due to racism) and general material disadvantage which may affect achievement levels in school.

Advantaged backgrounds   Indian and African-Asian children are more likely to come from business and professional middle-class family backgrounds, thereby gaining all the benefits that being middle-class confers in education. This variation in background may mean that some of the differences between ethnic groups in terms of educational achievement may have less to do with ethnicity as such, and more to do with social and economic disadvantage. However, this is not in itself adequate to explain all the differences between ethnic groups, as there are differences between ethnic groups from the same social class backgrounds.

While all the main ethnic groups are achieving more than ever before, the achievements of white and Indian Asian people have improved far more than those of Pakistani and Bangladeshi pupils, and the gap between them has actually widened. Social class differences cannot explain this, as Indian Asian students are doing better, and African-Caribbean and Pakistani and Bangladeshi students doing worse, than white students from the same social class background.

Language

In some Asian households, English is not the main language used, and in some black (African-Caribbean) households Caribbean English is used. The 2005 DfES report found that pupils for whom English was an additional language had lower attainment than pupils whose first language was English.

Language differences may cause difficulties in doing some schoolwork and communicating with the teacher, and white, middle-class teachers may mistake language difficulties for lack of ability in general, and therefore have lower expectations of some of their pupils.

Because Caribbean English is a different form of English, it may be unconsciously penalized in the classroom, because most teachers are white and middle class. The active discouragement of children from using their 'mother' tongue in school, and negative labelling, may provide obstacles to learning and motivation in school, as the self-fulfilling prophecy takes effect. However, the Swann Report found that while language factors might hold back some children, for the majority they were of little importance, and the 2005 report referred to above found the lower attainment of pupils for whom English was an additional language, compared to those for whom English was their first language, was narrower at Key Stage 4 than Key Stage 1, and therefore diminishes as children get older.

Family Life

African-Caribbean communities have a high level of lone parenthood, and this may pose financial and practical problems in supporting their children's education, no matter how much concern they may have about their children's progress. For African-Caribbean girls, who display higher levels of achievement than African-Caribbean boys, the fact that women are often the primary breadwinners in many African-Caribbean families may provide positive role models for girls and encourage higher levels of achievement – a recognition that they themselves will in future be major breadwinners. Asian family life has been characterized by close-knit extended families, which provide high levels of support for education, combined with cultural values encouraging higher levels of achievement.

The Swann Report (1985) and Pilkington (1997) suggested that some minority ethnic groups enjoy greater parental support than others. However, the 2005 DfES report found parental involvement with their children's education was greater in minority ethnic groups than in the population as a whole, and a higher proportion saw their children's education as mainly the parents' responsibility rather than the school's, and this was particularly true of African-Caribbean and Bangladeshi parents. A very high proportion (82 per cent) went to parents' evenings whenever there was an opportunity, although Pakistani and Bangladeshi parents were less confident about helping their children with homework.

Racism

A 'culture of resistance'   There are suggestions that racism in society as a whole may lead to low self-esteem among black pupils, and a hostility to schooling and the low-paid unskilled work it prepares them for. Stuart Hall, from a Marxist point of view, has discussed a 'culture of resistance' among African-Caribbean youth, leading to a rejection of schooling and to conflict within it when they are compelled to attend. It may well be that higher unemployment rates for African-Caribbeans contribute to a lack of motivation in school.

> **Racism** is believing or acting as though an individual or group is superior or inferior on the grounds of their racial or ethnic origins.

Teacher stereotyping, labelling and conflict in the classroom   Teachers often hold stereotypes of particular groups of students. Teachers have more positive expectations of Asians, particularly of Asian girls, generally seeing them as relatively quiet, well behaved and highly motivated. In contrast, research by Wright in four inner city primary schools found African-Caribbean pupils were often expected to be and labelled as troublemakers, and this may mean teachers take swift action against them. Research in primary and secondary schools has found an unusually high degree of conflict between white teachers and African-Caribbean students, and African-Caribbean children, unlike whites and Asians, are often punished not for any particular offence but because they have the 'wrong attitude'. A London Development Agency Education Commission report in 2004 said that relationships between African-Caribbean students and white teachers were characterized by 'conflict and fear'. An African-Caribbean student in this report pinpointed teacher stereotyping when he said: 'When it is white boys it is a group, but when it is black boys, it is a gang.' African-Caribbean (especially male) pupils are more likely to fight racism at school, and form anti-school subcultures. This may reflect the 'culture of resistance' mentioned above by Stuart Hall. These factors might explain the high level of exclusions among African-Caribbean students, since most permanent exclusions are for disobedience of various kinds, such as refusing to comply with school rules, verbal abuse, or insolence to teachers.

The Swann Report found only a small minority of teachers was consciously racist, but there is evidence of a good deal of unintentional racism, which can affect progress at school. Green, in an appendix to the Swann Report, found that some teachers with racist attitudes favoured and gave more time, individual attention and praise and encouragement to white pupils than to African-Caribbean boys and girls. Bhatti (1999) identified examples of pupils' own views of racist behaviour by teachers, which included being ignored and not being given the chance to answer questions in class, not being helped, not being given responsibility, and being unfairly picked on for punishment or a telling-off.

If teachers hold negative stereotypes, with consequent negative labelling, and have low expectations of black pupils ('slow learners'/'lack concentration'/'difficult to control'), this may lead to the development of low self-esteem among such pupils, and the labelling process may itself lead to the self-fulfilling prophecy, reinforced by the hostility to schooling among black students that such attitudes are likely to generate. This view was reinforced by the Ofsted and DfES reports of 2000 and 2005 which showed that the inequalities of attainment for African-Caribbean pupils become progressively greater as they move through the school system, deteriorating between Key Stage 1 and Key Stage 4. It would appear that the education system actively disadvantages black children.

The ethnocentric school curriculum

> **Multicultural education** involves a recognition of the diversity of cultures in society, and teaching about the culture of other ethnic groups besides that of the majority culture.
> **Ethnocentrism** is a view of the world in which other cultures are seen through the eyes of one's own culture, with a devaluing of the others.

Many schools have strong equal opportunities policies to tackle racism, and many schools have multicultural education, and try to include minority ethnic group cultures within the school curriculum. Despite attempts at multicultural education, many aspects of school life and the school curriculum remain ethnocentric.

In education, this involves school subjects and the hidden curriculum concentrating on white British society and culture, rather than recognizing and taking into account the cultures of other ethnic groups. For example, role models are frequently white; 'white' is good and 'black' is evil (as in the white knight versus the black knight); history is white and European; history and other textbooks still frequently carry degrading stereotypes of people from non-white races – portrayed often in subservient or 'primitive' roles; positive role models from the history, music, art and culture of black and other minority ethnic groups are frequently absent from the curriculum.

It has been suggested that this, along with the other factors discussed above, contributes to the low self-esteem of some minority ethnic children, and it means the school curriculum may be more attractive and culturally acceptable to some ethnic groups than others. Combining all the factors above may mean there is a culture clash between some minority ethnic groups and the white middle-class culture of the school. To apply Bourdieu's theory of cultural capital, while it might *appear* that all have an equal opportunity in education since they are assessed against the same culture and knowledge, the education system is not really neutral at all because its culture is predominantly white culture. These factors would contribute to explaining patterns of underachievement in education between ethnic groups.

Some words of caution

Explaining the underachievement of some minority ethnic groups is no easy task. It is likely to be a *combination* of the factors outlined above, with the different factors having different significance in particular circumstances. However, all the explanations need to be treated with caution. For example, while some teachers may hold racist beliefs, this does not necessarily mean they behave in a racist way in the classroom, and they may not allow the negative stereotypes of ethnic minorities they may hold to disadvantage children from minority ethnic groups. It should not be assumed all teachers are racist, and many make great and successful efforts to overcome any feelings of **racial prejudice** they hold and do all they can for all students. Racism is not as widespread in teaching as in some professions, like the police and legal professions, and teachers and schools have often been among the first to tackle racism and promote equal opportunities for all. More teachers from minority ethnic backgrounds act as positive role models for professional career success for black and minority ethnic students.

Negative labelling of ethnic minorities by teachers and others in the education system does not necessarily lead to the negative effects that the self-fulfilling prophecy suggests. The negative labels attached to some students from minority ethnic groups might not be accepted by those labelled. Research by Fuller (1980) among African-Caribbean girls in a London comprehensive school suggested that those labelled may reject the label and the low expectations of teachers, and combine a subculture of resistance to schooling with the hard work needed to overcome the obstacles placed before them and to achieve educational success. This partly arose because black girls recognized their future roles as key

Racial prejudice involves a set of assumptions about a racial or ethnic group which people are reluctant to change even when they receive information which undermines those assumptions.

breadwinners in black families. This demonstrates both that negative labels do not always have negative effects, and also explains why African-Caribbean females in general do better than their male counterparts in education. For example, 40 per cent of black African-Caribbean girls achieved five or more *A–C GCSE/GNVQs in 2004 compared to 25 per cent of African-Caribbean boys.

Activity

1 Go through the reasons suggested in these sections for the underachievement of some minority ethnic groups, and refer to figure 5.12 on p. 287. List the explanations in what you think is their order of importance. Explain and justify your reasons, and then suggest steps that might be taken in each case to overcome the obstacles you have listed.

2 Drawing carefully on what you have learnt in this chapter, try to draw up a 'league table' of achievement in education, drawing on both social class, gender and ethnicity. For example, middle-class Indian Asian girls are likely to come at the top, with working-class African-Caribbean males at the bottom. Try to fill in the rest, using categories of middle and working class, male and female, and white, Indian Asian, African-Caribbean, Pakistani and Bangladeshi ethnic groups.

3 Drawing on your own experience of schooling, can you identify any ways in which black and white students were/are treated differently by teachers or by other students? Is/was there any evidence of racism in your own school or college?

4 How ethnocentric is/was the curriculum in your school or college? Was there any evidence of knowledge of other cultures being taught in your school, appearing in textbooks and so on.

5 Go to the DfES standards website at www.standards.dfes.gov.uk/ethnicminorities and identify three policies that are currently being pursued to improve the educational achievements of minority ethnic groups. Explain how each policy might make such improvements.

Activity

1 Identify and explain three factors that may contribute to a culture clash between the culture of some minority ethnic groups and that of the school.

2 Identify and explain three material factors and three cultural factors that may contribute to the underachievement in education of some minority ethnic groups.

3 Answer the following essay question, in about one and half to two sides of A4 paper:
   Examine the view that the underachievement of some minority ethnic groups is mainly a result of family and social class background.

Private education: the independent schools

Around 7 per cent of the school population have chosen to opt out of the free, state-run comprehensive system and attend the fee-paying private sector of education – the independent schools. As Walford (2003) points out, there is a wide diversity of schools in the independent sector, some of which are so small that they are almost 'better thought of as parents home schooling their children'. As Walford says, there are 'schools that practise Transcendental Meditation and Buddhism; others that serve Seventh Day Adventists (a religious sect), Sikhs or Jews. There are more than 60 evangelical Christian schools and more than 50 Muslim schools.' Many of these schools arise because of parents expressing their choice of school, and while such schools may meet parental wishes, they do not necessarily lead to the elite careers associated with some of the most prestigious independent schools, which are the focus of attention here.

Most research and discussion of the private sector of education has been about what are known as the 'public schools', which, despite their name, are not in fact 'public' at all, but very expensive private schools. The reason for this attention is because, as Walford says, 'Entry to such schools has been seen as a passport to academic success, to high-status universities and to prosperous and influential careers.' The public schools are a small group of independent schools belonging to what is called the 'Headmasters' and Headmistresses' Conference' (HMC). Pupils at these schools are largely the children of wealthier upper and upper middle-class parents. These are long-established private schools, many dating back hundreds of years, which charge fees running into thousands of pounds a year. For secondary age students, annual fees varied from £6,000 to £21,000 per year in 2003. The two most famous boys' public schools are probably Eton (boarding fee £22,380 a year, plus extras, in 2004–5) and Harrow (£22,350 a year), and many of the 'top people' in this country have attended these or other public schools. A public school education means parents can almost guarantee their children will have well-paid future careers bringing them power and status in society.

The case for independent schools

The defenders of private education point to the smaller class sizes and better facilities of the public schools than those found in the state comprehensive system, which means children have a much better chance of getting into university. Many defend private education on the grounds that parents should have the right to spend their money as they wish, and improving their children's life chances through a free choice of schools is a sensible way of doing so.

The case against independent schools

Many remain opposed to private education, arguing that most people do not have the money to purchase a private education for their children, and it is wrong that the children of the well-off should be given more advantages in education than the poor. Despite many of the schools catering only for the well-off, they have traditionally had the same tax subsidies and benefits through charitable status as charities helping those in poverty or need. This charitable status has been estimated to be worth about 5–10 per cent on the average school fee (Palfreyman, 2003), or up to about £2,000 per pupil each year – an amount so generous that the government was suggesting in 2005 that these schools should use the full value of these tax subsidies to pay for the education of poor pupils in order to continue to qualify as charities. The taxpayer also pays the cost of training the teachers in these schools, since they attend state-run universities and colleges.

The quality of teaching in independent schools is often no better than in state-run comprehensives, and an Edinburgh University study found there is little difference in exam pass rates between middle-class pupils at state comprehensive schools and those in the independent sector. However, classes tend to be smaller than in comprehensives, allowing more individual attention, and the schools often have better resources and facilities. Eton College in 2003 had assets estimated at £162 million, with the added advantage of charitable status. These investments and fee income allow Eton to spend around £20,000 per year on each student, compared to the sum of around £3,000 spent on the average state school student in 2004. The opponents of private education argue more money should be spent on improving the state system so everyone has an equal chance in education.

Research has shown that even when children who go to private schools, especially the public schools, get worse examination results than children who go to comprehensive schools, they still get better jobs in the end. This suggests that the fact of attending a public school is itself enough to secure them good jobs, even if their qualifications are not quite as good as those of students from comprehensives.

Elite education and elite jobs

An **elite** is a small group holding great power and privilege in society.

A public school education remains a prime qualification for the **elite** jobs in society – that small number of jobs in the country which involve holding a great deal of power and privilege. Although only about 7 per cent of the population have attended independent schools (and public schools are only a proportion of those schools), many of the top positions in the civil service, the courts, the Church of England, industry, banking and commerce are held by ex-public school students.

In many cases, even well-qualified candidates from comprehensive schools will stand a poor chance of getting such jobs if competing with public school pupils. The route into the elite jobs is basically through a public school and Oxford and Cambridge universities (where about 50 per cent of students come from public schools). This establishes the 'old boys' network', where those in positions of power recruit others who come from the same social class background and who have been to the same public schools and universities as themselves. This shows one aspect of the clear relationship which exists between wealth and power in modern Britain, and how being able to afford a public school education can lead to a position of power and influence in society.

A public school education therefore means well-off parents can almost guarantee their children will have well-paid future careers bringing them similar levels of power and status in society as their parents. This undermines the principle of equality of educational opportunity, and any idea that Britain might be a meritocracy. This is because social class background and the ability to pay fees, rather than simply academic ability, become the key to success in education. Not all children of the same ability have the same chance of paying for this route to educational and career success. This would seem to demonstrate in a particularly stark way Bowles and Gintis's Marxist idea that the education system simply confirms and legitimizes social class of origin as social class of destination.

Activity

1 Go to www.etoncollege.com, the website of Eton College, or www.harrowschool.org.uk (Harrow School) and explore how the educational facilities and lifestyle at these schools differ from those of the school you go/went to (unless you went to one of these schools!).

2 Write a brief essay, about one side of A4, on the following:
Examine the arguments for and against the following view:
'The existence of private schools undermines the principle of equality of educational opportunity, because social class background rather than simply ability becomes the key to success in education. They only exist to help the wealthy and powerful pass on their wealth and power from one generation to the next. Private education should therefore be abolished.'

Chapter summary

After studying this chapter, you should be able to:

- explain what is meant by equality of educational opportunity
- describe and explain the strengths and weaknesses of the tripartite and comprehensive systems of education, and selection by ability in education
- identify the main changes in education since 1944, particularly those since 1988, and discuss the aims, consequences and criticisms of these reforms
- critically discuss the main purposes of education, as identified by the functionalist and Marxist perspectives
- explain what is meant by the 'hidden curriculum', and how it reflects and reinforces values and ideology outside schools
- explain what is meant by a meritocracy, and why Britain is not a meritocracy
- describe the facts about, and discuss a range of explanations for, social class, gender and ethnic group differences in educational achievement
- discuss the arguments for and against private education

Key terms

- anti-school subculture
- banding
- compensatory education
- counter-school subculture
- cultural capital
- cultural deprivation
- culture clash
- division of labour
- Education Action Zones
- Educational Priority Areas
- elaborated code
- elite
- equality of educational opportunity
- ethnocentrism
- habitus
- halo effect

- hidden curriculum
- ideological state apparatuses
- labelling
- meritocracy
- multicultural education
- particularistic values
- positive discrimination
- racial prejudice
- racism
- restricted code
- self-fulfilling prophecy
- sexism
- streaming
- subculture
- underachievement
- universalistic values

Coursework suggestions

1   Identify a range of factors that might make up what Bourdieu calls
    'cultural capital'. Through a questionnaire given to a sample of
    middle-class and working-class students, investigate whether they
    have the cultural factors you have identified. Discuss this in the
    framework of explanations for social class differences in educational
    achievement.

2   Observe classroom activities and try to see if boys and girls behave
    differently in class and are treated differently by teachers. For exam-
    ple, do they sit separately? Are boys or girls asked more questions? Are
    boys more disruptive? Does this vary between different subject classes
    and between male and female teachers? (If you plan to do classroom
    observation, applying Flanders's interaction analysis might be
    useful – see the box on p. 449 in chapter 8.)

3   Interview a sample of male and female students, asking them about
    what influenced them in making subject and exam choices.

4   Study labelling in a streamed school. How do those in lower streams
    react to being placed in those streams? Is there an anti-school
    subculture, and how does this influence their performance and
    behaviour at school? Is there a self-fulfilling prophecy?

5   Do a survey among the adult public, using different age, social class
    and ethnic groups, asking how they see education these days – are
    standards getting better, worse, or are they about the same compared
    to their own school days? What role do they think schools should be
    performing in society?

Exam Questions

EDUCATION

Time allowed: 1 hour 15 minutes   **Total for this Question:** *60 marks*

Item A

Despite a variety of educational reforms, there are still class-based differences in educational achievement. Social class is not the only factor affecting educational outcomes, of course; gender and ethnicity
also play a part. For example, evidence shows that the examination performance of girls has improved in
recent years, and girls generally are now performing better than boys at all stages of the education
process.   5

Nevertheless, it can be argued that social class remains the most important influence on a child's educational achievements. Despite the overall good performance of girls, for example, middle-class girls generally do better than working-class girls. It has been suggested that this can be explained by differences in
home background, such as the type of language spoken and parental aspirations.

Item B

Teachers' expectations of their pupils are often based on stereotypical views about pupils' gender, ethnicity and social class background. Using these stereotypes, teachers make assumptions about individual
pupils' abilities and conduct – often with little or no evidence. These assumptions enable teachers to label
pupils as 'hardworking', 'disruptive', 'bright', 'quiet', 'useless' and so on.

This might not be a problem if such labels had no effect, but much evidence suggests that they can exert a   5
powerful influence over pupils' achievements. In effect, pupils become what their teachers initially said
they were: they act out the label, often banding together with others who have been similarly labelled. Thus
labelling and other processes within schools are what determine who succeeds and who fails in education.

(a) Explain what is meant by 'stereotypical views' (**Item B**, line 1).   *(2 marks)*
(b) Identify **two** educational reforms which might reduce 'class-based differences in
    educational achievement' (**Item A**, line 1).   *(4 marks)*
(c) Suggest **three** reasons why girls' examination performance has improved in recent years
    (**Item A**, lines 3–4).   *(6 marks)*
(d) Identify **two** factors in pupils' home background which may affect their educational
    performance, **other than** those mentioned in **Item A**, and briefly describe the effect of
    each factor.   *(8 marks)*
(e) Examine sociological views of the different ways in which educational institutions can
    contribute to the economy.   *(20 marks)*
(f) Using material from **Item B** and elsewhere, assess the view that 'labelling and other
    processes within schools are what determine who succeeds and who fails in education'
    (**Item B**, line 8).   *(20 marks)*

(AQA AS Unit 2 January 2001)

EDUCATION

Time allowed: 1 hour 15 minutes   **Total for this Question:** *60 marks*

Item A

Most sociologists see material deprivation as a major cause of underachievement. However, according to cultural deprivation theory, some working-class and ethnic minority children fail because their parents do not socialise them into the appropriate norms, values and skills. For example, Douglas (1964) found that many working-class parents were uninterested in their children's progress and did little to support their education: they failed to attend parents' evenings, did not help them with their homework and did   5
not read to them.

As a result, such children are poorly equipped to take advantage of educational opportunities. For cultural deprivation theorists, government and educational bodies need to introduce policies to remedy the situation and give such children the chance to succeed.

However, while cultural deprivation has been used to explain class and ethnic differences in achievement,   10
most sociologists consider that when it comes to gender other factors are more important, particularly as the pattern of achievement has changed rapidly in recent years, with girls now generally out-performing boys at all levels of schooling.

Item B

According to functionalists, the education system encourages open competition while giving everyone an equal chance to succeed. As a result, all pupils can show what they are capable of achieving and what kind of future work role they are best suited for. The system is then able to provide each child with an education appropriate to their talents and to fit each individual with the knowledge, skills and attitudes they will need in their adult role.   5

Functionalists see this as having two main advantages. For the individual, it allows social mobility and rewards people according to their ability, not their social background. For society, it promotes a success-ful economy by ensuring each job is filled by someone with the appropriate talents. This leads to higher living standards for everyone.

(a) Explain what is meant by 'material deprivation' (**Item A**, line 1).   *(2 marks)*
(b) Suggest **two** reasons why many working-class parents may fail to attend parents' evenings,
    apart from lack of interest (**Item A**, line 5).   *(4 marks)*
(c) Identify **three** policies that government or educational bodies have introduced to
    overcome children's cultural deprivation (**Item A**, Lines 8–9).   *(6 marks)*
(d) Identify and briefly explain **two** reasons why girls are 'now generally out-performing
    boys at all levels of schooling' (**Item A**, lines 12–13).   *(8 marks)*
(e) Examine the role of processes in schools in producing different educational achievement
    among pupils from different social groups.   *(20 marks)*
(f) Using material from **Item B** and elsewhere, assess the view that the function of the
    education system is to select and prepare individuals for their future work roles.   *(20 marks)*

(AQA AS Unit 2 January 2005)

CHAPTER 6

Wealth, Poverty and Welfare

- The distribution of wealth and income, and explanations for it
- The welfare state
- Theoretical approaches to welfare
- The welfare state and social inequality
- Defining and measuring poverty
- Explaining poverty
- The debate over the underclass

Introduction

Many believe that large differences in wealth and income and the contrast between the very rich and the very poor have largely disappeared in modern

Britain. However, Britain remains one of the most unequal countries in the European Union, with stark contrasts between the expensive lifestyles of the rich minority, and the poverty and hardship of many of those who are unemployed, sick, old or low paid, who are lone parents, or who are homeless or living in decaying housing. This chapter will demonstrate that massive inequalities in wealth and income and widespread poverty remain in modern Britain, despite the existence of the welfare state.

The unequal distribution of wealth and income creates major differences in life chances between people. Life chances are the chances of obtaining those things defined as desirable and of avoiding those things defined as undesirable in any society. Life chances include the chances of obtaining things like good quality housing, good health, holidays, job security and educational success, and avoiding things like ill-health and unemployment. Life chances are about whether or not you have control over your life and are able to participate fully in society.

Wealth and poverty are two sides of the same coin. The causes of poverty cannot be separated from the causes of wealth, and reducing poverty necessarily involves a redistribution of wealth and income, since it is the unequal distribution of wealth and income that creates the extremes of poverty and wealth.

> **Wealth** is property in the form of assets which can be sold and turned into cash for the benefit of the owner.

Wealth and income

Wealth refers to property in the form of assets which can be sold and turned into cash for the benefit of the owner. The main forms of wealth are property such as housing and land, factories, bank deposits, shares in companies, and personal possessions.

> **Productive property** is property that provides an unearned income for its owner, such as factories, land, and stocks and shares.

- Productive property is wealth which provides an unearned income for its owner, for example houses which are rented, factories and land, or company shares which provide dividends.
- Consumption property is wealth for use by the owner, such as consumer goods like fridges, cars, or owning your own home, which do not produce any income.

> **Consumption property** is property for use by the owner which doesn't produce any income, such as owning your own car.

Income refers to the flow of money which people obtain from work, or from their investments.

> **Income** is a flow of money which people obtain from work, from their investments, or from the state.

- *Earned income* is income received from paid employment (wages and salaries).
- *Unearned income* is received from interest on savings and other personal investments, such as rent on buildings and land, interest on savings, and dividends on shares.

The distribution of wealth and income

Figure 6.1 shows that in 2002 the poorest 50 per cent of the population owned only 6 per cent of the wealth, while the richest 5 per cent owned 43 per cent. A quarter of the population possessed around three-quarters of the nation's wealth. The pattern becomes even more unequal when you exclude the value of people's homes, with nearly two-thirds (62 per cent) of wealth owned by just 5 per cent of adults. These figures are official figures from the Inland Revenue (the government's tax collectors), and they therefore underestimate the inequalities of wealth, as the wealthy have an interest in concealing their wealth to avoid taxation.

As figure 6.2 overleaf shows, income is also unequally distributed, with the richest fifth of income earners getting 42 per cent of all income in 2002–3 – more than twice their 'fair share' if income were equally distributed, and more than the bottom three-fifths of income earners got between them. The poorest fifth got only 8 per cent, less than a half of their 'fair share'.

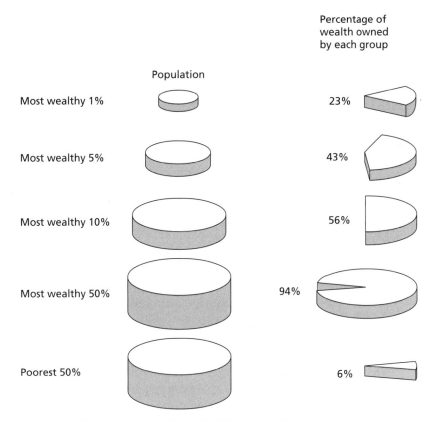

Figure 6.1 Distribution of wealth: United Kingdom, 2002
Source: Inland Revenue, 2004

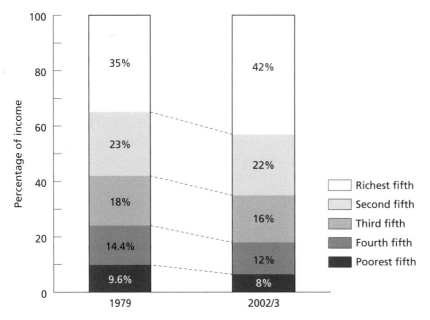

Figure 6.2 Change in distribution of income, by fifths of the population: United Kingdom, 1979-2002/3
Source: Households below Average Income, Department of Social Security, 1997 and Department for Work and Pensions, 2004

Who are the rich?

There are three main groups making up the rich:

- *The traditional aristocracy*   They are major landowners, such as the Duke of Westminster, who owns sizeable chunks of London, Cheshire, North Wales and Ireland, forests and shooting estates in Lancashire and Scotland and properties in North America and the Far East. According to the 2005 Rich List published by the *Sunday Times*, the Duke of Westminster's wealth amounts to an estimated £5.6 billion (£5,600,000,000).
- *The owners of industry and commerce*   These are the 'corporate rich' of the business world. This includes Sir Richard Branson of Virgin, Britain's seventh richest person in 2005, with estimated assets of £3 billion.
- *Stars of entertainment and the media*   These include former Beatle Sir Paul McCartney (£800 million), Sir Mick Jagger (£180 million), Sir Elton John (£185 million), and the relatively impoverished Sir Sean Connery on £82 million, Robbie Williams on £85 million and David and Victoria Beckham on £75 million.

Most wealth is inherited, with those inheriting doing nothing to earn their wealth. Most of the rich live on unearned income from investments rather than from employment. The starkness of these inequalities is made clear by the Queen, one of Britain's richest women, with personal assets estimated at £270 million. If she were to pop this into her local building society, she would receive at least £16 in unearned income each minute of every day every year (after tax) – about 190 times as much as someone on the national minimum wage in 2005, and she'd still have her original £270 million.

High earners and the self-made rich do not necessarily put in more work than those who receive low pay; it is simply that society places different values on people in different positions, and rewards them more or less highly. A senior executive in a large company or a rock star will probably not have to work as hard for his or her high income as an unskilled manual worker working long hours in a low paid job.

Activity

1 Go to Google (www.google.com) and search on the 'Rich list UK'. Have some fun finding out how rich your favourite celebrities are.
2 Do you agree or disagree with the view that it is wrong that the wealthy should be allowed to live off unearned income, and that large amounts of wealth should be able to be passed from parents to children? Do you think high earners really deserve their high rewards more than people who work in low paid jobs? Give reasons for your answers.

Attempts to redistribute wealth and income

The massive inequalities in wealth and income which have existed over the last century, and the inequalities in life chances these have caused, have provoked various measures by governments to redistribute wealth and income more equally. Some of these measures include:

● *inheritance tax*, which is a tax payable when people give gifts of wealth either before or after death, and is intended to limit the inheritance of vast quantities of wealth from one generation by the next
● *capital gains tax*, which is intended to reduce profits from dealing in property or shares, and is payable whenever these are sold
● *income tax*, which is payable on earned and unearned income; this is generally progressive, as it rises as earnings increase
● *social welfare benefits* from the state, like income support and job-seeker's allowance, which are generally seen as attempts to divert the resources obtained through taxation to the needy sections of society

Why have attempts to redistribute wealth and income failed?

Despite these measures, attempts to redistribute wealth and income have been largely unsuccessful. Little real redistribution has occurred, and what redistribution has taken place has mainly been between the very rich and the lesser rich.

Tax relief   The state allows tax relief, money normally used to pay income tax, on a wide variety of things such as business expenses, school fees and private pensions. These are expenses which only the better off are likely to have. This means that they pay a smaller proportion of their income in tax than a person who is poorer but who does not have these expenses.

Tax avoidance schemes   These are schemes which are perfectly legal, often being thought up by financial advisers and accountants to find loopholes in the tax laws and beat the tax system, thereby saving the rich from paying some tax. Such schemes involve things like living outside Britain for most of the year, investing in pension schemes to avoid income tax, investing in tax-free or low tax areas like the Channel Islands, giving wealth away to kin well before death to avoid inheritance tax, or putting companies or savings in other people's names, such as those of husband/wife, children or other kin.

Tax evasion   This is illegal, and involves people not declaring wealth and income to the Inland Revenue. This is suspected to be a common practice among the rich.

A failure to claim benefits   A final reason for the failure of attempts at wealth and income redistribution is that many people fail to claim the welfare benefits to which they are entitled. Some reasons for this are discussed later in this chapter.

Explaining the distribution of wealth and income

There are three main types of explanation for the unequal patterns of wealth and income distribution.

Functionalist explanations

Functionalist writers like Davis and Moore (1945) argue that inequalities in wealth and income are necessary to maintain society. According to Davis and Moore:

- Some positions in society are more functionally important than others in maintaining society. These require specialized skills that not everyone in society has the talent and ability to acquire.

- Those who do have the ability to do these jobs must be motivated and encouraged to train for these important positions with the promise of future high rewards in terms of income and wealth. There must therefore be a system of unequal rewards to make sure the most able people get into the most important social positions.

There are three main criticisms of this explanation:

1 There is no way of deciding which positions in society are more important, and this often rests on personal value judgements. There are many poorly rewarded occupations which can still be seen as vital in maintaining society. For example, a rich business executive can only become rich through the work of his or her employees, and a refuse collector is no less important than a doctor in maintaining society's health.
2 Some people have high levels of wealth and income, not because they have talent or occupy a position of 'functional importance', but because they have inherited their wealth. Having rich parents is still one of the major means of becoming wealthy.
3 Material rewards are not, as Davis and Moore suggest, the only means of motivating people to fill important social positions. People may be motivated by the prospect of job satisfaction, or by the attraction of giving service to others, as for example in teaching or nursing.

> **Activity**
>
> Do you think some jobs are more important than others in maintaining society? Do you think some jobs deserve higher rewards than others if people are to be motivated to train for them? Give examples of what you regard as important and unimportant jobs, giving reasons for your answer.

Weberian explanations

Market situation refers to the rewards that people are able to obtain when they sell their skills on the labour market, with the rewards they get dependent on the scarcity of their skills and the power they have to obtain high rewards.

Weberian explanations suggest that inequalities in wealth and income arise from differences in people's **market situation**.

Some people are able to get higher incomes when they sell their abilities and skills in the job market because they have rare skills, talents or qualifications that are in demand, such as doctors and lawyers. This might also happen because society values some skills and talents more highly than others and rewards them accordingly, as might be the case with business executives or company owners, or with football, film and music stars. Some 'celebrities' receive high rewards simply for being famous and in public demand, even though they lack any obvious talents.

The difficulty with the Weberian approach is that it does not easily explain the position of those who inherit their wealth and do not sell their skills on the labour market, as they live on unearned incomes rather than those earned through employment.

Marxist explanations

Marxist explanations suggest that the main reason for inequalities in wealth and income lies in the private ownership of the means of production – the key resources like land, property, factories and businesses which are necessary to produce society's goods. The concentration of ownership of the means of production in the hands of a small upper class is the basis of the inequalities of wealth, and this generates similarly high levels of income inequality through unearned income on investments. The difficulty with this approach is that it does not easily explain the wide inequalities in income that exist between people who do not own the means of production.

Activity

1 Classify each of the following situations as wealth, earned income or unearned income:
   - ownership of a chemical company
   - royalties received from publishing a sociology book
   - a boxer receiving £18 million for a boxing match
   - receiving £435 million for writing Harry Potter books
   - the Queen receiving £7.9 million from the government to support the royal household
   - Ownership of the publishing rights to the Beatles songs
   - an actor getting £20 million for making a film
   - rent received from ownership of a string of flats in London
   - dividends on shares held in a computer company
   - £1.4 million received by a footballer for sponsoring football boots
   - having £15 million worth of shares in a computer company
   - profits received from owning a national daily newspaper
   - £150 a week from working in a burger chain

2 Which out of the functionalist, Marxist and Weberian explanations do you find the most convincing in explaining the distribution of wealth and income in our society? Give reasons for your answer.

3 What assumptions and stereotypes do you have of the rich? Draw up your view of the features of rich people, such as their sources of wealth and income and their lifestyle. Where do you think your ideas and assumptions about the rich come from?

4 Do you think large inequalities in wealth and income are justified in society? Give reasons for your answer.

Activity

1 Explain, with examples, the difference between 'wealth' and 'income'.
2 Suggest three reasons why some jobs get higher rewards than others.
3 Identify two policies that might contribute to the redistribution of wealth and income.
4 Answer the following essay question, in about one and half to two sides of A4 paper: *Assess sociological explanations for the unequal distribution of wealth and income in contemporary Britain.*

The welfare state

What is the welfare state?

A welfare state is one that is concerned with implementing social policies guaranteeing the 'cradle to grave' well-being of the whole population, and particularly the elimination of poverty, unemployment, ill-health and ignorance. Such policies are generally implemented using resources collected through taxation.

The welfare state in Britain mainly began with the Beveridge Report of 1942. This recommended the development of state-run welfare services (backed up by voluntary organizations) aimed at the destruction of the 'five giants' of want, disease, squalor, ignorance and idleness, and the creation of a society where each individual would have the right to be cared for by the state from 'womb to tomb'. The welfare state as we know it today came into effect on 5 July 1948 – the date of the foundation of the National Health Service.

The welfare state provides a wide range of benefits and services, paid for by taxation. They include:

- A range of welfare benefits through the social security system for many groups such as the unemployed, those injured at work, the sick and disabled, widows, the retired, expectant mothers, lone parents and children.
- A comprehensive and largely free National Health Service, including antenatal and postnatal care, hospitals, local GPs, dentists and opticians (although some charges are payable – for example to dentists and opticians).
- A free and compulsory state education for all to the age of 16 (and subsidies after that age).
- Social services provided by local councils, such as social workers, and facilities for the mentally and physically disabled, the elderly and children. Local councils are also responsible for housing the

homeless, and for overseeing the adoption and arranging the fostering of children. The structure and key services of the welfare state (as they were in 2005) are shown in figure 6.3.

The Beveridge Report and the development of the welfare state in Britain were based on four main principles and assumptions:

- full employment
- universal welfare – cradle-to-grave provision
- free health care and education
- that women would be primarily housewives and mothers – as the Beveridge Report said, 'women would make marriage their sole occupation'.

Who provides welfare?

Although welfare is generally seen as provided only by the state, it is also provided informally through the family and community, and by a range of voluntary and private agencies as well. This range of provision is known as welfare pluralism.

> **Welfare pluralism** refers to the whole range of welfare provision, including informal provision by the family and community, welfare provided by the government, the voluntary sector and the private sector.

Informal welfare provision

Much welfare provision is provided informally by family, friends and neighbours. Feminist writers have emphasized that this often means care by women, as it is women who take on the main caring responsibilities in the family for the dependent elderly, the disabled and the sick. The Equal Opportunities Commission has suggested around three times more women than men are involved in this informal care. As seen above, the Beveridge Report included the patriarchal assumption that women would be primarily housewives and mothers, concerned with housework, childcare and looking after the family, with men supporting them through paid employment. This meant it was assumed married women didn't need the same level of social security benefits as men, as these would go to their husbands to support their families in times of need. Much welfare provision today still rests on this assumption, despite the fact that many married women now also work outside the home in paid employment.

The voluntary sector

Voluntary organizations are non-official, non-profit-making organizations, often charities, which are 'voluntary' in the sense that they are neither created by, nor controlled by, the government. They are staffed by both salaried employees and voluntary helpers, and are funded by donations from the public and grants from, or sale of services to, central and local government. Voluntary organizations try to fill some of the gaps left

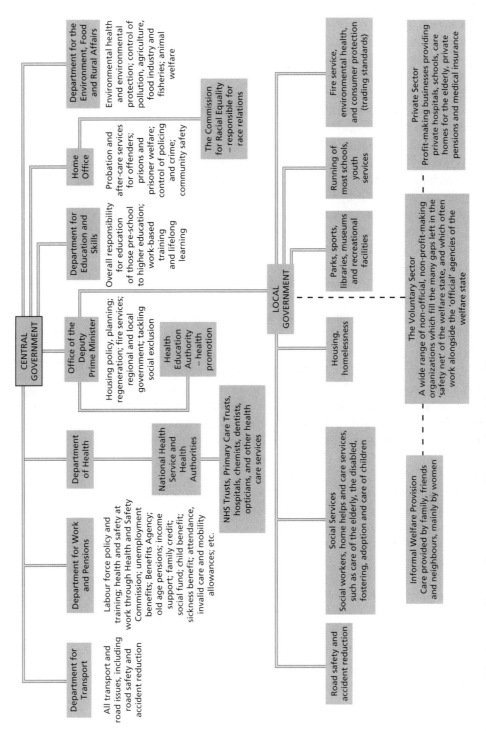

Figure 6.3 'Womb-to-tomb' care: the structure and key services of the welfare state

by the 'safety net' provided by the state, by providing help and information in areas where state assistance is too little or non-existent.

Voluntary organizations include groups such as the Salvation Army, which provides hostel accommodation and soup kitchens; Shelter, which campaigns for the homeless and helps with finding accommodation; Help the Aged and Age Concern; the Citizens' Advice Bureau (CAB); the NSPCC (the National Society for the Prevention of Cruelty to Children) and the Child Poverty Action Group, which promotes action for the relief of poverty among children and families with children. The churches also provide a range of welfare support, particularly to the elderly.

Voluntary organizations have the advantage of providing cheaper services than those provided by the state or private sectors, combined with high levels of expertise. They can therefore be better able to respond in specialized areas, like domestic violence, homelessness or AIDS, where state provision may be under pressure, inadequate or non-existent. However, voluntary organizations often lack adequate funds to be as effective as they might otherwise be, and they do not exist in all the areas where they are needed.

Voluntary organizations also play important roles as **pressure groups**. Many voluntary organizations lead public campaigns to improve welfare benefits and services for the poor and socially excluded. (Social exclusion is discussed later in this chapter.) Voluntary organizations play a major role in highlighting the weaknesses of the welfare state, and keeping problems such as poverty, homelessness and the care of the mentally ill in the public eye. They frequently provide expert knowledge and make recommendations to governments for changes to improve social welfare.

> **Pressure groups** are organizations which try to put pressure on those with power in society to implement policies which they favour.

The private sector

The private sector consists of profit-making private businesses, from which individuals or local and central government purchase welfare services. This sector provides welfare services such as private hospitals, schools, care homes for the elderly, private pensions and medical insurance. Those with conservative views (see the 'New Right' or market liberal approach, below) often see the private sector as cheaper, providing more choice, and more efficient and effective than state provision, because it has to compete for customers and provide a decent service if it is to survive in the face of competition. However, the need to make profits may mean cost-cutting takes a higher priority than the quality of services provided. Access to the private sector is only available to those who can afford it, and poor people may therefore not get services at all if the state doesn't provide or pay for them.

Activity

1   Do you think the state should be the main provider of welfare for all? What
    are the advantages and disadvantages of welfare provision by the state
    compared to the voluntary and private sectors?
2   Suggest reasons why informal welfare provision is mainly carried out by
    women. What consequences do you think this might have for women's
    lives and careers?

Theoretical approaches to welfare

There are four main approaches to the welfare state, and to the way
welfare services should be provided. The main differences are between
those who think welfare should be the responsibility of individuals,
provided by the private sector and with people buying services themselves, and those who think the state should provide welfare funded
through taxation.

The social democratic approach (the welfare model)

Social democratic approaches believe in the following:

Marginalization refers to
the process whereby some
groups are pushed by
poverty, ill-health, lack of
education, disability,
racism and so on to the
margins or edges of
society and are unable to
take part in the life
enjoyed by the majority of
citizens.

● *The government should be responsible for social welfare*, and for action
  to eliminate problems such as unemployment and poverty, providing
  care for the disabled, children in need, the elderly and other vulnerable and socially excluded groups facing **marginalization**.
● *Social inequality threatens the stability of society*, and wealth and
  income should be redistributed through progressive taxation (the
  more you earn, the more tax you pay), with benefits available to all
  to reduce social inequality and tackle poverty. Only the state has the
  power and resources to do this, and should provide 'womb to
  tomb' care.
● *Benefits should be available to all* (universal benefits), because selective, means tested benefits, which are only payable to those whose
  income falls below a certain level, create a stigma on those claiming
  them. This stigma means those in greatest need often fail to claim
  benefits to which they are entitled. Means testing also discourages
  people from taking low paid work when it becomes available, catching them in a poverty trap (see table 6.1 overleaf).
● *The need for more social cohesion* – universal provision, like free
  education, pensions, full employment and free health care, bring
  economic benefits through an employed, healthy and well-qualified
  workforce, and help to promote a more cohesive, less divided, society.

> ### Universal benefits and means testing
>
> *Universal benefits* are those available to everyone regardless of income, such as the basic state pension, child benefit and free health care and education.
>
>   *Means testing* involves people having to pass a test of their income and savings (their 'means') before receiving any benefits: only if these are low enough will they receive any benefits.

The New Right or market liberal approach

The New Right approach mainly developed in Britain in the years of the Conservative government between 1979 and 1997. This is also known as a market liberal approach because it believes that individuals should have the freedom to choose welfare provision from all those competing in the 'welfare market', and should take responsibility themselves for obtaining it, mainly through the private sector. According to this approach:

- *The generosity of the 'nanny' welfare state is seen as undermining personal responsibility and self-help*, and people's willingness to work to support themselves. Writers like Murray (1989, 1990) and Marsland (1989) argue that the welfare state has created a dependency culture and a work-shy underclass which wants to avoid work by living off welfare benefits. The generosity of the welfare state has undermined the importance of support from families, and encourages lone parenthood, as women have children they could not otherwise have supported, knowing they can get help from state benefits.
- *Taxation should be kept to the minimum*, and should not be wasted on providing welfare benefits to those who are able to support themselves.
- *State benefits should be restricted only to the very poor*, and those unable to work through sickness or disability, and should be means tested. The rest of the population should provide their own welfare services by buying them from the private sector, such as private medicine and private pension plans.

A **dependency culture** is a set of values and beliefs, and a way of life, centred on dependence on others, particularly benefits from the welfare state.

The **underclass** is a social group right at the bottom of the social hierarchy, whose members are in some ways different from, and cut off or excluded from, the rest of society.

Table 6.1 gives the case for and against means testing.

Marxist approaches

Marxist approaches tend to see the welfare state mainly as a way of buying off working-class protest, by reducing the risks to social order and political stability created by extreme poverty. By keeping the labour force healthy and efficient to the benefit of the capitalist class, the welfare state attempts

Table 6.1. The case for and against means testing of benefits

For (New Right or market liberal approach)	Against (social democratic or welfare model)
Benefits are targeted only on those who really need them. People who are able to work should support themselves. Money is saved on universal benefits which most people don't need and shouldn't have. More money is available to invest in the economy, create jobs and cut taxes	Means-tested benefits, which are received only by the very poor, may lead to some people being worse off if they take a low paid job. They may lose means tested benefits like housing or council tax benefits, and the extra they earn is not enough to compensate for the lost benefits. This 'poverty trap' discourages people from taking work. Universal benefits avoid this
Means testing stops voluntary unemployment being an option for some people, and fights the welfare dependency culture	Because of the poverty trap, means testing might drive people into a dependency culture and a reluctance to get a job
Families, communities and voluntary organizations are strengthened as alternative sources of support	Families and communities caught in the poverty trap are likely to be weakened by poverty and stress. Some will be encouraged to become 'benefit cheats' to get around means testing. Universal benefits keep everyone's standards up to an acceptable minimum level
Selective means-tested benefits will enable more benefits for the most disadvantaged, by no longer wasting money on those who can afford to support themselves	Often the most deprived do not take up or make full use of even universal benefits, as they're unsure of how to do so. Means-tested benefits attach a stigma to those who claim them, and make it even more unlikely they will claim benefits to which they are entitled

to make a system based on inequality, exploitation and conflict appear caring and just. The welfare state is then a form of social control – an attempt to keep the workforce efficient and trained, and the capitalist system stable, by giving workers a stake in society.

Feminist approaches

Feminist approaches emphasize the way the welfare state supports patriarchy, and the inadequacy of the welfare state in meeting the needs of women. They point to the way the benefit system is frequently based on contributions records built up by full-time workers, who are less likely to be women, and the way the founding principles of the welfare state, discussed earlier, were based on an assumption of women being financially supported by men, with important levels of care of the elderly, children, the sick and disabled being provided by women.

The social democratic or welfare model was that which underpinned the welfare state in Britain until 1979. Since then, the market model has become more dominant, with a greater emphasis on tackling the dependency culture, cutting the soaring levels of state spending on welfare provision, on encouraging provision by the voluntary and private sectors, and on more support through the family and community.

Activity

Refer to the following statements, and say in each case which model of welfare it most closely matches. Give reasons for your answers.

1 'Those who are working resent seeing neighbours, apparently as fit as themselves, living on incapacity benefit. It has become known as "bad back" benefit.'

2 'If it wasn't for the safety net of the welfare state, there would be widespread discontent and protest by working-class people against the inequalities and exploitation they face.'

3 'The welfare state simply doesn't recognize the amount of unpaid work that women do in the home.'

4 'If you withdraw benefits, people will be forced to bear the consequences of their behaviour. Gradually a traditional morality will re-emerge, whereby the two-parent family becomes the norm again, and bastards and single parents are stigmatized.'

5 'A lot of unemployment is produced by the very policies we are talking about. It is avoidable. You have little boys growing up who literally do not know how to work. They have not been socialized to get up at 7 o'clock and go into work even if they don't feel like it.'

6 'Get the poor off our overtaxed backs.'

7 'Investment, investment, investment in health, education, pensions and other public services is what this country needs. The government has done a lot, but a lot more needs to be done and this government will do it.'

8 'The government should stop squandering money on a spending binge, and invest in the economy to raise the living standards of all.'

9 'The state's welfare services should be financed largely from the income of those who can most afford to pay. The state should ensure that resources are redistributed from the rich and top salary earners to those in our society who suffer ill-health, unemployment, poverty and deprivation.'

The welfare state and social inequality

Social democratic approaches generally see the welfare state as a device for reducing social inequality through progressive taxation providing benefits for all, but particularly for the disadvantaged, through increased state spending on education, health, social security and other welfare services.

> ## Activity
>
> 1 Explain what is meant by 'welfare pluralism'.
> 2 Explain what is meant by the 'voluntary sector', and outline its role in welfare provision.
> 3 Explain the difference between universal and means-tested benefits.
> 4 Suggest two ways in which private sector welfare provision might create unequal access to welfare services.
> 5 Identify and explain two differences between the New Right (market liberal) and social democratic approaches to the welfare state.
> 6 Identify two feminist criticisms of the welfare state.
> 7 Write a short essay, of about one and a half sides of A4 paper, answering the following question:
> *Examine the view that social welfare is likely to be most effective when services are delivered by a range of providers rather than by the state alone.*

In other words, the welfare state is seen as *redistributive* – passing income from the rich to the poor – so society becomes more equal.

However, the welfare state has failed to do this. Means testing of benefits, prescription charges, dental charges, fees for universities and the abolition of student grants have all affected those on lower incomes the most. Some benefits, like the jobseeker's allowance (formerly unemployment benefit) and state pensions, are linked to income and previous employment, so those on lower incomes or with an interrupted paid employment record (for example, because they were raising children) get lower benefits.

Both basic and higher rates of income tax have been cut, and there has been an increase in indirect taxes like VAT (value added tax) and those on petrol, alcohol and tobacco. Indirect taxes are payable on people's spending rather than their income, and take up a greater proportion of the income of the poor compared with the better off. In these circumstances, the tax system has become less progressive, and in some ways hits the poor harder than the rich.

The inverse care law

The **inverse care law** suggests that those in the greatest need of help from the welfare state get the fewest resources allocated to them, while those whose need is least get the most resources.

In chapter 3 on health, the **inverse care law** was discussed. This suggests that those whose need is greatest get the least spent on them, and those whose need is least get the most spent on them. Julian Le Grand (1982) has argued that this inverse care law is found throughout the whole range of welfare state provision. He argues that most welfare spending consists of either universal benefits going to everyone (like the basic state pension, or free education and health care) or is spent in ways that provide services from which the middle class gains most. For example, people in the more advantaged middle class:

- receive more spending per head on health
- make better use of the health service, as they are more self-confident, effective and assertive in dealing with doctors, and therefore get longer consultations, ask more questions, receive more explanations from their doctors and are more likely to be referred for further treatment
- receive more spending per person in education, as their children are more likely to stay in education after school-leaving age, and they have more knowledge and confidence in dealing with educational professionals to get the best deals in education for their children
- benefit more from spending on roads and public transport (particularly rail travel), as they are more likely to be commuters and have cars
- benefit more from tax relief on private pensions and business expenses

Westergaard and Resler (1976) argue that the welfare system is largely concerned with transferring or redistributing resources *within* rather than *between* social classes, for example from one section of the working class to another, such as from those in work to those who are unemployed, and from the healthy to the sick. They see support for the old, the unemployed, the sick and disabled as being largely paid for by other working-class taxpayers, or through their own national insurance payments taken from their wages.

Inequalities between ethnic groups

In the chapter on health, there was a discussion of inequalities in health between ethnic groups. The weaknesses in health care discussed there are only part of the general pattern of disadvantage faced by some minority ethnic groups in the welfare state generally. Pakistani, Bangladeshi and African-Caribbean minority ethnic groups are marginalized, and encounter racism and discrimination in welfare provision. Literature is often not translated, and staff are often not trained in their cultural backgrounds. They are more likely to be unemployed, and so lose out on income-related benefits. Pakistani and Bangladeshi people are the poorest social groups in Britain.

Gender inequality

Feminist views have already been mentioned earlier in the context of the patriarchal assumptions of women as primarily wives, mothers and carers which have traditionally underpinned the welfare state. There are a number of other inequalities where women are concerned.

Women are more likely to work part-time rather than full-time, and to interrupt their working lives for childrearing or caring for dependent elderly relatives. A lack of free childcare often makes it difficult for women to take full-time jobs. This means they often lose out on a range of income-related benefits, like the earnings-related state pension and the job-seeker's allowance. Poverty is much more a problem for women than men, throughout their lives, but particularly in old age. (The 'feminization of poverty' is discussed later.) Feminists advocate making the welfare state more responsive to the needs of women, such as through the provision of better cancer screening, Well Woman clinics to meet women's health needs, and a recognition of women's unpaid work in the home.

The welfare state and poverty

Despite the welfare state, Abel-Smith and Townsend (1965) showed that in the 1960s poverty was still a major social problem in Britain. It remains so in contemporary Britain.

Until the end of the 1970s, the main thrust of state welfare policy was to tackle the problem of poverty. However, since the 1980s there has been a growing concern with the escalating costs of the welfare state. This was mainly due to rising unemployment in the 1980s, but in the 2000s it is mainly focused on the ageing population (a growing proportion of elderly people in the population). These have meant more benefits and pensions being paid out, with growing pressures on pension and health spending, but with less tax being collected to pay for them.

The Conservative governments of 1979–97 were strongly influenced by the ideas of the New Right. This meant the government wanted to cut back welfare spending, eliminate the dependency culture, and develop the principles of self-help. It preferred to target benefits only on the sick, disabled and the elderly and others unable to help themselves. The rest of the population was encouraged to rely more on their own resources rather than expecting to be supported by the state.

These years were marked by serious cuts in welfare spending and the value of welfare benefits. Income taxes were reduced, more benefits were means tested, and grants to the poor were replaced with loans. Charges were either introduced or increased for eye tests and dentists, and prescription charges were increased. Student grants were replaced with loans, and the Child Support Agency was set up, so that absent fathers rather than the state could carry the financial costs of looking after their children. State education was starved of cash.

By 1997, Britain had the highest levels of poverty in the European Union, and the largest gap between the highest and lowest paid since records began in 1886. Britain was one of the most unequal countries in the Western world.

The Labour government of 1997

A Labour government came to power in 1997, and began a process back towards a more social democratic model of welfare provision. A strong emphasis was placed on tackling the problems of those pushed to the margins of society and unable to fully participate in social life because of poverty, lack of education, old age or ill-health.

A large number of policies were implemented to tackle poverty and social exclusion, including:

- An increase in benefit and pension levels, a minimum income guarantee for pensioners, and big increases on spending on health and education.
- The introduction of Britain's first National Minimum Wage, to help the poorest paid.
- The introduction of a system of tax credits (allowances) to help the most disadvantaged.
- The establishment of 'New Deals' to help the young, lone parents, the long-term unemployed and the disabled to move from welfare into work.
- An increase in childcare and nursery education, with all 3 and 4 year olds guaranteed five half-days of nursery education a week.
- A Neighbourhood Renewal Strategy, to regenerate the most deprived communities, and to help improve the health and education of the most disadvantaged.
- A reduction in child poverty, with the aim of eliminating it within a generation.

> ### Activity
>
> Go to the government's social exclusion website, www.socialexclusion.gov.uk/, and identify two policies which are currently being followed to help the most disadvantaged in our society. Explain how they might do this and how successful they are.

Poverty

There are four basic issues in studying poverty:

1   defining poverty – what is it?
2   measuring poverty

3 explaining poverty
4 suggesting policy solutions for it

Changing views of poverty

Much of the early sociological research into poverty was a reaction against the idea that poverty was the poor's own fault – that they were simply idlers and scroungers, an 'undeserving' group who were themselves to blame for their own poverty, and therefore nothing should be done to help them. Two pieces of research showed the poor were in fact decent, hard-working families who were forced into poverty by circumstances beyond their control, such as irregular or low pay, ill-health or disability, unemployment or old age: the 'deserving poor'. These pieces of research were:

- Booth's *Life and Labour of People in London* – a study of poverty in London between 1886 and 1903.
- Joseph Rowntree's studies of poverty in York, carried out in 1899, 1936 and 1950.

Absolute poverty or subsistence poverty refers to a person's biological needs for food, water, clothing and shelter – the basic minimum requirements necessary to subsist and maintain life, health and physical efficiency. A person in absolute poverty lacks the minimum necessary for healthy survival.

Defining poverty (1): absolute or subsistence poverty

A person in absolute poverty lacks the minimum necessary for healthy survival. People in **absolute poverty** would be poor anywhere at any time – the standard does not vary much over time. The solution to absolute poverty is to raise the living standards of the poor above subsistence level.

Measuring absolute poverty

Various attempts have been made to measure absolute poverty. Rowntree, for example, used medical studies of nutrition to identify the cheapest

Absolute poverty
Photos: Gordon Browne

costs of a standard basic diet needed to maintain life, coupled with minimum housing, heating and clothing costs.

The absolute conception of poverty has some advantages, as it makes it relatively straightforward to make national and international comparisons, since basic physical or subsistence needs are fairly easy to identify. Such a view of poverty is generally the one most people consider when they think of poverty – the kind that is often found in less developed countries, for example in Africa, where famines and starvation occur and people lack the basic subsistence needs for biological survival.

Activity

1 Keep a record of everything you consume in one week – food, drinks, leisure activities, rent if you pay it, an estimate of how much electricity and gas you use, travel expenses and so on.
2 Find out how much all these things cost, perhaps by visiting a local supermarket.
3 Then try to find out how much you would be entitled to in welfare benefits each week. You may be able to find out from leaflets at a local social security office or a community centre or from the Citizens' Advice Bureau website www.adviceguide.org.uk/.
4 Discuss whether you could or would want to live on these benefit levels.

The weaknesses/disadvantages of the absolute conception of poverty

Difficulty in identifying basic subsistence needs It is difficult to identify objectively what basic subsistence needs are. For example, Rowntree's minimum budget was based on a list of nutritional and other requirements essential for life. He was criticized for relying heavily on the values and opinions of those who drew up the list. In particular, his list involved a no-waste budget, in which everything was fully used and food didn't go off or not get eaten. The list reflected the nutritional, cooking and shopping skills of middle-class researchers rather than the reality of the choice of food and the resources of the poor.

Value judgements Rowntree's views of food, clothing and shelter were those thought customary at the time. Even a basic budget may therefore reflect not simply minimal nutritional requirements, but value judgements of what an appropriate diet consists of.

It ignores the reality of people's lives 'Expert' views of the contents and costs of a minimum diet make assumptions that the poor have the same knowledge of nutrition as the experts, and that the poor can shop around and get the cheapest goods. It doesn't really take into account the knowledge people have, their shopping habits, how they actually spend the money they have, and the social, cultural and psychological factors which may influence this. For example, having a Christmas pudding may not be necessary to maintain health, but most people in Britain, including the poor, would want to have one. Is this wasteful and does it make assumptions that the poor should deny themselves diets that most people would regard as perfectly normal? The poor are often unable to buy at the cheapest prices anyway. (See the box 'Trapped in poverty: the poor pay more' on p. 343 later in this chapter.)

There is no clear subsistence minimum   There are wide differences between societies, and between groups in the same society, in what forms a subsistence minimum. Minimum diets, for example, will differ between men and women, by age, by the type of occupation a person has and so on. For example, an unskilled manual labourer doing heavy physical labour will require more calories each day than an office worker, and minimum nutritional and housing needs will be different between hot and cold climates.

It ignores social needs and cultural expectations   It treats people as if they were nothing more than biological machines, and ignores the fact that people are social beings, who live in groups which create needs beyond just physical survival. This involves mixing with people, entertaining them, eating with them, participating in community life and leisure activities, and meeting social obligations, such as buying wedding or birthday presents, or giving children parties. This will also involve expectations of appropriate food – eating cats or rats is not something most of us in Britain would see as acceptable behaviour, even though it might be quite nutritious. Value judgements and cultural expectations of what that minimum is therefore influence even a notion of a subsistence minimum.

These criticisms have led most sociologists and poverty researchers to adopt the idea of relative poverty.

Activity

Do you think poverty should be defined only in absolute terms? What other aspects, if any, of people's lives do you think should be considered in defining poverty?

Defining poverty (2): relative poverty

In this view, people are poverty-stricken when they lack things that wider society regards as the minimum necessary for a socially acceptable standard of living. Townsend (1979) has provided the classic definition of **relative poverty**:

> Individuals, families and groups in the population can be said to be in poverty when they lack the resources to obtain the types of diets, participate in the activities and have the living conditions and amenities which are customary, or at least widely encouraged or approved, in the societies to which they belong. Their resources are so seriously below those commanded by the average individual or family that they are, in effect, excluded from ordinary living patterns, customs or activities.

This type of poverty is a condition where individuals or families are deprived of the opportunities, comforts and self-respect which the majority of people in their society enjoy. Minimum needs are then related to the standard of living in any society at any one time, and will therefore vary over time and between societies, as standards of living change. For example, those living in slum housing in Britain would be regarded as poor in Britain, but their housing would appear as relative luxury to poor peasants in some developing countries. Similarly, running hot water and an indoor bathroom and toilet would have been seen as luxuries 150 years ago in Britain, but today are seen as basic necessities, and those without them would be regarded as poor by most people.

    The solution to relative poverty necessarily involves a more equal distribution of wealth and income, so no section of society is deprived in relation to the average standard of living. The debate about poverty necessarily becomes a part of the debate about social inequality.

    The relative definition of poverty is closely linked with the idea of **social exclusion**.

Dimensions of relative poverty apart from income: poverty as social exclusion

The ideas of relative poverty and social exclusion suggest there are wider social, cultural and psychological dimensions of poverty apart from just a low income. Poverty is not simply a matter of how much income people have, but can also involve a combination of other linked problems in their lives such as discrimination, poor skills, poor housing, bad health, family breakdown, social isolation, a poor environment, high crime neighbourhoods and poor quality and availability of public services like transport, hospitals, libraries, schools and play areas for children. These problems are linked, and each one can make the others worse, and create a vicious cycle in people's lives which it is hard for them to escape from. Two people

---

Relative poverty defines poverty in relation to a generally accepted standard of living in a specific society at a specific time. This takes into account social and cultural needs as well as biological needs, so that people can join in with the usual pattern of life in their society.

Social exclusion involves people being marginalized or excluded from participation in education, work, community life, access to services and other aspects of life seen as part of being a full and participating member of mainstream society. Those who lack the necessary resources are excluded from the opportunity to fully join in with society, and are denied the opportunities most people take for granted. It is about being cut off from what most people would regard as a normal life.

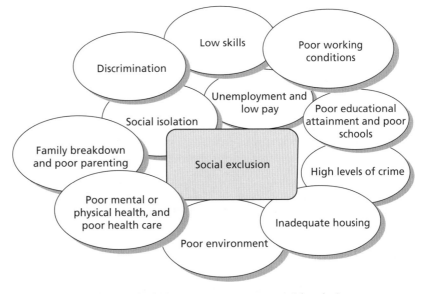

Figure 6.4 Dimensions of relative poverty: poverty as social exclusion

---

Activity

Refer to figure 6.4 and:

1 Suggest two ways that high crime areas and poor environments might be linked.
2 Suggest two ways that poor schools might be linked to poor parenting.
3 Suggest two ways that inadequate housing might be linked to poor health.
4 Suggest two reasons why poor health and a low income might contribute to social isolation.
5 Explain what is meant by 'social exclusion', and why relative poverty might be seen as social exclusion.

---

may have the same low income, but one may live in an isolated rural community with few facilities, no shop, no doctor's surgery, no car, irregular public transport, no local school and so on. The other may live in an urban area, with lots of facilities, easy transport or easy walking distances and so on. The poor may therefore live a deprived lifestyle apart from simply being short of money.

Figure 6.4 illustrates this range of linked dimensions of relative poverty, and how they can combine and overlap to create social exclusion.

Examples of poverty apart from income include the following.

Homelessness   In the year to June 2005, 115,340 households were officially accepted as homeless and in priority need by local authorities in

England. Breakdown of relationships, and mortgage and rent arrears can lead to loss of homes. This can make getting and holding down a job difficult, leading sometimes to a downward spiral.

Poverty in health care   Good health is important to an active life, but

- there are fewer doctors practising in inner city areas (where many of the poor live), and those who do are often overworked, because the poor have more health problems
- the poor are less likely to get time off work with pay to visit the doctor
- they face longer hospital waiting lists
- many are not fully aware of what health services are available to them, and the poor tend to be less vocal and articulate in demanding proper standards of care from doctors

Poverty at school   Education can offer a way out of poverty, but

- inner city schools often have older buildings and poorer facilities
- there is often a concentration of social problems in these schools, such as drugs and vandalism, and consequently a higher turnover of teachers
- parents are less able to help their children with their education, and have less money than better-off parents to enable the school to buy extra resources

Poverty at work   Poor working conditions include a neglect of health and safety standards and a high accident rate; working at night and long periods of overtime because the pay is so low; lack of trade union organization to protect the workers' interests; lack of entitlement to paid holidays; insecure employment; and no employers' sick pay or pension schemes.

Personal factors linked with poverty   These might include:

- *Poor health*   Examples are respiratory problems like asthma and infectious diseases, as a result of poor diet and damp, overcrowded housing.
- *Social isolation and boredom*   Making friends may be hard because there is no money to get involved in social activities.
- *Stress*   In the face of mounting bills and debts, stress can lead to domestic violence, family breakdown, and mental and physical illness.
- *Low self-esteem*   This can be brought on by dependence on others, the lack of access to the activities and facilities others have, and difficulties in coping with day-to-day life.

Measuring relative poverty

The idea of relative poverty is necessarily based on value judgements as to what constitutes a 'reasonable' standard of living. How do you decide what the minimum standards are in relation to the expectations of a particular society? There have been a number of attempts to come up with various measures of relative poverty, and these are outlined below.

Townsend's deprivation index   Townsend measured relative poverty in the UK using a 'deprivation index' of sixty indicators of lifestyle considered to be 'customary' for an acceptable standard of living. He reduced these to twelve which he saw as particularly important indicators of deprivation, clearly linked to low income, and then checked how many households lacked those items. This deprivation index is shown in the box overleaf.

Townsend's deprivation index was criticized heavily because:

- It was said to be measuring inequality not poverty.
- The choice of indicators was based on Townsend's own values and had more to do with taste than with poverty.
- It didn't allow for choice – for whether people lacked items because they couldn't afford them or because they simply didn't want them.
- It focused on people's individual behaviour, and ignored indicators of deprivation like the availability of and access to public services, such as public transport, hospitals, clinics and libraries.

The consensual measurement of relative poverty   The *Breadline Britain* studies by Mack and Lansley in 1983 and 1990, and *Poverty and Social Exclusion in Britain* by the Joseph Rowntree Foundation (Gordon et al., 2000), were attempts to overcome the criticisms of Townsend's deprivation index, particularly that it simply reflected his own preferences and values, and that it didn't allow for choice.

To avoid this, these surveys asked a representative sample of the public, not experts, to decide what items *they thought* were necessary for a minimum standard of living in Britain. The responses represented a consensus (widespread agreement) on what ordinary people thought made up the minimum standards required for life in Britain at the beginning of the twenty-first century.

The *Poverty and Social Exclusion* survey included only items that 50 per cent or more thought necessities, and then calculated how many people lacked three or more of these items, asking them whether this was because of choice or because they couldn't afford them. This research provided a valuable insight into how the public measures relative poverty. The list is shown in the box on page 329.

Townsend's deprivation index

1. Has not had a week's holiday away from home in the last twelve months.
2. (Adults only). Has not had a relative or friend to the home for a meal or snack in the last four weeks.
3. (Adults only). Has not been out in the last four weeks to a relative or friend for a meal or snack.
4. (Children only – under 15). Has not had a friend to play or to tea in the last four weeks.
5. (Children only). Did not have a party on last birthday.
6. Has not had an afternoon or evening out for entertainment in the last two weeks.
7. Does not have fresh meat (including meals out) as many as four days a week.
8. Has gone through one or more days in the past fortnight without a cooked meal.
9. Has not had a cooked breakfast most days of the week.
10. Household does not have a refrigerator.
11. Household does not usually have a Sunday joint (three in four times).
12. Household does not have sole use of four amenities indoors (flush WC; sink or washbasin and cold water tap; fixed bath or shower; and gas or electric cooker).

Source: P. Townsend, *Poverty in the United Kingdom* (Harmondsworth: Penguin, 1979).

Activity

Study Townsend's deprivation index:

1. Do you think the twelve items on Townsend's deprivation index provide useful indicators of poverty? Give reasons for your answers, with reference to each indicator.
2. Do you think such indicators provide an adequate view of poverty? Suggest ways of improving Townsend's index, and suggest five additional or alternative indicators that you think might provide a better guide to poverty in the 2000s.
3. In what ways do you think Townsend's own values might have influenced his choice of indicators? How do you think your own values might have influenced your choice of indicators in the previous question?

Income measurements – the 'official' poverty line The **poverty line** used in Britain in 2005, and by the European Union, was 60 per cent of average income (or strictly speaking, '60 per cent of median income after housing costs'). This line dividing those who are regarded as poor and those who are not was adopted as it was thought that at or below this level

A **poverty line** is a government-agreed dividing point between those who are poor and those who are not.

The *Poverty and Social Exclusion* survey list

1. Beds and bedding for everyone.
2. Heating to warm living areas of the home.
3. Damp-free home.
4. Visiting friends or family in hospital.
5. Two meals a day.
6. Medicines prescribed by doctor.
7. Refrigerator.
8. Fresh fruit and vegetables daily.
9. Warm, waterproof coat.
10. Replace or repair broken electrical goods.
11. Visits to friends or family.
12. Celebrations on special occasions such as Christmas.
13. Money to keep home in a decent state of decoration.
14. Visits to school, for example on sports day.
15. Attending weddings, funerals.
16. Meat, fish or vegetarian equivalent every other day.
17. Insurance of contents of dwelling.
18. Hobby or leisure activity.
19. Washing machine.
20. Collect children from school.
21. Telephone.
22. Appropriate clothes for job interviews.
23. Deep freezer/fridge freezer.
24. Carpets in living rooms and bedrooms.
25. Regular savings (of £10 per month) for rainy days or retirement.
26. Two pairs of all-weather shoes.
27. Friends or family round for a meal.
28. A small amount of money to spend on self weekly, not on family.
29. Television.
30. Roast joint/vegetarian equivalent once a week.
31. Presents for friends/family once a year.
32. A holiday away from home once a year not with relatives.
33. Replace worn-out furniture.
34. Dictionary.
35. An outfit for social occasions.
36. New, not second-hand, clothes.
37. Attending place of worship.
38. Car.
39. Coach/train fares to visit friends/family quarterly.
40. An evening out once a fortnight.
41. Dressing gown.
42. Having a daily newspaper.
43. A meal in a restaurant/pub monthly.
44. Microwave oven.
45. Tumble dryer.
46. Going to the pub once a fortnight.
47. Video cassette recorder.
48. Holidays abroad once a year.
49. CD player.
50. Home computer.
51. Dishwasher.
52. Mobile phone.
53. Access to the internet.
54. Satellite television.

Source: Adapted from David Gordon et al., *Poverty and Social Exclusion in Britain* (York: Joseph Rowntree Foundation, 2000). Reproduced by permission of the Joseph Rowntree Foundation.

Activity

1   Either alone or through majority agreement in a group, go through the
    Poverty and Social Exclusion survey list shown in the box, ticking those
    items which you think are necessities, which all adults should be able to
    afford, and no one should have to go without.
2   Compare your list with that of another person or group. How do your
    decisions compare with others? Were some items clear-cut and others
    borderline? Discuss the reasons for any differences of opinion about what
    count as necessities.
3   The *Poverty and Social Exclusion in Britain* national survey, conducted in
    2000, found that items 1–35 were considered necessities by 50 per cent or
    more of the population. At least two out of three members of the public
    classed items 1–25 as necessities which no one should have to go without.
    How far does your list agree or disagree with these national findings?
4   Do you think if you were in a very poor country you would have the same
    list of necessities? Give reasons for your answer.
5   What does this exercise tell you about the ways of measuring poverty in
    modern Britain?

of income people would be excluded from a minimum acceptable way of
life in the society they were living in. This involves a clear relative conception of poverty, but you should note the limitations discussed above of
using income alone as an indicator of poverty.

The strengths/advantages of the relative conception of poverty

The relative conception of poverty:

● Recognizes poverty as a social construction – this means it recognizes
  that measures of social deprivation are influenced by how other members of society define what is a 'normal' standard of living in any society.
● Recognizes that what constitutes poverty can change between societies and over time in the same society.
● Links poverty to wider issues of social exclusion.

The weaknesses/disadvantages of the relative conception of poverty

On the other hand, there are problems with the relative conception:

● It is not an indicator of poverty, but simply of social inequality. No
  matter how rich a society becomes, there will always be those who
  lack things that most people might want and have. Relative poverty
  will always exist as long as inequality exists.
● It is riddled with value judgements. Relative poverty standards reflect
  the values of 'experts', as in Townsend's deprivation index, or of the

public, as in the *Breadline Britain* and the *Poverty and Social Exclusion* surveys. Lacking three or more necessities was decided by the researchers as a significant indicator of poverty – but why not five, or six or seven or more?

- The 60 per cent of average income poverty line means some people will always be relatively poor, even as society gets richer. The 60 per cent level is fairly arbitrary – why not 50 per cent or 70 per cent?

Activity

1 Go through each of the statements (A–G) below, and explain in each case which definition of poverty is being used. Give reasons for your answer.
2 Explain in your own words what Moore (statement B) meant when he said, 'The poverty lobby would, on their definition, find poverty in Paradise.'
3 With reference to the statements below, identify five aspects of poverty apart from a low income.
4 How do you think those who use a relative definition of poverty might respond to Moore's claim in statement B that 'It is hard to believe that poverty stalks the land when even the poorest fifth of families with children spend nearly a tenth of their income on alcohol and tobacco.'
5 Explain, with examples, the view in statement C that 'The notion of being able to measure what is necessary to live and fully participate in society is fraught with difficulty, as this will to some extent depend on how the person chooses to live and on the researcher's own values.'

Statement A

Poverty curtails freedom of choice. The freedom to eat as you wish, to go where and when you like, to seek the leisure pursuits or political activities which others accept; all are denied to those without the resources . . . poverty is most comprehensively understood as a state of partial citizenship.'
(P. Golding, *Excluding the Poor*, Child Poverty Action Group, 1986)

Statement B

'Poverty in the old absolute sense of hunger and want has been wiped out, and it is simply that some people today are less equal. The lifestyle of the poorest 20 per cent of families represents affluence beyond the wildest dreams of the Victorians, with half having a telephone, car, and central heating and virtually all having a refrigerator and television set. It is hard to believe that poverty stalks the land when even the poorest fifth of families with children spend nearly a tenth of their income on alcohol and tobacco. It is absurd to suggest that a third of the population of Britain is living in or on the margins of poverty. Starving children and squalid slums have disappeared, What the poverty lobby is opposed to is simple inequality, and however rich a society becomes, the poor on their definition would never disappear. The poverty lobby would, on their definition, find poverty in Paradise.'

(Adapted from a speech by John Moore, a former social security minister)

Statement C

'Poverty cannot be defined simply in terms of survival. We need to look at whether individuals have the material resources to fully participate in society – this involves wider social needs (such as money to have a holiday, give children birthday parties, go the cinema, etc.) and goes beyond mere biological or physical survival. The notion of being able to measure what is necessary to live and fully participate in society is fraught with difficulty, as this will to some extent depend on how the person chooses to live and on the researcher's own values.'

Statement D

'They can only be counted as "poor" in relation to contemporary British standards of affluence, but compared to Victorian times they are rich beyond the dreams of avarice. Their condition is only shocking because it is not as comfortable as that of those who are better off. What those who talk of poverty in modern Britain find offensive is not so much the existence of poverty but the existence of inequality.'

(Adapted from Peregrine Worsthorne in the *Daily Telegraph*, 27 Oct. 1979)

Statement E

'Living on the breadline is not simply about doing without things; it is also about experiencing poor health, isolation, stress, stigma and exclusion.'

(Adapted from C. Oppenheim, *Poverty: The Facts*, Child Poverty Action Group, 1988)

Statement F

'To have one bowl of rice in a society where all other people have half a bowl may well be a sign of achievement and intelligence . . . To have five bowls of rice in a society where the majority have a decent, balanced diet is a tragedy.'

(M. Harrington, *The Other America*, London: Macmillan, 1962)

Statement G

'Poverty should be seen in relation to minimum needs established by the standard of living in a particular society, and all members of the population should have the right to an income which allows them to participate fully in society rather than merely exist. Such participation involves having the means to fulfil responsibilities to others – as parents, sons and daughters, neighbours, friends, workers and citizens. Poverty filters into every aspect of life. It is about not having access to material goods and services such as decent housing, adequate heating, nutritious food, public transport, credit and consumer goods.'

(Adapted from C. Oppenheim, *Poverty: The Facts*, Child Poverty Action Group, 1988)

Who are the poor in Britain?

In 2002–3 in Britain:

- 12,400,000 people were living in poverty (below 60 per cent of average income) – 22 per cent of the population
- 3,600,000 children (28 per cent of all children) were living in poverty

The identity of the major groups in poverty suggest that poverty is not caused by individual 'inadequacies', but by social circumstances beyond the control of the poor themselves. Poverty is essentially a problem of the working class, because other classes have savings, employers' pensions and sick pay schemes to protect them when adversity strikes or old age arrives. The groups who were living in low income households (on the poverty line – 60 per cent of average income) in 2002–3 are shown below:

- *The unemployed* – 10 per cent of those on low incomes were unemployed.
- *The low paid* – 39 per cent were in full-time or part-time work. Many of the poor work long hours in low paid jobs.
- *Pensioners* – 20 per cent were pensioners. Older pensioner couples over the age of 75, and single female pensioners, are the most vulnerable to poverty. Many elderly retired people depend on state pensions for support, and these are inadequate for maintaining other than a very basic standard of living.
- *Lone parents* – 20 per cent were lone parents. Lone parents with young children often face difficulties getting a full-time job because of the lack of affordable childcare facilities, or only work, at best, part-time, which generally gets lower rates of pay. Nine out of ten lone parents are women, who in any case get less pay than men.
- *Children* – 28 per cent of all children lived in poverty. Children living in lone parent families, or with parents who were unemployed or only working part-time, and in larger families with three or more children were the main groups.
- *Minority ethnic groups* – 59 per cent of households headed by someone of Pakistani or Bangladeshi ethnic origin were living in poverty.
- *Disabled people* – 27 per cent of individuals in households with a disabled adult lived in poverty. Disability often brings with it poorer employment opportunities, lower pay and dependence on state benefits.

Figure 6.5 overleaf illustrates which groups made up most of those living in poverty in 2002–3 by family type and by economic status. Figure 6.6 illustrates the risk of poverty facing those in particular social groups.

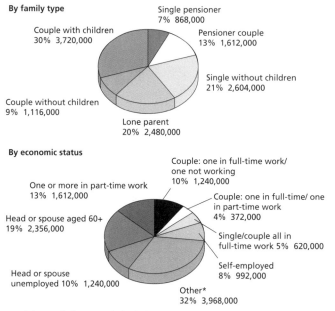

By family type

Single pensioner
7% 868,000

Couple with children
30% 3,720,000

Pensioner couple
13% 1,612,000

Single without children
21% 2,604,000

Couple without children
9% 1,116,000

Lone parent
20% 2,480,000

By economic status

Couple: one in full-time work/
one not working
10% 1,240,000

One or more in part-time work
13% 1,612,000

Couple: one in full-time/ one
in part-time work
4% 372,000

Head or spouse aged 60+
19% 2,356,000

Single/couple all in
full-time work 5% 620,000

Self-employed
8% 992,000

Head or spouse
unemployed 10% 1,240,000

Other*
32% 3,968,000

* Other = all those not included in previous groups, eg. long-term sick, disabled people, and non-working lone parent

Figure 6.5 Who are the poor? Number of individuals living below 60 per cent of average income after housing costs, 2002/3
Source: *Households Below Average Income*, Department for Work and Pensions, 2004

Activity

Refer to figure 6.5. In 2002–3:

1 What percentage of individuals in poverty were in pensioner couples?
2 What percentage of individuals in poverty were single without children?
3 How many individuals in poverty were lone parents?
4 How many individuals in poverty were in households with one or more in part-time work?

Refer to figure 6.6. In 2002–3:

5 Which family type had the greatest risk of individuals living in poverty?
6 Which family type had the lowest risk of individuals living in poverty?
7 Which group of individuals, by economic status, faced the greatest risk of poverty?
8 Which group of individuals, by economic status, faced the lowest risk of poverty?
9 What evidence is there in figure 6.6 that might be used to show that low pay is a cause of poverty?
10 Suggest how the evidence in figures 6.5 and 6.6 might be used to show that the poor are victims of unfortunate circumstances rather than being themselves to blame for their poverty. Could any of the evidence in the figures be used to support the opposite view?

By family type

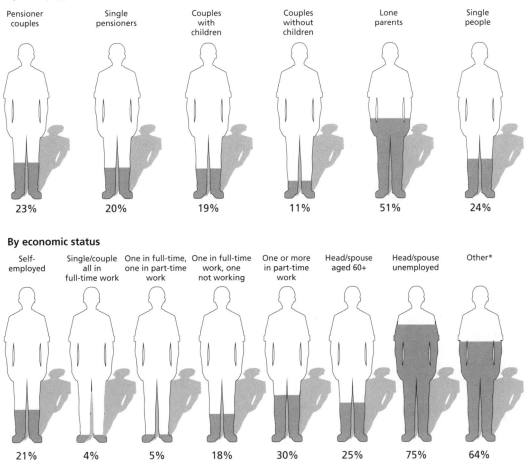

By economic status

* Other = all those not included in previous groups, eg. long-term sick, disabled people, and non-working lone parent

Figure 6.6 The risk of poverty: proportion of individuals in particular groups living in poverty (below 60 per cent of average income after housing costs), 2002/3
Source: Households Below Average Income, Department for Work and Pensions, 2004

The next section shows why women are more likely to face poverty than men.

The feminization of poverty

Women are far more likely than men to experience poverty. This is because:

● *They are likely to have the major responsibilities for housework and childcare.* This means that many women are forced to combine paid employment with childcare. They are therefore more likely to be in low paid and part-time work, and therefore to miss out on work-related welfare benefits.

- *They are the majority of homeworkers*, tied to the home by children or others dependent on them (such as the elderly). Many homeworking jobs are based on piecework (that is, payment for each product or part of a product made), are extremely low paid, and rarely carry such basic employment rights as holidays, pensions, and compensation for industrial accidents.
- *They are more likely than men to be lone parents* with sole responsibility for children, leading to reduced possibilities for employment, and dependence on state benefits.
- *They are more likely to sacrifice their own standard of living* to provide food, clothing and extras for the children. In many low income households, it is often mothers rather than fathers who bear the burden of trying to make ends meet.
- *They live longer than men and retire earlier.* They therefore spend a greater proportion of their lives beyond retirement age. However, because of the time they have taken off work to care for children, combined with low pay throughout their lives, they are less likely than men to have savings for old age, or to be entitled to employers' pensions, and so they are more likely to experience poverty in old age. Only half of women reaching retirement age in the ten years to 2010 will qualify for a full state pension when they retire.

Explaining poverty: cultural explanations

While the welfare state may have removed the worst excesses of absolute poverty, it has failed to solve the real problems of relative poverty. Why is this?

A good way to remember the various explanations of poverty is to think of them as 'blaming theories' – where is the blame placed for poverty? These can be grouped into cultural explanations, looked at here, and material explanations, which we turn to below.

Cultural explanations blame the culture of poverty, and the dependency culture generated by the *generosity* of the welfare state.

The culture of poverty

Early work on the cultural attitudes of the poor was first developed by Oscar Lewis (1961), as a result of his research among the urban poor in Mexico and Puerto Rico in the 1950s. Lewis suggests that the poor have a **culture of poverty** with its own norms and values and way of life. This

The **culture of poverty** is a set of beliefs and values thought to exist among the poor which prevents them from escaping from poverty.

> **Activity**
>
> 1 Explain what is meant by 'relative poverty' and identify and explain two criticisms of it.
> 2 Identify two groups of people who are more likely to be in poverty than others in modern Britain, and explain why this is so.
> 3 Explain what is meant by the 'poverty line'.
> 4 Identify three aspects of poverty *apart from* a low income.
> 5 In about two sides of A4 paper, answer the following essay question: *Critically assess the problems sociologists face in defining and measuring poverty.*

makes the poor different from the rest of society. He suggests the poor have the following cultural features:

- they are resigned to their situation, seldom taking opportunities when they arise
- they have a sense of *fatalism* – that nothing can be done to change their situation
- they are reluctant to work
- they don't plan for the future
- they make little effort to change their situation or take the initiative to try to break free of their poverty
- they are marginalized, and don't see themselves as part of or involved in mainstream society

Children grow up in this culture, which is passed on from generation to generation through socialization. This culture of poverty prevents those exposed to it from taking opportunities to escape from poverty when they arise, and the poor therefore remain poor because of their own values and behaviour. This 'victim blaming' approach was developed further by writers of the 'New Right'.

The dependency culture and the generosity of the welfare state

The New Right sees many of the poor as undeserving – a group of work-shy and lazy inadequates who are not deserving of support from the welfare state. 'New Right' supporter David Marsland (1989) argues that poverty arises from the *generosity* of the welfare state. Marsland claims:

- The generosity of 'handouts' from the 'nanny' welfare state has created a 'dependency culture'. This is where people abandon reliance on work, the family and the local community, and are content to live on welfare state 'handouts', rather than taking responsibility themselves for improving their situation. The more the welfare state provides benefits for people, the less they will do for themselves.

- Universal welfare benefits, which are payable to all regardless of income, such as education, health care and child benefits, take money away from investment in the economy and thus undermine the production of wealth.
- Universal welfare benefits should be withdrawn, and welfare benefits should be more selective and means tested, targeted on groups like the sick and disabled who are in genuine need, rather than given to those who are capable of supporting themselves.

The underclass (New Right version)   Charles Murray (1989), another New Right supporter, goes even further than Marsland. Murray has suggested that the attitudes and behaviour of the poor are responsible for their poverty, and that the poor form an anti-social, deviant underclass. This underclass is marked out by:

- high levels of illegitimacy, lone parenthood and family instability
- drunkenness and 'yob culture'
- crime, fiddling of the benefit system and drug abuse
- exclusion from school and educational failure
- work-shy attitudes leading to dropping out of the labour market and living off benefits

Murray is particularly scathing about lone parenthood, which he says arises from the high level of benefits, which encourage women to have children they could not otherwise afford. Murray argues that the generosity of the welfare state has created, supports and encourages this underclass, and the solution is to cut benefits to encourage self-reliance, or marriage or work.

New Right theories were very influential during the period of the Conservative governments in Britain between 1979 and 1997. There was a strong sense of the poor being punished for their poverty, with cuts in benefits and all welfare state spending, and a growing stress on the need for everyone, including the poor, to take more responsibility for themselves rather than relying on the state to help them out.

Activity

1. Suggest any ways in which you think the attitudes, beliefs and values of poor people might differ from those of the non-poor.
2. How might you carry out research to test the idea that the ideas of poor people are different from those of the non-poor? Work out a plan for carrying out research in this area.

Criticisms of cultural explanations of poverty

The differences have been exaggerated   The differences between the attitudes of the poor and non-poor have been exaggerated. Kempson, in research conducted for the Joseph Rowntree Foundation in 1996, found that the poor had attitudes to work much like the rest of the population. Robert Walker and colleagues (2000) found there was 'no real indication that a social underclass actually exists', and said the evidence for benefit dependency is 'slight'. He said: 'Life on benefit is mean and harsh. Consequently, people are much more keen to avoid claiming benefits than to choose them as a way of life. Most claimants who are able to work are eager to do so and routinely look for jobs when they can.'

Little evidence that children inherit their parents' attitudes   There is little evidence that the cultural attitudes of parents get passed on to their children, and parents often have higher ambitions for their children than they had for themselves. Rutter and Madge (1976) found that 'At least half of children born into a disadvantaged home do not repeat the pattern of disadvantage in the next generation. Over half of all forms of disadvantage arise anew in each generation.'

The poor want the same as everyone else   The poor want the same things as the rest of society, but factors like unemployment and social deprivation stop them from achieving them. For example, the poor cannot afford to save for a 'rainy day', planning for the future is difficult when the future is so hopeless or uncertain, and it is hard not to give up and become resigned to being unemployed after endless searching for non-existent jobs. It is the lack of resources that stops participation in society, not the culture of the poor or welfare state generosity. If there is any kind of dependency culture or culture of poverty, it is a *consequence* of poverty, not a *cause* of poverty.

Blaming the victims rather than the causes   Cultural explanations of poverty tend to blame the poor for their own poverty, and imply that if only the poor changed their values, then poverty would disappear. If these explanations are accepted, then the problem of poverty will be solved by policies such as cutting welfare benefits to the poor, to make them stand on their own two feet, and job training programmes to get them used to working. However, in most cases it is economic circumstances, not attitudes, which made them poor in the first place. Cultural explanations are convenient ones for those in positions of power, as they put the blame for poverty on the poor themselves. As Westergaard and Resler (1976) put it, 'the blame for inequality falls neatly on its victims.'

Unclaimed benefits

Many poor people do not claim the welfare benefits to which they are entitled, particularly those which are means tested. According to the Department for Work and Pensions' own estimates released in 2005, around one in five people were not claiming income-related benefits to which they were entitled in 2002–3 – between 3.25 and nearly 5 million people. This represented between £3.3 and £6.3 billion left unclaimed.

People may not claim benefits because of:

- the complexity of the benefits and tax system
- inadequate publicity
- the obscure language of leaflets and complex means-testing forms, which mean people often do not know what their rights are or the procedures for claiming benefits.

These bureaucratic hurdles are often so great that many people are deterred from claiming what they are entitled to. This is particularly important as the poor are among the least educated. The mass media periodically run campaigns about welfare 'fraudsters' and 'scroungers' – like 'Stuff the spongers' – which help to attach a stigma to claiming benefits which may deter some people, particularly the elderly, from doing so. The establishment of the Department for Work and Pensions 'Targeting benefit fraud' website (www.targetingfraud.gov.uk) may further contribute to attaching such a stigma.

Activity

Refer to the box 'Unclaimed benefits'. Suggest answers to the questions below, and then discuss them.

1   Do you agree or disagree with the view that the media give the impression that people receiving benefits are 'scroungers'?
2   Do you think most people receiving welfare benefits are deserving?
3   Do welfare benefits discourage people from taking more responsibility for their own lives?
4   Should people be expected to take a job even if they will be worse off than if they received benefits?
5   Go to the 'Targeting benefit fraud' website, www.targetingfraud.gov.uk. How much does the government estimate benefit fraud costs each year? Study the advertising campaigns, and discuss whether it might attach a stigma to all people claiming benefit. Do you think such advertising campaigns might stop people claiming benefits, even when they are entitled to them?

Explaining poverty: material explanations

Material explanations blame material constraints, the cycle of deprivation, the *inadequacy* of the welfare state, and the unequal structure of power and wealth in capitalist society.

Material constraints

As seen in the criticisms of cultural explanations above, it is material or situational constraints, the economic and social position of groups like the low paid, unemployed, sick and elderly, that influence the attitudes and behaviour of the poor. The hopelessness of the future undermines their ability and resolve to plan for the future. With a dead-end job or no job at all, and insufficient income to support a family, a person is unable to save and invest in the future or to support a stable family life. Resources are used up simply on week-by-week survival, concentrating the poor's attention on their immediate position. It is these factors that stop the poor from putting the mainstream values they share with everyone else into practice.

Any distinctive cultural features of the poor are therefore more likely to be a response to poverty rather than a cause of it. Once these material constraints are removed, by giving the poor decent housing, well-paid jobs, adequate benefits and some security in their lives, then any apparent culture of poverty or dependency culture will also disappear.

The cycle of deprivation

The theory of the **cycle of deprivation** suggests that poverty is cumulative, in the sense that one aspect of poverty can lead to further poverty. This builds up into a vicious circle of poverty from which the poor find it hard to escape, and it then carries on with their children.

Coates and Silburn in their early study of the St Ann's area of Nottingham, *Poverty: The Forgotten Englishmen* (1970), emphasized the circumstances in which the poor are trapped, and how these circumstances combine to form a web from which, regardless of attitudes or ability, there is little chance of escape. This has been called the **cycle of deprivation**.

For example, a child born in a poor family may have poor quality housing and diet. This may cause ill-health, and therefore absence from school. This means falling behind and failing exams, which in turn will mean a low paid job or unemployment, and therefore poverty in adult life. It then carries on with their children. Figure 6.7 overleaf illustrates examples of possible cycles of deprivation.

This cycle of deprivation is reinforced by the fact that poor people have to spend money in uneconomical ways – a matter in which they have little choice. The cost of living is higher for the poor than the non-poor, as illustrated in the box 'Trapped in poverty: the poor pay more' on page 343.

The problem with the cycle-of-deprivation explanation is that, while it explains why poverty continues, it does not explain how poverty begins in the first place.

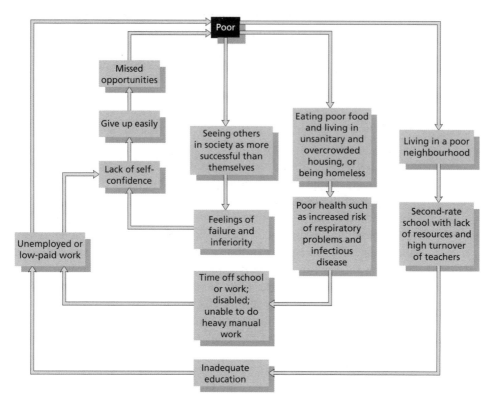

Figure 6.7 Cycles of deprivation

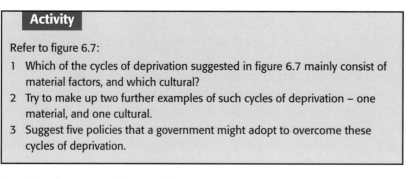

Activity

Refer to figure 6.7:

1 Which of the cycles of deprivation suggested in figure 6.7 mainly consist of material factors, and which cultural?
2 Try to make up two further examples of such cycles of deprivation – one material, and one cultural.
3 Suggest five policies that a government might adopt to overcome these cycles of deprivation.

The inadequacy of the welfare state

While the welfare state has provided some important assistance to the poor, and has removed the worst excesses of absolute poverty, widespread deprivation remains and the welfare state has failed to reduce the inequalities between the rich and the poor. Poverty persists, some argue, because benefit levels are too low to lift people out of poverty. From this viewpoint, the welfare state is not generous enough, and the poor get trapped in poverty by an inadequate, means-tested benefit system from which they

---

Trapped in poverty: the poor pay more

One of the great ironies of poverty is that the cost of living is higher for the poor than the non-poor, and this hinders the poor in their attempts to escape poverty. The poor pay more because:

- They often live in poor quality housing, which is expensive to heat and maintain.
- They live mainly in inner city areas, where rents are high.
- The price of goods and services is higher is poorer areas, due to factors like shoplifting and vandalism.
- They have to buy cheap clothing, which wears out quickly and is therefore more expensive in the long run.
- They have to pay more for food as they can only afford to buy it in small quantities (which is more expensive) and from small expensive corner shops as they haven't cars to travel to supermarkets. They also lack storage facilities like freezers for buying in bulk.
- They pay more for credit, as banks and building societies won't lend them money because they consider them a 'poor risk'. Loans are therefore often obtained from 'loan sharks' at exorbitant rates of interest.
- They suffer more ill-health, and so have to spend more on non-prescription medicines.
- The cost of house and car insurance is higher as a result of more theft and vandalism in poor areas.

---

find it hard to escape. This has led to an alternative view of the underclass to that suggested by Charles Murray.

The underclass (social democratic version) The social democratic view of the underclass is in keeping with the social democratic view of welfare discussed earlier in this chapter. This suggests the underclass consists of disadvantaged groups right at the bottom of the social class hierarchy whose poverty means they are excluded from taking part in society to the same extent as the non-poor.

Sociologists like Frank Field (1989) and Peter Townsend suggest this underclass consists of groups like the elderly retired, lone parents, the long-term unemployed, the disabled and the long-term sick. These groups are forced to rely on inadequate state benefits which are too low to give them an acceptable standard of living. This prevents them from participating fully in society, and leaves them prey to the poverty trap.

This view of the underclass differs from that of Charles Murray and the New Right, as it is not the attitudes of poor people which are to blame for their poverty, but the difficulties and misfortune they face which are beyond their control (like unemployment, illness or disability). The poor live depressingly deprived lifestyles, and want many of the things most people in society already have, like secure and decently paid jobs and opportunities. As Frank Field said, 'No one in their right mind believes that [the underclass] has volunteered for membership.'

It is a lack of opportunities and jobs, low pay and inadequate benefits, not their attitudes, which leaves them excluded from full participation in society. This view suggests social policies should tackle unemployment and low pay, improve the living standards of those on benefits (for example, through higher pensions and child benefits), and give incentives to the poor to get off benefits through decently paid jobs, and a national minimum wage. Only in this way will the excluded underclass disappear in our society.

Marxists such as Miliband (1974) and Westergaard and Resler are critical of the view that the poor are an underclass. They see the poor not as a separate, specially disadvantaged group, but simply as the most disadvantaged section of the working class, and argue that all working-class people face the risk of joining the ranks of the poor in circumstances of unemployment, sickness, disability, lone parenthood or old age.

Structural explanations: blaming the unequal structure of society

Structural explanations explain poverty as arising from the inequality of capitalist society, with its unequal distribution of wealth, income and power. Poverty is seen as an aspect of social inequality and not merely an individual problem of poor people. The problem of poverty is the same as the problem of riches, and the reason the poor remain poor is because they are either exploited by the rich (Marxist approach), lack skills and power (Weberian approach) or because they serve a necessary function in maintaining society (functionalist approach).

The Marxist approach   The Marxist approach, such as that adopted by Miliband and Westergaard and Resler, suggests:

- Wealth is concentrated in the hands of the ruling class, and this generates class inequality. Poverty is the inevitable result of capitalism, and low paid workers provide the source of profits which enables the rich to achieve high incomes.
- The privileged position of the wealthy ultimately rests on working-class poverty. The threat of poverty and unemployment motivates workers, and provides a pool of cheap labour for the capitalist class.
- The existence of the non-working poor helps to keep wages down, by providing a pool of reserve labour which threatens the jobs of the non-poor should their demands become excessively high.
- Poverty divides the working class, by separating off the poor from the non-poor working class, and preventing the development of

Activity

Item A

The underclass are a group who have developed a lifestyle and set of attitudes which means they are no longer willing to take jobs. They have developed a dependency culture, which means they are not prepared to help themselves but are prepared to live off the welfare state. Lack of morality, high crime levels, cohabitation and large numbers of lone parents are associated with this view of the underclass. Their 'sponging' attitudes and lack of social responsibility are to blame for their poverty. Most of the poor have only themselves to blame.

Item B

The underclass are a group whose poverty means they are excluded from taking part in society to the same extent as the non-poor, even though they want to. This group consists of people like the disadvantaged elderly retired, lone parent families, and the long-term unemployed. Their attitudes are the same as the rest of society, but they are forced to rely on inadequate state benefits which are too low to give them an acceptable standard of living. This prevents them from participating fully in society, and gives them little opportunity to fulfil their ambitions and escape the poverty trap.

Item C

'When I use the term "underclass" I am indeed focusing on a certain type of person defined not by his condition e.g. long-term unemployed, but by his deplorable behaviour in response to that condition, e.g. unwilling to take the jobs that are available to him . . . Britain has a growing population of working-aged, healthy people who live in a different world from other Britons, who are raising their children to live in it, and whose values are contaminating the life of entire neighbourhoods . . .'

1 Compare the three views of the underclass which are considered above. Identify in each case one researcher who might support that view. Explain your reasons.
2 Using the items and elsewhere, identify four features of the 'deplorable behaviour' (Item C) of the underclass.
3 Identify and explain three criticisms of Charles Murray's view of the underclass.
4 Outline the evidence that the attitudes of the so-called underclass are no different from those of the rest of society.
5 Identify the arguments and evidence you might use to show that the underclass is not a cause of poverty, but a result of poverty.
6 With reference to the items and elsewhere, identify and explain the solutions you would adopt to solve the problem of the underclass as identified in items A, B, and C. Explain in each case how the policy adopted might solve the problem.
7 With reference to the items, discuss which view you think provides the most accurate picture of poor people.

working-class unity and a class consciousness that might threaten the stability of the capitalist system.

The Weberian approach   Weberian approaches, such as that adopted by Townsend, suggest inequality arises from the different market position of individuals – the different skills that people have and the different rewards attached to them when they sell their labour in the job market. The poor frequently have a weak position in the labour market. They are marginalized because they lack the education and skills which might bring them higher rewards, and the demand for unskilled and unqualified labour is declining. For many, such as the sick, lone parents, the disabled, the elderly and the unemployed, their circumstances often mean they are excluded from competing in the labour market at all.

Poverty remains because the poor lack the power to change their position. They don't have the financial resources to form powerful groups to change public opinion, and they often lack the means to apply pressure on the rich, through strikes for example, as they are often not working or are in low paid and poorly organized workplaces.

Functionalist approaches   Functionalist writers like Gans (1973) and Davis and Moore argue that the existence of poverty has important functions in contributing to the maintenance and stability of society. This is because:

● The existence of poverty ensures that the most undesirable, dirty, dangerous or menial low paid jobs that most people don't want, but which are important to the smooth running of society, are performed. Poverty means some people have no other choice than to do these jobs.

● Poverty creates jobs in a range of occupations, such as social work, social security staff, the police and so on.

● The threat of poverty provides necessary incentives and motivation for people to work.

● The existence of the poor provides a living example to the non-poor of what not to be – an undesirable, deviant state to be avoided – and reinforces the mainstream values of honesty, hard work, seizing opportunities and planning for the future. As Gans said, 'The defenders of the desirability of hard work, thrift, honesty and monogamy need people who can be accused of being lazy, spendthrift, dishonest and promiscuous to justify these norms.'

● The existence of the low paid keeps some industries and services running. Hospitals, catering, agriculture and the clothing industry all depend on low paid workers.

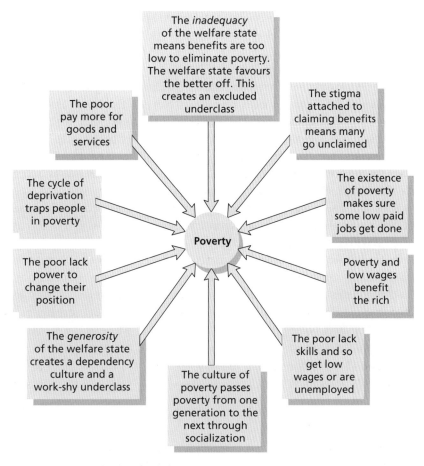

Figure 6.8 Why the poor remain poor

Poverty and value judgements

Defining and measuring poverty is inevitably a value-laden exercise. The definitions, measurement and explanations of poverty, and the social policies adopted to tackle the problem, rely to some extent on the value judgements of researchers and politicians. For example, if you adopt an absolute definition of poverty, then you will find very little in modern Britain. If you use the relative definition of 60 per cent of average income, you will find a lot (around 22 per cent of the population).

The solutions to poverty often reflect the political/ideological values of the researchers and their different interpretations of a similar range of evidence. The role of the welfare state in relation to poverty ultimately rests on judgements about what kind of society we should have. For example, New Right or conservative solutions to poverty frequently start with the assumption that the problem of poverty is primarily created by the nature of the poor themselves, and therefore the poor need harsh, punitive policies like cuts in benefits as an 'incentive' for them to change their behaviour.

More liberal or left-wing researchers are less likely to blame individuals for their poverty. They are more likely to focus on the structural constraints on the poor arising from the unequal nature of society. Such researchers are likely to see solutions to poverty in providing opportunities for the poor to escape their poverty, through means like the national minimum wage, better education, better health care, more job opportunities, more childcare support and higher pensions.

These different analyses and policy solutions often rest on a similar base of evidence, but the different values of the researchers lead to different interpretations of that evidence.

Does this mean that poverty research is therefore so value-laden as to be pointless? The answer is no, because the intense sociological, political and media debates about the definition, measurement and solutions to poverty have overcome the value judgements of individual researchers. Poverty research, regardless of values, has certainly exposed the extent to which many people in our society face social exclusion, and are cut off from what most of us take for granted as a normal life. This alone makes it a worthwhile and productive research area.

Activity

1 Explain what is meant by an 'underclass'.
2 Suggest two ways that the existence of poverty might be of benefit to society.
3 Explain the difference between cultural and material explanations of poverty.
4 Identify and explain three reasons why women are more likely than men to face poverty during their lives.
5 Make a chart in two columns. In the left column very briefly summarize the main definitions and the main explanations for poverty discussed in this chapter. In the right column, identify and explain briefly the solution which would be adopted for each definition and explanation.
6 In about one and half sides of A4 paper, answer the following essay question:
   Assess the view that the definition and measurement of poverty is inevitably a value-laden exercise.

Chapter summary

After studying this chapter you should be able to:

- outline and explain the inequalities of wealth and income in contemporary Britain, and suggest different explanations for them
- identify measures to redistribute wealth and income, and why they have not been very successful
- identify and discuss the features of the welfare state, including welfare pluralism
- identify and discuss the social democratic, New Right/market liberal, Marxist and feminist theoretical approaches to social welfare
- identify the arguments for and against means testing of welfare benefits
- discuss areas of inequality in the welfare state, including the inverse care law
- examine the role of the welfare state in tackling poverty
- identify and discuss the absolute, relative and consensual definitions and measurements of poverty, and the strengths and weaknesses of them
- explain what is meant by social exclusion
- identify a range of aspects of poverty apart from lack of income
- identify the major groups in poverty, and suggest reasons why these groups are in poverty
- explain why women are more likely to suffer poverty than men
- identify and critically discuss a range of cultural and material explanations for the continuation of poverty, including the culture of poverty, the dependency culture, the cycle of deprivation, the generosity or inadequacy of the welfare state, and structural explanations
- discuss different views of the underclass

Key terms

- absolute poverty
- consumption property
- culture of poverty
- cycle of deprivation
- dependency culture
- income
- inverse care law
- marginalization
- market situation

- poverty line
- pressure groups
- productive property
- relative poverty
- social exclusion
- underclass
- wealth
- welfare pluralism

Coursework suggestions

1   Plan a survey on people's attitudes to welfare spending, asking questions such as whether they would or would not be prepared to pay extra taxes for more spending on health, education and social benefits, whether benefits should be universal or means tested, what the role of the welfare state should be, and whether they would like the welfare state to reduce the gap between the highest and lowest income earners.

2   Investigate people's attitudes to welfare benefits, looking into things like whether they think welfare benefits are too high, whether too generous benefits encourage people to become dependent on the welfare state and stop taking responsibility for themselves, whether those on benefit are made to feel like second-class citizens, whether they think most people on benefits are 'fiddling' in one way or another, and so on.

3   Examine the role of a voluntary organization in the provision of social welfare.

4   Plan a survey on what people define as poverty, and whether they think it exists in Britain today. Draw up a list of items and ask people whether they think they are essential for a basic standard of living in Britain. You could use the list of items identified in the *Poverty and Social Exclusion* survey mentioned in this chapter.

Exam Questions

WEALTH, POVERTY AND WELFARE

Time allowed: 1 hour 15 minutes   **Total for this Question:** *60 marks*

Item A

DISTRIBUTION OF WEALTH (United Kingdom)

	1976	*1986*	*1996*
Marketable wealth			
Percentage of wealth owned by:			
Most wealthy 1%	21	18	19
Most wealthy 5%	38	36	39
Most wealthy 10%	50	50	52
Most wealthy 25%	71	73	74
Most wealthy 50%	92	90	93
Total marketable wealth (£ billion)	280	955	2042

Source: Adapted from *Social Trends* 30
(Office for National Statistics) © Crown copyright 2000

Item B

Some social scientists explain poverty in terms of the characteristics of the poor themselves. They see the problems facing the poor as lying in their personality or culture.

However, other social scientists take a structural or 'system-blaming' approach: they explain poverty in terms of social and economic forces beyond the individual. A recurring theme in this approach is that poverty is caused by social inequalities that are built into the structure of society. These system-blaming   5
theories propose radical remedies for change, such as a major equalizing of incomes and life-chances across the social divides of class, race and sex.

Some versions of this system-blaming approach take their analysis further. For example, writers like Holman and Gans have suggested that poverty performs important functions for capitalism or for various sections of the non-poor population.   10

Source: Adapted from H. Graham, *Health and Welfare* (Thomas Nelson) 1985

(a) Explain what is meant by 'wealth' (**Item A**).   *(2 marks)*
(b) Suggest **two** reasons for the existence of inequalities in wealth such as those shown in **Item A**.   *(4 marks)*
(c) Suggest **three** policies that governments might use to reduce the gap between rich and poor   *(6 marks)*
(d) Identify and briefly describe **two** functions that poverty may perform for 'sections of the
    non-poor population' (**Item B**, lines 9–10).   *(8 marks)*
(e) Examine the problems involved in defining and measuring poverty.   *(20 marks)*
(f) Using material from **Item B** and elsewhere, assess the view that 'poverty is caused by social
    inequalities that are built into the structure of society' (**Item B**, line 5).   *(20 marks)*

(AQA AS Unit 2 June 2001)

WEALTH, POVERTY AND WELFARE

Time allowed: 1 hour 15 minutes   **Total for this Question:** *60 marks*

Item A

Not everyone is equally likely to fall into poverty, just as not everyone has an equal chance of being rich. Certain social groups contain a much higher proportion of poor people. For example, women are more likely than men to experience poverty, as are members of some ethnic minority groups. Those who are dependent on benefits are more at risk of poverty, especially if these are means-tested rather than universal benefits, since the latter tend to be higher. Furthermore, those who are eligible to receive welfare bene-   5
fits and services of various kinds do not always take them up. Sociologists such as Rowntree have argued that some people who theoretically have enough to meet their needs, fail to do so because they do not spend their income appropriately – for example on cheap but nutritious foodstuffs – and as a result they find themselves in poverty.

Item B

Sociologists from a social democratic or liberal perspective argue that the welfare state was set up to eliminate or reduce poverty by redistributing some of the wealth of the better off to the poor by means of progressive taxation and welfare benefits and services. By contrast, New Right thinkers and politicians argue that the welfare state, far from being a solution to the problem of poverty, is in fact a major cause of poverty. For example, high taxation on the profits or salaries of business people will discourage them   5
from setting up or expanding their businesses. This in turn means fewer jobs will be created, thus producing higher levels of unemployment and poverty. Similarly, high levels of welfare benefits will act as a disincentive to the unemployed to find work, since they can live comfortably without doing so.

(a) Explain briefly what is meant by 'universal benefits' (**Item A**, lines 4–5).   *(2 marks)*
(b) Identify **two** reasons why some poor people 'do not spend their income appropriately'
     (**Item A**, line 9).   *(4 marks)*
(c) Suggest **three** reasons why 'women are more likely than men to experience poverty'
     (**Item A**, lines 2–3).   *(6 marks)*
(d) Identify and briefly explain **two** reasons why 'those who are eligible to receive welfare
     benefits and services of various kinds do not always take them up' (**Item A**, lines 5–6).   *(8 marks)*
(e) Examine some of the ways in which poverty, wealth and income may be defined and
     measured.   *(20 marks)*
(f) Using material from **Item B** and elsewhere, assess the view that the welfare state is the
     cause of poverty rather than the solution to poverty.   *(20 marks)*

(AQA AS Unit 2 January, 2004)

Work and Leisure

Defining work, non-work and leisure

Defining work, non-work and leisure is no simple matter. People generally think of work as 'paid employment', but there are many activities done by those in paid work which are also carried out by those who don't receive payment for them. For example, people employed as cleaners or child-minders, as gardeners or as painters and decorators will be paid for their work, but those doing these same jobs in their own homes will not. Similarly, young people playing football for leisure is somewhat different from a professional footballer playing a match, even though both might enjoy the activity. So what we regard as work perhaps depends not so much on what we actually do, the tasks or activities we perform, but the social context in which we do it, how others see it, and how we personally experience it – is it freely chosen or not? Do we enjoy it or not? Do we have control over it or not? Are we paid for it?

Work

Pahl and Gershuny (1980) and Pahl (1984) identify four main areas of what we may regard as work:

- Paid employment for the production of goods and services in the *formal or officially approved economy*, where people's earnings are subject to national insurance and payment of income tax.
- Paid employment for the production of goods and services in the *'black economy'* – the informal or unofficial cash economy, where people's earnings are paid in cash without the payment of tax and insurance. Such people may be in receipt of welfare benefits, or simply working 'off the books' to avoid income tax and VAT.
- *Unpaid work in the home* – domestic labour involving the unpaid production of goods and services such as meals, housework, childcare and DIY.
- *Unpaid work outside the home*, where goods and services are provided for neighbours and friends in exchange for them doing other work for you, or where voluntary work is carried out for community organizations, charities, churches or political parties.

Non-work

All time outside these work activities is not necessarily leisure time. There are some activities which we have to perform which don't involve payment and in which we have little choice. Such activities include washing, eating, sleeping, food shopping, taking the children to school and travelling to work.

Leisure

Leisure time or leisure activities generally involve some element of free choice, pleasure and relaxation. The same activity may be regarded as work by one person but as leisure by another. For example, watching a professional football match would be leisure for most people, but not for the newspaper reporters or TV camera operators who have to cover the match, or for the players. This means that what counts as a leisure activity will depend not so much on the activity itself, but the way people see it themselves – the *meaning* the activity has for them.

Three periods of time

We might therefore think of work, non-work and leisure as three different aspects of time:

- *Work time* is that involving the paid or unpaid production of goods and services – time 'sold' or otherwise committed to others.
- *Non-work time* is committed time that involves necessary activities such as attending to self-care, travelling to work and other necessary commitments.
- *Leisure time* is that free of practical commitments, such as work or study, involving activities which are self-imposed and freely chosen, which the individual considers to be personally enjoyable.

Activity

1 Keep a record for one week of the time you spend on all your various activities. Classify them under the headings 'work time', 'non-work or committed time' and 'leisure time'.
2 Keep a record of those activities which you find difficult to classify under any of these headings, explaining why you found them difficult to classify.
3 Do you consider studying sociology and other AS levels as a work or a leisure activity?
4 What do your findings tell you about:
   - the amount of real leisure time you have?
   - the restrictions on expanding your leisure time?
   - the difficulties of distinguishing between work and leisure?

The importance of work

Work is an important element in occupying, directing and structuring the individual's time – the demands of working life involve a high degree of discipline if paid jobs are to be kept. It is, for most people, the single biggest commitment of time in any week, and it is perhaps one of the most important experiences affecting people's entire lives. How money is earned, how much, in what working conditions, and how long it takes decide in many ways the kind of life a person will lead. For example, the hours worked and whether working conditions are good or bad can have major effects on health. Shiftwork, nightwork, long hours of overtime, and work carrying risks of industrial disease, accidents and stress can have serious consequences for a person's health and life expectancy. Work will also influence the amount of money people have to enjoy non-work time, how much they might be able to save for retirement, and the amount of pension they will get.

Work and identity

When we meet people for the first time, one of the first things we usually find out about them is what they do for a living. In fact, it is quite likely that most people we meet as adults are a result of contacts made through work. The time and money available to enjoy leisure activities are related to our work.

Work is therefore often a central part of our identity – how we see ourselves and how other people define us. This is most clear when people lose their jobs, which undermines their sense of personal identity and self-esteem, and their status in society, as well as affecting their family life, their health and their ability to participate in social life. It is work that enables us to obtain the income necessary to buy the consumer goods and services – including leisure goods and services – which support the lifestyles which are also important aspects of our identity. Figure 7.1 illustrates the importance of work.

Activity

1   Refer to figure 7.1, and briefly explain, with examples, each of the ways identified that work might influence our lives.
2   To what extent do you think people's work is central in forming their identity – how they and others define and see them? Do you think work is more important than people's leisure activities and lifestyle in forming their identity?
3   What are the most important factors influencing how you define and see your own identity, and how others see you? Think about any job you may have, your student status, your lifestyle, and leisure choices like clothes, music, the clubs you go to, and so on.

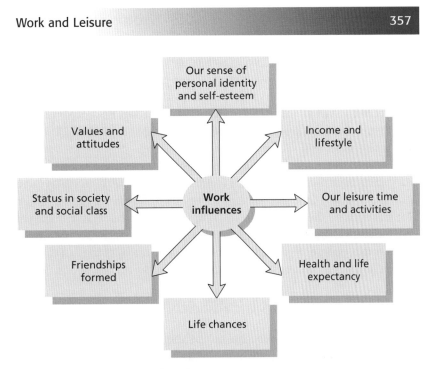

Figure 7.1 The importance of work

The changing nature of work and leisure

> **Industrialization and an industrial society**
>
> Industrialization creates an industrial society, which has the following features:
> - The production of goods is mainly carried out using technology (machinery) rather than using manual craft skills.
> - The workforce is urban, in industrial towns and cities, rather than rural, in agriculture in the countryside.
> - Work is based mainly in factories and offices, rather than in the home.
> - The workforce is dependent for its livelihood on earnings gained through working for others, rather than self-produced goods, foodstuffs and services.

Work and leisure in pre-industrial society

In pre-industrial Britain, up to about the beginning of the nineteenth century, the division between work and leisure was much more blurred than it is today. The family home was a unit of production, and most activities were carried out through all family members cooperating together and working to produce those goods necessary for their own needs. The family home was where most people worked, or in a workshop attached to it, or in agriculture on small family farms in rural communities. Non-agricultural work involved the use of craft skills, using manual skills and hand tools. The worker had full control of the production process, and enjoyed a sense of control, creativity, involvement and satisfaction at making a complete product from start to finish. There were relatively few occupations, with most people bonded together in what Émile Durkheim (1858–1917) called mechanical solidarity.

People did not generally go out to work in the sense they do today. They had greater control over when to work and when not to work, and this varied at different times of the year, depending on harvest times and the weather. Workers decided their own pace and hours of work, and could combine it with leisure activities. Work and leisure were therefore more closely linked. For example, people might mix business and pleasure by going to a country fair not only to enjoy themselves but also to sell a few of their goods.

> **Mechanical solidarity** is where societies are integrated by individuals identifying with one another through sharing a similar occupation, lifestyle and experiences. It is mainly found in traditional rural or agricultural societies.

Work and leisure in industrial society

Industrialization created the separation of home and work, as work moved outside the home into factories and offices. People began selling their labour to employers in exchange for wages, and so became dependent on employers for their livelihoods. Employers took control of the time, pace, conditions, machinery used and place of people's work. Leisure came to be a separate part of life – a clearly defined period of time which was separate from working life.

Workers in the new industrial towns were concentrated in factories, where the division of labour developed rapidly. Rather than the mechanical solidarity of life in pre-industrial society, society was moving towards what Durkheim called organic solidarity.

As work in the nineteenth century became more factory-based, specialized and fragmented, workers lost independence and control over the work they did. The employers had the say over their place of work, and the days and hours they worked. The workers no longer owned or controlled the products they produced, or the way in which they were produced, with all the products and the profits going to the factory owners. This led to what Marx called 'alienation', which will be discussed later in this chapter.

In the new industrial towns, conditions for working-class people were appalling, with low pay, high death rates, and dangerously unhealthy living and working conditions. Non-work time for the workers was often spent in dangerous, deviant and unhealthy leisure activities, such as excessive drinking, gambling and fighting. This conflicted with the needs of the factory owners for a disciplined workforce who arrived regularly and on time for work.

From the mid-nineteenth century onwards, leisure time therefore became increasingly controlled and directed in the interests of employers,

> The **division of labour** is a term referring to the way work is divided up into a large number of specialized tasks, each of which is carried out by one worker or group of workers.
> **Organic solidarity** is where societies are integrated by individuals depending on one another because people have specialized skills in different occupations, with different lifestyles and experiences. People rely on others for a wide range of goods and services, and on other workers to help them complete finished products at work. It is mainly found in industrial societies with an advanced division of labour.

with more organized leisure activities, like sports clubs, provided to channel the workers' leisure into less harmful activities. Since that time, leisure has become more organized and commercialized, and there is now a huge leisure industry in its own right, producing goods and services to fill expanding leisure hours and to meet a wide variety of consumer tastes.

The workers were understandably reluctant to submit to the power and control of the factory owners which emerged during the industrialization process. After all, the workers did not own the means of producing goods or services, and lacked any say over what they produced and the conditions in which they produced them. Control, discipline, productivity and motivation of the workforce therefore became major concerns for owners and managers, as they sought to keep complicated and expensive machinery running, goods produced, or services provided. This issue of management and control of the workforce is discussed below.

> **Productivity** refers to how much workers produce – their output in terms of items made or processed – in a given time period.

Activity

1 Suggest two reasons why it is sometimes difficult to distinguish between work and leisure.
2 Suggest three ways in which work may be important in forming an individual's identity.
3 Explain briefly what is meant by an industrial society.
4 Explain what is meant by the division of labour.
5 Explain briefly the difference between 'mechanical' and 'organic' solidarity.
6 Identify and briefly explain two ways that leisure may have changed since industrialization.

The management and organization of work

Abercrombie and Warde et al. (2000) have identified four types of strategy for controlling the workforce:

- *Direct control* is where there is direct supervision of the workforce by owners or managers themselves. This is typically found in small businesses. This form of control is not very common today in larger companies.
- *Technical control* is where the nature of jobs and the speed of work are controlled by the application of technology, with each worker given a limited range of tasks to do involving little skill. This was most successfully achieved by what has become known as Taylorism and Fordism, involving scientific management, which are discussed below.
- *Bureaucratic control* is where workers are controlled by a hierarchy of authority in the firm, with every worker having an immediate

> **Taylorism** or scientific management has the following main features:
> - Work is broken down into its simplest elements, with workers given clear and simple instructions on exactly how they should do their job.
> - Managers plan and coordinate these different tasks done by workers, who have no control over their work, and knowledge of it is transferred to management.

superior, and formal rules controlling the worker's job. The workforce is divided by competition between workers for promotion.

- *Responsible autonomy* is where workers are given a much wider degree of discretion and responsibility and are less controlled by direct supervisors. The workforce is more self-policing, and the knowledge necessary to produce goods or services is often held in the workforce itself.

Technology and the control of work

The idea of using technology (machinery) not only to produce goods but also as a means of controlling the workforce was first developed by Frederick William Taylor (1856–1915), who believed that the principles of what he called **scientific management** should be applied to work.

Taylorism and scientific management

Taylor believed that the best means by which management could control the workforce and ensure the maximum output of goods was by defining every task in work down to the smallest detail, and working out how long each task should take. This became known as a 'time and motion' study. He suggested management should reduce the power of workers over their work process by removing as much skill as possible from the worker's

> **Scientific management** is a theory first developed by Frederick William Taylor, who believed the management of workers in an industrial firm and the tasks they perform should follow scientific principles. These involved tight control of the workforce, and performance of work tasks to run in the same way as a piece of industrial machinery might run. It is also commonly known as Taylorism or Fordism (see below).

Taylor's scientific management principles were first introduced in the mass production of Henry Ford's Model-T (these are pictures of its production in the 1920s), and this then became known as Fordism
Photos: Courtesy Ford Motor Company

Fordism has the following main features:

Fordism has the following main features:
- Single products are produced on a mass scale by fixed machinery in the form of assembly lines.
- Work is broken down into tasks which are as small, simple and easily learnt as possible.
- Workers are controlled closely by managers and supervisors.
- Managers and supervisors plan, coordinate and control the production process.
- The speed of work is controlled by the speed of the assembly line, which is itself controlled by management.
- Workers lack skills, knowledge of the production process and control over the speed of work, and are removed from decision-making at work.

Deskilling is the removal of skills from work by the application of new machinery which simplifies tasks.

job, and breaking each task that was done into such small, simple and repetitive tasks that they could be completed with hardly any skills at all. Workers would then become like extensions of the machinery they were operating. This would increase the control of management over workers, by concentrating in management all decision-making and knowledge of the production process, with the former skills of the workforce removed and transferred on to machinery.

Taylor's scientific management principles were first applied in practice in 1908 in the United States by Henry Ford, who used assembly lines to produce the world's first mass-produced car – the Model-T Ford. These techniques of production and control became known as **Fordism**, and gave rise to two related issues: the way the workforce could be 'deskilled' by technology, and the growing alienation of the workforce.

Fordism

Henry Ford revolutionized car making by mass producing cheap, standardized cars on assembly lines, where the work was broken down into such small and repetitive tasks that each task required very little skill or training, keeping labour costs relatively low. Ford's first cars cost only about half the price of cars that were produced previously using craft skills, but there was little choice of model, style or colour. Ford famously summed up this mass-produced standardized car when he said his Model-T was available in 'any colour you like, as long as it's black'. By 1929, over 15 million standard Model-T cars had been produced on assembly lines using mainly unskilled labour.

Braverman: the deskilling and degradation of work

Braverman (1974) took a Marxist view, arguing that control of the workforce, through the application of scientific management principles and a highly specialized division of labour, led to what he called the **deskilling** and degradation of work.

Deskilling was aimed at controlling the workforce, increasing production and raising profits through cutting labour costs, as unskilled workers are cheaper and more replaceable than skilled workers. Braverman saw the mass-production assembly lines used for producing the Model-T Ford as an early example of the degradation and deskilling of work, with the process spreading to many areas of work during the twentieth century.

Compared to the manual craft skills used by workers in pre-industrial and early industrial society, where workers were responsible for the production of a complete product from start to finish using manual skills, it is not difficult to see how many jobs were deskilled. Computerized machinery and fully automated production processes mean that many traditional manual skills have become transferred to machinery. For example, the typesetting and printing of newspapers used to be a highly skilled process, giving print workers a lot of control over their work. The introduction of computer technology effectively eliminated these skills and control by the workers, and newspapers are now set on computer screens, and printed by automated processes.

Deskilling has also gone on in many non-manual jobs, with the skills of secretaries removed by word processors and voice-activated computer software. Bank clerks have been deskilled by the removal of 'brain work' through the application of sophisticated computer accountancy programs, and many bank jobs have disappeared altogether with the development of cashpoint machines. Shop workers have been deskilled through barcode checkouts.

Activity

1 To what extent do you think work has been deskilled? Try to think of some examples of this.
2 Suggest ways workers might react to work which requires little skill, involvement and job satisfaction.
3 How do you think employers might motivate workers in deskilled and boring jobs?

Criticisms of Braverman and the deskilling thesis   Braverman's deskilling thesis has been controversial, and there is a variety of criticisms of his suggestion that the application of technology has deskilled the workforce:

- In the nineteenth century, most workers were in unskilled or semi-skilled jobs anyway, so there has been no deskilling relative to earlier times.
- Rather than removing skills, technology has created new skills, such as computer programming, and some jobs have been reskilled. For example, typists have had to develop information and communications technology (ICT) skills to operate computerized word-processing packages.
- The Fordist model of mass production is old-fashioned and disappearing, and employers are increasingly using more flexible methods of production. Employers today look for a wider range of skills and higher levels of training in their workforce, particularly to operate new and more complex technology in the production process.
- It depends on how you define a 'skill' – some groups of workers have been more successful in getting their jobs defined as 'skilled' in negotiations with management. In general, men's jobs have often been defined as more skilled than those done by women.
- There has been a decline in semi- and unskilled manual work, and an increase in skilled work. Gallie (1994) found little evidence to support Braverman's deskilling thesis, with many workers saying their work had

become more skilled (upskilling), with more qualifications needed to get their jobs, and more time spent on training to learn how to do them.

● Other Marxist sociologists argue that deskilling is only one means of controlling the workforce among a variety of methods.

Human relations theory

Braverman's suggestion that deskilling and the application of the principles of scientific management are the main means of controlling the workforce has been challenged by those who argue there are a variety of techniques used by management to control the workforce. The human relations approach, originally developed by Elton Mayo in the 1920s, found that workers were often more effectively controlled and more productive (that is, they would produce more) if they felt valued by management.

In 1927, Elton Mayo led a team of researchers in the Hawthorne plant of the Western Electric Company of Chicago to try to find the factors affecting the productivity of workers. They set up a test area involving five workers who knew they were being investigated. Working conditions were matched with the rest of the factory, and then the researchers made changes in factors such as room temperature, lighting, work hours, rest breaks and other features. They found output went up *even when conditions were made worse*. It turned out the most important factor affecting production was not environmental factors or the technology used, but the *presence and interest of the researchers themselves*: being the focus of attention increased productivity (this 'Hawthorne effect' is discussed in the next chapter, see pages 418–19).

Activity

Identify the difficulties that the 'Hawthorne effect' might cause sociologists when they carry out interviews and observation on social groups. In what ways might this undermine the truthfulness or *validity* of the findings of social research?

Mayo concluded that if management showed more care and attention to the personal and social needs of workers, and work was made more enjoyable, then productivity could rise. The human relations approach suggested that workers might become more self-disciplined, more committed to their work and more productive by moving away from boring and repetitive assembly-line production, and if work was made a more rewarding experience by devices such as:

● *Job enrichment* – giving workers more independence and responsibility for decision-making in their work and the way they organize it, and the chance to use their own initiative rather than being closely directed by managers and controlled through the use of technology.

- *Job rotation* – giving workers a wider variety of jobs to do.
- *Job enlargement* – including a wider range of tasks within a job.
- *Teamwork* – where a team of workers is responsible for completing a product, rather than individuals having responsibility for a single, boring task.

Responsible autonomy

Friedman (1977) is also critical of Braverman's deskilling thesis and his idea that the workforce is controlled through technology. Friedman argues that employers achieve more effective control and higher levels of efficiency of the workforce by involving workers more in their work, rather than by the application of scientific management and Fordist approaches. He suggests workers will identify more with a company and their work, and therefore require less direct supervision and control, if management gives them some **responsible autonomy**.

Responsible autonomy means workers are given a limited degree of control over their work, and the opportunity to use their own initiative and to organize their own work routines through teamwork.

Activity

1 Identify and explain two features of 'scientific management'.
2 Explain, with examples, what is meant by the 'deskilling' of work.
3 Suggest two ways that work might not have been deskilled.
4 Explain what is meant by the human relations approach to the management of work.
5 Explain what is meant by 'job enrichment'.
6 Identify two features of Fordism.
7 Explain what is meant by the 'productivity' of a workforce.
8 Explain what is meant by 'responsible autonomy' at work, and suggest two reasons why it might improve the productivity of a workforce.

Alienation and job satisfaction

Job satisfaction is concerned with how much enjoyment, involvement, creativity and pleasure people get from their work. An *extrinsic or instrumental attitude* to work is one in which the most important thing about a job is high wages. An *intrinsic attitude* to work is one in which the most important feature of a job is the amount of pleasure, fulfilment and satisfaction it offers. High pay is not seen as the only, or most important, reason for doing the job. **Alienation** is the clearest form of lack of work satisfaction.

The Marxist view of alienation

Marx believed alienation came about because workers lacked power and were exploited at work. The workers have little control over the work they

Alienation is the condition where workers have no job satisfaction or fulfilment from their work. Work becomes meaningless and workers have an extrinsic or instrumental attitude to their work. Work is simply a means of earning money rather than a personally rewarding, satisfying and creative activity in its own right.

do, and they own neither the products they produce nor the means of producing them, with all the products and the profits going to the factory owner – the capitalist. In many cases, the workers cannot even afford to buy the products they spend all day producing. Marx believed that only in a communist society, where industry was owned by all the people rather than private individuals, could work be really satisfying and fulfilling.

Blauner's view of alienation

Technological determinism is the view that the technology or machinery used in production is the major influence in explaining workers' attitudes and involvement in work.

Blauner (1964) believed the degree of alienation and job satisfaction was influenced by the technology (machinery) involved in work, and the amount of control it gives workers over their work. Blauner's theory is summarized in table 7.1.

From his study of a variety of industrial settings, Blauner suggested that the degree of alienation changed with the use of different production technology, in what is known as **technological determinism**.

Craft production is the production of goods by human skill using hand tools.

Craft production　In **craft production**, a worker makes or is responsible for a complete product from start to finish, using manual skills and hand tools. An example would be making and finishing a pair of shoes by hand. The high level of skill in using hand tools, and the creativity, responsibility and control of the craft worker in the work situation mean such work often has a high degree of job satisfaction. Blauner used the example of the printing industry in his research as an example of craft production – at the time

Table 7.1. Blauner's theory of alienation

Aspect of work	Aspect of alienation
The amount of control workers have	*Powerlessness*　The worker has no control over decisions made at work; for example, over working conditions, work tasks or management decisions
The level of meaning and purpose workers see in their work	*Meaninglessness*　Work is seen as pointless and boring, as it often involves making only one small part of a finished product
The extent to which workers are socially integrated into work – how far they are involved with other workers	*Isolation*　The worker feels isolated from fellow workers. Friendships are hard to form, and the worker feels like a cog in a machine
The extent to which the worker feels his or her full potential is fulfilled at work, through a sense of creativity and self-expression in their work	*Self-estrangement*　The worker feels his or her full potential is not being fulfilled, with no personal creativity or self-expression in the work – a feeling that anyone could do the job

it lacked the computer technology it uses today. He found such workers had full charge of the printing process, with command over the speed of their work and an absence of external control by management. They had a sense of control, pride and purpose in their work and the skills they used, and felt a sense of identification with their fellow printers. They therefore had high levels of job satisfaction.

Mechanization   Blauner did research on mechanization in the textile industry, where he found workers had little control or decision-making in their work or freedom of movement during the working day. Work was routine and repetitive, requiring little skill, variety or creativity. Such workers showed higher levels of alienation than craft workers.

> **Mechanization** involves the production of goods by machines, which take over the manual skills involved in craft production.

Assembly-line production   Assembly-line production is a further development of mechanization. Blauner used the example of the car industry here, which used Fordist assembly-line production methods. As products travel along a moving conveyor belt, each worker uses machines to carry out the same small task until the product is finished at the end of the line. Workers lack control over the speed of their work, because the speed of the assembly line decides how fast they must work. Each worker makes only a small part of the finished product, using few skills. This makes it hard for workers to identify with the products they have produced, using technology over which they have no control. They have little freedom of movement, as they have to keep working on the assembly line, and there is social isolation from other workers. Because the tasks required of each worker are so routine and simple, requiring little creativity, skill or training, such work is often boring, repetitive and unsatisfying. Assembly-line workers face the highest levels of alienation, and have a highly instrumental approach to work – getting high wages is the only point in doing the work.

Automation   Blauner used the example of the chemical industry to illustrate automation, though the application of robot technology in modern car manufacture might be used as another example. Automation has become very common in production now due to the development of computer technology.

Blauner argues that automation removes some of the more repetitious and boring aspects of work. Workers have responsibility and control in running, supervising and maintaining the complex machinery used in automated industries. They are not tied to the machine and work in teams, so they have greater opportunity to mix with other workers. Their control over and responsibility for the whole process gives such workers a sense of meaning and identification with their work, high levels of job satisfaction and low levels of alienation.

> **Automation** is the process where machinery and computers not only make goods, but also control the speed of production, the input of raw materials and the correction of any mistakes, with very little human supervision.

Criticisms of Blauner's concept of alienation

Blauner's view that the technology used in work is the major influence on levels of alienation and job satisfaction has been the subject of a range of criticisms.

Marxist criticisms   Marxist writers argue that Blauner gives too much emphasis to the technology used as a cause of alienation. They claim that the main cause of alienation is the private ownership of the means of production, with workers lacking control over what they produce and how they produce it, and having no share in the profits made from their labours.

There is too much emphasis on technology   Blauner ignores the importance of other factors apart from technology that influence job satisfaction. These include those that arise from outside the workplace itself, such as what workers expect from the job in the first place. For example, if workers expect their jobs to be boring, then they may be quite satisfied with them because they expected nothing else. Women in part-time work may find even boring jobs satisfying, as their job may provide them with an opportunity to escape from domestic labour, and give them more independence in the family, and an opportunity to meet other people outside it. A range of factors influencing levels of alienation and job satisfaction are shown in figure 7.2

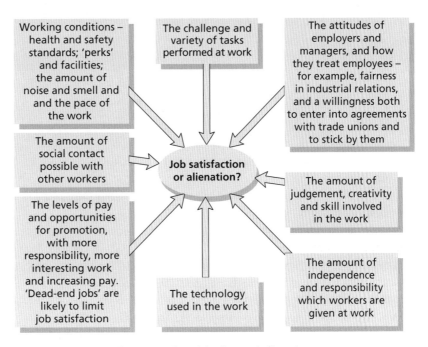

Figure 7.2 Factors influencing job satisfaction and alienation

Automated industries are also alienating   Nichols and Beynon (1977) carried out their own study of automated chemical plants and found little evidence of reduced alienation through more skill and responsibility at work. They found much work in the chemical industry involved no skill at all; the variety of tasks workers did just meant workers were going from one boring job to another, and many of them experienced isolation in work they found boring and stressful.

Gallie (1978) found most workers in automated industries were indifferent to their work. The shift work required by the need to keep automated processes running twenty-four hours a day was harmful to workers' health and disruptive of family and social life. Gallie suggested management styles and whether workers were involved in decision-making were far more important influences on the degree of job satisfaction and alienation than the technology used.

Times have changed   Many now argue that Blauner's work is really out of date, as his view of the most extreme form of alienation was based on an early model of Fordist assembly lines. Some argue the organization of work has changed since Blauner's time, even on assembly lines, and that computer technology has meant work today involves much higher levels of satisfaction. These new forms of the management and organization of work have become known as post-Fordism (discussed below).

How workers respond to alienation

Workers do not take alienating work lying down, and there is a wide range of methods used to resist it. Many of these are forms of industrial conflict, as illustrated in figure 7.4 later in this chapter. These include:

- producing poor quality, faulty goods, or providing a poor service to customers
- taking unofficial breaks ('going to the toilet'), and extending official ones to get some relief
- high levels of absenteeism and 'skiving off', with large numbers of workers 'off sick'
- leaving the job because it is so boring – a high turnover of workers is common in alienating work
- conflict with management, with workers using trade unions to 'get back' at management, through actions such as lack of cooperation, strikes and working to rule
- industrial sabotage – actions aimed at destroying the workplace, machinery or goods produced – literally 'putting a spanner in the works'

- attempts to achieve more creativity outside work in leisure activities to compensate for the lack of meaning and creativity in work, such as DIY activities or gardening

How employers respond to alienation

To motivate and maintain discipline and control of the workforce, and keep up productivity, essential for the efficient running of their businesses, employers have adopted a number of strategies to attempt to overcome or minimize alienation among the workforce and increase their involvement in their work. Such strategies include:

- teamwork
- job rotation
- job enlargement
- job enrichment
- worker participation in management decision-making
- 'flexitime' (where workers have some discretion over when they work, such as some long days and some short ones, provided they work the normal total hours each week)
- profit-sharing schemes, to encourage workers to identify themselves as having a stake in the firm's success

Post-Fordism and flexible specialization

Many argue that the Fordist production techniques considered by Braverman to be at the root of deskilling, and by Blauner to be the main source of alienation, are increasingly out of date and no longer appropriate to the demands of modern consumers.

Fordist production methods had the following problems:

- they often led to high labour turnover and conflict with management due to the boring and unskilled nature of the work
- workers were often insufficiently trained
- workers lacked motivation and commitment to their work
- workers who were trained in only very narrow tasks were unable to resolve problems when things went wrong

The experience of Japanese industry showed that a well-trained and committed workforce is often better at resolving production problems than managers, who were removed from the immediate production process. The desire to produce large quantities of mass-produced goods was often at the expense of the quality of those goods.

While the assembly-line technique and the application of Taylor's scientific management principles were effective for producing a very limited

Activity

1   How might sociologists research whether alienation exists in a workforce? Suggest ways you might do this, and identify any difficulties you might face.
2   The table provides a possible approach to investigating alienation and job satisfaction. Devise a questionnaire around the issues below, and give it to or interview people in four different types of job. Ask them additionally what *they* think are the main factors influencing job satisfaction.
3   Present your findings in your group, and discuss the main influences on job satisfaction.

Indicator of alienation	Job 1	Job 2	Job 3	Job 4
Control over the work tasks they do				
Ability to influence management decisions				
Whether they identify and find meaning in the products they produce				
How far they are integrated into work and find it a pleasant, rewarding and sociable experience				
Whether they find the work personally fulfilling				

4   To what extent do you think the various measures adopted by some employers to overcome alienation at work might be successful? Go through each of the four features of alienation identified by Blauner (table 7.1 on page 365), identifying in each case how employers might overcome each one.
5   What do you think is the long-term solution to alienation?

Activity

1   Explain what is meant by the terms 'job satisfaction' and 'alienation'.
2   Identify and explain four factors that may influence whether people find job satisfaction in their work.
3   Explain what is meant by 'mechanization'.
4   Suggest two ways in which workers might respond to alienating work.
5   Suggest two reasons why employers might want to tackle a lack of job satisfaction among their employees.
6   In about one and a half sides of A4 paper, answer the following essay question:
    Examine sociological explanations for the different levels of job satisfaction workers may get from their work.

Flexible specialization
involves a flexible
workforce with a range of
skills able to use
multipurpose machinery
to produce a range of
specialized products and
to perform a range of jobs,
with some control over
decision-making in teams.

Post-Fordism is a system
of production using
flexible specialization,
where computer-
controlled multipurpose
machinery produces
specialized products, able
to adapt quickly to
changing consumer tastes
in production.

range of relatively cheap products on a mass scale, consumers have become more demanding and want more personalized, or customized, specialized and high quality goods, rather than the 'any colour you like as long as it's black' approach of Fordism.

Writers such as Piore and Sabel (1984), Piore (1986), J. Atkinson (1985) and Warde (1989) argue that work is now organized along the lines of **flexible specialization**. Flexible specialization in **post-Fordism** involves five main features.

- flexible products
- flexible technology
- flexible skills
- flexible workforce numbers
- changing organization and management of work

Flexible products

There is now a requirement for smaller quantities of customized goods produced for more specialized and changeable consumer tastes. This reflects the way people are increasingly establishing their identities through consumer lifestyles and choices, rather than accepting the standardized, mass-produced products found in the Fordist model.

Flexible technology

Computer technology is being used to make production more flexible. The same machinery is used to perform a range of different tasks, and gives firms the flexibility to quickly change product lines in line with changing consumer demands. The emphasis is now on producing limited runs of a wider variety of customer-focused specialist products, customized for the individual tastes of consumers.

Flexible skills

As product lines change frequently in keeping with consumer demands, multiskilled workers are required who can perform a range of tasks and jobs. Core workers (see overleaf) require a wider range of skills, enabling them to perform a variety of tasks. They are given more control over their work to encourage them to use their initiative in developing innovatory ideas and products. Piore and Sabel see computer technology and more flexible specialization increasing job satisfaction, as a multiskilled and flexible core workforce is involved in more craft-like production of specialized goods.

Flexible workforce numbers

As there are growing pressures for a wider range of ever-changing specialized, customized consumer products, so there is a need for more specialist

A flexible workforce?

suppliers and subcontractors, and for a more flexible workforce. The work-force becomes divided into core workers and periphery workers. Rather than the full-time permanent workforce typical of Fordism, the proportion of full-time workers has been reduced, and there is more use of temporary, part-time and subcontracted workers – periphery workers.

Core workers and the primary labour market   Core workers are seen as 'core' to the firm's continuing success. They have good job security and promotion prospects, are involved in decision-making and are multi-skilled, trained in a variety of tasks, giving them the flexibility to work in a variety of jobs. They are more likely to have 'responsible autonomy' through teamwork, with less centralized management control as found in the Fordist model. White males are more likely to occupy such jobs. Such workers form part of what has been called the primary labour market.

Periphery workers and the secondary labour market   Periphery work-ers tend to be less well trained, with lower skill levels than core workers, with lower pay and less job security. They are less likely to be involved in decision-making at work, and are more strictly supervised by manage-ment. Companies will have little obligation to them. Feminist writers like Walby (1989) suggest that women are more likely to make up such a workforce, as they are more restricted to part-time work because of their responsibilities for housework and childcare. Minority ethnic groups are also found more as part of the peripheral labour force. Periphery workers

> **Core workers** are the well paid and qualified, skilled workers who make up the full-time, permanent employees in a workplace.

> The **primary labour market** is the relatively secure section of the labour market, involving full-time work, good pay and working conditions, job security, training and career opportunities.

> **Periphery workers** are employees who are often part-time, or on short-term or temporary full-time contracts, and employed on a casual, temporary basis, and therefore easily dispensable and replaceable.

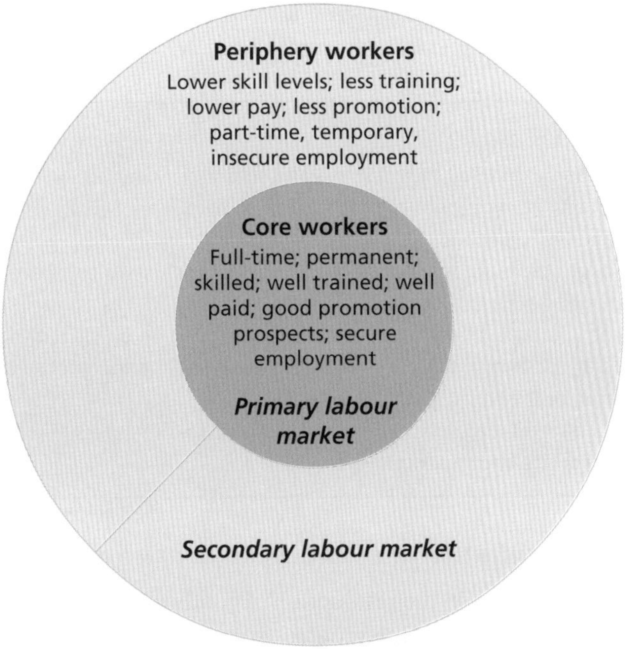

Figure 7.3 Core and periphery workers and primary and secondary labour markets

The **secondary labour market** is the insecure section of the labour market, involving part-time, or short-term or temporary work, lack of job security, lower levels of training, poorer pay and few promotion opportunities.

form part of what has been called the secondary labour market. See figure 7.3

The casualization of the workforce   In 2005 in Britain, about one in four people in employment was working part-time, and there were nearly 1.5 million temporary workers. According to the Labour Force Survey, about a quarter of temporary workers were temporary because they could not find a permanent job, and about 15 per cent of men were working part-time because they could not find a full-time job. This *casualization* of the workforce – that is, people being employed by companies only as and when required, on temporary or part-time contracts to do specific short-term tasks – was one of the main changes in the labour market in Britain at the turn of the twenty-first century. This trend appears likely to continue, with growing numbers of people facing several changes of job in their lifetimes, a lack of job security, and increasing part-time or temporary work. This gives management the flexibility to respond to rapidly changing consumer demands, employing more periphery workers and subcontractors when demand for particular products rises, and losing them or using different subcontractors as demand changes. Firms are also less likely to employ staff directly themselves, preferring to contract out the work to other, cheaper and more specialist firms. For example, rather than employing their own cleaning and catering staff, firms are more likely to contract the work out to firms that specialize in such work.

Activity

1 Identify and explain all the reasons you can think of why (a) women and (b) minority ethnic groups are more likely to be periphery workers than men and white people.
2 How might the attitudes of periphery workers to their work and the company differ from those held by core workers?
3 How do you think the fact that you were employed on only a part-time or temporary basis might affect your attitude to work and the goods you produced or the services you provided?
4 What benefits, if any, do you think flexibility in working hours might provide for (a) workers and (b) employers.

Changing organization and management of work

The need for flexibility in the production of goods to meet more personalized, specialized and ever changing consumer demands has resulted in changes in the organization and management of work:

- Workers are given more 'responsible autonomy' in their work, with more independence and decision-making by workers themselves, including more flexible working hours.
- There is less bureaucratic or hierarchical control by management (rules and regulations handed down by management) of core workers. There is more teamwork, with groups of employees taking responsibility for the development and production of products.
- There are more flexible working hours, as workers are required to respond quickly to changing product demand.

The world's largest computer software company, Microsoft, illustrates these new flexible working arrangements well. Microsoft is open twenty-four hours a day, and employees choose their own working hours. They work in teams which are responsible for developing products. Workers are not strictly controlled by managers, but are controlled by responsibility and commitment to their fellow team members. They have responsible autonomy – they are trusted by management, and encouraged and supported in using their skills in product development. Their success is judged by the effectiveness of the team's work in delivering the end product which they were given responsibility for developing.

Table 7.2 summarizes the main differences between Fordism and Post-Fordism.

Table 7.2. Fordism and post-Fordism

	Fordism	*Post-Fordism*
Technology	Fixed machinery producing one product – assembly line production	Computer-controlled, multipurpose machines
Type of production	Mass production	More limited, specialized production, changing with consumer tastes, styles and fashions
Products	Relatively cheap, standardized products produced in large quantities for a mass consumer market	Variety of specialized, high quality products, geared to consumer demands for customized products
Work tasks	Fragmented, repetitive, limited range of deskilled tasks	Reskilling or multiskilled tasks and multitasking flexible workforce able to do range of jobs
Workers' involvement	No control by workers, tight control by managers	Workers given more responsibility, with some control and decision-making by workers working in teams/groups; consultation and participation of workers in decision-making
Job security and contract	Relatively secure, full-time work, depending on the sale of goods; pay rates collectively negotiated through trade unions	Full-time core workers secure, but peripheral workers insecure, on part-time, temporary or short-term individual contracts

Criticisms of post-Fordism

Some contend that the extent of these changes in the management and flexibility of work and production has been exaggerated. Writers like Pollert (1988), Wood (1989) and Dex and McCulloch (1997) argue:

- The demand for mass-produced products and mass production techniques has not disappeared, but continues in a wide range of industries, such as the mass production of food and drink, CD and DVD players, cars, DIY goods, home furnishings, computers and so on. Mass production techniques have actually been extended to new industries, such as catering and food production. For example, burger chains like McDonald's use assembly-line techniques, with workers requiring little skill or initiative to heat and

Any colour you like: the Ford Focus

A good example of post-Fordist flexible production, which contrasts markedly with Henry Ford's original Model-T Ford of the 1920s, is production of the Ford Focus – Britain's best-selling car in 2004. The Ford Focus in 2004 was available in eight different models, of varying engine sizes and type. There was a choice of three- and five-door models, plus an estate version. There were six body designs, and three choices of interior design. There was a variety of 'styling packs' available, four types of optional alloy wheels, and a range of 'comfort' options, such as air deflectors, sound systems, sensors, climate control, sunroofs (manual and electric) and sunblinds. There was a choice of twelve colours, with options for metallic or non-metallic finishes.

Configure your car on the internet

This vast range of options and possible combinations meant each car could be built uniquely customized to the individual tastes of consumers. Customers could even configure their own personalized car on the internet (www.ford.co.uk – and look for configurator).

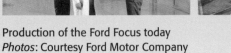

Production of the Ford Focus today
Photos: Courtesy Ford Motor Company

serve products mass produced in factories supplying all McDonald's branches.

- Flexibility is often restricted to the largest firms, which are the only ones who can afford the huge investment required in purchasing the new complex machinery capable of changing product lines quickly and without disruption.

- Rather than full-time work becoming more skilled, Pollert claims that the overall skill levels of the workforce have not increased, and Thompson (1993) argues that jobs have not been reskilled but workers are simply expected to perform a wider range of tasks requiring little skill.
- Employers have only a limited, short-term commitment to their employees, with growing insecurity for workers, and a decline in the permanent and full-time job for life. Workers now face the likelihood of periods of redundancy and starting again in a range of different jobs in the course of their lives.

The future of work

Braverman sees the future as holding a growing deskilling and degradation of work, as seen in Fordist methods of production and control. This contrasts markedly with the post-Fordist model, with Piore and Atkinson seeing a growth in flexible specialization and the multiskilling of the workforce, and Friedman forecasting growing control by workers through their involvement in decision-making and responsible autonomy.

Zuboff's (1988) study of the application of computer technology in the United States found that such technology could either deskill work or create more skilled work. It can be used to increase the power of management in monitoring, controlling and disciplining the workforce ever more closely, or give the workforce more flexibility in working hours and involve it more in decision-making and control of their work through increased access to information. The effects of technology will vary between jobs and workplaces according to the management priorities identified and how management chooses to use technology. There are choices about how technology is used, and ultimately it comes down to the issue of who owns and controls work, and the choices those with power make.

There are, therefore, quite different interpretations of the way the management and organization of work are changing. While some work may be deskilled, with workers being downgraded and more closely controlled by employers, other work may require more skills, with workers given responsible autonomy and control in the workplace, and flexibility in their working hours and conditions. In industries using traditional assembly-line mass production techniques, the Braverman view is likely to be accurate. However, in newer, 'high-tech' industries, the flexibility of the post-Fordist model is more likely to prevail.

Whatever the future holds, there is growing insecurity in the world of work today, and the days of permanent full-time jobs for life have gone. More workers are now likely to face retraining, changes in jobs, and increasing risks of redundancy, or temporary and short-term contracts.

Activity

1   Explain what is meant by a 'core worker'.
2   Identity two features of the secondary labour market.
3   Identify two features of post-Fordism.
4   Identify and explain two differences between Fordism and post-Fordism.
5   Suggest two ways that changing consumer demands have changed the way products are produced.
6   In about one and half sides of A4 paper, answer the following essay question:
    Examine sociological explanations of how and why work has become more flexible in recent years.

The effects of changing technology on society

The development of technology has had important effects on the nature of work, but there are wider effects on society:

- As technology changes, new skills are needed and old skills become redundant. Retraining of workers becomes increasingly important.
- The workforce will need to have a wider range of skills, and be adaptable and flexible enough to adapt to rapidly changing technology.
- There has been a decline in the numbers of unskilled and semi-skilled manual workers, as machines have taken over their jobs.
- Employees are facing more flexible work patterns, with more shift-work, nightwork, six-day working and overtime to keep complex automated processes running twenty-four hours a day. For example, in 2000, one in five employees was working for companies open twenty-four hours a day, seven days a week. This is blurring the distinction between work and leisure time for many people. Work, leisure, entertainment, shopping and other aspects of our lives are increasingly becoming 24/7 round-the-clock activities.
- New technology is revolutionizing our lifestyles. For example, the major supermarkets now offer twenty-four-hour shopping, either in their stores or via the internet, consumers can shop online for every type of product, cash dispensers mean we are no longer tied by banking hours and online banking is available at all times. Information and communications technology has transformed learning in schools and colleges, with the internet used as a key learning tool and information source.
- New technology enables consumers to have a much wider choice of specialized and customized products to support and enhance their identities and lifestyles, and these are becoming both cheaper and of better quality.

Activity

Read the following passage, and answer the questions beneath.

'Technological advances have always threatened jobs, but the real question is not whether computers will end work – but how they will change it. Do they really make us more efficient? The blistering pace of productivity growth has been attributed to the widespread use of computer technology, but new analysis of the effect of computers on productivity in 400 large US companies shows that is only half the story.

'Firms which introduced computerized systems alongside opportunities for employees to get involved – self-managing teams, devolved decision-making – ended up with a sharp rise in output per head. But the ones which simply stuck computers on desktops, with no change in organizational structure, were, on average, less productive than firms which hadn't installed computers at all. Bosses would have been economically better off standing in the car park, tearing up £50 notes. The study proves the truth about technology: it's what you do with it that counts.

'In one recent global survey, three-quarters of respondents said computers had made their lives better, but one in ten said that advances in computer and internet technology had enabled them to "work more". Information technology potentially makes us 24-hours-a-day, 365-days-a-year employees. It allows us to work as we wish. Perhaps at a steady pace, perhaps in intense bursts followed by long walks in the park. We can use our desktop or laptop computers as much for leisure as for work. When computers are used creatively, they can allow all of us to work more flexibly and humanely. But it's not up to the computer. It is up to us.'

(Adapted from 'The way we work', by Richard Reeves in the *Guardian*, 6 February 2001).

1 What two reasons does the article above suggest account for 'the blistering pace of productivity growth'?
2 In what ways might computer technology enable us to 'work more flexibly and humanely'?
3 Suggest ways computer technology might 'make us 24-hours-a-day, 365-days-a-year employees'.
4 In what ways do you think information and communications technology has changed the way students study?
5 Outline all the ways you can think of that changes in technology have affected, and are affecting, your lifestyle. Think about things like mobile phone technology, MP3 players and downloaded music, the internet, computer technology generally, and the mass media.
6 Do you think technological change will have good or bad effects on society generally and the individual's experience of work? Give reasons for your answer.

Conflict at work

Conflict between employers or managers and workers, and sometimes between different groups of workers, is a common feature of most workplaces. Such conflict shows itself in a variety of ways, illustrated in figure 7.4.

Strikes

The clearest, most visible indicator of conflict at work is strike action. R. Hyman (1972) defines a strike as a temporary stoppage of work by a group of employees in order to apply pressure on employers to express and resolve a grievance or enforce a demand. *Official strikes* are those approved by a trade union leadership; *unofficial strikes* are not.

Strike statistics, which are produced by the Office for National Statistics, can be a misleading indicator of the extent of industrial conflict. This is because they are based on reports by employers, and some may choose not to report strikes to conceal the extent of conflict, while others may report even very short work stoppages to give an unfavourable impression of trade unions.

There are also different definitions of strikes used in different countries, and different ways of calculating the extent of strikes. These might include,

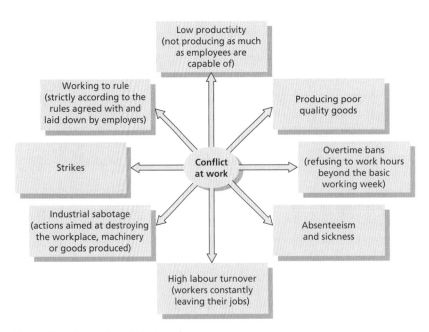

Figure 7.4 Signs of conflict at work

for example, the number of working days lost (a working day is one person working for one day), the number of workers involved, and the number of work stoppages.

The number of strikes has declined in Britain in recent years. Changes in trade union laws have made it much more difficult for trade unions to take strike action, and to enforce it when they do. For example, the requirement to hold secret postal ballots before taking strike action, limitations on the legal immunity of striking workers, and limits on picketing have all made it more difficult for workers to take effective strike action. The growing flexibility of the workforce and the division into core and periphery workers, discussed earlier in this chapter, have meant core workers in the primary labour market have less cause for grievances at work. Part-time or temporary periphery workers in the secondary labour market are often too vulnerable and dispensable to risk taking strike action.

Trade unions

Trade unions are organizations of workers formed for the protection of their members' interests. The strength of trade unions lies in the fact that they represent the interests of large numbers of workers in a workplace, who can then act together as one force to negotiate with management. The unity of workers is the union's strength. Unions use a variety of techniques to protect their members' interests. These include local or national negotiations with employers over pay and terms and conditions of employment, backed up with action such as overtime bans or strikes when necessary. Unions may take legal action against employers who act unfairly or unlawfully, or who breach health and safety regulations. Unions also provide a range of legal and financial assistance to their members.

The causes of conflict at work

Much of this chapter so far has suggested that the changing nature of work in industrial societies created a fundamental problem for employers. This is the problem of how to control a workforce who are carrying out boring and monotonous work when they neither own the products produced nor the means of producing them.

From a Marxist perspective, employers and employees have fundamentally different interests. Employers want to get the maximum productivity from their workforce at the lowest possible cost, and they exploit the workforce by paying them less than the full value of their work, providing profits for the employer. The workforce naturally wants to achieve as high wages as possible – but this will mean less profit for the employer. This means the employer–employee relationship has an inbuilt conflict of interest.

This underlying conflict of interest creates ongoing difficulties for employers in securing the goodwill and cooperation of their employees. Most people may go to work every day simply to earn a living, and put up with the inequalities of work without thinking about them. Nevertheless, some features of the workplace are associated with higher levels of conflict:

- threatening behaviour by management, such as factory closure, redundancies and sackings, arbitrary discipline (carried out without regard to proper rules and agreed procedures), and victimization of individuals
- inadequate health and safety standards
- speeding up of work
- over-rigid and inflexible or unfair management control
- whether workers are organized in trade unions; these provide a means of communication with management and of channelling grievances and resolving conflicts through agreed procedures
- the degree of alienation experienced at work
- levels of pay, and the quality of working conditions
- the terms and conditions of employment, such as the length of working hours, pension and sick pay schemes, promotion prospects and training opportunities, and the availability of canteen and sports facilities

---

Activity

1 Identify three types of conflict at work.
2 Suggest ways workers might try to get their own back against employers who are too strict and unfair.
3 Suggest two ways that the technology used in work might cause conflict.
4 Imagine you were the personnel manager in a company, or a trade union representative. Draw up a plan with a number of recommendations for making the company conflict-free. Explain in each case how you think your suggestions would help to eliminate conflict.
5 On about one and a half sides of A4 paper, answer the following essay question:
   Examine sociological explanations for conflict at work.

Unemployment

Nothing shows the importance of work more than the loss of a job, or not being able to find one. Being made redundant is nearly always a shattering experience for the individual, particularly for older people who stand poorer chances of finding another job than those who are younger.

Unemployment statistics

Unemployment statistics are politically very sensitive, because high numbers of unemployed are nearly always seen as a sign that governments and politicians are falling to manage the economy well.

Official unemployment statistics are now published in two main forms:

- The *claimant count*   This defines the unemployed as those who are available for and actively seeking work, and who are in receipt of Jobseeker's Allowance.
- The *ILO (International Labour Organization) count*   This defines the unemployed as those who are without work in a particular week, who want a job, who have actively sought work in the last four weeks and are available to start work in the next two weeks, whether or not they are in receipt of Jobseeker's Allowance.

These two different counting methods produce different numbers of unemployed. For example, in October 2005 there were 890,100 unemployed in the United Kingdom according to the claimant count, but 1,433,000 according to the ILO count.

While official unemployment statistics provide a useful indicator of trends in unemployment, there are some concerns over the truthfulness or *validity* of the official statistics in providing a true picture of the numbers of unemployed people. For example, the claimant count excludes those who can't claim unemployment-related benefits, such as married women who may not have enough national insurance contributions to qualify for such benefits, or those under 18. It also excludes men over 60 who do not have to register as unemployed, and so are not counted.

Some suggest that the official statistics *overstate* the number of unemployed, as a few who appear in the statistics may be working illegally in the 'black economy' while claiming welfare benefits at the same time. Others may be nearing retiring age, and are not really looking for work at all.

However, the official statistics almost certainly *underestimate* the extent of unemployment, since they exclude a number of groups:

- Those in part-time work who are really looking for full-time work – a form of disguised unemployment. About one in four workers in October 2005 in the UK was working part-time, 23 per cent of whom were men, and 77 per cent women. Most women working part-time don't want full-time work, but according to the Labour Force Survey, 6 per cent of women and 15 per cent of men were working part-time because they couldn't find a full-time job – 594,000 people.

- Those on government job training schemes, who can't find a proper job but don't count as unemployed.
- Those reluctantly staying on at school or college because they can't find jobs.
- Those officially classified as 'economically inactive'. This includes those who don't want a job, like those looking after a family, or who are sick, or students, but also those who want a job but are not actively seeking work or immediately available to start work – there were around 2 million people in this category of hidden unemployment in October 2005.

If these groups were to be counted, then claimant count unemployment figures would rise by nearly four times, and the ILO count more than double.

Despite its limitations, the ILO count is a more valid indicator of the numbers of the unemployed than the claimant count, as it includes all those who are actively seeking and available for work, whether or not they are entitled to claim benefits.

Who is most at risk of unemployment?

Not all groups in the population, nor those in different areas of the country, face the same risks of unemployment. Some groups and areas are far more likely to face unemployment than others.

- *Manual workers* are more vulnerable than non-manual, with semi-skilled and unskilled manual workers facing higher risks than skilled manual and non-manual workers, since they are more disposable and more easily replaceable. Generally, the risk of unemployment reduces as you move up the social class scale.
- *Men* are more vulnerable than women, because men are more likely than women to be in higher paid, full-time employment in the manufacturing industries which are most at risk during periods of economic recession.
- *Young people (18–24)* are vulnerable because they lack training and experience, and cannot compete with those already trained. They are also likely to be the most recent employees, and therefore as 'last in' they are also likely to be 'first out' when unemployment strikes.
- *Older people (over 55)* are more vulnerable than people under that age, as they have a limited working life. Employers are reluctant to retrain them if their skills are redundant, or to offer them jobs if they are unemployed.
- *Non-white people are more vulnerable than white people* – an effect of racism and educational underachievement. In 2004, about 4 per cent

of white people were unemployed, compared to 5 per cent of Indian Asians, 10 per cent of African-Caribbeans, 12 per cent of Pakistanis and around 15 per cent for Bangladeshis.

- *The north* tends generally to be hit harder when unemployment strikes than the more prosperous south. (This is sometimes referred to as the north–south divide.) As figure 7.5 shows, in October 2005 the

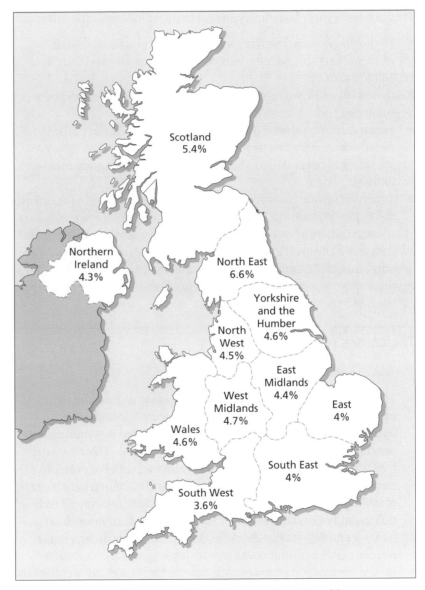

Figure 7.5 ILO unemployment rate by region: percentage of workforce unemployed, October 2005
Source: Data from Labour Force Survey

North East had the highest rate of unemployment in the United Kingdom, followed by Scotland.

- *The disabled* are about twice as likely to face unemployment as those who are not disabled.

Types of unemployment

There are four types of unemployment, each of which has a different cause:

- *Frictional unemployment* is short-term unemployment arising when workers are changing jobs and have not yet started their new employment.
- *Cyclical unemployment* occurs during periods of depression in the economy.
- *Seasonal unemployment* occurs during different seasons of the year – variations arising when people become employed or unemployed according to seasonal demand for labour, such as in agriculture or tourism.
- *Structural unemployment* occurs when workers don't have the skills to do the jobs that are available (this is known as *sectoral unemployment*), or where jobs are not available in the areas where unemployed people live (*regional unemployment*). Structural unemployment can only be tackled by policies such as retraining programmes to reskill the workforce, or the development of new industries in areas of high unemployment.

The causes of unemployment

There are various causes of unemployment:

- *The development of new technology*, which may remove the number of workers required to perform tasks, replacing them with fully automated work processes using computer technology. Automation has removed the need for many unskilled and semi-skilled manual jobs, and many non-manual jobs have also been hit. For example, cash dispensers have caused huge redundancies among banking staff, many routine clerical jobs have been replaced with computer technology, and sales staff have been reduced through computerized barcode and self-service checkouts in supermarkets. However, care is needed in this explanation, as new technology has also created a range of new occupations, such as the need for computer technicians and support staff, trainers, software and computer games developers, and skilled workers able to operate and control the new technology. New technology also creates a demand for new consumer leisure goods, such as mp3 players, CD and DVD players, home computers, Playstations, Xboxes, GameCubes, mobile phones and so on. Meeting this demand itself creates jobs.

- *The decline of manufacturing industry*, with international competition from manufactured goods from countries with lower wage costs, such as Japanese and Korean cars and consumer electrical goods from China, hitting British manufacturing industry.
- *The decline of traditional heavy industries*, such as mining, docking and the steel industry, in the face of cheaper imported products.
- *The increase in the working population*, including more married women working and more people living longer and working up to and beyond retirement age.
- *The growing flexibility and casualization of employment*, where there is disguised unemployment through part-time work and the growth in the proportion of periphery workers.

The effects or consequences of unemployment

The consequences of unemployment for individuals and society are shown in table 7.3 overleaf. For those in the poorest paid occupations, the experience of losing their jobs is likely to be more severe than those in better paid occupations, as the low paid will have smaller redundancy payments and be less likely to have savings to ease the period while they search for new work. Men and women may also experience unemployment in different ways. Women are less likely to see their identities as so totally tied in with paid employment, and to define their role in the family as primary wage earner. Similarly, young single people with no family responsibilities or mortgage repayments, who are relatively new to the world of work, will cope better with job loss than people in their fifties who have been in work for most of their lives.

Leisure, identity and consumption

What is leisure?

Leisure time was defined at the beginning of this chapter as time 'free of practical commitments, such as work or study, involving activities which are self-imposed and freely chosen, which the individual considers to be personally enjoyable'. What counts as a leisure activity will therefore depend to a great extent on the meaning people attach to the activities they do, rather than the activity itself. For example, someone who is obliged to do it every day may see cooking for a family as a real chore, but

Table 7.3. The consequences and effects of unemployment

For individuals	For society
The loss of the identity, status and self-esteem which are obtained through work may undermine a person's self-confidence. The endless search for work and the stigma of dependence on welfare benefits and social services are likely to undermine self-esteem further and contribute to growing demoralization and despair	*More discipline at work*, with declining influence and membership of trade unions and fewer strikes, as people worry about their jobs. Declining, or not increasing, wage levels and poorer conditions at work, as employers no longer have to make efforts to attract workers
Poverty, mounting debts and hardship arising from the loss of an adequate regular income may create stress and anxiety in coping with daily life. The loss of a home may result for homeowners or tenants if mortgages or rent cannot be paid	*More alienation and dissatisfaction at work*, as people have less opportunity to change jobs and get stuck in jobs they no longer enjoy or want
Social isolation and social exclusion, with the loss of friendships formed through work, particularly as there is little money to spend on leisure and social activities, such as going to the pub or clubs with friends. More free time, but with little money to enjoy it, may result in boredom	*An increase in social divisions*, with growing gaps between the rich and the poor, and those in work and those without jobs. Political unrest. The high levels of unemployment in the 1980s in Britain were accompanied by periodic outbreaks of rioting in many of the inner cities
A loss of identity obtained through consumer goods and lifestyle, which may no longer be affordable	*More racism and scapegoating*, as people try to find easy answers to their unemployment and try to lay the blame on vulnerable groups, such as minority ethnic groups, asylum-seekers and young people
More ill-health and depression, brought on by a poorer diet, stress, and the despair arising from the loss of routine and a sense of purpose, direction and social identity	*More social problems* such as poverty, homelessness and mental illness, and rising rates of crime, suicide, alcoholism and drug abuse
Increasing stress in the family – there may be confusion over roles in the family, for example the 'role swapping' which may occur with working female partners and unemployed males. 'Getting under one another's feet' may be a problem, particularly if both partners are unemployed	*More family breakdowns, higher divorce rates, and more violence in the home*, with abuse against women and children, due to rising levels of stress in the family
	Rising demands on the welfare state, but fewer people in work to pay the taxes to fund benefit payments and rising health costs

those who are not compelled to do it every day might see it as an enjoyable leisure activity. Similarly, some people may be so involved in and enjoy their work so much that they take it up as a leisure activity, such as professional musicians, or teachers who take students on school trips in their holiday time. Women who have responsibility for housework and

---

Activity

1 Imagine you were to lose your job, or left school or college and were unable to find work while your friends were working. List all the ways this would affect or change your life.

2 Suggest three ways that high levels of unemployment might cause instability and conflict in a society.

3 Identify two ways that unemployment might exclude individuals from leisure and social activities enjoyed by most people in society.

4 Suggest two ways that unemployment might affect an individual's sense of identity.

5 Identify and explain two reasons why official unemployment statistics may not show all those who are unemployed.

6 Identify two groups who face a higher risk of unemployment than others, and in each case explain why.

7 In about one and half to two sides of A4 paper, answer the following essay question:
Examine sociological explanations of the causes and social consequences of unemployment.

---

childcare (domestic labour) may even see part-time paid employment as a leisure activity – an enjoyable opportunity to escape from domestic labour, gain some independence and interact with others.

The changing pattern of leisure

Shorter working hours

In the last century or so, the working week for most workers has been shortened, with full-time workers working an average of about 38 hours a week in 2005 (though a fifth work more than 45 hours a week), compared to about 46 hours a week in 1961. This means people have more time for leisure activities today. Longer holidays and more part-time work have also increased leisure time, though the 'flexibility' of working patterns means this leisure time is more likely to be spread across all times of the day and across all seven days of the week.

Higher standards of living

Paid holidays have increased, and higher incomes have raised standards of living. This has enabled people to take advantage of increased leisure time to pursue more varied and ambitious activities. Widespread car ownership, for example, has opened up a range of leisure activities, and more working-class people have access through package holidays to locations across the globe that were once only available to the rich.

Changes in technology

Rapid changes in technology have occurred, removing the satisfaction, creativity and identification with work which people once enjoyed in pre-industrial societies, and more people are attempting to achieve these and establish their identities through creative leisure pursuits.

The leisure industry

These changes have meant that the leisure industry, including travel and tourism as well as leisure and fitness centres and shops for consumer leisure spending, has been one of the fastest growing industries in the last forty years.

Marxist writers like Clarke and Critcher (1985) point out that leisure has become a highly organized and commercialized multinational industry, employing millions of people worldwide, and concerned with making profits. Sport, for example, is a huge international and highly profitable business, with merchandising of goods, and global TV and satellite deals worth millions of pounds. Tourism, and the associated airline and hotel chains, are a major global industry.

The mass production methods used in industry (discussed earlier) have themselves been applied to leisure activities, through the mass production of a whole range of consumer goods and services to fill our leisure time. These range from mobile music to fitness equipment; from package holidays to spectator sports and 24-hour global mass media, including the internet; from theme parks to coffee shops and burger bars.

The flexible specialization and diversity of choice of post-Fordism are also now found in the leisure industry, with specialized products available for every consumer choice. For example, even in leisure products aimed at the mass market, there is a range of customized, individualized leisure activities, such as specially tailored package holidays, and theme parks which cater for a range of different interests. People are increasingly defining themselves, and others are defining them, by the ways they participate in these leisure-based consumer lifestyles.

Leisure activities have also become more privatized, with most people now engaged in home-based leisure activities, rather than taking part in community or other activities outside the home. The most popular leisure activity in Britain is watching television.

Leisure and identity

Much of this chapter has suggested that work is a major factor in defining individuals' personal identities – how people define themselves and how others see and define them. However, writers like Rojek (1995) and Roberts (1978, 1986) believe that leisure activities, the products we consume and the lifestyles we follow are far more significant in defining our identities today.

Postmodernists argue that people now express themselves and achieve creativity and individuality through their adoption of a wide range of leisure activities and lifestyles. Their identities are established through their consumption of the huge diversity of consumer leisure goods and services now on offer, such as music, household decor, holiday destinations or clubs, the shops they buy from and the activities they follow. Going clubbing in Ibiza gives quite a different indication to others of who you are than having a week in Blackpool; shopping from the Oxfam charity shop projects a different image from buying your clothes at Gap; bungee jumping or surfing or 'extreme' sports suggest a different identity from knitting or being a 'couch potato' television viewer.

Through their leisure activities and participation in consumer culture, people can make individual choices about who they want to be and how they want others to see them. In the postmodern 'pick and mix' consumer society, people can become whatever they want to be, adopting lifestyles and identities built around the almost unlimited choice of leisure activities and consumer goods available.

> **Activity**
>
> 1 Explain, with examples, what you understand by the 'pick and mix' consumer society.
> 2 Do you think 'shopping' has become a leisure activity in its own right? Think about your own shopping behaviour and the importance it has, or hasn't, for you.
> 3 To what extent are your own personal identity and the way others see you defined by your status as a student or worker, or are they defined more by your lifestyle and the consumer goods you buy? Give reasons and suggest evidence for your answer.

How much free choice is there in choosing identities and lifestyle?

Rojek and Roberts, and postmodernist writers, suggest that most people now have an almost unlimited free choice of leisure activities and lifestyle, and of the identity and image they wish to adopt for themselves and to project on to others through their consumer spending. Such a view suggests there is no real social pattern of leisure, and that people are unrestrained in their lifestyle choices by social factors such as their family, level of income, work, age, sex, ethnic group or social class. However, Marxist writers Clarke and Critcher argue that large corporations shape and manipulate people's consumer choices in leisure through advertising, which creates endless demand for new 'must have' products and services.

> **Activity**
>
> Working in a group, discuss answers to the following questions:
> 1 What are the 'must have' products which you would like to own, and why?
> 2 To what extent do you think owning these products is important in the way others see you?
> 3 Do you think you are manipulated by advertising into buying leisure goods and services, and taking part in some leisure activities rather than others?

The view that we now have unrestrained choice in our leisure activities, and that we are completely free to adopt any lifestyle and identity we like through our leisure choices and consumer spending, ignores a range of factors which still have important influences, or constraints, on the consumption patterns, lifestyles and identities we can adopt and project on to others through our leisure activities. These are considered below.

Factors influencing the choice of leisure activity

Occupation and work experience

Parker (1971, 1976) believes that people's occupations and the way they experience their work, such as the amount of independence and satisfaction they have in it, have important influences on their non-work behaviour and leisure. He suggests there are three patterns in the link between work and leisure, which he calls the opposition, neutrality and extension patterns. These are shown in table 7.4

Criticisms of Parker Parker's emphasis on the way the experience of work influences leisure patterns has been heavily criticized, particularly for

Table 7.4. Patterns of relationship between work and leisure

Work–leisure pattern	Nature of work	Typical occupations	Nature of leisure
Opposition	Physically hard and dangerous male-dominated occupations; hostility to work	Mining, deep sea fishermen, steelworkers	Opposition to work. Leisure is a central life interest – a sharp contrast in opposition to work, and an opportunity to escape from the hardships of work
Neutrality	Boring and routine work, with little job satisfaction, leading to apathy and indifference to work	Routine clerical workers, assembly-line workers, supermarket staff	Nothing much to do with work (neutral); leisure for relaxation with home and family, like DIY or going out with the family
Extension	Work involving high levels of personal commitment, involvement and job satisfaction	Professionals and managers – doctors, teachers, social workers, business executives	Because work is so interesting and demanding, leisure is work related, and there is a blurring of the distinction between work and leisure. Work extends into leisure time, and may be used to improve work performance. For example, business executives playing golf or eating out with clients, teachers using their own time to run school trips/holidays with students, or preparing lessons or developing computer skills at home

> **Activity**
>
> 1 List all the ways you can think of that our working lives might influence our leisure activities. Explain in each case the influences you identify.
> 2 Parker suggests that work extends into and becomes merged with leisure because people find their work is so satisfying. Suggest examples of occupations where you think this might be the case, giving your reasons.
> 3 What other reasons, apart from enjoyment of work, might there be for work extending into leisure time?

putting too much importance on work experience, and not paying enough attention to factors other than work that might shape leisure patterns.

- *Parker overemphasizes the importance of work in shaping leisure activities* – in Britain in 2005 only about 61 per cent of the population over age 16 were in employment, and one in four of these was working part-time. Experiences at work can therefore not explain the leisure activities of substantial sections of the population, including those who are retired, those in full-time education, full-time housewives, others who are economically inactive, and the unemployed.
- *Parker oversimplifies the influence of work on leisure*, even for those in full-time paid employment. Roberts (1978, 1986) and Clarke and Critcher (1985) say he doesn't take into account the choices that people can make in leisure activities, and such activities vary even among those in the same occupation.
- *Parker's research is focused primarily on men in full-time paid employment* – feminist writers like McIntosh (1988) and Deem (1990) say Parker does not take into account the way gender influences leisure, particularly as many women work only part-time and their leisure is far more influenced by the demands of domestic labour (housework and childcare), and control by men, than paid employment.

Social class

Social class differences in leisure have been exaggerated, but differences in income, car ownership, educational qualifications and working hours, such as shiftwork, evening and weekend working and flexible working, mean that middle-class and working-class people often follow different leisure activities. For example, they are likely to read different books, magazines and newspapers, watch different TV programmes and films at the cinema, join different organizations, eat and drink in different pubs, wine bars and restaurants, and travel to different holiday destinations. Fitness and leisure centres tend to be used more by middle-class people. Some leisure activities are denied to the working class simply because of the high costs involved. For example, the high membership fees of private golf clubs, and the expense of activities such as flying and motor racing effectively bar such activities to the working class, and much of the middle class.

Scraton and Bramham (1995) argue that recent views that people have a free choice of leisure, and create their own identities through participating in leisure-based consumer activities like shopping, ignore the fact that this is only available to the most well-off members of society. For most people, such choices are not an option, as they lack the resources to make free choices in leisure activities. The level of income remains a major constraint on leisure, and restricts people's ability to get involved in what have become highly commercialized leisure activities. For many people, shopping, for example, is about seeking out the cheapest bargains to stretch limited incomes to feed and clothe themselves and their children. Those in the poorest social classes, who are unemployed or in low paid work, have few opportunities to establish their personal identities through buying into consumer products.

Age

Age has an obvious influence on the choice of leisure activities. The leisure of young single people tends to be spent outside the home in the company of their peer group. They may gain some economic independence through either a wage packet or benefits obtained on training schemes, but lack the financial commitments and responsibilities of children and household bills, and the burden of paying rent or a mortgage. This means young people are more leisure-centred than perhaps any other age group except the retired. They are therefore more likely to have the opportunity of forming their identities through participation in leisure-based consumer lifestyles, expressed through the purchase of clothes and music, and the clubs, pubs and concerts they go to.

The family life cycle

The family life cycle will also influence leisure activities and opportunities. Young couples setting up households together, and having children, will face more restrictions on leisure activities, with household costs, mortgages and the costs of children. As children become less dependent on their parents, and as mortgages get paid off, people will have more disposable income to spend on leisure activities and consumer goods. Ill-health as people get older, with reduced income in retirement, may once again limit leisure opportunities.

Gender

Gender has an important influence on the choice of leisure activity. As a result of gender role socialization, men and women show different leisure interests and some leisure activities are more associated with one sex than the other.

Feminist researchers have noted that women generally have less time and opportunity for leisure activities than men, as they often have responsibility for housework and childcare, and sometimes for dependent elderly relatives or the sick and disabled, on top of paid employment. Women also earn less than men, which further restricts their opportunity to participate in commercial leisure activities.

Research by Deem (1986) in Milton Keynes found that women's leisure activities were often combined with aspects of childcare, such as driving the children to leisure centres and going swimming with them. This does raise questions of how far such activities are really freely chosen and enjoyable leisure activities, rather than aspects of unpaid domestic labour. As housework and childcare have no starting and finishing hours, and as many women combine this with full-time or part-time paid employment, many women find it hard to see leisure as a distinct period of time, and what leisure they have is often limited to home and family based activities.

Deem's research in Milton Keynes, and Green, Hebron and Woodward's (1990) research in Sheffield, found that patriarchy and patriarchal control (dominance and control by men) restricted women's leisure opportunities to 'approved' activities. Male partners often felt threatened by women's independent participation in leisure activities that might bring them into social contact with other men. Activities like clubbing and going to pubs in a 'night out with the girls' are often not approved of by men, but doing a night class at the local college or going to keep-fit classes are seen as OK.

Patriarchy also restricts women's independence and choice in leisure activities through the harassment women may face in public places, such as getting 'chatted up' if they go into pubs, clubs or leisure centres on their own, or the risks they face in walking home alone at night.

Activity

1 Identify and explain two ways that the leisure activities of males and females differ.
2 The evidence suggests women have less leisure time and opportunities than men. What effects do you think this might have on women forming individual identities and lifestyles?

Ethnicity

Ethnicity has important influences on leisure activities, and people will often make cultural choices of leisure activity in accordance with the ethnic group to which they belong, influencing their tastes in food, music and films. Some minority ethnic groups may find their activities restricted by racism.

Asian women are more likely to be restricted to home and family based activities because of culturally defined roles. Roberts (1983) found that many Asian workers will put in long working hours so they can afford, and have time, to visit kinfolk in their countries of origin.

However, younger British-born people from minority ethnic groups may be adopting less culturally defined leisure choices and lifestyles, and forming identities that are less constrained by the cultural inheritance of their parents' culture.

Activity

1 Identify and explain three factors that may influence an individual's choice of leisure activity.
2 Explain briefly what is meant by 'leisure has become a commercialized activity'.
3 In about one and a half sides of A4 paper, answer the following essay question:
   Examine the view that a person's social position is still the main influence on their leisure patterns.

Chapter summary

After studying this chapter, you should be able to:

- explain the difficulties in defining work, non-work and leisure
- explain the importance of work, and how it influences people's identity
- explain the changing nature of work and leisure
- explain features of the management and organization of work, including the way technology is used as a means of control of the workforce
- explain what is meant by the 'human relations' approach to management
- critically discuss the debates over the causes and consequences of deskilling and alienation
- identify the features of Fordism and post-Fordism
- discuss the effects of changing technology on work and society
- discuss the causes and consequences of conflict at work
- discuss the types, causes and consequences of unemployment, and the groups most at risk of unemployment
- identify the difficulties in defining leisure
- discuss the changing patterns of leisure

- discuss the role of leisure and consumption in forming people's identities
- discuss the social factors influencing leisure patterns

Key terms

- alienation
- automation
- core workers
- craft production
- deskilling
- division of labour
- flexible specialization
- Fordism
- mechanical solidarity
- mechanization
- organic solidarity
- periphery workers
- post-Fordism
- primary labour market
- productivity
- responsible autonomy
- scientific management
- secondary labour market
- Taylorism
- technological determinism

Coursework suggestions

1 Interview a sample of people in different types of work, or in the same type, asking them about the kinds of thing they like or dislike about their job. Link this in with Marx's and Blauner's theories of alienation.

2 Carry out a study of the introduction of new technology into a workplace, its advantages and disadvantages, and workers' attitudes to it.

3 Carry out a survey among some unemployed people, asking about how they spend their time, the reasons they are unemployed, the problems they encounter, etc. Link this to theories of unemployment, work and leisure.

4 Do a survey of people's leisure activities, and do unstructured interviews with some of them to uncover how important they see leisure as being in establishing their identities.

5 Carry out unstructured interviews with a sample of people, perhaps from different age groups or ethnic groups or of different sexes, asking them about how they see the differences between work, non-work and leisure, and the influences on their choice of leisure activities. Link this to debates about work, non-work and leisure.

A number of the activities in this chapter could easily be adapted and developed into coursework proposals.

Exam Questions

WORK AND LEISURE

Time allowed: 1 hour 15 minutes   **Total for this Question:** *60 marks*

Item A

Unemployment may sometimes result from technological changes in work processes. For example, the introduction of computer-aided printing techniques in the newspaper industry in the 1980s resulted in heavy job losses and a pattern of enforced 'leisure', especially among skilled male manual workers. On the other hand, the new technology also creates jobs, including whole new occupations that had not previously existed, such as computer programmers. Many of the new occupations have been filled by   5
female workers. These trends help to explain the differences in the rates of official rewarded employment and unemployment between men and women. However, the official figures are widely criticized for not giving an accurate picture of how many people are unemployed, which groups are most affected (such as specific ethnic or age groups), or changes over time. Similarly, official rates of economic activity, which include both the employed and unemployed, may also be misleading.   10

Item B

Frederick W. Taylor founded the 'scientific management' approach to the organisation and management of work. He believed that it was the responsibility of management to organise and control the work process and that this could not be left to the workers themselves. In his view, there was 'one best way' of performing any work task and it was management's job to discover it by applying scientific principles to the design of work processes. For example, tools should be carefully designed for the specific job – Taylor   5
even spoke of the 'science of shovelling'. He argued that workers and tasks must be closely matched; for example, those with low intelligence should be given simple, repetitive tasks. He believed that workers are motivated only by economic rewards and that payment by results was the most effective method of motivating them to work hard and raise their productivity. In his view, 'scientific management' would bring an end to industrial conflict, since higher productivity would bring both higher profits to employers and   10
higher wages to employees.

(a) Explain what is meant by 'productivity' (**Item B**, line 9).   *(2 marks)*
(b) Suggest **two** reasons why different ethnic groups have different rates of unemployment
     (**Item A**, line 9).   *(4 marks)*
(c) Suggest **three** reasons why the leisure patterns of the unemployed may differ from those
     of the employed.   *(6 marks)*
(d) Identify and briefly explain **two** reasons why official unemployment figures may not
     give an accurate picture of unemployment (**Item A**, lines 7–8).   *(8 marks)*
(e) Examine the reasons for different levels of alienation and works satisfaction experienced
     by different groups of workers.   *(20 marks)*
(f) Using material from **Item B** and elsewhere, assess the usefulness of the 'scientific
     management' approach to an understanding of the organisation and management
     of work.   *(20 marks)*

(AQA AS Unit 2 January 2003)

WORK AND LEISURE

Time allowed: 1 hour 15 minutes **Total for this Question:** *60 marks*

Item A

Leisure patterns are influenced by social differences and inequalities. For example, unskilled workers tend to have different leisure pursuits from those in professional occupations, and some groups may be leisure-poor while others are leisure-rich. Similarly, women's leisure patterns tend to differ from those of men.

Leisure patterns also vary along with the type of society in which they are found. For example, in pre-industrial societies, leisure tended to be informally organised and based in the community or family. In modern industrial or post-industrial societies, while this type of leisure still exists, new forms of leisure and new ways of organising it have emerged.   5

Item B

Marx saw production technology in capitalist society as a means of controlling workers and raising profits. Labour costs could be reduced by replacing skilled workers with machines. Workers would lose control over their work as they became little more than machine minders. Members of the working class would become increasingly similar as they were all deskilled to the level of unskilled workers.

Harry Braverman agrees that since the early 20th century there has been a steady degrading or deskilling   5
of work. He argues that employers have used Frederick W. Taylor's principles of scientific management to take control of the labour process and to remove skills from workers.

Source: Adapted from P. Taylor et al., *Sociology in Focus* (Causeway Press) 1995

(a) Explain what is meant by 'leisure-poor' (**Item A**, line 2–3). *(2 marks)*
(b) Identify **two** features of 'scientific management' (**Item B**, line 6). *(4 marks)*
(c) Suggest **three** ways in which leisure may have changed since industrialisation
    (**Item A**, lines 5–7). *(6 marks)*
(d) Identify and briefly explain **two** reasons why 'women's leisure patterns tend to differ from
    those of men' (**Item A**, line 3). *(8 marks)*
(e) Examine some of the causes and effects of unemployment. *(20 marks)*
(f) Using material from **Item B** and elsewhere, assess the view that work has become
    increasingly deskilled over the last 100 years. *(20 marks)*

(AQA AS Unit 2 May 2004)

CHAPTER **8**

Sociological Methods

- Participant observation
- Non-participant observation
- Longitudinal studies
- Case studies and life histories
- Methodological pluralism and triangulation
- Doing your own research

MUCH of this book has concentrated on what sociologists have already found out about society. But how do sociologists go about finding these things out in the first place? Sociological methods are the variety of tools or techniques sociologists use to find out something about an area which remains relatively unexplored, to describe some aspects of social life, or to discover the causes of some social event, such as the causes of crime or ill-health. This chapter will examine the various research methods that sociologists use to collect evidence. These are summarized in figure 8.1

Influences on the choice of research method

The main research methods flow from two different theoretical approaches to the study of society. These two approaches are known as positivism and interpretivism. Positivists and interpretivists often use different research

Positivism is an approach in sociology that believes society can be studied using similar scientific techniques to those used in the natural sciences, such as physics, chemistry and biology.

Interpretivism is an approach emphasizing that people have consciousness involving personal beliefs, values and interpretations, and these influence the way they act. They do not simply respond to forces outside them.

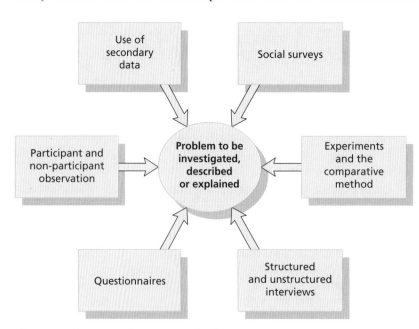

Figure 8.1 The range of research methods

methods because they have different assumptions about the nature of society, which influences the type of data they are interested in collecting.

Positivism and research methods

Positivists believe that just as there are causes of things in the natural world, so there are external social forces, making up a society's social structure, that cause or mould people's ideas and actions. Durkheim, a positivist, called these external forces social facts.

Social facts are phenomena which exist outside individuals and independently of their minds, but which act upon them in ways which constrain or mould their behaviour. Such phenomena include social institutions like the law, the family, the education system and the workplace.

Positivists believe social institutions create expectations of how individuals should behave and limit their choices and options, with social control making individuals behave in socially approved ways.

Durkheim said the aim of sociology should be the study of social facts, which should be considered as things, like objects in the natural world, and could in most cases be observed and measured quantitatively – in number/statistical form. The feelings, emotions and motives of individuals cannot be observed or measured, and should therefore not be studied. These are in any case the result of social facts existing outside the individual, such as the influences of socialization, the law, the mass media, family, the experiences of work and so on.

Examples of positivist approaches might be to look at whether people in some social classes suffer more illness than those in other classes, or are more likely to commit crime, by looking at statistics on health and crime. Similarly, positivist research on relationships in the family might collect statistical data on who does what around the home, the length of time spent by partners on housework and childcare and so on.

Positivists argue that without quantification, sociology will remain at the level of insight, lacking evidence, and it will be impossible to replicate (or repeat) studies to check findings, establish the causes of social events, or make generalizations.

Quantitative data are anything that can be expressed in statistical or number form or can be 'measured' in some way, such as age, qualifications, income or periods of ill-health. Such data are usually presented in the form of statistical tables, graphs, pie charts and bar charts.

Just as the data of the natural sciences are drawn from direct observation and can be measured and quantified, so positivists use research methods which involve the collection of quantitative (statistical) data to test their ideas. Such quantitative methods are more likely to involve large-scale or macro research on large numbers of people. These methods include:

- the experiment
- the comparative method
- social surveys
- structured questionnaires
- formal/structured interviews
- the use of official statistics

Interpretivism and research methods

Interpretivists believe that, because people's behaviour is influenced by the interpretations and meanings they give to social situations, the researcher's task is to gain an understanding of these interpretations and meanings, and how people see and understand the world around them. Sociology should therefore use research methods which provide an understanding from the point of view of individuals and groups. This process is called **verstehen** (pronounced *ver-stay-un*).

Instead of collecting statistical information, interpretivists suggest there is a need to discuss and get personally involved with people in order to get at how they see the world and understand it. Examples might be to look at whether people in some social classes tolerate or dismiss ill-health more than those in other classes, or are more likely to be arrested because of the way police see them. Similarly, interpretivist research on relationships in the family might carry out in-depth interviews with family members, finding out how they feel about doing jobs around the home, whether they see housework and childcare as shared out equally or not and whether they'd want them to be.

The methods interpretivists use are therefore those which involve the collection of **qualitative data**. This consists of words giving in-depth description and insight into the attitudes, values and feelings of individuals and groups, and the meanings and interpretations they give to events. Such qualitative methods include:

- participant and non-participant observation
- informal (unstructured/in-depth) interviews
- open-ended questionnaires
- personal accounts like diaries and letters.

These are more likely to involve in-depth small-scale or micro research on small numbers of people.

The interpretivists question the value of the research methods used by positivists, such as structured questionnaires and interviews. This is because they impose a framework on research – the sociologist's own view of what is important, rather than what may be important to the individuals being researched.

Figure 8.2 shows the broad links which exist between the two different theoretical approaches of positivism and interpretivism, other wider theories of society identified with them, and the research methods most likely to be used.

Verstehen is the idea of understanding human behaviour by putting yourself in the position of those being studied, and trying to see things from their point of view.

Qualitative data are concerned with people's feelings, meanings and interpretations about some event, and try to get at the way they really see things. Such data are normally in the form of the sociologist's description and interpretation of people's feelings and lifestyles, often using direct quotations from the people studied.

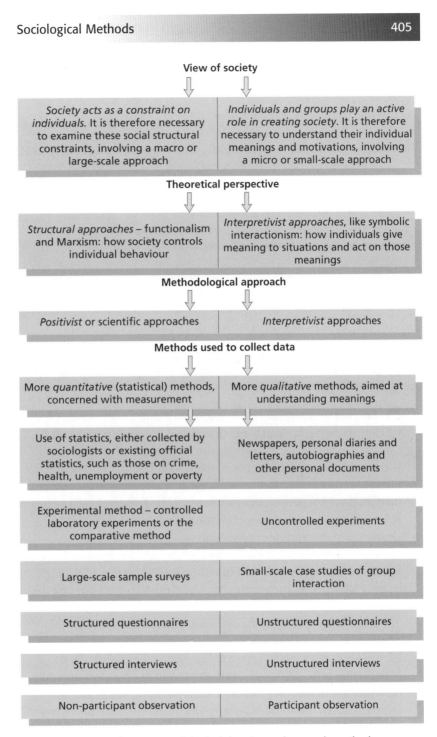

Figure 8.2 The link between sociological theories and research methods: a summary

---

Activity

Imagine you wanted to do a study of how tasks are divided up between men and women in the home. You are interested in:

- housework and other household jobs
- childcare (not just who does it, but who takes responsibility for making sure children have new clothes, shoes, the right gear for school, get food they like and so on)
- decision-making
- dealing with family conflicts and emotions

Suggest ways that positivists and interpretivists might approach these issues differently, and what types of methods they might use to obtain their information.

Other influences on the choice of research method

It is not simply theoretical issues that influence the choice of methods sociologists use. This will also depend on a range of non-theoretical factors:

- *The time and funding that are available* to complete the research will influence the scale of the research and the types of method used. For example, large-scale research is expensive, and beyond the means of most sociologists. Research for military or defence purposes will attract funding more easily than research into help for disabled people. Government-backed research is likely to open more doors to researchers and produce more sponsorship than private individuals or small research departments are able to achieve by themselves. Government-backed research often favours quantitative data gathered through large-scale surveys, such as the British Crime Survey funded by the Home Office.
- *The availability of existing data* on a topic may limit or decide the method.
- *The values and beliefs of the researcher* will inevitably influence whether she or he thinks issues are important or unimportant and therefore worthy of study or not. Townsend (1979), for example, clearly believed the study of poverty was important, and his values are reflected in his devotion to poverty research throughout his academic life.
- *Sociologists are professionals with careers and promotion prospects* ahead of them, and they face a constant struggle to get money to fund their research. There is therefore an understandable desire to prove

their own hypotheses right. The desire for promotion may influence what topics are seen as useful to do research on, as will the current state of knowledge and what constitutes a 'trendy' or lucrative research area.

● *The pressure to publish findings* and publishers' deadlines may mean research is not as thorough as it ought to be.

Figure 8.3 illustrates some of these influences on the choice of research topic and the methods used.

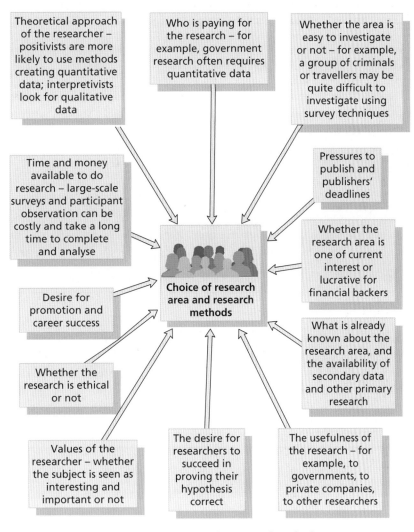

Figure 8.3 Influence on choices of research topic and method

Activity

Refer to figure 8.3 and:

1   Suggest two ways that sources of funding for research might influence that research.

2   Suggest two reasons why investigating some social groups may be much more difficult than others.

3   Answer in about one and a half sides of A4 paper the following essay question:
    Examine the view that the main influences on a researcher's choice of research method are practical considerations.

Key issues in social research

There are three key issues that should always be considered when carrying out or assessing research. These are the issues of reliability, validity and the ethics of research.

Reliability

Reliability is concerned with *replication*: whether another researcher using the same method for the same research on the same group would achieve the same results. For example, if different researchers use the same questionnaire on similar samples of the population, then the results should be more or less the same if the techniques are reliable.

> **Reliability** refers to whether another researcher, if repeating research using the same method for the same research on the same group, would achieve the same results.

Validity

Validity is concerned with notions of truth: how far the findings of research actually provide a true picture of what is being studied. Data can be *reliable* without being valid. For example, official crime statistics may be reliable, in so far as researchers repeating the data collection would get the same results over and over again, but they are not valid if they don't give us the full picture of the extent of crime.

> **Validity** is concerned with notions of truth: how far the findings of research actually provide a true picture of what is being studied.

Ethics

The ethics of research are concerned with morality and standards of behaviour, and when sociologists carry out research they should always consider the following points:

> **Ethics** concerns principles or ideas about what is morally right or wrong.

- They should take into account the sensitivities of those helping with their research. For example, it would not be appropriate to ask about attitudes to abortion in a hospital maternity ward where women may be having babies or have suffered miscarriages.

- Findings should be reported accurately and honestly.
- The physical, social and mental well-being of people who help in research should not be harmed by research; for example, by disclosing information given in confidence which might get the person into trouble, or cause them embarrassment.
- The anonymity, privacy and interests of those who participate in your research should be respected. You should not identify them by name, or enable them (or an institution) to be easily identified.
- As far as possible, your research should be based on the freely given consent of those studied. Researchers should make clear what they're doing, why they're doing it, and what they will do with their findings.

Primary data is that which is collected by sociologists themselves – it only exists because the sociologist has collected it.

Secondary data is that which the sociologist carrying out the research has not gathered himself or herself, but which already exists.

Primary and secondary data

Primary data is usually obtained by carrying out a social survey, using questionnaires and interviews, or by participant observation.

Secondary data is collected from secondary sources. Figure 8.4 shows a range of these sources that might be used by sociologists in carrying out research.

Both types of data can take either quantitative (statistical) or qualitative (non-statistical) forms.

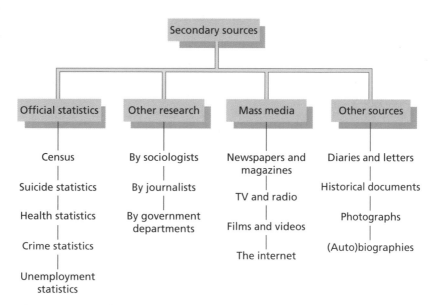

Figure 8.4 Secondary sources of data

Qualitative secondary sources

Qualitative secondary sources include newspapers, novels, literature, art, autobiographies, letters, diaries, radio and TV programmes, parish registers, historical documents, previous sociological studies, school records, social work files, police records, minutes of meetings, and some official government reports.

The advantages and uses of qualitative secondary sources

- Qualitative secondary sources may provide valuable, or the only, sources of information in an area. For example, historical documents are often the only way of investigating the past, and without them it would be very difficult to find out about history. Laslett's and Anderson's work on the family would have been impossible without reference to records going back several centuries.
- They are useful for interpretivists who wish to gain insights into the worldview or ideologies of those who produced them. Some historical documents and autobiographies can be particularly useful for these purposes.
- They may be very useful for assessing people's concerns or worries. For example, the letters pages and agony columns of newspapers and magazines may give valuable insights into the thinking of their readers (or the thinking of the editor on what she or he chooses to print).

The disadvantages and limitations of qualitative secondary sources

Scott in *A Matter of Record* (1990) suggests four criteria for judging secondary data in general, but his points are very useful in assessing secondary qualitative data:

- *Authenticity*   Is the evidence genuine or a forgery? For example, diaries apparently by Adolf Hitler were purchased for millions of pounds and published in 1983 after being certified authentic by top historians. They were later found to be a complete forgery.
- *Credibility*   Is the evidence believable, sincere and honest? Does it contain biases, distortions and exaggerations by the writers to deceive or mislead readers? Is the evidence reliable? Who was a document written for? Does it simply reflect the values and beliefs of those who

produced it? The mass media, for example, are often seen as very biased (one-sided) sources of evidence, and material written for publication may be very different from material meant to be private. For example, autobiographies and published diaries of politicians should be treated with some scepticism, as they're likely to be very selective in the material included; at the same time, they may show how the politicians' minds worked, which might be useful for interpretivist research.

- *Representativeness*   Is the document typical of those appearing at the time? Is the evidence complete or merely a partial, biased account? Are other documents missing? Many historical documents have been destroyed, and governments often ban the publication of official records for a number of years after the events they relate to. What about those people in the past who couldn't read or write? Does the secondary data available simply reflect the views of the privileged minority in the past who were able to read and write well enough to produce diaries, letters and other documents?
- *Meaning*   What do documents mean? Do they have the same meaning now as they did at the time they were first produced?

Content analysis

Content analysis is a way of trying to analyse the content of documents and other qualitative material by quantifying it. This is done, for example. by sorting out categories, and then going through documents, books, magazines, television programmes and so on systematically, recording the number of times items in each category appear. Examples might include feminist researchers analysing reading books for children and seeking evidence of gender-role stereotyping: they might use categories such as male leader/female led, female works or plays indoors/male outdoors, and so on.

The Glasgow University Media Group has adopted this type of method in analysing television news. They video-recorded all TV news bulletins for a year and then made a content analysis, categorizing reports on industrial unrest and evaluating them. Their research showed statistical evidence of television's biases towards management and against workers, with managers, for example, more often portrayed in calm, peaceful surroundings and workers in noisy conditions against a background of traffic noise. This gave the impression that managers were more 'rational' and calm than workers. This research challenged the mass media's claims of impartiality and balance in news reporting.

Activity

1 Go through the following examples, marking each as primary or secondary *and* quantitative or qualitative data.
   - exam results of schools in your area published in a local newspaper
   - newspaper stories from the 1930s
   - information collected by you showing the proportions of students doing different AS-level subjects
   - teenage magazines
   - statistics produced by the local NHS trust showing inequalities in health
   - video-recordings of a week's news reports
   - letters in a newspaper complaining about the risks to health of mobile phone masts
   - the published diaries of a former prime minister
2 Explain, with reasons, in what circumstances you might, or might not, consider each of the above pieces of data to be (a) reliable, and (b) valid, as sources of evidence.
3 Outline what ethical problems and problems of validity of the data collected, if any, there might be in each of the following situations:
   - a researcher joining a religious group to study it, concealing their role as a researcher
   - a researcher joining the police force to discover if there was evidence of racism among police officers, and then publishing his or her research
   - standing outside a gay club and noting the car numbers of drivers using the club, then using a friend in the police force to get hold of their addresses for a follow-up questionnaire on what it's like being gay
   - pretending to be ill and going to the doctor to investigate how doctor's decide whether someone is ill or not
4 Do you consider there are ever any situations where a researcher might be justified in deceiving people to obtain research data? Explain your answer with examples of particular situations.

Quantitative secondary sources

Quantitative secondary sources include a huge range of statistical data produced by groups like companies, charities and pressure groups. A major source of such data is the mass of official statistics collected by

Activity

Go to www.statistics.gov.uk, the website of the Office for National Statistics, and identify (a) five government statistical publications, and (b) statistics for the current year (or the most recent year for which data are available) on unemployment, suicide, health, crime, divorce and marriage.

national and local government and other official agencies. These include census data, statistics on births, marriages and deaths, and social services, unemployment, education, crime and health statistics.

The advantages and uses of official statistics

- Official statistics are important for planning and evaluating social policy, such as responding to housing needs, transport and education planning and meeting the care needs of the elderly.
- They are frequently the only available source of data in a particular area.
- They are readily available and cheap to use. There is no need to spend time and money collecting data, and some data, such as census data, would be impossible for an individual to collect.
- They are often comprehensive in coverage, and therefore more likely to be representative.
- They often cover a long timespan, and therefore allow the examination of trends over time, such as those on crime, unemployment, health and divorce. They can be used for 'before and after' studies, for example, to judge the effect of government policies on reducing inequalities in health or the extent of poverty.
- They allow intergroup and international comparisons to be made, such as between working-class and middle-class family sizes, or suicide, divorce and crime rates between countries. They can therefore be used for the comparative method in sociology (discussed later in this chapter).

The problems and limitations of official statistics

If official statistics are basically accepted at face value as a true, or valid, record of events (as some researchers do with crime statistics and other official statistics), problems are likely to centre on their presentation, accuracy and completeness. For example, attempts have been made to overcome the inadequacy of the official crime statistics and make them more accurate by using **victim surveys** like the British Crime Survey to discover the 'dark number' of unrecorded crimes.

A **victim survey** is one that asks people to say whether they have been a victim of crime, whether they reported it to the police or not.

Many sociologists would argue any statistics, and especially official statistics, can't be taken at face value as they are socially constructed and may be politically biased. For example:

- Official statistics are collected for administrative purposes rather than for purposes of sociological research – so the definitions and classifications adopted may be unsuitable for sociological research.
- Official statistics are produced by the state. This means they may be 'massaged' to avoid political embarrassment to the government (see,

for example, the discussion of unemployment figures below). The political process also affects which statistics are collected and which are not – for example, data on working days lost through strikes rather than industrial injuries; on social security 'scroungers' rather than tax evaders; on house-building rather than homelessness; on the poor but not the rich, and so on.

- Interpretivists argue that statistics are not 'objective facts' but simply social constructions: the product of a process of interpretation and decision-making by those with authority. The following examples illustrate why sociologists should treat official statistics with some caution and pages 73–4 showed the limitations of official statistics on divorce.

Suicide statistics

J. M. Atkinson (1978) and other interpretivists argue that suicide statistics are simply social constructions reflecting the behaviour of coroners, doctors, relatives, etc., and their definitions of suicide. They tell us more about the decision-making processes of the living than the intentions of the dead and the real number of suicides (see the activity on page 416).

Unemployment statistics

Between 1979 and 1997, the method of calculating unemployment statistics was changed about thirty times, with each change creating a statistical drop in unemployment. 'Claimant count' unemployment figures only include those who sign on at job centres, are eligible for jobseeker's allowance, and are immediately available to start work. They therefore exclude many married women, people who have retired early, those reluctantly staying on at school or college because of no jobs, those on government training schemes, and those reluctantly working part-time. They have therefore massively underestimated the real extent of unemployment, to the advantage of the government at the time. The International Labour Organization (ILO) definition of unemployment, which includes all those who are actively seeking work and available to start, whether or not they receive jobseeker's allowance, gives far higher numbers of the unemployed. If the 'economically inactive' are included as well – a category which includes those who want work but are not immediately available to start work or aren't actively seeking it – then the numbers of the unemployed are higher still.

Health statistics

Health statistics can be inaccurate because:

- They depend on people persuading doctors they are ill, and are therefore simply a record of doctors' decision-making.

- Doctors may diagnose illnesses incorrectly, reflecting the state of the doctor's knowledge – and therefore recorded illnesses may not be accurate. Many AIDS deaths may have been recorded as pneumonia or another illness before doctors 'discovered' AIDS. Recent research has suggested that deaths from AIDS may have occurred in the 1950s in Britain, although the disease was not really 'discovered' until the 1980s.
- Not all sick people go to the doctor and not all people who persuade the doctor they're sick are actually so – some may be malingerers or hypochondriacs.
- Private medicine operates to make a profit, and therefore is perhaps more likely to diagnose illness, as patients receiving treatment produce profits.

Crime statistics

Official crime statistics can be inaccurate for a number of reasons, and have to be treated very carefully by sociologists, because they do not show the full extent of crime in society. The following outlines these problems.

They only include crimes known to the police   Only around a quarter of all crimes are reported to the police, and even fewer are recorded by them as offences. There is a 'dark number' of undiscovered, unreported and unrecorded crimes. Victim surveys like the British Crime Survey show that many offences go unreported, such as vandalism, theft from the person, theft from motor vehicles, crimes of domestic violence, rape, and many burglaries.

Low clear-up rates   Only about one in five of all crimes is 'cleared up', with offenders caught. This leaves open the possibility that the other 80 per cent of known offences are committed by very different 'criminal types' from those who come before the courts.

Unreported crime   People may not report offences to the police because:

- They may think that the incident is too trivial to report; for example, where the incident did not involve loss or damage, or the loss was too small.
- They may think there is little point in reporting the incident because they feel the police could not do anything about it, either by recovering their property or by catching the offenders.
- They may fear embarrassment or humiliation at the hands of the police or in court, as happens, for example, in cases of rape and domestic violence.

- They fear they will themselves be in trouble. This may happen, for example, in crimes where there is no obvious victim and both parties benefit, such as the illegal supplying of drugs, or giving and accepting bribes. Illegal drug users who get ripped off by drugs dealers are extremely unlikely to report the incident, as they would get themselves into trouble.

- They may fear reprisals if the crime is reported, as in crimes of domestic violence.

- They may feel it is a private matter they would rather deal with themselves, such as assault between friends.

- They may not be aware an offence has been committed against them – people may have had 'lost' property stolen, been robbed by hoax gas meter readers or ripped off by cowboy builders without even realizing it.

- The crime may have no single victim or be seen as 'legitimate' (justified), such as tax evasion, or not paying customs duty.

- They may wish to protect the public reputation of the institution in which the offence occurs. For example, computer fraud in banks may be dealt with unofficially, without involving the police, in case the bank's customers lose confidence that their money is safe in its hands. A similar example might be a student caught with illegal drugs in a school or college, where reporting to the police might give a bad impression to parents and harm the reputation of the institution.

Activity

1 Go to www.homeoffice.gov.uk/crime, the Home Office 'crime and policing' website, track down the latest British Crime Survey, and find the five main reasons included in the latest survey for why the public don't report crime, and the two offences or groups of offences that are most likely to go unreported.

2 Read the following passage and then answer the questions beneath:

'Suicide is, by definition, the death of a person who intended to kill himself or herself. The problem for coroners is they can't ask dead people if they meant to kill themselves, so they can only guess at the truth by looking for "clues" in the circumstances surrounding the death. Atkinson has suggested there are four main factors which coroners take into account when deciding whether a death is a suicide or not:

- *Whether there was a suicide note.*
- *The way the person died, for example by hanging, drowning or a drug overdose. Death in a road accident rarely results in a suicide verdict.*
- *The place the death occurred and the circumstances surrounding it; for example, a drug overdose in a remote wood would be more likely to be*

seen as a suicide than if it occurred at home in bed. A coroner might also consider circumstances such as whether the person had been drinking alcohol before taking the drugs, and whether the drugs had been hoarded or not.

- *The life history and mental state of the dead person, such as her or his state of health, and whether the victim was in debt, had just failed exams, lost a job, got divorced and was depressed or not.*

Coroners do not always agree on the way they interpret these clues. For example, Atkinson found one coroner believed a death by drowning was likely to be a suicide if the clothes were left neatly folded on the beach, but another coroner might attach little importance to this.'

(a) How is suicide defined in the passage?

(b) Why do you think coroners attach such importance to suicide notes?

(c) Suggest two reasons why the presence or absence of a suicide note might be an unreliable 'clue' to a dead person's intention to die.

(d) Suggest ways, with reasons, in which relatives and friends might try to persuade a coroner that a death was not a suicide but an accident.

(e) On the basis of the evidence in the passage, suggest reasons why
   (i) some deaths classified as suicides may have been accidental, and
   (ii) some deaths classified as accidents may in fact have been suicides.

(f) With reference to the evidence in the passage, suggest reasons why sociologists should be very careful about using official statistics on suicide as a record of the real number of suicides in society.

3 In about one and a half sides of A4 paper, answer the following essay question:
Assess the usefulness of official statistics for sociologists in their research.

The experimental (laboratory) method of research

A **hypothesis** is an idea which the researcher guesses might be true, but which has not yet been tested against the evidence.

The experiment is the main means of conducting research in the natural sciences. In natural science, experiments are used to test a **hypothesis** in laboratory conditions in which all variables or causes are under the control of the researcher. By manipulating variables and studying and measuring the results, the researcher tries to test a hypothesis by isolating the causes of some phenomenon under investigation (such as, why pigs get fat).

The researcher will take two groups that are alike in every way: one is the *control group* and the other is the *experimental group*. The researcher will then alter some factor (the *independent variable*) in the experimental group to see if the variable being investigated (the *dependent variable*) changes compared to the control group (for example, alter heat in pigsties to see if this affects pigs getting fat). If nothing changes in the experimental group, then that variable can be dismissed as a cause of the thing being investigated, and other variables can be tested (for example, type of food). Through this experimental method, the researcher can eventually arrive at an explanation for the issue being investigated that has been tested against evidence, since any difference between the two groups after the experiment can only be because of the experimental variable, as the two groups were otherwise identical before the experiment.

Such laboratory experiments in the natural sciences have the advantage of:

- enabling scientists to test their hypotheses in controlled conditions
- making it easy to isolate and manipulate variables to isolate the causes of events
- being repeatable (replicable) and therefore able to be checked by other researchers
- enabling comparisons to be made with other similar experimental research

Problems of using the experimental method in sociology

- In the social sciences, and sociology in particular, it is often difficult to isolate a single cause of a social issue like crime, or underachievement in school, and it is extremely difficult to isolate variables for testing. For example, crime and low achievement in school are the result of a range of causes.
- Experiments need to treat one group differently from another similar group and compare results. However, this poses ethical problems for sociologists, as it may have negative effects on the experimental group. People may also object to being experimented on.
- Experiments are often only possible in small-scale settings with very limited, specific aims, but sociologists are often interested in wider settings like achievement in education and the causes of crime or ill-health, and such small-scale settings may be unrepresentative.

A particular problem is the Hawthorne effect.

The Hawthorne effect and the problem of validity

Sociologists want to study people in their 'normal' social context, but the laboratory and experimental conditions are artificial situations. People, unlike chemicals and many animals, can and do know what is going on in an experiment. The knowledge that an experiment is taking place, even if

> The **Hawthorne effect** is where the presence of a researcher, or a group's knowledge that it is the focus of attention, changes the behaviour of a group.

it is not fully understood, may mean people behave differently from their usual, everyday behaviour. They may deliberately sabotage the experiment, or 'play up' for the researcher. The very presence of the observer may become the principal independent variable in social scientific experiments. The classic example of this 'experimental effect' is the Hawthorne effect, which is explained in the box.

The Hawthorne effect

In 1927, a team of researchers led by Elton Mayo set up an experiment in the Hawthorne plant of the Western Electricity Company of Chicago, to try to find the factors affecting the productivity of workers. Using a control group and an experimental group, they set up a test area involving five workers who knew the experiment was taking place. Working conditions were matched with the rest of the factory, then the researchers varied factors such as room temperature, lighting, work hours, rest breaks, etc. They found output went up *even when conditions were made worse*. It turned out the most important variable affecting production was not environmental factors etc. but the *presence and interest of the researchers themselves*: being the focus of attention increased productivity. This influence of the researchers on research is known as the Hawthorne effect.

Such circumstances throw some doubt on the validity of using the experimental method for sociological research, and it is hardly ever desirable or possible to perform laboratory experiments in sociology. However, some experimental techniques have been used in sociology in the form of field experiments.

Field experiments

Field experiments are those conducted in the real world under normal social conditions, but trying to follow similar procedures to the laboratory experiment. They have mainly been carried out by interpretivists, who are interested in how meanings and labels, like 'bright' or 'mentally ill', get attached to people, and how others then react to them. This is illustrated in the work of Rosenthal and Jacobson and of Rosenhan, described in the box 'Examples of field experiments in sociology overleaf'.

The comparative method

The comparative method rests on the same principles as the experiment, and is an alternative to it. However, instead of setting up artificial experiments or situations, the researcher collects data about different societies

Examples of field experiments in sociology

In the 1960s, Rosenthal and Jacobson wanted to test the hypothesis that teachers' expectations had important effects on pupils' academic performance. They told teachers that 20 per cent of children had been tested and shown to have high intelligence and were expected to make rapid progress in the next year compared to other students. In fact, the students had been chosen totally at random, and were no different from the other students. Within a year, those students whom the teachers were told were bright made very rapid progress compared to other students. This was seen as evidence that pupil progress was affected by teacher expectation, and teachers' predictions of pupil progress could actually influence the progress they made – a self-fulfilling prophecy. This research posed ethical problems, as it may well have been that teachers' high expectations of the students labelled 'bright' may have been linked with low expectations of those labelled not bright, and had negative consequences on their progress – a self-fulfilling prophecy with negative effects on student progress. (See Rosenthal and Jacobson, *Pygmalion in the Classroom* (1968).)

Rosenhan was interested in discovering how the staff of mental hospitals made sense of and labelled people as mentally ill. He arranged for perfectly sane 'patients' to fake the symptoms of schizophrenia (hearing voices), and they were admitted to hospital, unknown to staff as fakes. Once admitted to hospital, they behaved normally. All were diagnosed as schizophrenics, even though they were perfectly healthy. Rosenhan reversed the experiment, telling hospital staff they could expect patients who would be faking illness. The staff eventually thought they had identified the fake patients, but all those they identified were actually genuine patients who wanted help. (See Rosenhan, 'On being sane in insane places' (1973).)

Activity

1   Identify and explain three reasons why the experimental method may not be suitable for sociological research.
2   Refer to the examples of field experiments by Rosenthal and Jacobson, and Rosenhan:
- What aims did Rosenthal and Jacobson have in carrying out their piece of research?
- In what ways do you think their research might be useful to others?
- Do you think there are any ethical difficulties in either piece of research?
- To what extent do you think it might be possible to generalize these pieces of research to the whole of society? Would you need more information to answer this question?

or social groups in the real world, or the same society at different times (this is called the historical method). The researcher then compares one society or group with another in an attempt to identify the conditions that are present in one society but lacking in the other, as a way to explain the causes of some social event.

This approach is most commonly used by positivists concerned with trying to isolate and identify the causes of social events and behaviour.

An example of the use of the comparative method is Durkheim's study of suicide. Durkheim could hardly experiment with people to see what kinds of factors made them commit suicide, and he couldn't control the social situations in societies whose suicide rates he wished to compare. All he could do was to compare official suicide statistics in various societies and examine what seemed to be the most frequent factors linked with high suicide rates. He collected suicide statistics from a number of European countries and, by comparing variables such as religion, marital status and geographical location, he concluded that differences in suicide rates could be partly explained by differences in religious belief between societies.

Surveys and sampling methods

Surveys are a means of collecting primary data from large numbers of people, usually in a standardized statistical form.

Surveys are most commonly done using questionnaires or structured interviews.

Who uses the survey method?

Because surveys produce quantitative statistical data, they are the method most favoured by positivists.

Townsend used the survey method to produce a mass of statistical data, with questionnaires carried out by trained interviewers, about the causes and extent of poverty in his classic study *Poverty in the United Kingdom* (1979). Many people use surveys apart from sociologists, for instance the government when it carries out the ten-yearly census, market researchers who want to test people's attitudes to products, and election pollsters trying to find out how people will vote in elections.

Representativeness and sampling

In some cases, it may be possible to interview every member of the population under investigation because it is such a small group, such as a class of college students, or because the organization doing the research has the resources to investigate everyone. For example, the government surveys the entire population of Britain in the census every ten years.

Sociologists rarely have the time or money to question everyone in large-scale and expensive surveys, so they usually collect information from a **sample**.

If it is a **representative sample**, containing all the relevant characteristics of the whole **survey population**, such as age and gender groups, ethnic groups and social class, then the results obtained from the sample can be generalized or applied to the whole survey population.

The representativeness of a sample can be affected by:

- *Sample size*   Too small a sample may mean that it is not representative, and in general the larger the sample taken, the more representative it will be. However, a sample is at its ideal size when making it any larger won't produce much more accurate or representative results than if the entire survey population had been questioned.

- *The sampling frame*   A commonly used **sampling frame** includes the Register of Electors, which includes the names and addresses of all adults over the age of 18 in Britain who are registered to vote in elections. Another nationwide sampling frame, which is now the most complete one available in Britain, is the Royal Mail's Postcode Address File, which lists all addresses in the UK. Doctors' lists of patients are also commonly used as sampling frames, as most people are registered with a doctor. It is extremely important that a sampling frame should be complete: no individuals or particular groups of individuals should be missing. Otherwise, the sample drawn from the sampling frame may be unrepresentative of the entire survey population. For example, a telephone directory would be an unreliable sampling frame if the researcher wanted to select a sample which was representative of the entire adult population, as it only contains those who have a landline, and excludes those who may not be able to afford or want a telephone, or who are ex-directory and therefore not included in the phone book, or who only have a mobile phone.

- *The sampling method used*   Careful **sampling methods** mean that often the information provided by the sample can be generalized with great accuracy to the whole survey population. For example, opinion polls on the voting intentions of electors often produce extremely accurate predictions of the outcome of general elections from questioning samples of only about 1,500 people, drawn from millions of adult voters.

The problem for sociologists is how to obtain as representative a sample as possible, and this is achieved by various sampling methods.

Sampling methods

Figure 8.5 summarizes the main sampling methods discussed below, with examples.

> A **sample** is a smaller *representative* group drawn from the survey population (the whole group under investigation).

> The **survey population** is the whole group being studied, and will depend on the hypothesis the researcher wishes to investigate.
>
> A **sampling frame** is a list of names of all those included in the survey population from which the sample is selected.
>
> A **representative sample** is a smaller group drawn from the survey population which contains a good cross-section of the survey population, such as the right proportions of people of different ethnic origins, ages, social classes and sexes. The information obtained from a representative sample should provide roughly the same results as if the whole survey population had been questioned.
>
> **Sampling methods** are the techniques sociologists use to select representative individuals to study from the survey population.

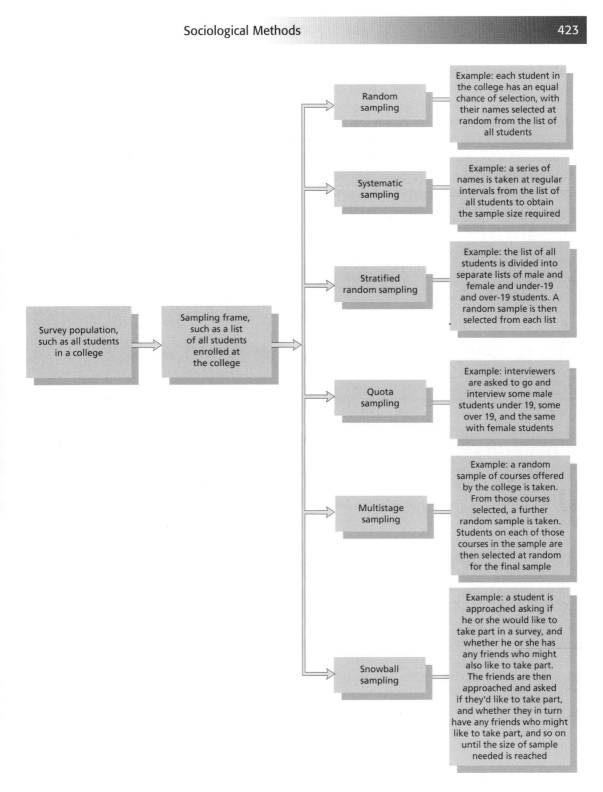

Figure 8.5 Examples of sampling methods

Random sampling   Random sampling simply means that every individual in the survey population has an equal chance of being picked out for investigation. For example, all names are put in a hat and enough names picked out to make up the sample size required. This is most commonly done by numbering all the names in the sampling frame and then getting a computer to select numbers at random to fill the sample size. However, such a method is subject to the laws of chance, which may result in an unrepresentative sample – there may be too many people of one sex, age group or social class or who live in the same area. For example, a small survey of a school might by chance select only black females, and miss out black males and white males and white females.

Systematic sampling   Systematic sampling is where names are selected from the sampling frame at regular intervals until the size of sample is reached, for example by selecting every tenth name in the sampling frame. This has much the same risk of being unrepresentative as a random sample. For example, every tenth name might, purely by chance, happen to be a white and middle-class person.

Stratified random sampling   Stratified random sampling is a way of attempting to avoid the possible errors caused by simple random sampling. This is achieved by subdividing (stratifying) the sampling frame into a number of smaller sampling frames drawn up on particular bases, such as social class, age, sex, ethnic group or education, according to their proportions in the population under investigation. The criteria used will depend on the factors being investigated. Individuals are then drawn at random from each of these sampling frames. For example, in a survey of doctors, we may know from earlier research that 8 per cent of all doctors are Asian, and so the sociologist must make sure 8 per cent of the sample are Asian. To do this, the sociologist will separate out the Asian doctors from the sampling frame of all doctors, and then take a random sample from this list of Asian doctors to make up 8 per cent of the sample of all doctors in the survey population. In this way, the final sample is more likely to be representative of all doctors in the survey population. Stratified random sampling has the advantage over simple random sampling of being much more representative, because all the characteristics of the survey population are more certain to be represented in the sample. See the box 'Obtaining a stratified random sample' and figure 8.6, which shows an example.

Quota sampling   In quota sampling, interviewers are told to go and select people who fit into certain categories according to their proportion in the survey population as a whole, such as so many men and women

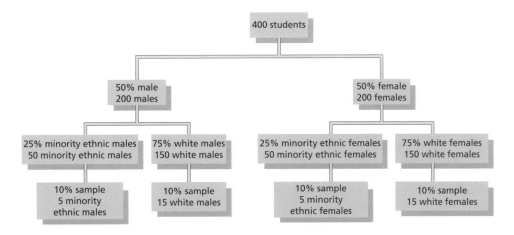

Figure 8.6 An example of stratified random sampling

Obtaining a stratified random sample

Suppose there were 400 students in a school. Of these, 50 per cent are male and 50 per cent are female. In each group, 75 per cent are white and 25 per cent are from minority ethnic groups. You want a 10 per cent representative sample (40 people).

Figure 8.6 shows how you might obtain a stratified random sample by dividing up the sampling frame of 400 names, first into two sampling frames (by sex), and then by subdividing each again into two (by ethnic group). You then take a 10 per cent random sample from each of the final four sampling frames.

This stratified random sample of 40 people (10 per cent of the original 400 students) should be representative of the sex and ethnic characteristics of the entire school population, as these features of the survey population are now certain to be included in the 10 per cent sample.

---

over the age of 45. The choice of the actual individuals selected is left to the honesty of the interviewer (unlike other sampling methods where actual named individuals are identified). The problem with quota sampling is that it is not necessarily representative. For example, the quota might be filled by stopping people while shopping during the week, but this would exclude those not shopping or who are at work. The fact that the choice of person rests on the interviewer's discretion means there may be bias in the choices they make. For instance, they may not approach people who don't look very welcoming, even though they fit the category, or they might ignore those who refuse to cooperate and simply find another person who fits the quota. This could well lead to a bias in the sample.

> ### Non-representative sampling
>
> In some cases a non-representative sample might be useful in sociological research: for example, selecting a group for a particular purpose which is not representative, but because it has the particular characteristics you want to study. For example, in studying a hypothesis like 'roles in the family are more likely to be equal among younger middle-class couples', it might be useful to study a group that is young and middle class, to test or disprove the hypothesis, or gain insights into those couples.

Multistage or cluster sampling   Multistage or cluster sampling involves selecting a sample in various stages, each time selecting a sample from the previous sample until the final sample of people is selected. For example, in a national survey of school students, you might first take a random sample of schools, then take a random sample of students in those sample schools.

Snowball sampling   Snowball sampling is used when a sampling frame is difficult to obtain or doesn't exist, or when a sample itself is very difficult to obtain. The researcher may identify one or two people with the characteristics they're interested in, and ask them to introduce them to other people willing to cooperate in the research, and then ask these people to identify others. For example, Laurie Taylor in *In the Underworld* (1984) used this technique to investigate the lifestyles of criminals. There was no readily available sampling frame of criminals. He happened to know a convicted criminal, who was willing to put him in touch with other criminals who were willing to cooperate in his research. These criminals in turn put him in touch with other criminals, and so his sample gradually built up, just as a snowball gets bigger as you roll it in the snow.

Such samples may be useful, but they are not random or representative. They rely on volunteers recommending other volunteers to the researcher, and the sample is therefore self-selecting, and this may create bias. For example, such volunteers may have particular views for or against a particular issue and that may be why they volunteered.

Figure 8.7 shows how a major national annual survey, the British Social Attitudes Survey, used a combination of multistage, systematic and random sampling to obtain a final sample of 3,146 individuals drawn from nearly all people over the age of 18 in Britain.

The stages of a survey

Before carrying out a large-scale survey, it is important to carry out a **pilot survey** (sometimes called a pilot study).

A **pilot survey** is a small-scale practice survey carried out before the final survey to check for any possible problems.

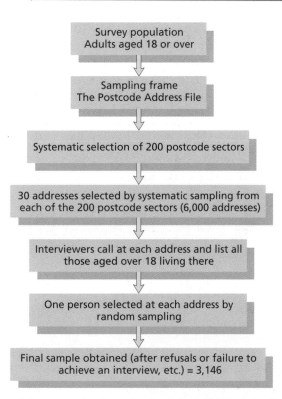

Figure 8.7 Obtaining a sample: the example of the British Social Attitudes Survey

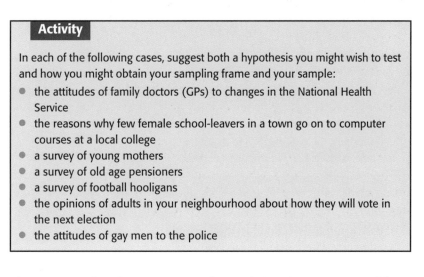

Activity

In each of the following cases, suggest both a hypothesis you might wish to test and how you might obtain your sampling frame and your sample:

- the attitudes of family doctors (GPs) to changes in the National Health Service
- the reasons why few female school-leavers in a town go on to computer courses at a local college
- a survey of young mothers
- a survey of old age pensioners
- a survey of football hooligans
- the opinions of adults in your neighbourhood about how they will vote in the next election
- the attitudes of gay men to the police

The purpose of a pilot survey or a pilot study is to iron out any problems which the researcher might have overlooked, and avoid wasting time and money in the final survey. For example, some of the sample may have moved away or died, there may be problems with non-response or non-cooperation by respondents, or some questions may be unclear.

After the pilot survey is completed, the results are reviewed, any necessary changes are made, and the main survey can then proceed. The stages of a survey are shown in figure 8.8.

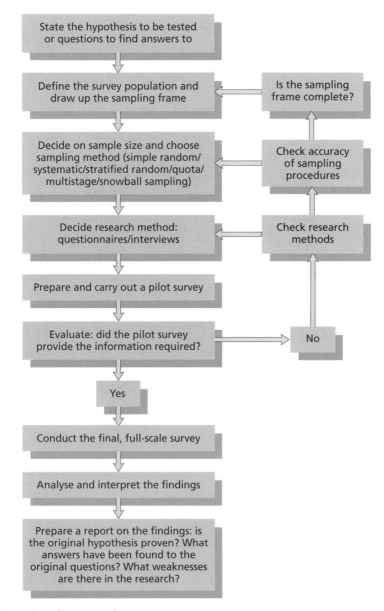

Figure 8.8 The stages of a survey

Problems of the social survey

There are three major problems faced by social survey researchers in achieving 'scientific' accuracy:

- *Validity*   Surveys need to be very carefully planned if they are to obtain data which are valid – which really represent what they claim to represent. The statistical data produced by surveys are questioned by interpretivists, who would argue statistical data lack the depth to describe accurately people's meanings and motives, and that they use categories which are imposed by the sociologists.
- *Generalization*   This is concerned with representativeness: how far the findings of a piece of research can be generalized to other sections of the survey population rather than simply restricted to the sample selected. For example, the sample selected may be too small, or unrepresentative, or people selected may have moved, died, etc., in which case the results may not be able to be generalized.
- *Reliability*   Whatever the survey finds should be found by anyone else conducting the same survey again. This may be a particular problem where face-to-face interviews are used. This issue is discussed below under 'interviewer bias'.

Activity

1   Explain what is meant by a 'representative sample'.
2   Suggest two reasons why sociologists might use a sample when doing a survey.
3   Suggest two reasons why sociologists might undertake a 'pilot study'.
4   Explain what is meant by a 'quota sample'.
5   Identify three factors that may influence the representativeness of a sample.

Questionnaires

The nature and use of questionnaires

Most surveys involve the use of a questionnaire of some kind. A questionnaire is a list of pre-set questions to which the *respondents* (the people answering the questions) are asked to supply answers – either by filling in responses themselves (a self-completion questionnaire) or by giving information to an interviewer, either face to face or over the telephone. When administered by an interviewer, these take the form of interviews.

Researchers using questionnaires see them as a comparatively cheap, fast and efficient method (compared to other methods like unstructured interviews or participant observation) for obtaining large amounts of quantifiable data on relatively large samples of people.

The questionnaire is one of the main tools of measurement in positivist sociology, as data obtained by structured questionnaires are easily quantified and can be analysed more 'scientifically' and objectively than qualitative data.

Questionnaire design: some principles and problems

Great care is needed in questionnaire design. Because the idea is to present all respondents with the same questions and therefore obtain comparable data, questionnaires can't be changed once a survey has begun. They should be kept as simple and clear as possible, otherwise those being interviewed or filling in the questionnaire themselves will be unlikely to complete it.

A pilot survey is therefore very important to clear up problems and avoid wasting time and money on a poorly designed questionnaire. Pilot studies are used to test questions, make sure their meaning is clear, and to ensure layout and wording are suitable for the intended sample.

The section below identifies some important issues in designing a questionnaire.

Designing a questionnaire

As short as possible, with clear layout and instructions   Completing the questionnaire should be made as easy as possible for the respondent:

- The questionnaire should be clearly laid out and well printed. Instructions for completing it should be easily understood by the respondent, and it should be easy to follow and complete.
- The number of questions should be kept to the minimum required to produce the information. Respondents may be unwilling to answer long lists of questions, or may stop giving serious thought to their answers.
- Start the questionnaire with the simplest questions and shortest answers first, leaving the more complicated questions or more detailed answers until the end. Otherwise people may be put off right from the beginning.
- There should be just enough alternative answers (including 'don't know') to allow respondents to express their views and to provide the information required.

Clear and neutral language, and the avoidance of 'leading questions'
The form of questions needs careful thought:

- Questions should be simple and direct – capable of being answered 'yes' or 'no', by a choice from fixed responses, or with short open-ended answers.
- Questions should be phrased in neutral terms – otherwise respondents might feel they are expected to give a particular answer. Questions which encourage people to give a particular answer are called 'leading questions', and they are likely to produce distorted or invalid (untruthful) results. A question like 'Why do you think sex before marriage is wrong?' is a poor, leading question because it encourages people to accept that sex before marriage is wrong because of the way the question is worded.
- Questions should be clear in meaning and phrased in simple, everyday language, avoiding technical or unfamiliar words which people may not understand. For example, a question like 'Do you have joint conjugal roles in your household' is a bad question because people are unlikely to understand what 'conjugal roles' are. Similarly, a question like 'Do you watch television a lot?' is a poor question, as people might interpret 'a lot' in different ways – it is better to specify actual time periods such as 1-2 hours, 3–4 hours a day and so on.
- Questions should only be asked which the respondents are likely to be able to answer accurately – for example, to give responses or opinions on things they might reasonably be expected to know about, or remember accurately.
- Questions should mean the same thing to all respondents. The researcher can't automatically assume that questions will have the same meaning to the respondent as they do to the researcher.
- Offensive questions should be avoided.

Confidentiality   Those being surveyed should be reassured that their answers will be kept confidential or anonymous.

Types of questionnaire

There are two main types of questions used in questionnaires: pre-coded or structured questions, and open-ended questions. Both types of question may be combined in the same questionnaire.

Pre-coded questionnaires

Pre-coded questionnaires are highly structured, and involve individuals being asked a number of pre-set questions with the choice of a limited

Questionnaires should always be phrased in simple, everyday language

---

Activity

1 Refer to the section 'Designing a questionnaire' on pages 430–1. Draw up a five-question questionnaire on attitudes to poverty (or some other sociological topic of interest to you).
2 Test your questionnaire on five people.
3 Identify and explain any difficulties you come across in your questionnaire, and amend your questions as necessary.
4 Suggest as many criticisms as you can of the following questions:
 • 'Do you read newspapers often?'
 • 'Have you been diseased recently?'
 • 'What do you think of help given to the disabled?'
5 In the light of your criticisms, write new questions, and a choice of answers, to overcome the difficulties you have identified.

---

number of multiple-choice answers. They are sometimes known as closed, structured or multiple-choice questionnaires. Table 8.1 summarizes their advantages and disadvantages.

Open-ended questionnaires

Open-ended questionnaires are less structured than pre-coded questionnaires. Although open-ended questionnaires will still usually have a number of pre-set questions, there is no pre-set choice of answers. This allows individuals to write their own answers or dictate them to an

Table 8.1. The strengths and weaknesses of pre-coded questionnaires

Advantages and strengths	Disadvantages and problems
• They are fairly quick to complete. • They produce standardized data that is easy to classify and produce in quantitative statistical form. • They allow data to be collected to produce new theories or to test existing hypotheses. • They enable comparisons to be made between different groups and populations. Since individuals are answering the same questions, and using the same choices of answers, their answers should show real differences between people rather than differences arising because of the way the questions were formulated or asked. • The statistics produced should be reliable and other researchers can check the findings, and repeat the research if they wish.	• The meaning of questions may not be clear to some respondents. Extra questions cannot be asked or added to get the respondents to expand or explain themselves more fully. • The *imposition problem*. This is the risk that, when asking questions, researchers might be imposing their own views and framework on the people being researched, rather than getting at what they really think. The limited choice of answers imposes strict and artificial limits on what kind of information can be given or collected, as the constraints don't allow the respondent to develop or qualify their answers. The answer the respondent wants to give may simply not be there. This poses problems of *validity*, as the researcher may be imposing a choice of answers which may not really apply to that particular respondent.

Table 8.2. The strengths and weaknesses of open-ended questionnaires

Advantages and strengths	Disadvantages and problems
• They produce more valid data, since the respondent is using his or her own words to express what they really mean rather than being given a pre-set choice of answers reflecting what the researcher thinks important. The *imposition problem* is less serious. • They produce more detail and depth than pre-coded questionnaires.	• The range of possible answers often makes it difficult to classify and quantify the results of such questionnaires. For example, the meaning of the answers may be unclear. • Because of the wide variety of answers, it may be difficult to compare results with other similar research.

interviewer. They are sometimes known as unstructured question-naires. Table 8.2 summarizes their advantages and disadvantages.

The postal/mail or self-completion questionnaire

This kind of questionnaire is either left with the respondent and picked up later, or sent through the post with a pre-paid addressed envelope for the reply, or it may be sent and returned via e-mail. The respondent will complete the questionnaire himself or herself. The strengths and weak-nesses of postal questionnaires are shown in table 8.3.

Table 8.3. The strengths and weaknesses of postal questionnaires

Advantages and strengths	Disadvantages and problems
• They are a relatively cheap method compared to paying interviewers, particularly for collecting data from large numbers of people spread over a wide geographical area. • Results are obtained quickly: most that get returned at all get returned within a couple of weeks. • People can reply at their leisure and not just when an interviewer is present, so more precise answers may be obtained (especially if documents need to be consulted). • Questions on personal, controversial or embarrassing subjects are more likely to get a better response than if an interviewer is present. • There is no problem of interviewer bias (see the later discussion on this).	• There is a major problem of *non-response* in postal questionnaires (a 50 per cent response is very good). Those replying may be an unrepresentative sample of the survey population, for example in being more educated, or interested in the topic being researched, or having a particular axe to grind. This poses major problems for the *representativeness* and *validity* of the results. • People may not give valid replies, due to forgetfulness or dishonesty, or because of different interpretations or meanings attached to the questions. There is no interviewer present to prompt replies or explain questions. • There is no way of knowing whether the right person completed the questionnaire – they may have let someone else do it.

The validity of questionnaire research

Interpretivists question whether questionnaires produce a valid picture of the social world and human behaviour. They make the following major criticisms of questionnaire research.

Imposition

Positivist-based questionnaires risk what has been called the **imposition problem**. This is because they have already decided what the important questions are before the research, and questionnaires don't really discover the way respondents see the world. Such researchers are therefore simply imposing their own structure (what they think is important) on what they are investigating, possibly affecting the *validity* of the research (see below). It is therefore difficult to develop hypotheses during research, and respondents cannot provide information they haven't been asked for. It is also impossible for respondents to express feelings and subtle shades of opinion in statistical form. It is, for example, impossible to measure subjective factors such as the nature and strength of religious belief.

> The **imposition problem** refers to the risk that the researcher, when asking questions, might be imposing their own views or framework on the people being researched, rather than getting at what they really think.

Validity

There is no guarantee people will tell the truth in questionnaires. People may give answers they think are socially acceptable – what they think they ought to say, rather than what they really believe or how they behave in real life. This poses problems about the validity of the research. In 1983, for example, following major public concerns about children viewing unsuitable 'video nasties', questionnaire research was carried out, with results which suggested that 40 per cent of 6-year-old children had seen some of the famous 'video nasties'. This had major repercussions in the press and Parliament, leading to legislation. The research was later repeated by other sociologists on another sample of 11-year-olds. They found 68 per cent claimed to have seen 'video nasties' – but the researchers had named films which didn't even exist.

There may be different meanings attached to the wording of questions, which may influence the results. For example, many people prefer to call themselves 'middle class' when offered the choice of middle class or lower class, but when offered 'working class' more are prepared to put themselves in this category. Researchers need to be aware of how such meanings may differ between classes, ethnic groups, age groups and so on if their questionnaires are to produce valid data.

Activity

1 Identify and explain three reasons why questionnaire research may not produce valid data.
2 Suggest three reasons why unstructured questionnaires might produce more valid data than structured questionnaires.
3 Explain what is meant by the 'imposition problem' in questionnaire-based research.
4 In about one and a half sides of A4 paper, answer the following essay question:
   Assess the usefulness of unstructured questionnaires in sociological research.

Interviews

Questionnaires may also form the basis of interviews by social researchers. Interviews are one of the most widely used methods of gathering data in sociology. There are two main types of interviews: structured or formal interviews, and unstructured or in-depth, informal interviews.

Structured or formal interviews

Structured or formal interviews are based on a structured, pre-coded questionnaire (the interview schedule). They are much like postal questionnaires administered by an interviewer. The interviewer asks the questions set in the same order each time, and does not probe beyond the basic answers received: a formal question and answer session. Table 8.4 summarizes the advantages and disadvantages of these interviews.

Table 8.4. The strengths and weaknesses of structured interviews

Advantages and strengths	*Disadvantages and problems*
• They are generally the most effective way of getting questionnaires completed and the problem of non-response found with postal questionnaires is much rarer. Skilled interviewers can persuade people to answer questions, and problems of illiteracy are overcome.	• The interview schedule/questionnaire may impose limits on what the respondent can say, as the interviewer cannot probe beyond the basic questions asked. This means there is a limited depth of understanding of what the respondent may mean.
• Data so obtained is often seen as more *reliable*, since all respondents will be answering the same questions, so results can be compared with other groups. The research can, if necessary, be replicated by other interviewers to check the findings.	• They are more time-consuming and costly than postal questionnaires – interviews are often slow, and interviewers have to be paid. Many more people can be questioned with a postal questionnaire for the same cost.
• They are useful for obtaining answers to questions about facts like the age, sex and occupation of those being interviewed.	• There is the possibility of interviewer bias (see below).
• They usually involve pre-coded questions and answers which make them relatively easy to put into quantitative statistical form (note the *positivist* implication here).	
• There is less of a problem with interviewer bias than in unstructured interviews, as there is little involvement of the interviewer with the interviewee beyond basic politeness (see the later discussion on interviewer bias).	

Interviewers may not always get the cooperation they hope for . . . especially if they choose the wrong moment

Unstructured or informal (in-depth) interviews

An unstructured interview is like a guided conversation. The interviewer has topics in mind to cover (the 'interview schedule') but few if any pre-set questions. If there is a questionnaire at all, it will be of the open-ended, unstructured variety. The interviewer will seek to put the respondent at ease, in a relaxed, informal situation, and will then ask open-ended questions which may trigger off discussions or further questions. The interviewer aims to obtain further depth or detail than is possible in a postal questionnaire or in a structured interview, and draw out the respondent's feelings, opinions and confidences. This approach was used by Oakley in *From Here to Maternity* (1981), a study of the experience of becoming a mother in British society. Table 8.5 overleaf shows the strengths and weaknesses of these interviews.

Developing a hypothesis in unstructured interviews

During the research which led to her theory of conjugal roles (the roles played by each partner in marriage) and social networks, Bott (1957) interviewed twenty couples in London. It was only because the link between social networks and conjugal roles emerged in the course of her interviews that Bott was able to develop her theory. This would have been impossible using questionnaires, since she wouldn't have known what questions to ask, as she hadn't developed a hypothesis on social networks before she began interviewing.

Activity

1. Make up a short five-question structured questionnaire (with a choice of answers) to find out about attitudes to poverty (you might adapt the questionnaire you drew up in the earlier activity on 'Designing a questionnaire').
2. Test this out on five people, using a structured interview, and record your findings.
3. Now, using the same questions as 'prompts', do unstructured interviews with two people. Be prepared to probe further and ask extra questions and enter discussions. Record your findings.
4. Compare the data collected by each type of interview, and the time it took to complete the interviews. Is there any difference between the information collected by these two types of interview, and the time taken to carry them out? Explain why you think this might be the case.
5. Identify and explain three reasons why a sociologist might use an unstructured interview rather than a structured interview in sociological research.
6. Identify two ways that unstructured interviews might be unreliable as a method of research.

Table 8.5. The strengths and weaknesses of unstructured interviews

Advantages and strengths	*Disadvantages and problems*
• Their greater flexibility increases the validity of the data obtained compared to structured interviews. This is because they provide more opportunity for the respondent to say what they really think and feel about an issue (note the *interpretivist* implication). For example, Oakley found in *From Here to Maternity* that unstructured interviews enabled her to develop close relationships of trust and openness with the women concerned, and allowed women to speak for themselves openly and personally about motherhood. • There is the possibility of probing much deeper than a structured questionnaire. • Ambiguities in questions and answers can be clarified, and the interviewer can probe for shades of meaning. • The ideas of the sociologist can develop in the course of the interviews. The interviewer can adjust questions and change direction as the interview is taking place if new ideas and insights emerge. It is possible a new hypothesis might emerge during the research. By contrast, structured interviews have already decided the important questions. • Interviewers may be able to assess the honesty and validity of replies during the course of the interview: this may be difficult with structured interviews.	• Unstructured interviews are time-consuming and costly, and this may mean fewer interviews are conducted, raising problems of representativeness. • They may be less reliable than structured interviews as questions may be phrased in a variety of ways and the researchers are more involved with the respondents. Differences between respondents may therefore simply reflect differences in the nature of the interview and the questions asked, rather than real differences between people. • It is difficult to replicate such interviews. The success of an informal interview depends heavily on the personality and personal skills of the interviewer, such as in getting people to answer questions that produce useful information, and in keeping the conversation going. Another researcher repeating the interviews may therefore not get the same results again, so findings from such research may therefore not be comparable with other groups (a criticism *positivists* might make). • It is difficult to compare and measure the responses of different interviewees. Unstructured interviews are therefore more popular with *interpretivists*, who are concerned with increasing their understanding of respondents and obtaining qualitative data. *Positivists* don't often use this method, except for exploratory research to develop a hypothesis for further investigation (using other methods).

General problems of interviews

The general problems of interviews centre on two main, and related, issues: the validity of the data obtained, and in particular, the problem of interviewer bias.

Validity

- Interview data are often taken by positivists as revealing the attitudes and behaviour of people in everyday life. However, interpretivists would argue that an interview is a very artificial situation, and what people say in an interview may have little to do with their real or normal behaviour. There is no guarantee people will give a true account in interviews, and they may lie, forget or otherwise mislead the interviewer. This poses problems for the validity of the data obtained by interviewing techniques.
- It is unlikely that anyone in an interview situation will give honest answers to questions that involve very personal or embarrassing issues.
- Interviews involve words and phrases, and meanings may vary between social groups. A structured interview, where there is little opportunity to qualify meaning, might not provide comparable data when administered to members of different social groups. For example, words like 'bad' and 'wicked' are used in different ways by younger and older people.
- Members of different social groups may attach different importance to the content of questions. For example, mental illness carries less stigma among Puerto Ricans than among the Jews, the Irish or black people in the United States. This means Puerto Ricans are more willing to admit to the symptoms of mental illness – but this doesn't mean there is necessarily more mental illness among them. This again raises doubts about the validity of some interview data, as it may simply reflect how much people are willing to admit to things to an interviewer, rather than real differences between people.

Interviewer bias

Interviewer bias refers to the answers given in an interview being influenced or distorted in some way by the presence or behaviour of the interviewer.

Interview bias refers to the way answers in an interview may be influenced or distorted in some way by the presence or behaviour of the interviewer. Interviews involve face-to-face social interaction between people, and the success of interviews often relies on the personal skills of the interviewer. The results of an interview will also partly depend on the way participants define the situation, and their perceptions of each other. For example, the interviewer's personality, sex, age, ethnic origin, tone of voice, facial expressions, and dress (suit or jeans) all impose a particular definition of the situation on the respondent, and this may influence the responses given. Status differences, such as age and ethnicity, between the respondent and the interviewer can lead to bias too. For example, an adult carrying out interviews with school students may not be given honest answers. The interviewer may give the impression, however unwittingly or unintentionally, of wanting to hear a certain answer.

In such circumstances, it is possible that the interviewees might adapt their answers to impress the interviewer by giving answers they think the interviewer wants to hear and would approve of, rather than giving their real opinions. This is perhaps unsurprising, as nearly everyone likes to obtain the approval of the person they're talking to.

There is therefore a danger (particularly with unstructured interviews) that the interviewer and the interview context may unduly influence the interviewee (the person being interviewed). This may mean that differences between interviews reflect differences in the way the interviews were conducted rather than real differences in what the respondents were actually saying. This interaction situation can therefore affect the quality, validity and reliability of the data.

An example of this arose in the course of the 1992 general election in Britain, when all the opinion polls (mainly using face-to-face interviews) predicted a narrow Labour victory, when in fact the Conservatives won. Subsequent research suggested that Conservative voters were more reluctant to admit in interviews that they were going to vote Conservative at a time when the Conservative government was very unpopular, and when admitting voting for them appeared to be flying in the face of public opinion.

All the above suggests that in interview research it is very difficult for the researcher to avoid influencing what is obtained as data. It could therefore be argued that the data obtained by interviews are socially constructed – created and influenced by the presence, actions and behaviour of the interviewer, and the context in which the interview is conducted.

Overcoming interviewer bias   To overcome interviewer bias, interviewers are carefully trained to be non-directive. This means not to offer opinions, or show approval or disapproval of answers received. 'Be friendly but restrained', showing a polite indifference to the answers received, is often the advice given to interviewers to reduce the risks of interviewer bias.

However, Becker (1970) suggests a more aggressive style of interviewing is more likely to squeeze information out of respondents which may not otherwise have been volunteered. This involves 'playing dumb', playing the devil's advocate by taking positions on issues, or 'winding people up' in the hope of prompting the respondent into saying more. Another way of avoiding interviewer bias is to avoid face-to-face interviews altogether, and use telephone interviews instead. This has, since the 1992 general election, been a more common practice among opinion poll researchers.

Concluding remarks on interviews

The more structured the interview, the more easily can results be quantified statistically and comparisons made. However, the tighter the structure, the less the respondent can state and develop what she or he 'really means'. The degree of structure of interviews will vary from highly structured to very unstructured depending on whether the researcher feels the need is for quantification, or for an understanding of meanings. This will depend on the theoretical perspective of the researcher – whether he or she adopts a more positivist or more interpretivist approach to understanding society. However, the other influences identified in figure 8.3 earlier in this chapter (page 407) will also affect the type of interview approach adopted.

Activity

1 Suggest two reasons why information obtained by interviews may not be valid.
2 Explain briefly what is meant by 'interviewer bias'.
3 Consider the following situations, and in each case: (a) suggest possible ways in which interviewer bias might occur and distort the results of the interview, and (b) suggest what steps might be taken to help remove or reduce the bias.
   - a white person being questioned by a black interviewer about her or his racial attitudes
   - an adult interviewing students in a school
   - an adult interviewer asking young people about their attitudes to illegal drug use
   - a female interviewer asking a married or cohabiting couple about how household tasks are divided up between them
   - an older woman asking questions of a young lone mother about the way children should be brought up
4 In about one and a half sides of A4 paper, answer the following essay question:
   Assess the usefulness of unstructured interviews in sociological research.

Participant observation

Participant observation involves a researcher actually joining the group or community she or he is studying, and participating in its activities over a period of time. The researcher tries to become an accepted part of the group to see the world the way members of the group do.

The theoretical context of participant observation

Participant observation is typically used by interpretivists to develop an understanding of the world from the point of view of the subjects of the research. Interpretivists argue that a sociological understanding of society can only be gained by understanding people's meanings. They suggest the most effective way of doing this is for researchers to put themselves in the same position as those they are studying. The idea is to get 'inside' people's heads to see the world as they do and how they make sense of it. Rather than testing hypotheses against evidence and searching for the causes of social events, *verstehen* (an understanding developed through empathy or close identification) and qualitative research are what sociology should be about.

The problem for interpretivists who choose participant observation is not the positivist concern with scientific detachment, but how to become involved enough to understand what is going on as seen through the eyes of group members, and not letting the researcher's own values and prejudices distort the observations.

The stages of participant observation and related problems

The stages of participant observation can be summed up in terms of *getting in*, *staying in* and *getting out* of the group concerned.

Getting in

Joining a group raises many questions about the researcher's role. The researcher may adopt an **overt role** where the researcher declares his or her true identity to the group and the fact he or she is doing research. Alternatively, the researcher may adopt a **covert role** (concealing his or her role as a researcher), or a 'cover story' (partially declaring his or her role as a researcher, but concealing elements of it).

A covert role   A covert role is most likely to be adopted where criminal or highly deviant activities are involved, such as the research by Humphreys on homosexuals in *The Tea Room Trade* (1970). The researcher who called himself 'James Patrick' in *A Glasgow Gang Observed* (1973) had to keep even his name secret, as he feared for his personal safety when studying violent gangs in Glasgow. Adopting a covert role has the advantage of avoiding the risk of people's behaviour changing because they do not know they are being studied.

If a covert role is to be adopted and maintained, the researcher has little choice but to become a full participant in the group, because there is a risk of the research being ruined if the covert researcher's real identity and purpose are discovered. This may involve participation in illegal or unpleasant activities. It is also difficult to ask questions and take notes without arousing suspicion, and there are also moral and ethical concerns over observing and reporting on people's activities in secret, without obtaining their consent first.

An **overt role** is one where the researcher reveals to the group being studied his or her true identity and purpose.

A **covert role** is one where the researcher conceals from the group being studied his or her true identify as a researcher, to gain access to the group and avoid disrupting its normal behaviour.

An overt role   Adopting an overt role has the advantage that things might be hidden from a member of a group in a way that they might not be from a trusted and known outsider – since she or he will have nothing to gain in the group. Other advantages are that the researcher may be able to ask questions or interview people, and avoid participation in illegal or immoral behaviour, without arousing suspicion. Ethically and morally, it is right that people should be aware they are being studied.

Adopting an overt role does have problems though. For example, there is always the possibility that the behaviour of those being studied may be affected, raising questions over the validity of the research. As Whyte admitted in *Street Corner Society* (1955), quoting the gang leader 'Doc': 'You've slowed me up plenty since you've been down here. Now when I want to do something, I have to think what Bill Whyte would want me to know about it and how I can explain it . . . Before I used to do things by instinct.'

After deciding the nature of the role, the next problem is getting access to the group. The presence of a stranger needs explanation, and researchers need to establish 'bona fide' credentials for getting access to the group. This may involve gaining friendships with key individuals. For example, Whyte was able to do his research because of his contacts with the gang leader 'Doc'. Participant observation in some contexts may require permission from higher authorities. This may mean the researcher is identified with authority, which may affect the behaviour of those being observed. For example, participant observation by an adult of students in a school will require the permission of the headteacher. This may mean the researcher is identified with the staff rather than the students.

Staying in

The observer has to develop a role which will involve gaining the trust and cooperation of those observed, to enable continued participation in and observation of the group. Initially this will involve learning, listening and getting a sense of what's going on: 'Initially, keep your eyes and ears open but keep your mouth shut' was Doc's advice to Whyte in *Street Corner Society*.

Problems of 'staying in' involve issues such as the need for extensive note-taking, which may be disruptive of the behaviour of the group, and how far to involve yourself without either losing the trust of the group or the objectivity of a researcher. Maintaining the trust of the group may involve getting involved with acts that the researcher doesn't agree with. Eileen Barker (1984), for example, gave a talk to the Moonies which reinforced the beliefs of one Moonie, despite Barker's protests that she didn't believe a word of what she had said. Staying in might also involve the observer with unpleasant acts or people, and possibly criminal behaviour. For example, Whyte actually did some 'personating' – voting twice in an election – as this was common practice in the group he was studying.

Getting out

'Getting out' of the group involves issues such as leaving the group without damaging relationships, becoming detached enough to write an 'impartial' and accurate account, and making sure members of the group cannot be identified. There may be possible reprisals against the researcher if criminal activities are involved. Patrick faced threats to his personal safety after adopting a covert role in a Glasgow street gang and when his research was finally published in *A Glasgow Gang Observed* (1973).

Four classic studies of participant observation research

William Whyte, *Street Corner Society* (1955)

This is a study of an Italian-American street corner gang in Boston in the United States. Whyte spent three and a half years in the area as a participant observer, including living in an Italian house with the group he was studying and he became a member of the gang.

Laud Humphreys, *The Tearoom Trade: A study of Homosexual Encounters in Public Places* (1970)

Humphreys wanted to study the gay subculture, and observed the sexual activity of gay men in ninety public toilets (the 'tearooms') in American cities in the 1960s. He initially adopted a covert role as a 'gay voyeur' (someone who liked watching sex between men) and 'watch-queen' – a lookout for other men in case of police interference. Humphreys became an accepted part of the gay scene in Chicago, through visiting gay bars and other parts of the gay scene. Adopting a more overt role, he also interviewed some men. Humphreys noted the car numbers of many gay men who used the 'tearooms' and, through police contacts, was able to get their addresses and background information for interview research a year later as part of a health survey. Humphreys had to disguise his appearance during this survey so he wouldn't be recognized by men he had met.

James Patrick, *A Glasgow Gang Observed* (1973)

James Patrick used a covert role to study a violent and delinquent teenage Glasgow gang over a period of four months between October 1966 and January 1967.

Eileen Barker, *The Making of a Moonie* (1984)

This is a study of members of the Unification Church, a controversial religious sect headed by the Rev. Moon. Barker used overt participant observation over a period of six years, accepting the risk this could mean the people she was studying could be affected by her presence.

Activity

Refer to the four participant observation studies by Whyte, Humphreys, Patrick and Barker in the box.

1   Suggest ways that the personal characteristics of the researcher may have been important in enabling him or her in each case to do the research.
2   What problems might there be in generalizing the findings of such studies to other similar social groups?
3   What difficulties do you think the researchers might have found in each study in:
    ● getting into the group?
    ● staying in the group?
    ● getting out of the group without damaging personal relationships?
4   Write about one side of A4 paper on any (a) ethical difficulties and (b) problems of validity there might have been with any of these examples of research.

The strengths and weaknesses of participant observation

Table 8.6 summarizes participant observation's advantages and disadvantages.

Table 8.6. The strengths and weaknesses of participant observation

Advantages and strengths	*Disadvantages and problems*
● The sociologist gains first-hand knowledge of the group being studied. By building a relationship of trust, more in-depth, valid data can be obtained than by other research techniques. It is the method least likely to impose the sociologist's own views on the group being studied, therefore providing a more valid understanding of a social group. ● It allows hypotheses and theories to emerge from the research as it goes along. This enables the researcher to discover things she or he may not even have thought about before. As Whyte noted in *Street Corner Society*, 'As I sat and listened, I learned the answers to questions that I would not even have had the sense to ask if I had been	● Positivists argue there are problems with the validity and reliability of participant observation studies. For example, there is no real way of checking the findings, as there is no real evidence apart from the observations and interpretations of the researcher. What one researcher might regard as important may be missed or seen as unimportant by another. Even direct quotations from group members are often written down later, and may be only partially recalled – the researcher may remember what she or he *thought* was said. ● The presence of a researcher, if she or he is known to the group, may in some ways change the group's behaviour simply because they know they are being studied. This 'Hawthorne effect' may lead to problems for the validity of the research. For example, Whyte admits in *Street Corner Society* that knowledge of his presence and intentions may well have changed the behaviour of the gang.

Table 8.6. (continued)

Advantages and strengths	Disadvantages and problems
getting my information solely on an interviewing basis.' ● It is the best way to get at the meanings that a social activity has for those involved in it, through seeing the world through the eyes of members of the group. ● It may be the only possible method of research. For example, criminal and other deviant activities may be very difficult to investigate using other methods like interviews and questionnaires. ● People can be studied in their normal social situation over a period of time, rather than the rather artificial and 'snapshot' context of a questionnaire or interview. ● There is less of a chance that the people being studied can mislead the researcher than there is using other methods. This might therefore produce more valid data.	● There is a danger of the researcher becoming so involved with the group, seeing the world only as the group does, and developing such loyalty to it, that she or he may find it difficult to stand back and report findings in a neutral way. 'Going native' – becoming so involved that all detachment is lost – is a possible problem. The researcher may then stop being a participant observer and become a non-observing participant. ● It is very time-consuming and expensive compared to other methods, as it involves the researcher being physically present in the group for long periods. ● Because only a small group is studied, it may not be representative, so it is difficult to make generalizations. ● There may be ethical issues if people do not know they are being observed, and therefore will not have the opportunity to give their consent to the research. ● In personal terms, such research may be difficult for the researcher – for example, mixing with people they would rather not be with, getting involved in distasteful or illegal activities (in order to fit in), or even facing personal danger – as James Patrick did in *A Glasgow Gang Observed*. Humphreys was actually arrested during his research on gays.

Reliability and validity in participant observation

Positivists tend to be critical of participant observation because they argue the data obtained is rarely quantified and is unreliable. Participant observation depends heavily on the sensitivity, skills, personality and personal characteristics of the observer, and this makes it very difficult to replicate a participant observation study in order to check the findings. As Whyte said in *Street Corner Society*: 'To some extent my approach must be unique to myself, to the particular situation, and to the state of knowledge existing when I began research.'

Participant observation is always to some extent selective observation – the researcher's interpretation of the significant and important things happening in a group. What one participant observer reports or interprets as significant may not be seen as such by another. Positivists would ask how interpretivists can prove they have interpreted the attitudes and experiences of others correctly. Participant observers use devices like extensive note-taking to accumulate evidence to help to ensure that their research is reliable as well as valid and can be checked by others. Other sociologists are, though, ultimately left to rely on the memory, observational and interpretive skills of the researcher, and this raises problems for the validity and reliability of the research that are difficult to resolve.

Activity

1 Identify and explain two criticisms positivists might make of participant observation as a research method.
2 Identify and explain two reasons why interpretivists might argue that participant observation is the most effective method of understanding and explaining social life.
3 Suggest two reasons sociologists who employ participant observation might give to claim their work is as 'scientific' as any positivist research.
4 Suggest all the ways you can that the social characteristics of the researcher might make it difficult to conduct participant observation.
5 With examples, explain the advantages of adopting (a) a covert role and (b) an overt role in participant observation.
6 What are the ethical and moral issues which make participant observation difficult, particularly if using a covert role?
7 Explain what is meant by the risk in participant observation that 'the researcher may stop being a participant observer and become a non-observing participant'.
8 Look at the weaknesses and disadvantages of participant observation listed earlier. Suggest ways that a skilled participant observer might be able to overcome the problems identified.
9 Much participant observation research has been done on deviant groups. Suggest reasons why this might be the case.
10 In about one and half sides of A4 paper, answer the following essay question:
   Assess the usefulness of participant observation in sociological research.

Activity

'Of course it was known that I was not a Moonie. I never pretended that I was, or that I was likely to become one. I admit that I was sometimes evasive, and I certainly did not always say everything that was on my mind, but I cannot remember any occasion on which I consciously lied to a Moonie. Being known as a non-member had its disadvantages, but by talking to people who had left the movement I was able to check that I was not missing any of the internal information which was available to rank-and-file members. At the same time, being an outsider who was "inside" had enormous advantages. I was allowed (even, on certain occasions, expected) to ask questions that no member would have presumed to ask either his leaders or his peers. Furthermore, several Moonies who felt that their problems were not understood by the leaders, and yet would not have dreamed of being disloyal to the movement by talking to their parents or other outsiders, could confide in me because of the very fact that I was both organisationally and emotionally uninvolved.'

(Eileen Barker, *The Making of a Moonie*, Oxford: Blackwell, 1984)

1　With reference to the passage above, explain in your own words the advantages Barker found in adopting an overt role.
2　What ethical problems are involved in Barker's admission that she was 'sometimes evasive'?
3　Barker says, 'Being known as a non-member had its disadvantages.' What disadvantages do you think she might have come across (either read the research, or think and guess!).
4　Do you consider there are any circumstances in which adopting a covert role in research might be justified? Explain your answer.
5　Humphreys took car numbers of gay men who used public toilets to obtain gay sex and, through police contacts, was able to get their addresses and background information for interview research a year later as part of a health survey. What ethical difficulties do you think this poses?

Non-participant observation

Some sociological research is carried out by observation alone (without the researcher participating). The main reason for this is to reduce or eliminate the risk that people will be affected by the presence of a researcher or new member of their social group. It may also be used when groups might be unwilling to cooperate in research (though this raises ethical issues). Non-participant observation also allows sociologists to observe people in their normal social situations, and avoid the Hawthorne effect. This can only be achieved fully when the observation is carried out without the knowledge of the observed, for example from a distance, by blending into the background, through one-way glass or using video cameras. If the observer is visibly present, even though not participating, there is still the possibility that his or her presence will influence what is happening.

A problem with this method is that it does not allow the researcher to investigate the meanings people attach to the behaviour that is being observed. The data produced may well reflect simply the assumptions and interpretations of the researcher, raising serious issues over the reliability and validity of the data.

An example of non-participant observation

Flanders (1970) studied interaction in classrooms. He produced a list of ten categories of interaction, and he then observed lessons and ticked the category that best described what was happening at particular times. These categories, with explanations, are listed below. Categories 1–7 are concerned with what the teacher is saying or doing, and categories 8 and 9 with what students are saying or doing.

1 *Accepts feelings* (teacher accepts an attitude or feeling of a student).

2 *Praises or encourages* (teacher praises/encourages student behaviour, including jokes, smiles, nods of the head and similar teacher responses).

3 *Accepts/uses idea of student* (teacher accepts and uses/builds on/develops ideas suggested by a student).

4 *Asks question* (teacher uses own ideas to ask questions of a student, to which an answer is expected).

5 *Lecture* (teacher gives own facts, opinions and explanations – the teacher, not student, makes the first move).

6 *Gives direction* (teacher gives commands or orders to student).

7 *Criticizes or justifies authority* (teacher criticizes student to make student behaviour more acceptable, or justifies teacher's own behaviour/actions).

8 *Student response* (student responds to teacher's questions or ideas).

9 *Student initiated* (student makes the first move to express his or her own ideas/opinions, asks teacher questions or introduces a new topic).

10 *Silence or confusion* (a category to describe times when interaction can't be easily understood or categorized by the observer, such as periods of silence or confusion).

The observer then produces a tally chart to show what type of interaction (1–10) is going on in the classroom in particular time periods, for example every minute of a lesson. This produces a quantitative account of teacher–student interaction during the course of a lesson, which can then be used for comparison with other teachers and lessons.

Longitudinal studies

Most sociological researchers study a group of people for a short period of time, producing a 'snapshot' of events. It is therefore difficult to study change over time.

The longitudinal study attempts to overcome this problem by selecting a sample from whom data are collected at regular intervals over a period of years. Table 8.7 summarizes the method's advantages and disadvantages.

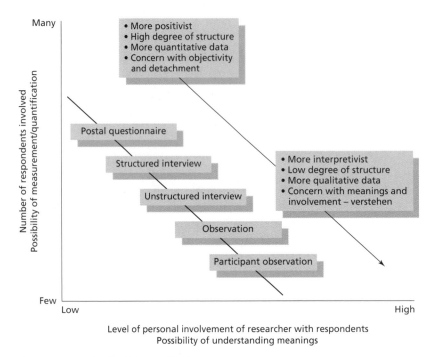

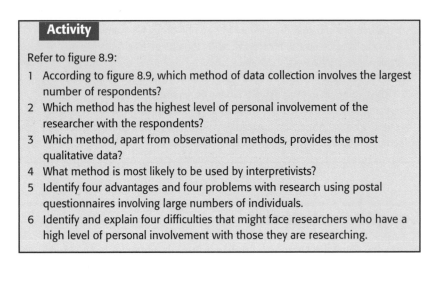

Figure 8.9 Methods of data collection

Activity

Refer to figure 8.9:

1 According to figure 8.9, which method of data collection involves the largest number of respondents?
2 Which method has the highest level of personal involvement of the researcher with the respondents?
3 Which method, apart from observational methods, provides the most qualitative data?
4 What method is most likely to be used by interpretivists?
5 Identify four advantages and four problems with research using postal questionnaires involving large numbers of individuals.
6 Identify and explain four difficulties that might face researchers who have a high level of personal involvement with those they are researching.

Table 8.7. The strengths and weaknesses of longitudinal studies

Advantages and strengths	*Disadvantages and problems*
• They make it possible to study change over time. • As long as the sample remains the same, researchers can be sure that the changes measured do not result from changes in the composition of the sample. • They may provide more valid data in some circumstances. Studies which ask people about past events rely on human memories, and people may also distort or exaggerate past events. Longitudinal studies help to avoid this, as there are previous studies to refer back to.	• It is necessary to select a sample who are available and willing to assist in the research project over a long period. However, it is likely that the original sample size will drop as people die, can't be traced, or become unwilling to cooperate. This may reduce the representativeness of the sample. • Those in the sample are conscious of the fact that they are being studied. This may change their behaviour because they think more carefully about what they do (especially if they know they may be questioned about it in the future). This Hawthorne effect may bring into question the validity of the findings. • There is the problem of cost. Most funding agencies are unwilling to take on a commitment over a long period of time.

Examples of longitudinal studies

J. W. B. Douglas studied the educational progress of a sample of children through their school careers, studying them at the ages of 8, 11 and 16. The findings of Douglas and his colleagues were published in *The Home and the School* (1964) and *All our Future* (1968).

The census, carried out every ten years since 1801 (with the exception of 1941), is in effect a longitudinal study of the entire population. This enables researchers to trace broad patterns of social change, and to make comparisons between the social conditions of one period and another.

Case studies and life histories

A case study involves the intensive study of a single example of whatever it is the sociologist wishes to investigate. A case study can be carried out using almost any method of research, though the more interpretivist, qualitative methods are more common, such as in-depth unstructured interviews or participant observation. Life histories are case studies which focus on one individual. Life histories are most commonly obtained through in-depth unstructured interviews and guided conversation, backed up with reference to personal documents such as diaries and letters. Great importance is placed on the person's own interpretations and explanations of her or his behaviour.

Case studies and life histories do not claim to be representative. However, researchers using these approaches do claim that an in-depth account of a single example can make an important contribution to our knowledge about an area. Table 8.8 lists the strengths and weaknesses of these methods.

An example of a case study

Learning to Labour (1977) by Paul Willis was a case study of a group of male students in a single school in Wolverhampton. It stimulated widespread debate about the relationship between schooling and capitalism, how students resist schooling, and the formation of counter-school subcultures, and encouraged the development of theories by other sociologists.

Table 8.8. The strengths and weaknesses of case studies and life histories

Advantages and strengths	*Disadvantages and problems*
• A particular study can be used to test the usefulness of theories of social life. Willis's study, for example, challenged previous approaches to explaining how working-class young people got working-class jobs through the education system. • They may be useful in generating new hypotheses which can then be tested by further research. • They enable the researcher to see the world from the point of view of the individual or group, and give far more detail and understanding than can be obtained by surveys or quantitative measurements.	• They may not be representative, and it may therefore not be possible to generalize on the basis of their findings. • They may not be reliable or valid. Life histories view the past from the standpoint of the present. This raises questions about the accuracy of recall of facts, and the benefit of hindsight might generate a reinterpretation of the past. This might raise questions about the validity of such research.

Methodological pluralism and triangulation

It is easy to get the impression that sociological research is divided into two opposing camps, with positivists pursuing methods generating quantitative data, and interpretivists using methods generating qualitative data.

In the real world of practical research, most sociologists will use a range of methods to collect a range of different kinds of data, regardless of whether they are quantitative or qualitative – whatever methods seem best

Methodological pluralism is the term used to describe the use by sociologists of a variety of methods in a single piece of research.

Triangulation is the use of two or more research methods in a single piece of research to check the reliability and validity of research evidence.

suited and most practical for producing the fullest possible data to understand the subject being studied. This is known as **methodological pluralism**, and is very useful for increasing sociological understanding of social life.

Sociologists will also often use a variety of methods, and different types of data, to check that the results obtained by a particular method are valid and reliable. For example, participant observation might be used to investigate further, or check the accuracy or validity of statistical (quantitative) evidence collected by questionnaires in a survey, or to observe to check whether people act as they said they did in an interview. This approach of using a range of methods (usually two or three) to check findings is called **triangulation**.

Methodological pluralism and triangulation frequently go hand in hand, because the use of several methods producing different types of data (methodological pluralism) not only gives a fuller picture of what is being explained but, *at the same time*, is a valuable approach for checking the reliability and validity of research findings (triangulation).

Examples of these two approaches are considered below:

- Humphreys in *The Tearoom Trade* (1970) used a combination of questionnaires, unstructured interviews and participant observation.
- Eileen Barker, in her 1984 study of the Moonies, used participant observation (lasting six years) to gain first-hand insight, living in various Moonie centres in Britain and abroad. Barker supplemented this with in-depth interviews to investigate the background of individual Moonies, and to help form hypotheses to guide her participant observation, and used questionnaires to obtain further information from a larger sample.
- Hobson's (2000) research on teacher training courses used questionnaires to obtain the views of over 300 trainee teachers in four teacher training institutions. He supplemented this with informal interviews with twenty trainee teachers to gain in-depth knowledge of the trainee teachers' views. Participant observation was also used to observe the training process and the trainees' responses to it. As a result, Hobson 'discovered things that I might not have thought to ask or have been told by trainees through the use of other methods'. He was able to check the responses of individual trainees in closed questionnaires with what they said in the interviews and how they acted on the training course. Hobson also used secondary data in his research. In this way, Hobson argues, the use of several methods enabled him to check the validity of his findings and produce a fuller and more accurate picture of teacher training courses.

Figure 8.10 overleaf illustrates a range of possible uses of methodological pluralism and triangulation.

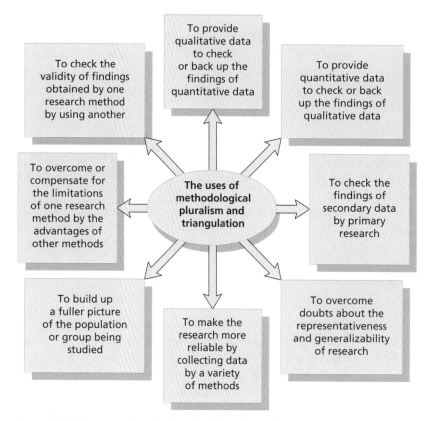

Figure 8.10 The uses of methodological pluralism and triangulation

---

Activity

Refer to figure 8.10 and:

1 Imagine you were doing some research on how household tasks were divided up between men, women and children in the home, and what they each thought about it. Suggest at least three different methods you might use to collect the information, saying what information you might expect to collect using each method.

2 Give examples of ways you might apply each of the main uses of methodological pluralism and triangulation suggested in figure 8.10 to the research area in question 1. Write a brief sentence explaining each use, in each case drawing on an example based on the research area in question 1.

3 Explain two ways in each case that methodological pluralism and triangulation might help to improve the (a) validity, (b) reliability, and (c) representativeness of a piece of research.

Doing your own research

As part of the AQA AS Sociology course, you have the option of preparing a research proposal – an outline of a piece of small-scale research you might undertake. This should be no longer than 1,200 words, and it carries 30 per cent of the final AS marks. If you do this well, you should have laid the groundwork for your research project in the second year of the A-level course, though you are not obliged to do the same topic. This chapter should provide you with all the information you need to deal with the research methods aspects of this, and you should choose one of the topic areas included in this book to develop your research proposal. There are suggestions of suitable topics at the end of every chapter except chapter 1 and this chapter, but you can of course devise your own.

The AQA requires the research proposal to be organized under the following headings, and expects candidates to stick strictly to the number of words allocated to each section. You should include the word count at the end of each section, and the overall total number of words at the end.

1 Hypothesis or aim

This section should include:

- Your choice of an area for research.
- Either a *single* hypothesis (an idea you guess might be true, but which hasn't yet been tested by research evidence) or a *single* aim (a question relating to the area of interest you want to find out about) which could form the basis of sociological research into the area you have chosen.
- A brief summary of the reason(s) for choosing that area of research and aim or hypothesis.

Maximum length: 100 words.

2 Context and concepts

This section should include:

- Accurate summaries of two pieces of material relevant to your chosen area which provide a suitable context or background framework for the research. These might include research studies, statistics and other secondary sources of information. You should carefully explain how your pieces of material are linked to your aim or hypothesis.
- Clear and full definitions of two or three concepts relevant to the research idea, with explanations of why they are relevant. Concepts are the sociological terms and ideas used to describe and explain social life,

which make up the 'jargon' of the subject. Practically every key term in this book, found in the glossary, can be used as a concept in this section.

Maximum length: 400 words.

3   Main research method and reasons

This section should include:

- A brief description of the main research method you might use, and an explanation of why you chose it. You should show a good understanding of your chosen method, and explain how it is an appropriate sociological method to research the hypothesis or aim you have stated in section 1. You should refer to both theoretical and practical reasons for your choice of method, but make sure these reasons are clearly linked to the actual piece of research you might be doing.
- Details relating to this method. For example, if you plan a survey, then you should give brief details of sample size and sampling method, and the type of questionnaire or interview you would use. If you plan to use participant observation, suggest ways of getting into the group, whether you would use an overt or covert role, and so on. If you plan to use secondary sources, give details of the type of information you might expect to find and use.

Maximum length: 400 words.

4   Potential Problems

In this section you should provide brief details of the problems you might expect to face in carrying out your research. These might include problems like non-response in a self-completion questionnaire, difficulties in obtaining a representative sample, whether your presence, age or sex might influence behaviour, whether there's a risk of interviewer bias, any difficulties obtaining secondary data, time, cost, ethical issues and so on. Make sure the problems you identify are actually relevant to your research proposal, and the real problems you might come across if you were actually carrying out the research necessary to explore your hypothesis or aims. For example, a general discussion of the problems of interviewer bias will not get you as many marks as a discussion of the problems you might have interviewing the particular people you plan to research, how your own personal characteristics might make your interviews difficult, or difficulties you might identify in selecting your particular sample.

Maximum length: 300 words.

Total word count: 1,200 words.

An example of a coursework proposal

The following is a (slightly modified) genuine coursework proposal, which was awarded top marks in every section – confirmed by an AQA moderator. This shows you what you should aim for. The comments in **Bold type** refer to the AQA marking scheme, and indicate why each section achieved top marks. Note that each section, and the entire proposal, is exactly the target number of words – as the AQA mark scheme points out, 'candidates should be reminded of the need to adhere to the 1200 word limit, as one of the skills they are being tested on is the ability to capture the most important points in a concise way.'

Hypothesis

This proposal is about lone mother perceptions of the effects of social deprivation on their children.

The family remains a key social institution in Britain, despite growing family diversity. Lone parents account for 25% of those with dependant children, with 90% of them headed by women. The high risk of poverty lone parents face, alongside social stigma and political prejudice, despite increasing family diversity, means lone parent families remain contentious. This provides the basis for my hypothesis:

'Lone-parent mothers do not believe they are materially or emotionally disadvantaging children, despite inherent risks of poverty and the harmful effects of family ideology.'

(100 words)

This identifies a very clear and relevant sociological focus (issues around lone parenthood) and a very clear hypothesis, backed up with wholly appropriate reasons for choosing it.

Context and concepts

The Joseph Rowntree Foundation study *Private Lives and Public Responses: Lone Parenthood and Future Policy* (1997), by Ford and Miller, draws from a large body of research highlighting the current facts and debates surrounding lone parent families. The report recognises that lone-parenthood is a life-cycle stage common to many children, and that such families are often subject to 'poverty, debt and hardship'. It suggests that these children are neither neglected nor undisciplined. Furthermore, 'lone-parents spend almost as much on their children as do married parents, and try to protect their children from poverty by spending less on themselves.'

The New Deal for Lone Parents (NDLP) is Labour's policy aimed at promoting self-help. Office for National Statistics figures for January 2001 illustrate the success of the NDLP. Of the 205,490 interviewed, 89% agreed to participate, 95% being women. 45% have so far left the NDLP for permanent employment. These 'snapshot' figures highlight many contemporary lone-parents' positive attitudes and desire for work, to increase their own and their children's standard of living.

The concept of Family Ideology refers to the dominant set of beliefs, values and images promoting the 'ideal' family. This 'ideal family' is the conventional and patriarchal 'cereal-packet' family. This stereotypical model is very misleading, as it is not typical of the majority of household structures. This ideology is very influential on social policy, but is harmful to all those living outside the 'ideal'. Lone mothers have been repeatedly discriminated against in such policies, and frequently attacked by the mass media and New Right politicians for not being able to support their children properly.

Growing family diversity somewhat reduces the harmful effects of this ideology. This concept recognises the emergence of alternative family forms and household arrangements within Britain. Rapoport and Rapoport originally identified five dimensions of diversity: cultural, class, life cycle, cohort and organisational. Lone parent families are the prime example of the latter, making up the majority of alternatives. Growing acceptance and support of minority lifestyles has enabled many women to escape dependence upon male partners and successfully raise their children alone, with less fear of condemnation or stigmatisation. Furthermore, the changing and more tolerant social climate has produced greater acceptance of lone-mothers' choices. The growing acceptance of family diversity seems to be transforming society's previously prejudiced attitudes to lone parenthood, and reducing the stigma attached to lone mothers and the accusation that they do not care for their children properly.

(400 words)

This shows a very good knowledge and understanding of two relevant pieces of material (the Joseph Rowntree study and the social policy of the New Deal for Lone Parents). These are accurately and concisely presented, and linked and relevant to the hypothesis, and provide a clear context for the research, showing lone parents are very concerned for their children. Two concepts are included – family ideology and family diversity – and they are both clearly defined and appropriately

developed, with references to the New Right and to Rapoport and Rapoport's research, and both are relevant to the hypothesis.

Main research method

I intend to conduct a series of unstructured questionnaires, administered by interviewers. This method involves an interpretivist approach to exploring my hypothesis. Using this method, I aim to explore the beliefs of lone mothers about whether they are materially or emotionally disadvantaging their children, by allowing them to reveal their true feelings by answering in their own words about how they see the effects of their lone-parent status on their dependants.

This method will collect qualitative data, and should produce more valid information than other methods, as it allows the lone mothers to express their true thoughts in some depth, thus avoiding problems of imposition. The interviewer-conducted questionnaire helps to overcome any ambiguities in questions, and allows answers to be clarified and explored in more depth, ensures completion, and avoids problems like illiteracy or misinterpretation. Some pilot interviews would be carried out to check any difficulties with the questionnaire or interviewing techniques.

Although the material would largely be in qualitative form, some quantitative data may be obtained by including some preset questions to retain an element of structure, and representativeness achieved by acquiring a representative sample from the survey population. This would make it possible to generalise the results to all lone mothers. However, such generalisations must be viewed cautiously because qualitative data is often unreliable, as other researchers will have difficulty in replicating any findings.

My survey population will be all lone mothers currently with dependent children, and the sampling frame will be attained from DSS records of such mothers claiming lone parent benefit or other related benefits. A representative sample would be obtained by using a combination of cluster and stratified random sampling, and a realistic sample size would be between approximately 400 and 700 lone mothers.

Stratified random sampling is particularly important to this survey. Distinctions must be made between class, ethnicity, age, geographical location and particularly each lone parent's status, e.g. divorced, widowed, or never-married. Each group and sub-group must proportionally represent their number in the entire survey population.

Relevant secondary sources to support and test my findings include existing studies by bodies such as the Joseph Rowntree Foundation (see *Child Poverty and its Consequences*, 1999), and the Institute for Family Policy Research, who may also provide funding for my primary research. Action groups such as Family and Youth Concern, and the National Council for One Parent Families could also be particularly useful sources of existing qualitative information.

(400 words)

This shows a very good knowledge and understanding of the appropriateness of an unstructured questionnaire carried out by an interviewer, picking up theoretical issues (qualitative/quantitative data, avoidance of imposition, and interpretivism) and issues of validity and the importance of representativeness of the sample. Details of the implementation of the proposed methodology are clear and accurate, and perfectly suitable to the hypothesis. Sampling issues and how to obtain a sampling frame are well considered. The sample size is unrealistic for a student (and probably unnecessary in qualitative research), but this doesn't matter as this is a proposal for research, and the student doesn't have to actually carry it out. Nonetheless, the proposal suggests ways the survey might be funded. The methodology also refers to existing secondary sources that might be referred to.

Potential problems

Problems concerning generalisation may arise if the 400–700 lone-mother sample is simply too small a number to be representative, if too many of the sample refuse or are unable to take part, or if some of the lone-mothers statuses have recently changed, e.g. now cohabiting, or they have formed a reconstituted family.

Reliability could prove a major problem with the open-ended nature of the questionnaire. In allowing lone-mothers the freedom to answer questions as unrestrictedly and truthfully as possible, it makes the classification and verification of results very difficult for future researchers. This may cause any findings to lack reliability in the eyes of more scientific-based positivist researchers.

Interviewer bias remains a universal problem for all interview research. It refers to the unavoidable dilemma caused by the very presence of an interviewer affecting or influencing the respondent's answers, and thereby affecting the validity, and especially reliability, of the results. Some interviewees may not reveal their true feelings in an interview, for fear of appearing a 'bad mother' – particularly to a 17-year-old male. Mothers are unlikely to want to admit to having deprived or failed their children, and this poses potential problems for the validity of the research.

Ethical problems arise over whether it is right to fuel the clinging stigma attached to the worthiness of lone mothers, by probing uncomfortable and controversial issues with them. Some mothers may find the underlying implications of such questioning insulting.

Practical problems must also be considered when attempting such a large-scale piece of research. Interviews are lengthy, and interviewers and administration costs expensive. Such time and monetary constraints may affect the number of interviews possible, and thereby the representativeness of the sample. The interpretivist flavour of my hypothesis may deter financial backing from Governmental or charitable sources, who tend to favour more positivist-based research.

(300 words)

(Total words: 1,200)

The proposal identifies a very good range of potential problems, relevant and linked to the hypothesis: representativeness if the sample doesn't work out, and consequent problems of generalisation, problems of checking qualitative research linked to concerns by positivist researchers, interviewer bias, ethical issues, problems of validity, and the practical and political problems of funding arising from the qualitative nature of the research.

Overall, this is an excellent coursework proposal, following the guidelines exactly, showing a good grasp of sociological theory and methods, and it would be unreasonable and unrealistic to expect much more in 1,200 words.

Chapter summary

After studying this chapter, you should be able to:

- discuss a range of theoretical and practical considerations that sociologists consider in conducting research
- explain the difference between positivism and interpretivism, and how these two approaches use different research methods
- distinguish between quantitative and qualitative data, and the advantages and limitations of each
- identify the difference between primary and secondary sources, and the strengths and limitations of the data obtained from each
- explain the problems of reliability and validity of research evidence
- identify the ethical considerations sociologists must consider when carrying out social research
- explain the advantages, uses and limitations of official statistics, with examples

- explain the uses and problems of the experimental method in sociology
- explain how the comparative method might be used as an alternative to the experimental one
- explain the main features and stages of the social survey, and the various sampling methods sociologists use to gain representative samples
- explain the uses, strengths and weaknesses of different types of questionnaires and interviews, including the problems of imposition and the validity and reliability of these methods
- explain fully the problem of interviewer bias
- explain the uses, strengths and weaknesses of participant observation as a research method, including theoretical and practical problems, and the issues of validity and reliability
- discuss the strengths and weaknesses of longitudinal studies, case studies and life histories
- explain what is meant by methodological pluralism and triangulation, and why sociologists might want to use a range of methods in sociological research
- plan your own research drawing on the various methods outlined in this chapter

Key terms

- covert role
- ethics
- Hawthorne effect
- hypothesis
- imposition problem
- interpretivism
- interviewer bias
- methodological pluralism
- overt role
- pilot survey
- positivism
- primary data
- qualitative data
- quantitative data
- reliability/replication
- representative sample
- sample
- sampling frame
- sampling methods
- secondary data
- social facts
- survey population
- surveys
- triangulation
- validity
- verstehen
- victim survey

Exam Questions

SOCIOLOGICAL METHODS

Answer **all** parts of the Question.
Time allowed: 1 hour

Total for this question: *60 marks*

Item A

Dobash and Dobash studied domestic violence. Their mistrust of quantitative secondary data about domestic violence led them to collect their own evidence primarily through interviews. In this extract they discuss aspects of their research methodology.

'Our intention was to explore the factors related to violence against women and the best way to achieve this was to conduct interviews. We did not begin with an extensive interview schedule. Instead, we held   5
open-ended unstructured interviews and discussions with people who had first-hand knowledge of wife-beating – battered women themselves. We also talked to professionals who had experience of working with families characterised by violence.

'Our approach met several problems. The sensitive nature of the study – violent behaviour between family members – posed many problems that could reduce the representativeness of the sample we   10
created. A further difficulty was that the unstructured interviews each lasted from two to twelve hours and all of them had to be recorded. We eventually carried out 28 interviews in the pilot study.'

Item B

Ken Pryce investigated the Calvary United Brotherhood, a small Pentecostalism Christian church in Bristol. In this extract he examines some issues associated with his choice of method.

'The method adopted for the research was covert participant observation, an approach often used in the study of small-scale social groups and interactions. Because it places the researcher inside the group being studied, participant observation gives the sociologist the opportunity to gain accurate insights into   5
the experiences of group members.

'I began attending the Calvary church services on a regular basis, posing as a true believer. Despite my initial acceptance into the Calvary church, there was still some curiosity as to my real motive for joining. The reason I always gave was that although I was from a very religious background my education had drawn me away from religion but now I just felt like going to church again.   10

'However, I was still very aware of the ethical problems with my covert approach and eventually I explained my role as a researcher to the church leader. He responded by saying he would do anything he could to help. He went about this by carefully concealing my research intentions from other members of the church. However, having made my research purpose overt to him, I found that he wanted something in return – my baptism and permanent membership of the church.'   15

(a) Explain what is meant by an 'interview schedule' (**Item A**, line 5).   *(2 marks)*

(b) Suggest **two** reasons why the researchers in **Item A** might have found it difficult to create a sample that was representative of all victims of domestic violence.   *(4 marks)*

(c) Suggest **three** difficulties Dobash and Dobash might have had in analysing data from lengthy unstructured interviews that lasted 'from two to twelve hours' (**Item A**, line 11).   *(6 marks)*

(d) Identify and briefly explain **two** advantages of using 'open-ended unstructured interviews and discussions' (**Item A**, line 6) in sociological research. *(8 marks)*

(e) Examine the advantages and disadvantages of official statistics as a source of data for the sociologist. *(20 marks)*

(f) Using material from **Item B** and elsewhere, assess the usefulness of participant observation in sociological research. *(20 marks)*

(AQA AS Unit 3 June 2001)

SOCIOLOGICAL METHODS

Answer **all** parts of the Question.
Time allowed: 1 hour   **Total for this question:** *60 marks*

Item A

Catherine Clark and Sally Leat studied the classroom experiences of children with special educational needs. This extract is taken from their discussion about which form of observational research they should use.

'Having decided to use observation to investigate the classroom behaviour of this type of pupil, a decision had to be made about the type of observation to be used. Observation techniques fall into two broad   5
categories, structured and unstructured. However, structured observation often has a very narrow focus. For pupils with learning difficulties it is important that the observational techniques used should be sufficiently flexible to take the surprising and unexpected into account. The kind of structured observational schedule used to study classroom behaviour has often been too rigid.

'Consequently, an open-ended, unstructured approach appeared to offer the best means of including a   10
wide range of behaviour, as well as allowing us to link the behaviour we observed with the classroom context. As with many sociological studies, our research was carried out with only a small sample of research subjects. Even so, we found that unstructured observation can generate important research into teacher–pupil relationships, particularly when the sociologist is participating in the situation they are researching.   15

'A further decision we had to make was between overt and covert approaches to research.'

Source: Adapted from C. CLARK and S. LEAT, 'The use of unstructured observation in teacher assessment', in C. TILSTONE, *Observing Teaching and Learning* (David Fulton, London) 1998

Item B

Kaldenburg and his colleagues investigated the extent to which there is a relationship between age and response rate to mailed questionnaires. To do this, they analysed the response rates of people aged 60 to 93 years of age to a questionnaire posted to them concerning their pensions.

'A random sample of 1,000 was drawn from a population of 23,000 retired public employees in the files of a pensions company in a large city in the USA. A four-page questionnaire booklet was mailed to the   5
sample. The questionnaire was designed using large fonts and employed clear and easy instructions.

'The survey included a variety of question formats including overall satisfaction questions using a five-point scale from "very satisfied" to "very unsatisfied", as well as open-ended questions. The questionnaire also carried a question that asked whether the survey had been completed by the person to whom
it was mailed.   10

'The number of questionnaires returned after a single mailing was 465 out of the original 1,000 sent out. A response rate of 46.5% is generally considered to be very high and this might have resulted from the interest elderly people have in the provision of their pensions. We also found that response rates declined
with age.'   14

Source: Adapted from Kaldenburg et al., 'Mail survey response rate patterns in a population of the elderly', *Public Opinion Quarterly,* 58 (University of Chicago Press) 1994

(a) Explain what is meant by a 'structured observational schedule' (**Item A**, lines 8–9).   *(2 marks)*
(b) Explain the difference between 'overt and covert approaches to research' (**Item A**, line 16).   *(4 marks)*

(c) Suggest **three** reasons why sociological research is often carried out using 'only a small sample of research subjects' (**Item A**, lines 12–13). *(6 marks)*

(d) Identify and briefly explain **two** advantages some sociologists see in 'participating in the situation they are researching' (**Item A**, lines 14–15). *(8 marks)*

(e) Examine the reasons why sociologists might use personal and historical documents in their research. *(20 marks)*

(f) Using material from **Item B** and elsewhere, assess the usefulness of mailed questionnaires in sociological research. *(20 marks)*

(AQA AS Unit 3 May 2002)

Glossary

Words in blue within entries refer to terms found elsewhere in the glossary.

absolute poverty   Poverty defined as lacking the minimum requirements necessary to maintain human health. *See also* relative poverty.

achieved status   Status which is achieved through an individual's own efforts. *See also* ascribed status.

agenda-setting   The list of subjects which the mass media choose to report and bring to public attention.

alienation   A lack of power and satisfaction at work.

anomie   Confusion and uncertainty over social norms.

anti-school subculture   A set of values, attitudes and behaviour in opposition to the main aims of a school.

arranged marriage   A marriage which is arranged by the parents of the marriage partners, with a view to compatibility of background and status. More a union between two families than two people, and romantic love between the marriage partners is not necessarily present.

ascribed status   Status which is given to an individual at birth and usually can't be changed. *See also* achieved status.

automation   Production of goods by self-controlling machines with little human supervision.

banding   A system of grouping students in schools according to their ability.

'beanpole' family   A multi-generation extended family, in a pattern which is long and thin, with few aunts and uncles, reflecting fewer children being born in each generation, but people living longer.

bias   A subject being presented in a one-sided way, favouring one point of view over others, or deliberately ignoring, distorting or misrepresenting issues.

birth rate   The number of live births per 1,000 of the population per year.

bourgeoisie   In Marxist theory (*see* Marxism), the class of owners of the means of production.

capitalists   The **social class** of owners of the **means of production** in industrial societies, whose primary purpose is to make profits.

class conflict   The conflict that arises between different **social classes**. It is generally used to describe the conflict between the **bourgeoisie** and **proletariat** in Marxist views of society (*see* **Marxism**).

class consciousness   An awareness in members of a **social class** of their real interests. *See also* **false consciousness**.

classic extended family   A **family** where several related **nuclear families** or family members live in the same house, street or area. It may be horizontally extended, where it contains aunts, uncles, cousins, etc., or vertically extended, where it contains more than two generations. *See also* **modified extended family**.

communes   Self-contained and self-supporting communities, where all members of the community share property, childcare, household tasks and living accommodation.

communism   An equal society, without **social classes** or **class conflict**, in which the **means of production** are the common property of all.

compensatory education   Extra educational help for those coming from disadvantaged groups to help them overcome the disadvantages they face in the education system and the wider society.

conjugal roles   The **roles** played by a male and female partner in marriage or in a cohabiting couple.

consumption property   Property for use by the owner which doesn't produce any **income**, such as owning your own car. *See also* **productive property**.

core workers   The well-paid and qualified, skilled workers who make up the full-time, permanent employees in a workplace. *See also* **primary labour market**, **periphery workers**.

counter-school subculture   A set of **values**, attitudes and behaviour in opposition to the main aims of a school.

covert role   Where the researcher in a participant observation study keeps her or his identity as a researcher concealed from the group being studied. *See also* **overt role**.

craft production   The production of goods by human skill using hand tools.

cultural capital   The knowledge, language, attitudes and **values**, and lifestyle which give **middle-class** and **upper-class** students who possess them an inbuilt advantage in a middle-class controlled education system. Associated with the French Marxist Bourdieu (*see* **Marxism**). *See also* **habitus**.

cultural deprivation   The idea that some young people fail in education because of supposed deficiencies in their home and **family** background, such as inadequate **socialization**, failings in pre-school learning, inadequate language skills and inappropriate attitudes and **values**.

culture   The language, beliefs, **values** and **norms**, **customs**, **roles**, knowledge and skills which combine to make up the 'way of life' of any society.

culture clash   A difference and conflict between the cultural **values** of the home and those of educational institutions. *See also* **culture**.

culture of poverty   A set of beliefs and **values** thought to exist among the poor which prevents them escaping from poverty.

customs   **Norms** which have existed for a long time.

cycle of deprivation   An explanation of how one aspect of poverty, such as poor housing, can lead to further poverty, such as poor **health**, building up into a cycle which makes it difficult for the poor to escape from poverty.

death rate   The number of deaths per 1,000 of the population per year.

dependency culture   A set of **values** and beliefs, and a way of life, centred on dependence on others. Normally used by **New Right** writers in the context of those who depend on welfare state benefits.

deskilling   The removal of skills from work by the application of new machinery which simplifies tasks.

determinism   The idea that people's behaviour is moulded by their social surroundings, and that they have little free will, control or choice over how they behave.

deviance   Failure to conform to social **norms**.

deviancy amplification   The process by which the mass media, through exaggeration and distortion, actually create more crime and **deviance**.

disability   A physical or mental **impairment** which has a substantial and long-term adverse effect on a person's ability to carry out normal day-to-day activities.

disease   A biological or mental condition, which usually involves medically diagnosed symptoms.

division of labour   The division of work or occupations into a large number of specialized tasks, each of which is carried out by one worker or group of workers.

divorce rate   The number of divorces per 1,000 married people per year.

domestic labour   Unpaid housework, including cooking, cleaning, childcare and looking after the sick and elderly.

dominant ideology   The set of ideas and beliefs of the most powerful groups in society, which influence the ideas of the rest of society. Usually associated with Marxist ideas (*see* **Marxism**) of the **ruling class** and how the ruling class can impose its own ideas on the rest of society.

Education Action Zones   Areas which face a range of social problems, such as poverty and unemployment, in which schools are given extra money and teachers to help children overcome difficulties at school arising from their home backgrounds. In 2005, they became Excellence in Cities Action Zones (EiCAZs).

Educational Priority Areas   An early form of Education Action Zone, these were discontinued in the early 1980s.

elaborated code   A form of language use involving careful explanation and detail. The language used by strangers and individuals in some formal context, like a job interview, writing a business letter, or a school lesson or textbook. Associated with the work of Bernstein. *See also* restricted code.

elite   A small group holding great power and privilege in society.

equality of educational opportunity   The principle that every child, regardless of her or his social class background, ability to pay school fees, ethnic background (*see* ethnicity), gender or disability, should have an equal chance of doing as well in education as her or his ability will allow.

ethics   Principles or ideas about what is morally right and wrong.

ethnicity   The shared culture of a social group which gives its members a common identity in some ways different from other groups.

ethnocentrism   A view of the world in which other cultures are seen through the eyes of one's own culture, with a devaluing of the others. For example, school subjects may concentrate on white British society and culture rather than recognizing and taking into account the cultures of different ethnic communities (*see* ethnicity).

expressive role   The nurturing, caring and emotional role, often linked by functionalists (see functionalism) to women's biology and seen as women's 'natural' role in the family. *See also* instrumental role.

extended family   A family grouping including all kin (*see* kinship). There are two main types of extended family: the classic extended family and the modified extended family. *See also* 'beanpole' family, nuclear family.

false consciousness   A failure by members of a social class to recognize their real interests. *See also* class consciousness.

family   A social institution consisting of a group of people related by kinship – ties of blood, marriage or adoption.

family ideology   A set of dominant beliefs and values about what the family and family life *should* be like.

feminism   The view that examines the world from the point of view of women, coupled with the belief that women are disadvantaged and their interests ignored or devalued in society. *See also* liberal feminism, Marxist feminism, radical feminism.

flexible specialization   Production methods involving more specialized products to meet changing consumer demands, using technology that can be quickly adapted to producing new products, with workers having a range of skills, and demand for workers fluctuating as consumer demands change. *See also* post-Fordism.

folk devils   Individuals or groups posing an imagined or exaggerated threat to society.

Fordism   The application of Taylorism to the mass production of standardized goods using assembly line technology, involving few skills and repetitive work by employees. First developed by Henry Ford in car production in the 1920s, hence the term Fordism.

functional prerequisites   The basic needs that must be met if society is to survive.

functionalism   A sociological perspective which sees society as made up of parts which work together to maintain society as an integrated whole. Society is seen as fundamentally harmonious and stable, due to the value consensus established through socialization. *See also* Marxism, structuralism.

gate-keeping   The power of some people, groups or organizations to limit access to something valuable or useful. For example, doctors act as gate-keepers as they have the power to allow or refuse entry to the sick role, and the mass media have the power to refuse to cover some issues and therefore not allow the public access to some information.

gender   The culturally created differences between men and women which are learnt through socialization.

globalization   The growing interdependence of societies across the world, with the spread of the same culture, consumer goods and economic interests across the globe.

habitus   The cultural framework (*see* culture) and set of ideas possessed by each social class, into which people are socialized (*see* socialization) and which influences their tastes in music, newspapers, films and so on. Bourdieu, a French Marxist (*see* Marxism), argued the dominant class has the power to impose its own habitus in the education system, giving those from upper-class and middle-class backgrounds an inbuilt advantage over those from working-class backgrounds.

halo effect   When pupils become favourably stereotyped (*see* stereotype) on the basis of earlier impressions by the teacher, and are rewarded and favoured in future teacher–student encounters.

Hawthorne effect   When the presence of the researcher, or a group's knowledge that it has been specially selected for research, changes the behaviour of the group, raising problems of the validity of social research.

health   Being able to function normally within a usual everyday routine.

hegemony The acceptance of the **dominant ideology** by the **working class**, as a result of the power of the **ruling class** to persuade others to accept and consent to its ideas.

hidden curriculum Attitudes and behaviour which are taught through the school's organization and teachers' attitudes but which are not part of the formal timetable.

high culture Cultural products (*see* **culture**), mainly media based, seen as of lasting artistic or literary value, aimed at small, intellectual, predominantly **upper-class** and **middle-class** audiences, interested in new ideas, critical discussion and analysis. *See also* **mass culture**.

household An individual or group living at the same address and sharing facilities.

hypothesis An idea which a researcher guesses might be true, but which has not yet been tested against the evidence.

iatrogenesis Any harmful mental or physical condition induced in a patient through the effects of treatment by a doctor or surgeon.

identity How individuals see and define themselves and how other people see and define them.

ideological state apparatuses Agencies of the state which serve to spread the **dominant ideology** and justify the power of the dominant **social class**.

ideology A set of ideas, **values** and beliefs that represent the outlook, and justify the interests, of a social group.

illness The subjective feeling of being unwell or unhealthy (*see* **health**) – a person's own recognition and definition of a lack of well-being.

impairment Some abnormal functioning of the body or mind, either that one is born with or arising from injury or **disease**.

imposition problem When asking questions in interviews or postal questionnaires, the risk that the researcher might be imposing their own views or framework on the people being researched, rather than getting at what they really think.

income A flow of money which people obtain from work, from their investments, or from the state. *See also* **wealth**.

infant mortality rate The number of deaths of babies in the first year of life per 1,000 live births per year.

instrumental role The provider/breadwinner **role** in the family, often associated by functionalists (*see* **functionalism**) with men's role in family life. *See also* **expressive role**.

integrated conjugal roles **Roles** in marriage or in a cohabiting couple where male and female partners share domestic tasks, childcare, decision-making and **income** earning.

interpretivism A sociological **perspective** that suggests that to understand society it is necessary to understand the meanings people give to their behaviour, and how this is influenced by the behaviour and interpretations of others. The focus of research is therefore on individuals or small groups rather than on society as a whole. *See also* positivism, social action theory.

interviewer bias   The answers given in an interview being influenced or distorted in some way by the presence or behaviour of the interviewer.

inverse care law   In relation to the welfare state and health care, the suggestion that those whose need is least get the most resources, while those in the greatest need get the fewest resources.

kibbutz   A community established in Israel, with the emphasis on equality, collective ownership of property, and collective childrearing.

kinship   Relations of blood, marriage or adoption.

labelling   Defining a person or group in a certain way – as a particular 'type' of person or group.

labour power   People's capacity to work. In Marxist theory (*see* Marxism), people sell their labour power to the employer in return for a wage, and the employer buys only their labour power, not the whole person.

laws   Official legal rules, formally enforced by the police, courts and prison, involving legal punishment if the rules are broken.

liberal feminism   A feminist approach (*see* feminism) which seeks to research the inequalities facing women, and enable women to achieve equal opportunities with men, without challenging the system as a whole. *See also* Marxist feminism, radical feminism.

life chances   The chances of obtaining those things defined as desirable and of avoiding those things defined as undesirable in a society.

life expectancy   An estimate of how long people can be expected to live from a certain age.

macro approach   A focus on the large-scale structure of society as a whole, rather than on individuals.

marginalization   The process whereby some people are pushed to the margins or edges of society by poverty, lack of education, disability, racism and so on. *See also* social exclusion.

market situation   The rewards that people are able to obtain when they sell their skills in the labour market, depending on the scarcity of the skills they have and the power they have to obtain high rewards.

Marxism   A structural theory of society which sees society divided by conflict between two main opposing social classes, due to the private ownership of the means of production and the exploitation of the non-owners by the owners. *See also* functionalism, structuralism.

Marxist feminism   A Marxist approach (*see* Marxism) to the study of women, emphasizing the way they are exploited both as workers and as women. *See also* feminism, liberal feminism, radical feminism.

mass culture (popular culture)   Cultural products (*see* culture), mainly media based, produced as entertainment for sale to the mass of ordinary people. These involve mass-produced, standardized, short-lived products of no lasting value, which are seen to demand little critical thought, analysis or discussion. *See also* high culture.

matriarchy   Power and authority held by women. *See also* patriarchy.

means of production   The key resources necessary for producing society's goods, such as factories and land.

mechanical solidarity   Where people are bonded together through a similarity of lifestyle and occupation. *See also* organic solidarity.

mechanization   The process where production of goods by hand is replaced by production by machinery.

media representations   The categories and images that are used to present groups and activities to media audiences. These representations influence the way we think about these activities and groups, and are often linked to stereotypes.

meritocracy   A society where social positions are achieved by individual merit, such as educational qualifications, talent and skill.

methodological pluralism   The use of a variety of methods in a single piece of research.

micro approach   A focus on small groups or individuals, rather than on the structure of society as a whole.

middle class   Those in non-manual work – jobs which don't involve heavy physical effort, are usually performed in offices and involve paperwork or computer work of various kinds. *See also* social class, upper class, working class.

minority ethnic group   A social group which shares a cultural identity (*see* culture) which is different in some respects from that of the majority population of a society.

modified extended family   A family type where related nuclear families, although living apart geographically, nevertheless maintain regular contact and mutual support through visiting, the phone, e-mail and letters. *See also* classic extended family.

monogamy   A form of marriage in which a person can only be legally married to one partner at a time. *See also* polyandry, polygamy, polygyny, serial monogamy.

moral panic   A wave of public concern about some exaggerated or imaginary threat to society, stirred up by exaggerated and sensationalized reporting in the mass media.

mortification A process whereby a person's own identity is replaced by one defined by an institution, such as a hospital or prison.

multicultural education Education which involves teaching about the **culture** of other ethnic groups (*see* **ethnicity**) besides that of the majority culture.

negative sanctions Punishments of various kinds imposed on those who fail to conform to social **norms**. *See also* **positive sanctions**, **sanction**.

New Right A political philosophy found in the work of some sociologists, but mainly associated with the years of Conservative government in Britain between 1979 and 1997. This approach stresses individual freedom, self-help and self-reliance, reduction of the power and spending of the state, the free market and free competition between private companies, schools and other institutions, and the importance of traditional institutions and values.

news values The **values** and assumptions held by editors and journalists which guide them in choosing what to report and what to leave out, and how what they choose to report should be presented.

norms Social rules which define correct and approved behaviour in a society or group.

norm-setting The process whereby the mass media emphasize and reinforce conformity to social **norms**, and seek to isolate those who don't conform by making them the victims of unfavourable public opinion.

nuclear family A **family** with two generations, of parents and children, living together in one **household**. *See also* **extended family**.

objectivity Approaching topics with an open mind, avoiding **bias**, and being prepared to submit research evidence to scrutiny by other researchers.

organic solidarity Where people are bonded together because they depend on one another, as they all have different occupations and rely on each other for a wide range of goods and services which they don't themselves produce. *See also* **mechanical solidarity**.

overt role Where the researcher in a participant observation study reveals her or his identity as a researcher to the group being studied. *See also* **covert role**.

particularistic values Rules and **values** that give a priority to personal relationships. *See also* **universalistic values**.

patriarchy Power and authority held by males. *See also* **matriarchy**.

periphery workers Workers who are part-time, or on temporary or short-term contracts, employed on a casual, temporary basis and therefore easily dispensed with and replaced. *See also* **secondary labour market**, **core workers**.

perspective   A way of looking at something. A **sociological perspective** involves a set of theories which influences what is looked at when studying society.

pilot survey   A small-scale practice **survey** carried out before the final survey to check for any possible problems.

polyandry   A form of marriage in which a woman may have two or more husbands at the same time. *See also* **monogamy**, **serial monogamy**.

polygamy   A form of marriage in which a member of one sex can be married to two or more members of the opposite sex at the same time. *See also* **monogamy**, **serial monogamy**.

polygyny   A form of marriage in which a man may have two or more wives at the same time. *See also* **monogamy**, **serial monogamy**.

popular culture   *See* **mass culture**.

positive discrimination   Giving disadvantaged groups more favourable treatment than others to make up for the disadvantages they face.

positive sanctions   Rewards of various kinds to encourage people to conform to social **norms**. *See also* **negative sanctions**, **sanction**.

positivism   An approach in sociology that believes society can be studied using similar scientific techniques to those used in the natural sciences, such as physics, chemistry and biology. *See also* **interpretivism**.

post-Fordism   A system of production involving computer-controlled multipurpose machinery, specialized products, a multiskilled flexible workforce able to do a range of jobs, and given some control over decision-making in teams. *See also* **flexible specialization**.

postmodernism   The belief that society is changing so rapidly and constantly that it is marked by chaos and uncertainty, and social structures are being replaced by a whole range of different and constantly changing social relationships. Societies can no longer be understood through the application of general theories like **Marxism** or **functionalism**, which seek to explain society as a whole, as it has become fragmented into many different groups, interests and lifestyles. Society and social structures cease to exist, to be replaced by a mass of individuals making individual choices about their lifestyles.

poverty line   The dividing point between those who are poor and those who are not. The poverty line used in Britain today, and by the European Union, is 60 per cent of average income.

pressure groups   Organizations which try to put pressure on those with power in society to implement policies they favour.

primary data   Information which sociologists have collected themselves. *See also* **secondary data**.

primary deviance   Deviant behaviour which is not publicly labelled (see labelling) as deviant. *See also* secondary deviance.

primary labour market   The relatively secure section of the labour market, involving full-time work, good pay and working conditions, job security, training, and career opportunities. *See also* secondary labour market, core workers, periphery workers.

primary socialization   The early forms of socialization in the family and close community. *See also* secondary socialization.

privatization   The process whereby households and families become isolated and separated from the community and from wider kin (*see* kinship), with people spending more time together in home-centred activities.

privatized nuclear family   A self-contained, self-reliant and home-centred family unit that is separated and isolated from its extended kin, neighbours and local community life.

productive property   Property which provides an unearned income for its owner, such as factories, land and stocks and shares. *See also* consumption property.

productivity   How much workers produce – their output in terms of items made or processed – in a given time period.

proletariat   The social class of workers who have to work for wages as they do not own the means of production.

qualitative data   Information concerned with the meanings and interpretations people have about some issue or event.

quantitative data   Information that can be expressed in statistical or number form.

racial prejudice   A set of assumptions about an ethnic group (*see* ethnicity) which people are reluctant to change even when they receive information which undermines those assumptions.

racism   Believing or acting as though an individual or group is superior or inferior on the grounds of their racial or ethnic (*see* ethnicity) origins.

radical feminism   A feminist approach (*see* feminism) which focuses on the problem of patriarchy. For radical feminists, the main focus of research is on the problem of men and male-dominated society. *See also* Marxist feminism, liberal feminism.

reconstituted family   A family where one or both partners have been previously married, and bring with them children of the previous marriage.

relative poverty   Poverty defined in relation to a generally accepted standard of living in a specific society at a particular time. *See also* absolute poverty.

reliability Whether another researcher, if repeating or replicating research using the same method for the same research on the same group, would achieve the same results.

replication *see* reliability.

representative sample A smaller group drawn from the survey population, of which it contains a good cross-section. The information obtained from a representative sample should provide roughly the same results as if the whole survey population had been surveyed.

responsible autonomy Where workers are given a limited amount of control over their work, and the opportunity to use their own initiative and to organize their own work routines through teamwork.

restricted code A form of language use which takes for granted shared understandings between people. Colloquial, everyday language used between friends, with limited explanation and use of vocabulary. *See also* elaborated code.

role conflict The conflict between the successful performances of two or more roles at the same time, such as worker, student and mother.

role models Patterns of behaviour which others copy and model their own behaviour on.

roles The patterns of behaviour which are expected from individuals in society.

ruling class The social class of owners of the means of production, whose control over the economy gives them power over all aspects of society, enabling them to rule over society.

ruling class ideology The set of ideas and beliefs of the ruling class.

sample A small representative group drawn from the survey population for questioning or interviewing.

sampling frame A list of names of all those in the survey population from which a representative sample is selected.

sampling methods The techniques sociologists use to select representative individuals to study from the survey population.

sanction A reward or punishment to encourage social conformity. *See also* negative sanctions, positive sanctions.

scapegoats Individuals or groups blamed for something which is not their fault.

scientific management A theory first developed by Frederick William Taylor, who believed the management of workers in an industrial firm and the tasks they perform should follow scientific principles involving tight control of the workforce, and performance of work tasks in the same way as a piece of industrial machinery. It is also commonly known as Taylorism or Fordism.

secondary data   Data which already exist and which the researcher hasn't collected herself or himself. *See also* primary data.

secondary deviance   Deviant behaviour which is labelled (*see* labelling) as such by others. *See also* primary deviance.

secondary labour market   The insecure section of the labour market, involving part-time, short-term or temporary work, lack of job security, lower levels of training, poorer pay and few promotion opportunities. *See also* primary labour market, core workers, periphery workers.

secondary socialization   Socialization which takes place beyond the family and close community, such as through the education system, the mass media and the workplace. *See also* primary socialization.

secularization   The process whereby religious thinking, practice and institutions lose social significance.

segregated conjugal role   A clear division and separation between the roles of male and female partners in a marriage or in a cohabiting couple.

self-fulfilling prophecy   People acting in response to predictions of their behaviour, thereby making the prediction come true. Often applied to the effects of streaming in schools.

serial monogamy   A form of marriage where a person keeps marrying and divorcing a series of different partners, but is only married to one person at a time. *See also* monogamy, polyandry, polygamy, polygyny.

sex   The biological differences between men and women.

sexism   Prejudice or discrimination against people (especially women) because of their sex.

sexual division of labour   The division of work into 'men's jobs' and 'women's jobs'.

sick role   The pattern of behaviour which is expected from someone who is classified as ill.

social action theory   A perspective which emphasizes the creative action which people can take, and that people are not simply the passive victims of social forces outside them. Social action theory suggests it is important to understand the motives and meanings people give to their behaviour. *See also* interpretivism, structuralism.

social class   A broad group of people who share a similar economic situation, such as occupation, income and ownership of wealth. *See also* middle class, upper class, working class.

social construction   The way something is created through the individual, social and cultural (*see* culture) interpretations, perceptions and actions of people. Official statistics, notions of health and illness, deviance and suicide are all examples of social phenomena that only exist because people have constructed them and given these phenomena particular labels.

social control The process of persuading or forcing individuals to conform to **values** and **norms**.

social exclusion The situation where people are marginalized (*see* **marginalization**) or excluded from full participation in education, work, community life and access to services and other aspects of life seen as part of being a full and participating member of mainstream society. Those who lack the necessary resources are excluded from the opportunity to fully participate in society, and are denied the opportunities most people take for granted.

social facts Social phenomena which exist outside individuals but act upon them in ways which constrain or mould their behaviour. Such phenomena include **social institutions** such as the **family**, the law, the education system and the workplace.

social institutions The organized social arrangements which are found in all societies, such as the **family** and the education systems.

social mobility Movement of groups or individuals up or down the social hierarchy.

social policy The package of measures taken to solve **social problems**.

social problem Something that is seen as harmful to society in some way, and needs something doing to sort it out.

social structure The network of **social institutions** and social relationships that form the 'building blocks' of society.

socialization The process of learning the **culture** of any society. *See also* **primary socialization, secondary socialization**.

sociological perspective A set of theories which influence what is looked at when studying society.

sociological problem Any social issue that needs explaining.

status The amount of prestige or social importance a person has in the eyes of other members of a group or society. *See also* **achieved status, ascribed status**.

stereotype A generalized, oversimplified view of the features of a social group, allowing for few individual differences between members of the group.

streaming A system of grouping students in schools by ability for all subjects.

structural differentiation The way new, more specialized **social institutions** emerge to take over functions that were once performed by a single institution. An example is the way some functions of the family have been transferred to the education system and the welfare state.

structuralism A **perspective** which is concerned with the overall structure of society, and sees individual behaviour moulded by **social institu-**

tions like the **family**, the education system, the mass media and work. *See also* **functionalism, Marxism**.

structuration A **perspective** between **structuralism** and **social action theory** which suggests that, while people are constrained by social institutions, they can at the same time take action to support or change those institutions.

subculture A smaller **culture** held by a group of people within the main culture of a society, in some ways different from the main culture, but with many aspects in common.

surplus value The extra value added by workers to the products they produce, after allowing for the payment of their wages, and which goes to the employer in the form of profit.

survey A means of collecting **primary data** from large numbers of people, usually in a standardized statistical form.

survey population The section of the population which is of interest in a **survey**.

symbolic interactionism A sociological **perspective** which is concerned with understanding human behaviour in face-to-face situations, and how individuals and situations come to be defined in particular ways through their encounters with other people.

symmetrical family A **family** where the **roles** of husband and wife or cohabiting partners have become more alike (symmetrical) and equal.

Taylorism The breaking down of work into its simplest elements, with workers given clear and simple instructions on exactly how they should do their jobs. Managers take over all decision-making and coordinate the work, and all knowledge of the work is transferred to management. *See also* **Fordism, scientific management**.

technological determinism The view that the technology used in production is the major influence in explaining workers' attitudes and involvement in work.

triangulation The use of two, or usually more, research methods in a single piece of research to check the **reliability** and **validity** of research evidence.

underachievement The failure of individuals or groups to fulfil their potential – they do not do as well in education (or other areas) as their talents and abilities suggest they should.

underclass A social group right at the bottom of the **social class** hierarchy, who are in some ways cut off or excluded from the rest of society.

universalistic values Rules and **values** that apply equally to all members of society, regardless of who they are. *See also* **particularistic values**.

upper class   A small social class who are the main owners of society's wealth. It includes wealthy industrialists, landowners and the traditional aristocracy. *See also* middle class, working class.

validity   This is concerned with notions of truth – how far the findings of research actually provide a true picture of what is being studied.

value consensus   A general agreement around the main values of society.

value freedom   The idea that the beliefs and prejudices of the sociologist should not be allowed to influence the way research is carried out and evidence interpreted.

values   General beliefs about what is right or wrong, and about the important standards which are worth maintaining and achieving in any society.

verstehen   The idea of understanding human behaviour by putting yourself in the position of those being studied, and trying to see things from their point of view.

victim survey   A survey which asks people if they have been victims of crime, whether or not they reported it to the police.

wealth   Property in the form of assets which can be sold and turned into cash for the benefit of the owner. *See also* income.

welfare pluralism   The range of welfare provision, including informal provision by the family and community, the welfare state, the voluntary sector and the private sector.

working class   Those working in manual jobs – jobs involving physical work and, literally, work with their hands, like factory or labouring work. *See also* middle class, social class, upper class.

Bibliography

This bibliography cites only texts explicitly referred to in this book in case students wish to read original material.

Abel-Smith, B. and Townsend, P. (1965) *The Poor and the Poorest*, London: G. Bell & Son.

Abercrombie, N., Warde, A. et al. (2000) *Contemporary British Society* (3rd edn), Cambridge: Polity.

Acheson Report (1998) *Independent Inquiry into Inequalities in Health*, London: Stationery Office.

Althusser, L. (1971) *Lenin and Philosophy and Other Essays*, London: New Left Books.

Anderson, M. (1971) *Family Structure in Nineteenth Century Lancashire*, Cambridge: Cambridge University Press.

Anderson, M. (ed.) (1980) *Sociology of the Family* (2nd edn), Harmondsworth: Penguin.

Ariès, P. (1973) *Centuries of Childhood*, Harmondsworth: Penguin.

Atkinson, J. (1985) 'The changing corporation', in D. Clutterbuck (ed.), *New Patterns of Work*, Aldershot: Gower.

Atkinson, J. M. (1978) *Discovering Suicide*, Basingstoke: Macmillan.

Ball, S. J. (1981) *Beachside Comprehensive: A Case-Study of Secondary Schooling*, Cambridge: Cambridge University Press.

Ballard, R. (1982) 'South Asian families', in Rapoport et al. (1982).

Barber, M. (1996) *The Learning Game*, London: Victor Gollancz.

Barker, E. (1984) *The Making of a Moonie*, Oxford: Blackwell.

Barrett, M. and McIntosh, M. (1982) *The Anti-Social Family*, London: Verso.

Becker, H. S. (1970) *Sociological Work*, Chicago: University of Chicago Press.

Becker, H. S. (1971) 'Social class variations in the teacher–pupil relationship', in School and Society Course Team, Open University (ed.), *School and Society*, London: Routledge & Kegan Paul.

Bernstein, B. (1971) 'Education cannot compensate for society', in School and Society Course Team, Open University (ed.), *School and Society*, London: Routledge & Kegan Paul.

Best, L. (1993) 'Dragons, dinner ladies and ferrets: sex roles in children's books', *Sociology Review*, 3, no. 3.

Bhatti, G. (1999) *Asian Children at Home and at School: An Ethnographic Study*, London: Routledge.

Blauner, R. (1964) *Alienation and Freedom*, Chicago: University of Chicago Press.

Bott, E. (1957/1978) 'Conjugal roles and social networks', in P. Worsley (ed.), *Modern Sociology* (2nd edn), Harmondsworth: Penguin.

Boulton, M. G. (1983) *On Being a Mother*, London: Tavistock.

Bourdieu, P. (1971) 'Systems of education and systems of thought' and 'Intellectual field and creative project', in M. F. D. Young (ed.), *Knowledge and Control*, London: Collier-Macmillan.

Bowles, S. and Gintis, H. (1976) *Schooling in Capitalist America*, London: Routledge & Kegan Paul.

Brannen, J. (2003) 'The age of beanpole families', *Sociology Review*, Sept.

Braverman, H. (1974) *Labour and Monopoly Capital*, New York: Monthly Review Press.

Browne, K. and Bottrill, I. (1999) 'Our unequal, unhealthy nation: class inequality, health and illness', *Sociology Review*, 9, no. 2.

Cicourel, A. V. and Kitsuse, J. I. (1971) 'The social organisation of the high school and deviant adolescent careers', in School and Society Course Team, Open University (ed.), *School and Society*, London: Routledge & Kegan Paul.

Clarke, J. and Critcher, C. (1985) *The Devil Makes Work: Leisure in Capitalist Britain*, Basingstoke: Macmillan.

Coard, B. (1971) *How the West Indian Child is Made Educationally Sub-normal in the British School System*, London: New Beacon Books.

Coates, K. and Silburn, R. (1970) *Poverty: The Forgotten Englishmen*, Harmondsworth: Penguin.

Cohen, S. (1972) *Folk Devils and Moral Panics*, London: MacGibbon & Kee.

Colley, A. (1998) 'Gender and subject choice in secondary education', in J. Radford (ed.), *Gender and Choice in Education and Occupation*, London: Routledge & Kegan Paul.

Collins, R. (1972) 'Functional and conflict theories of stratification', in B. R. Cosin (ed.), *Education, Structure and Society*, Harmondsworth: Penguin.

Cooper, D. (1972) *The Death of the Family*, Harmondsworth: Penguin.

Critcher, C., Bramham, P. and Tomlinson, A. (1995) *The Sociology of Leisure*, London: Chapman & Hall.

Davis, K. and Moore, W. E. (1945/1967) 'Some principles of stratification', in R. Bendix and S. M. Lipset (eds), *Class, Status and Power* (2nd edn), London: Routledge & Kegan Paul.

Deem, R. (1986) *All Work and No Play*, Milton Keynes: Open University Press.

Deem, R. (1990) 'Women and leisure – all work and no play', *Social Studies Review*, 5, no. 4.

Department of Health (1992) *The Health of the Nation*, London: HMSO.

Department of Health (1998) *Our Healthier Nation*, London: Stationery Office.

Dex, S. and McCulloch, A. (1997) *Flexible Employment: The Future of Britain's Jobs*, Basingstoke: Macmillan.

Douglas, J. W. B. (1964) *The Home and the School*, London: MacGibbon & Kee.

Douglas, J. W. B., Ross, J. and Simpson, H. (1968) *All our Future*, London: Peter Davies.

Duncombe, J. and Marsden, D. (1995) 'Women's "triple shift": paid employment, domestic labour and "emotion work" ', *Sociology Review*, 4, no. 4.

Edgell, S. (1980) *Middle-Class Couples*, London: Allen & Unwin.

Elston, M. (1980) 'Medicine: half our future doctors', in R. Silverstone and A. Warde (eds), *Careers of Professional Women*, London: Croom Helm.

Eversley, D. and Bonnerjea, L. (1982) 'Social change and indications of diversity', in Rapoport et al. (1982).

Ferguson, M. (1983) *Forever Feminine: Women's Magazines and the Cult of Femininity*, London: Heinemann.

Ferri, E., Bynner, J. and Wadsworth, M. (2003) *Changing Britain, Changing Lives*, London: Institute of Education.

Field, F. (1989) *Losing Out: The Emergence of Britain's Underclass*, Oxford: Blackwell.

Finn, D. (1984) 'Leaving school and growing up', in I. Bates et al. (eds), *Schooling for the Dole*, Basingstoke: Macmillan.

Finn, D. (1987) *Training without Jobs*, Basingstoke: Macmillan.

Flanders, N. A. (1970) *Analysing Teaching Behaviour*, New York: Addison Wesley.

Fletcher, R. (1966) *The Family and Marriage in Britain*, Harmondsworth: Penguin.

Francis, B. (2000) *Boys, Girls and Achievement: Addressing the Classroom Issues*, London: Routledge/Farmer.

Friedman, A. (1977) *Industry and Labour*, Basingstoke: Macmillan.

Fuller, M. (1980) 'Black girls in a London comprehensive school', in R. Deem (ed.), *Schooling for Women's Work*, London: Routledge & Kegan Paul.

Gallie, D. (1978) *In Search of the New Working Class*, Cambridge: Cambridge University Press.

Gallie, D. (1994) 'Patterns of skill change: upskilling, deskilling or polarisation?', in R. Penn, M. Rose and J. Ruben (eds), *Skill and Occupational Change*, Oxford: Oxford University Press.

Gans, H. J. (1973) *More Equality*, New York: Pantheon.

Gatrell, C. J. (2004) *Hard Labour: The Sociology of Parenthood, Family Life and Career*, Maidenhead: Open University Press.

Gibson, A. and Asthana, S. (1999) 'Schools, markets and equity: access to secondary education in England and Wales', presentation to American Educational Research Association Annual Conference, Montreal, reported in the *Guardian*, 6 July.

Gibson, C. (1994) *Dissolving Wedlock*, London: Routledge.

Giddens, A. (2001) *Sociology* (4th edn), Cambridge: Polity.

Gillborn, D. and Gipps, C. (1996) *Recent Research on the Achievements of Ethnic Minority Pupils*, London: Office for Standards in Education.

Gillborn, D. and Mirza, H. S. (2000) *Mapping Race, Class and Gender: A Synthesis of Research Evidence*, London: Office for Standards in Education.

Glasgow University Media Group (1976) *Bad News*, London: Routledge & Kegan Paul.

Glasgow University Media Group (1980) *More Bad News*, London: Routledge & Kegan Paul.

Goffman, E. (1961) *Asylums*, Harmondsworth: Penguin.

Goode, W. J. (1963) *World Revolution and Family Patterns*, New York: Free Press.

Goode, W. J. (1971) 'A sociological perspective on marital dissolution', in M. Anderson (ed.), *Sociology of the Family*, Harmondsworth: Penguin.

Gordon, D. et al. (2000) *Poverty and Social Exclusion in Britain*, York: Joseph Rowntree Foundation.

Graham, H. (1985) *Health and Welfare*, Basingstoke: Macmillan.

Graham, H. (1993) *Hardship and Health in Women's Lives*, Hemel Hempstead: Harvester Wheatsheaf.

Green, E., Hebron, S. and Woodward, D. (1990) *Women's Leisure, What Leisure?* Basingstoke: Macmillan.

Hargreaves, D. (1967) *Social Relations in a Secondary School*, London: Routledge & Kegan Paul.

Hargreaves, D. (1976) 'Reactions to labelling', in M. Hammersley and P. Woods (eds), *The Process of Schooling*, London: Routledge & Kegan Paul.

Hart, N. (1985) *The Sociology of Health and Medicine*, Ormskirk: Causeway Press.

Heath, S. (2004) 'Transforming friendship – are housemates the new family?', *Sociology Review*, Sept.

Hobson, A. (2000) 'Multiple methods in social research', *Sociology Review*, 10, no. 2.

Humphreys, L. (1970) *The Tearoom Trade: A Study of Homosexual Encounters in Public Places*, London: Duckworth.

Hyman, H. H. (1967) 'The value systems of different classes', in R. Bendix and S. M. Lipset (eds), *Class, Status and Power* (2nd edn), London: Routledge & Kegan Paul.

Hyman, R. (1972) *Strikes*, London: Fontana.

Illich, I. (1976) *Limits to Medicine*, London: Marion Boyars.

Katz, E. and Lazarsfeld, P. F. (1955) *Personal Influence: The Part Played by People in the Flow of Mass Communication*, New York: Free Press.

Keddie, N. (1971) 'Classroom knowledge', in M. F. D. Young (ed.), *Knowledge and Control*, London: Collier-Macmillan.

Keddie, N. (ed.) (1973) *Tinker, Tailor . . . the Myth of Cultural Deprivation*, Harmondsworth: Penguin.

Kelly, A. (1987) *Science for Girls*, Milton Keynes: Open University Press.

Kempson, E. (1996) *Life on a Low Income*, York: Joseph Rowntree Foundation.

Labov, W. (1973) 'The logic of nonstandard English', in Keddie (1973).

Laing, R. D. and Esterson, A. (1970) *Sanity, Madness and the Family*, Harmondsworth: Penguin.

Laslett, P. (1965) *The World We Have Lost*, London: Methuen.

Laslett, P. (1972) 'Mean household size in England since the sixteenth century', in P. Laslett (ed.), *Household and Family in Past Times*, Cambridge: Cambridge University Press.

Le Grand, J. (1982) *The Strategy of Equality*, London: Allen & Unwin.

Leach, E. R. (1967) *A Runaway World?* London: BBC Publications.

Lewis, O. (1961) *The Children of Sanchez*, New York: Random House.

Licht, B. G. and Dweck, C. S. (1987) 'Some differences in achievement orientations', in M. Arnot and G. Weiner (eds), *Gender under Scrutiny*, London: Hutchinson.

Lobban, G. (1974) *Data Report on British Reading Schemes*, London: Times Educational Supplement.

Lull, J. (1990) *Inside Family Viewing: Ethnographic Research on Television's Audiences*, London: Routledge.

Lull, J. (1995) *Media, Communication, Culture*, Cambridge: Polity.

Mack, J. and Lansley, S. (1985) *Poor Britain*, London: Allen & Unwin.

Mack, J., Lansley, S. and Frayman, H. (1992) *Breadline Britain 1990s – the Findings of the Television Series*, London: London Weekend Television.

Marsland, D. (1989) 'Universal welfare provision creates a dependent population. The case for', *Social Studies Review*, 5, no. 2.

McIntosh, S. (1988) 'A feminist critique of Stanley Parker's theory of work and leisure', in M. O'Donnell (ed.), *New Introductory Reader in Sociology* (2nd edn), Walton-on-Thames: Nelson.

McKeown, T. (1976) *The Modern Rise of Population*, London: Edward Arnold.

McKeown, T. (1979) *The Role of Medicine*, Oxford: Blackwell.

McQuail, D. (1972) *The Sociology of Mass Communications*, Harmondsworth: Penguin.

Miliband, R. (1974) 'Politics and poverty', in D. Wedderburn (ed.), *Poverty, Inequality and Class Structure*, Cambridge: Cambridge University Press.

Mills, C. W. (1970) *The Sociological Imagination*, Harmondsworth: Penguin.

Mitchell, R., Shaw, M. and Dorling, D. (2000) *Inequalities in Life and Death: What if Britain Became More Equal?* Bristol: Policy Press.

Mitsos, E. (1995–6) 'Boys and English – classroom voices', *English and Media Magazine*, 33 and 34.

Mitsos, E. and Browne, K. (1998) 'Gender differences in education – the underachievement of boys', *Sociology Review*, 8, no. 1.

Murdock, G. P. (1949) *Social Structure*, New York: Macmillan.

Murray, C. (1989) 'Underclass', *Sunday Times Magazine*, 26 Nov.

Murray, C. (1990) *The Emerging British Underclass*, London: Institute of Economic Affairs.

Navarro, V. (1976) *Medicine under Capitalism*, New York: Prodist.

Nazroo, J. (1997a) *Ethnicity and Mental Health*, London: Policy Studies Institute.

Nazroo, J. (1997b) *The Health of Britain's Ethnic Minorities: Fourth National Survey of Ethnic Minorities*, London: Policy Studies Institute.

Newburn, T. and Hagell, A. (1995) 'Violence on screen – just child's play?', *Sociology Review*, 4, no. 3.

Nichols, T. and Beynon, R. (1977) *Living with Capitalism*, London: Routledge & Kegan Paul.

Oakley, A. (1974) *The Sociology of Housework*, Oxford: Martin Robertson.

Oakley, A. (1981) *From Here to Maternity*, Harmondsworth: Penguin.

Oakley, A. (1984) *The Captured Womb: A History of the Medical Care of Pregnant Women*, Oxford: Blackwell.

Oakley, A. (1989) *Women Confined*, Oxford: Martin Robertson.

Oppenheim, C. (1988) *Poverty: The Facts*, London: Child Poverty Action Group.

Oppenheim, C. and Harker, L. (1996) *Poverty: The Facts*, 3rd edn, London: Child Poverty Action Group.

Pahl, R. E. (1984) *Divisions of Labour*, Oxford: Blackwell.

Pahl, R. E. and Gershuny, J. I. (1980) 'Britain in the decade of three economies', *New Society*, 3 Jan.

Palfreyman, D. (2003) 'Independent schools and charitable status: legal meaning, taxation advantages, and potential removal', in G. Walford (ed.), *British Private Schools – Research on Policy and Practice*, London: Woburn Press.

Parker, S. (1971) *The Future of Work and Leisure*, London: MacGibbon & Kee.

Parker, S. (1976) 'Work and leisure', in E. Butterworth and D. Weir (eds), *The Sociology of Work and Leisure*, London: Allen & Unwin.

Parsons, T. (1951) *The Social System*, London: Routledge & Kegan Paul.

Patrick, J. (1973) *A Glasgow Gang Observed*, London: Eyre Methuen.

Philo, G. (ed.) (1999) *Message Received: Glasgow Media Group Research, 1993–1998*, London: Longman.

Pilkington, A. (1997) 'Ethnicity and education', in M. Haralambos (ed.), *Developments in Sociology*, vol. 13, Ormskirk: Causeway Press.

Piore, M. (1986) 'Perspectives on labour market flexibility', *Industrial Relations*, 45, no. 2.

Piore, M. and Sabel, C. F. (1984) *The Second Industrial Divide*, New York: Basic Books.

Pollert, A. (1988) 'The flexible firm: fixation or fact?', *Work, Employment and Society*, 2, no. 3.

Rapoport, R. and Rapoport, R. N. (1971) *Dual Career Families*, Harmondsworth: Penguin.

Rapoport, R. and Rapoport, R. N. (1976) *Dual Career Families Re-examined*, Oxford: Martin Robertson.

Rapoport, R. N., Fogarty, M. P. and Rapoport, R. (eds) (1982) *Families in Britain*, London: Routledge & Kegan Paul.

Roberts, K. (1978) *Contemporary Society and the Growth of Leisure*, London: Longman.

Roberts, K. (1981) *Leisure (2nd edn)*, London: Longman.

Roberts, K. (1983) *Youth and Leisure*, London: George Allen & Unwin.

Roberts, K. (1986) 'Leisure', in M. Haralambos (ed.), *Developments in Sociology*, vol. 2, Ormskirk: Causeway Press.

Rojek, C. (1985) *Capitalism and Leisure Theory*, London: Tavistock.

Rojek, C. (1995) *Decentring Leisure: Rethinking Leisure Theory*, London: Sage.

Rosenhan, D. L. (1973) 'On being sane in insane places', *Science*, 179.

Rosenthal, R. and Jacobson, L. (1968) *Pygmalion in the Classroom*, London: Holt, Rinehart & Winston.

Rutter, M. and Madge, N. (1976) *Cycles of Disadvantage: A Review of Research*, London: Heinemann.

Rutter, M. et al. (1979) *Fifteen Thousand Hours: Secondary Schools and their Effects on Children*, Shepton Mallet: Open Books.

Scheff, T. J. (1966) *Being Mentally Ill*, Chicago: Aldine.

Scott, J. (1990) *A Matter of Record: Documentary Sources in Social Research*, Cambridge: Polity.

Scraton, S. and Bramham, P. (1995) 'Leisure and postmodernity', in M. Haralambos (ed.), *Developments in Sociology*, vol. 11, Ormskirk: Causeway Press.

Shakespeare, T. (1998) *The Disability Reader: Social Science Perspectives*, London: Cassell.

Sharpe, S. (1976) *Just Like a Girl*, Harmondsworth: Penguin.

Sharpe, S. (1994) *Just Like a Girl* (2nd edn), Harmondsworth: Penguin.

Shorter, E. (1977) *The Making of the Modern Family*, London: Fontana.

Spender, D. (1982) *Invisible Women: The Schooling Scandal*, London: Writers and Readers.

Stanworth, M. (1983) *Gender and Schooling*, London: Hutchinson.

Sugarman, B. (1970) 'Social class, values and behaviour in schools', in M. Craft (ed.), *Family, Class and Education*, London: Longman.

Swann Committee (1985) *Education for All: Report of the Committee of Inquiry into the Education of Children from Ethnic Minority Groups*, London: HMSO.

Szasz, T. (1972) *The Myth of Mental Illness*, London: Paladin.

Taylor, L. (1984) *In the Underworld*, London: Unwin.

Thompson, P. (1993) 'The labour process: changing theory, changing practice', *Sociology Review*, 3, no. 2.

Townsend, P. (1979) *Poverty in the United Kingdom*, Harmondsworth: Penguin.

Townsend, P., Davidson, N. and Whitehead, M. (1990) *Inequalities in Health: The Black Report and The Health Divide*, Harmondsworth: Penguin.

Tudor-Hart, J. (1971) 'The inverse care law', *Lancet*, 1.

Walby, S. (1989) 'Flexibility and the changing sexual division of labour', in S. Wood (ed.), *The Transformation of Work*, London: Unwin Hyman.

Walford, G. (ed.) (2003) *British Private Schools: Research on Policy and Practice*, London: Woburn Press.

Walker, R., Howard, M., Maguire, S. and Youngs, R. (2000) *The Making of a Welfare Class?* Bristol: Policy Press.

Warde, A. (1989) 'The future of work', *Social Studies Review*, 5, no. 1.

Westergaard, J. and Resler, H. (1976) *Class in a Capitalist Society*, Harmondsworth: Penguin.

Whyte, W. F. (1955) *Street Corner Society* (2nd edn), Chicago: University of Chicago Press.

Wilkinson, R. G. (1996) *Unhealthy Societies*, London: Routledge.

Willis, P. (1977) *Learning to Labour: How Working Class Kids Get Working Class Jobs*, Farnborough: Saxon House.

Wood, S. (1989) 'The transformation of work', in S. Wood (ed.), *The Transformation of Work?* London: Unwin Hyman.

Young, M. and Willmott, P. (1973) *The Symmetrical Family*, Harmondsworth: Penguin.

Zuboff, S. (1988) *In the Age of the Smart Machine*, New York: Basic Books.

Here is the word list for the activity on p. 11, given in the correct order.

Objectivity	role conflict	working class
value freedom	values	upper class
social institutions	norms	underclass
social structure	social control	social classes
socialization	positive	social mobility
gender	negative sanctions	status
identity	deviance	ascribed status
ethnicity	social class	status
minority ethnic group	life chances	achieved status
roles	social classes	

Here is the solution to the crossword puzzle on p. 107:

```
K I B B U T Z                   R           D
  I             H O U S E H O L D           E
  R                           L       K     P
B O T T   P A R S O N S   E X P R E S S I V E
  H       R                   M       N     N
    S E R I A L M O N O G A M Y O       S   D
          M                   D       H     E
      S   A   D I V O R C E R A T E   E   I N
  G A Y   R   O               L       P     T
P     M   Y   M               S
A     M   S   E       C               C   E
T   R E C O N S T I T U T E D         O   X
R   T   C   T         R     N   D     N   T
I   R   I   I O A K L E Y   E   I     J   E
A   I   A   C         A     W   V     U   N
R   C   L   L         L     M   O     G   D
C O H A B I T A T I O N   P   M A R R I A G E
H   L   Z   B         A   N   C   L   D
Y       A   O     L E A C H       E   R
        T   U         K           O
        I   R   N U C L E A R F A M I L Y
        O             T               E
    L O N E P A R E N T   F E M I N I S M
```

Index

...ex

see sociological pers

...lot survey
...476
...o the mass

498